AF352461

Art and Devotion
at a Buddhist Temple in the
Indian Himalaya

Contemporary Indian Studies

*Published in association with the
American Institute of Indian Studies*

Recipient of the Edward Cameron Dimock, Jr. Prize in the Indian Humanities,
awarded by the American Institute of Indian Studies and published
with the Institute's generous support.

ART AND DEVOTION AT A
BUDDHIST TEMPLE
IN THE INDIAN HIMALAYA

MELISSA R. KERIN

INDIANA UNIVERSITY PRESS

Bloomington & Indianapolis

This book is a publication of

Indiana University Press
Office of Scholarly Publishing
Herman B Wells Library 350
1320 East 10th Street
Bloomington, Indiana 47405 USA

iupress.indiana.edu

The paper used in this publication meets
the minimum requirements of the American
National Standard for Information
Sciences—Permanence of Paper for Printed
Library Materials, ANSI Z39.48–1992.

Manufactured in the
United States of America

Cataloging information is available
from the Library of Congress

ISBN 978-0-253-01306-4 (cloth)
ISBN 978-0-253-01309-5 (ebook)

1 2 3 4 5   20 19 18 17 16 15

To my beloved Elsa

CONTENTS

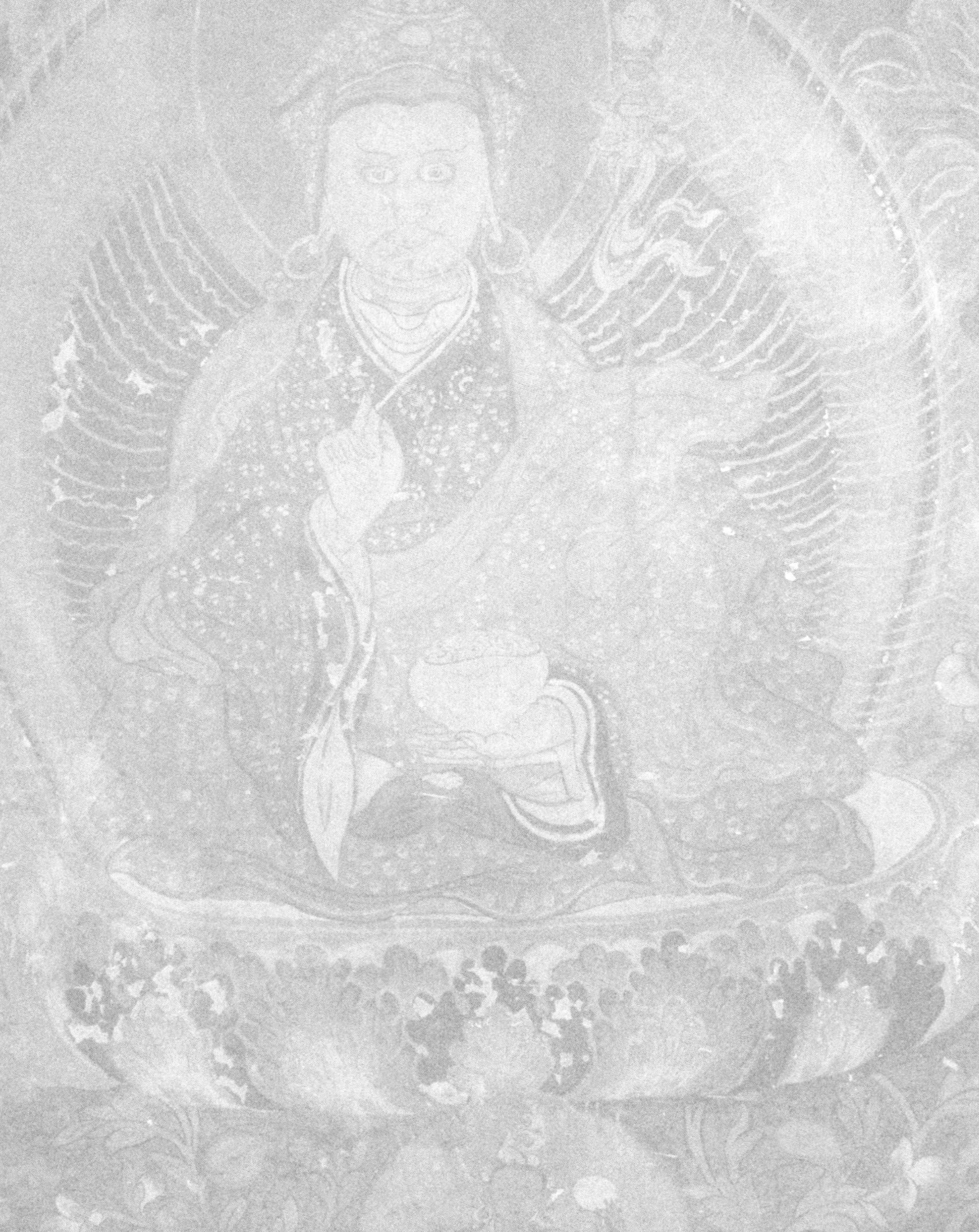

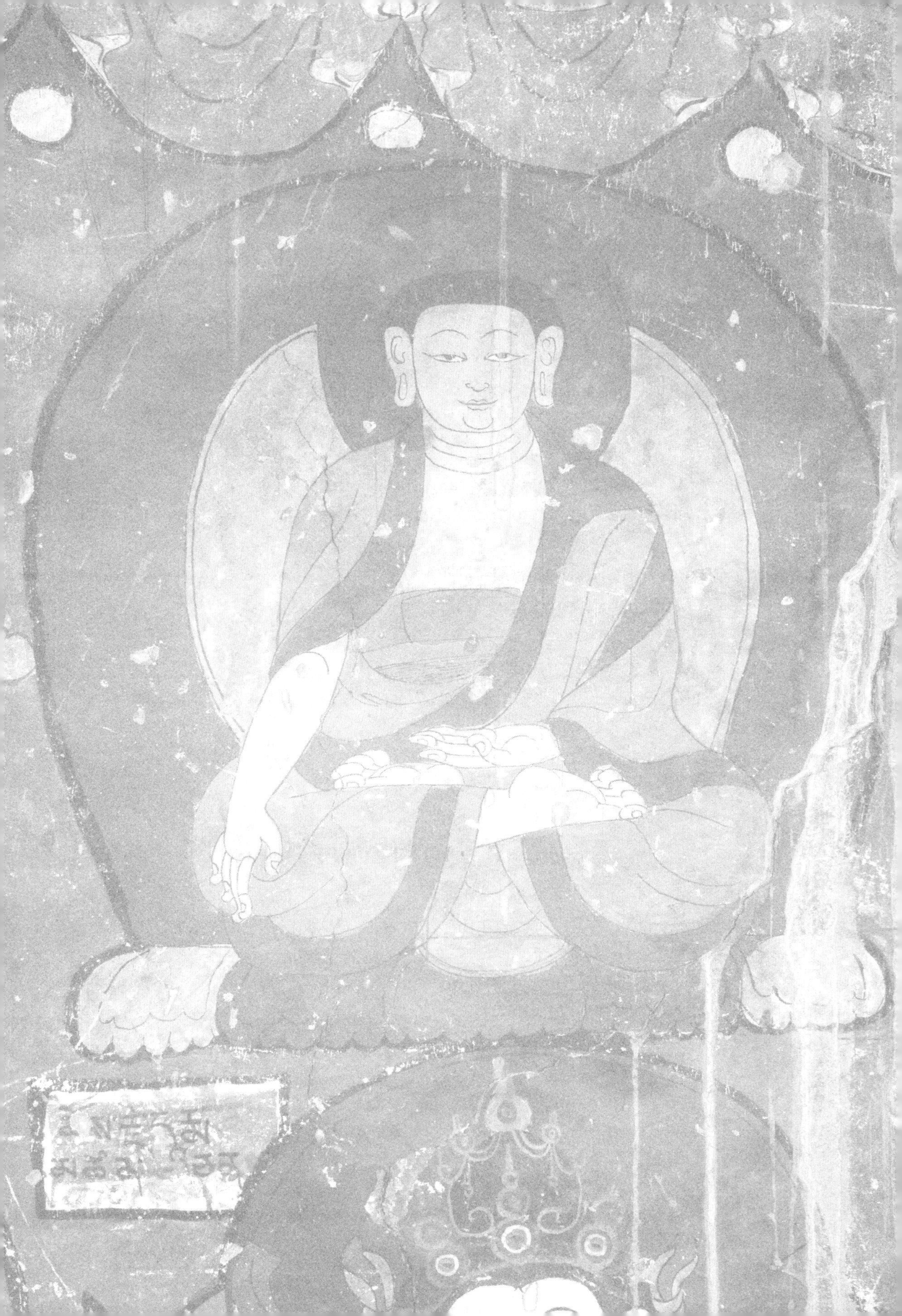

All photographs are by John Henry Rice unless noted as the following:

MRK: Melissa R. Kerin
RNL: Rob N. Linrothe
WHAV: Western Himalayan Archive, Vienna

Plates

Figures

Many people have offered their guidance and support over the years it has taken me to bring this book to fruition. The two people who stand out most are Professor Deborah Klimburg-Salter (Universität Wien, Kunstgeschichte) and Professor Michael Meister (University of Pennsylvania, Department of the History of Art). Only now—as a professor, advisor, and researcher in my own right—can I truly appreciate all that they have done for me. On the other side of the desk, as it were, I realize the fine balance of challenging, encouraging, and guiding students as they shape and define their projects. Michael's and Deborah's insights, warnings, questions, suggestions, and challenges helped me contour my project, but also gave me a solid conceptual and methodological foundation from which I could continue working on this material. I cannot express my gratitude enough for their counsel and continued support.

Many colleagues in India and Tibet made my fieldwork productive and fruitful. The people of Nako, and in particular Lama ji, kindly answered my questions, invited me into their homes and temples, offered me tea, and openly shared with me their information and stories about Nako and its artistic heritage. Professor Jampa Samten of the Central Institute for Higher Tibetan Studies in Sarnath generously met with me to discuss the Rgya 'phags pa (Gyapagpa) iconographic program and gave me critically important information and bibliographic resources on the 'Bri gung (Drigung) tradition and its history in West Tibet. Dr. Tashi Sampel, the director of the Songtsen Library in Dehra Dun, met with me to discuss my many questions about Drigung lineage. Moreover, he put me in touch with several important Drigung teachers and historians. One of these lamas cum historians was Ven. Thogden Rimpoche of Ladakh, who answered my many questions. While in Ladakh, architect John Harrison shared with me his knowledge of various Drigung sites. Several of his drawings appear in this volume. Romi and Kalpana Khosala were very hospitable to me when I met them in Himachal Pradesh. Drawings produced by his architectural firm are also used in this book. Lastly, Guge Tsering Gyalpo from Lhasa's Tibetan Academy of Social Sciences talked with me at length over the few months I was there in 2006, about Drigung history in the Guge region.

None of my fieldwork, archival research, or writing would have been possible without the generosity of several institutions. Grants through the University of Pennsylvania's Department of Art History subsidized two archival trips to Rome, Vienna, and London, as well as a summer-long trip to Central and West Tibet. A Fulbright-Hays Doctoral Dissertation Research Abroad Fellowship (2004–5) allowed me the opportunity to conduct research in Kinnaur, Spiti, and Ladakh. Through the Mellon/ American Council of Learned Societies Dissertation Completion Fellowship (2007–8) I had an uninterrupted year to write. In 2008–9, I was again the fortunate recipient of the American Council of Learned Societies' generosity in the form of the Recent Doctoral Recipients Fellowship, which allowed me time to write this manuscript. The staff at the Western Himalayan Archive Vienna has also been incredibly generous with allowing me to use and reproduce many of their images, which are featured in this book. Without their generosity chapters 4 and 5 could never have been written. Moreover, Verena Widorn, Susy Novotny, and Verena Ziegler have always made me feel very welcomed.

Support from two institutions financed the production of this book, for which I am deeply grateful. In 2010 the American Institute of Indian Studies awarded me the Edward C. Dimock, Jr. Book Prize in the Indian Humanities, which came with it a substantial publishing stipend. Lastly, the provost's office at Washington and Lee University generously contributed a substantial publishing subsidy.

Through Washington and Lee I also had the opportunity to work with a great group of students in my *Art and Martial Culture of Tibet* seminar. Together we discussed various sections of this book. They bravely offered their critiques and raised questions, which helped me think through and revise portions of chapter 4. I am also fortunate to have been able to discuss my work with my colleagues in the Departments of Art and Art History and Religion at Washington and Lee University.

Editors and staff at Indiana University Press have been wonderful to work with. I thank Rebecca Tolen, Sarah Jacobi, Nancy Lightfoot, and Dawn Ollila for their hard work and thoughtful suggestions, which have made for a better book in the end.

Colleagues from the University of Pennsylvania, the Universität Wien, and beyond, have provided incisive feedback and helpful suggestions at various stages of writing. Several colleagues invited me to present chapters of the book at lectures and conferences, which gave me the opportunity to work through and refine aspects of my argument. Others offered much needed camaraderie, good humor, and perspective. I thank Suzanne Bessenger, Dan Ehnbom, Pika Ghosh, Kim Gutchow Emily Hage, Amy Heller, Christian Luczanits, Meredith Malone, Andy Quintman, Kurtis Schaeffer, Tamara Sears, Kurt Tropper, Kevin Vose, and Verena Widorn. Lastly, I thank Rob Linrothe, who has over the years provided invaluable suggestions and an encouraging voice. Several of his photos have also been used in this book.

Lastly, I thank my family, in the greatest sense of the word. Over recent years I have leaned on them heavily. I especially thank my mom, Claire Kerin, for all her prayers, meditation, and endless love. I thank my late father, Robert Kerin, who with my mom traveled to India and Nepal to understand better this second home of mine. And there are many others—Robert, Judy, Blu, Mike, Lisa, Phil, Ashley, Tim, Amelia, Emily, Jules, Kevin, Anne, Mark, Kelly—whose loving fellowship made a huge difference. My most ardent supporter, though, must be my daughter, Elsa Sofia, who was thrilled to learn that I was writing a book. "What's the story about?" she eagerly asked. Perhaps one day she might pick this up to see exactly what this story was about. If she does, I hope she might linger upon the book's dedication. You are my heart, Elsa. I cannot thank you enough.

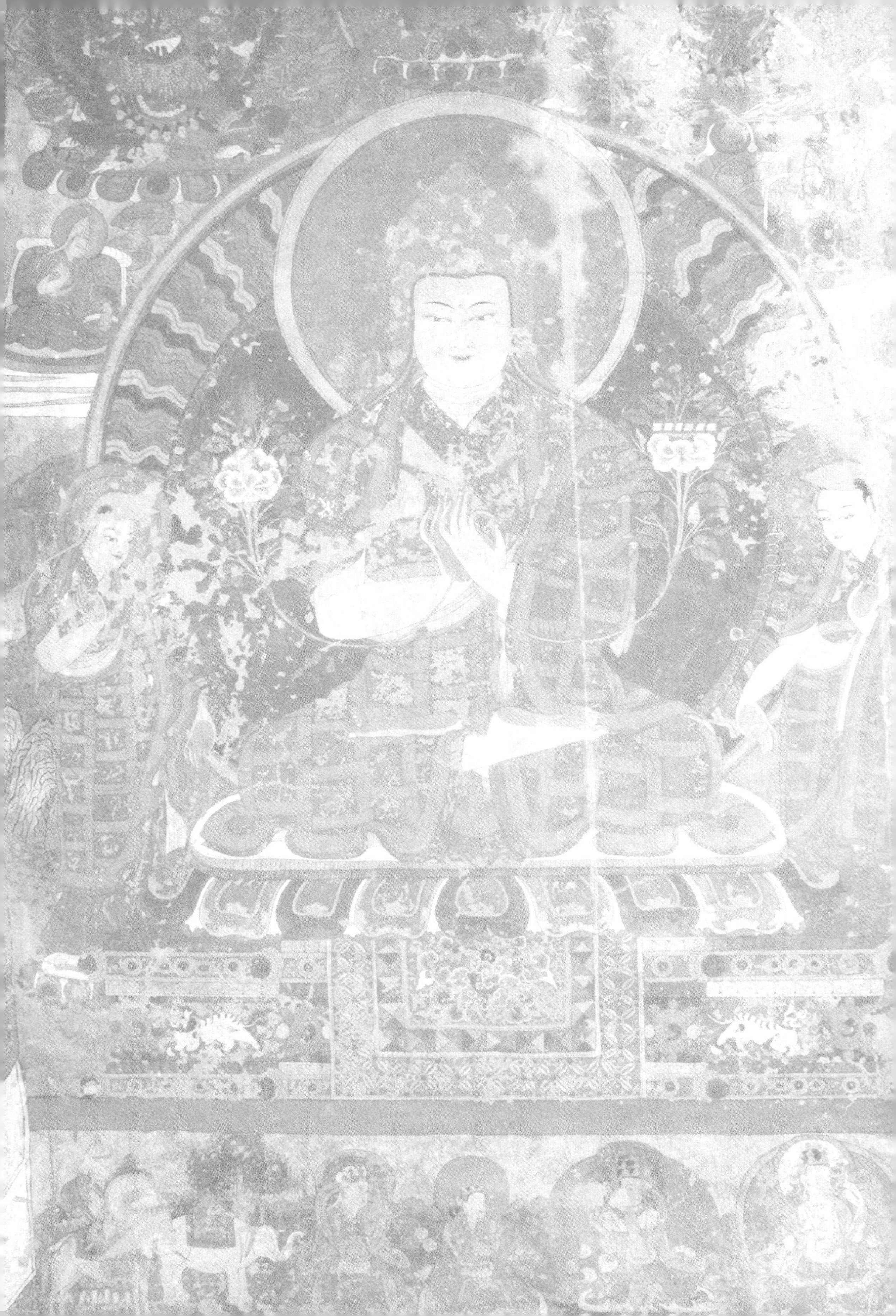

I employ the Wylie transliteration system for the first occurrence of Tibetan words in each chapter. The romanized phonetic version of the word (which is based on Central Tibetan pronunciation) appears in parentheses after the transliterated form. It is the unitalicized romanized version of the Tibetan word that is then used throughout the remainder of the chapter. Both Wylie and romanized phonetic forms of Tibetan words are included in the index.

The primary exception for using Wylie transliteration is in the case of place names, for which there are often many variant spellings. I have referred to regions and villages by their conventional Romanized spellings.

As the nomenclature for describing Vajrayāna Buddhism has changed over the years, it should be noted that I use the term "tradition" to refer to its main branches, such as Bka' brgyud (Kagyu), and "school" to describe the small, subgroups within these larger traditions, such as 'Bri gung (Drigung). When necessary, I have omitted the nominalizing "pa" after tradition or school names.

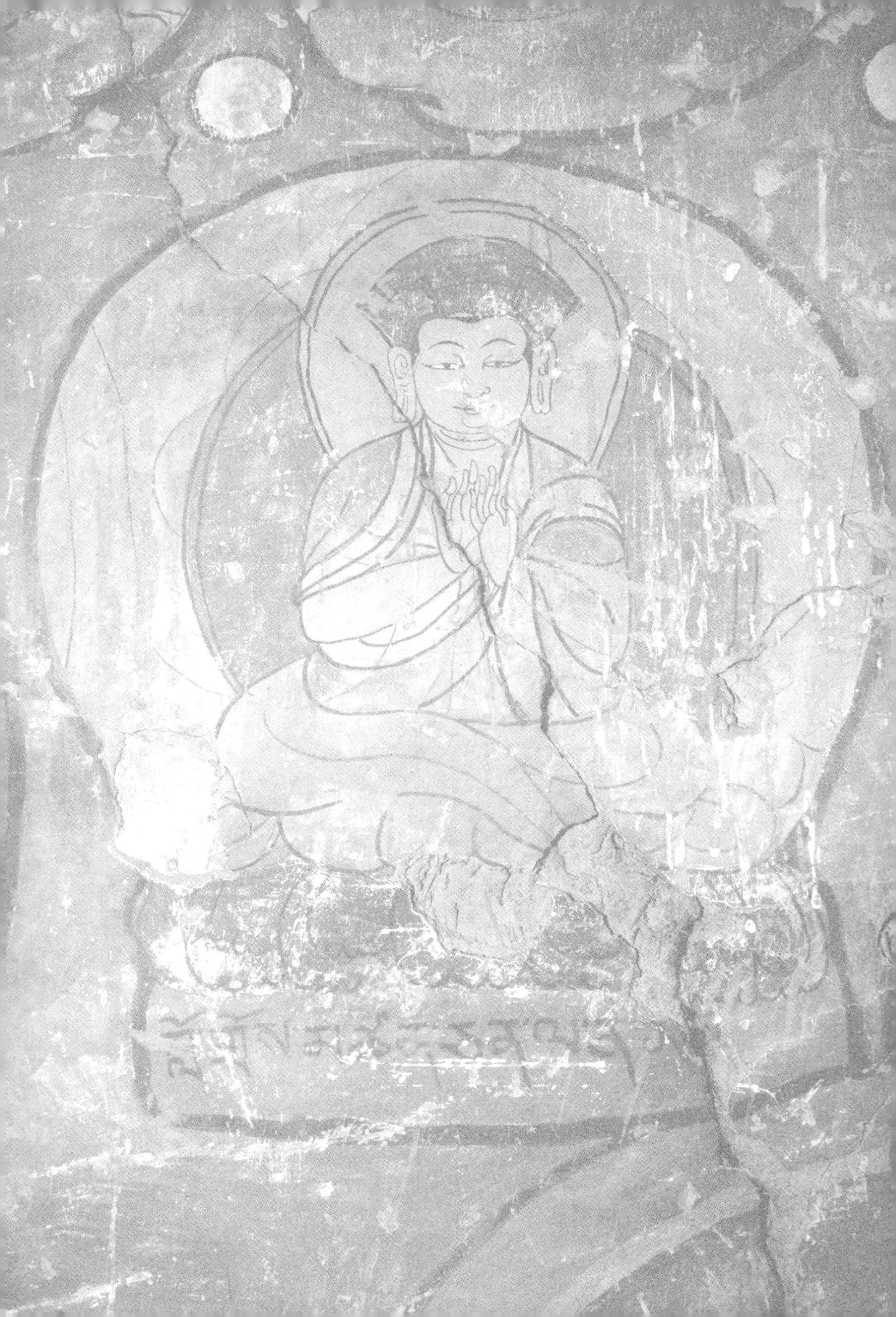

Art and Devotion
at a Buddhist Temple in the
Indian Himalaya

Introduction

This book investigates the complex devotional, artistic, and political histories of a set of late-sixteenth-century wall paintings at the Rgya 'phags pa (Gyapagpa) Temple in Nako, a village in the Khu nu (Kinnaur) District of India's Himachal Pradesh state (plate 1). The paintings that form the focus of this book have only occasionally been included in cursory surveys of the region; they have not, however, received any rigorous academic analysis.[1] By contrast, coeval paintings at courtly and religious centers such as Tsaparang and Tabo have been studied, to varying degrees, for their art historical and religious significance. There are several notable factors contributing to the omission of the Gyapagpa wall paintings from the academic record. The first is that these paintings were not the products of grand courtly patronage. Consequently, little historical evidence about the paintings, such as inscriptions or chronicles, survives. Moreover, the materials and craftsmanship of these paintings pale in comparison to those of other neighboring sites with strong royal affiliations. Lastly, these paintings were produced when Nako was located on the margins of both mainstream political and religious activity.

What, then, could these unknown, faded, and marginal paintings have to teach us? This book will demonstrate that these murals are among the rarest sources of historical documentation for this area and sixteenth-century period, as well as for a specific type of Tibetan Buddhism practiced in Kinnaur (fig. 0.1). Analysis of this overlooked temple and its paintings has provided significant insights into religious practices

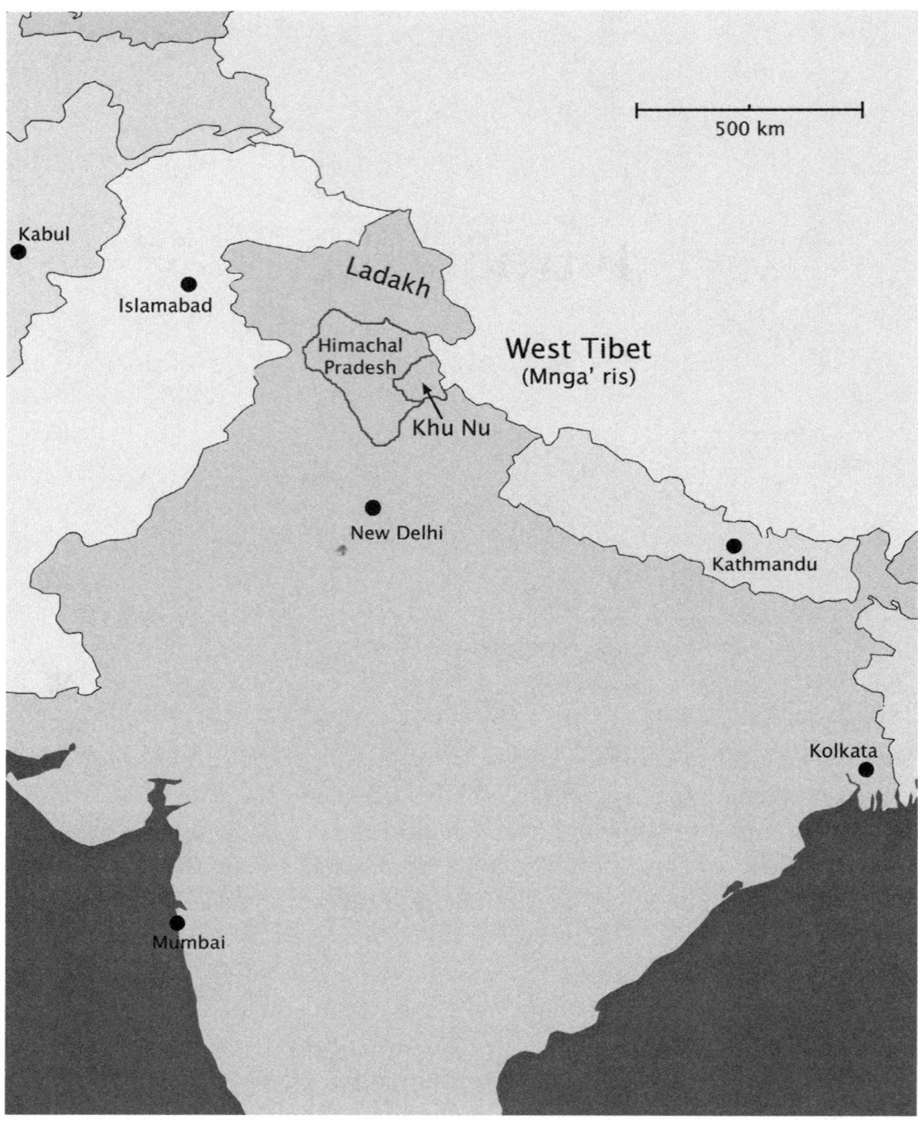

Figure 0.1. Map of Khu nu (Kinnaur), Ladakh, and Mnga' ris (Ngari).

of Nako, past and present, as well as larger patterns of regional and transregional interactions among western Himalayan Buddhist centers during the late medieval period. Consequently, this book elucidates how the Gyapagpa paintings are indices of important political, artistic, and religious developments that are critical to accurately contouring the hitherto elusive sociopolitical complexion of India's western Himalayan region—a region often omitted from Indian histories.[2] More generally, this project serves to broaden and nuance interdisciplinary discourses concerning the complex relationships between material culture and identity formation, ideology, and devotional praxis.

Temple

Nako is located in India's Kinnaur District, much of which is part of the larger Tibetan cultural zone that spreads from the modern-day Tibetan Autonomous Region (Xizang) in the People's Republic of China into India's Lahaul-Spiti, Zangskar, and Ladakh. As is the case in much of this Indo-Tibetan area, Nako's populace practices Buddhism and speaks both Hindi and a local dialect of Tibetan. A dramatic mountainous landscape surrounds Nako, but most impressive is the sharp peak of Leo Purgyal, the highest mountain in the area, that rises just above the village. This majestic site, however, is not the first visual encounter a visitor has in Nako. Rather, upon arriving in the village, once the diesel fumes from the jeep or bus have settled, one is initially met with concrete storefronts and modest guesthouses. These new façades belie the antiquity and vibrancy of the actual village. It is only when one penetrates into the densely knit residential quarters, views the terraced, cultivated fields, and visits the numerous Buddhist temples scattered throughout the village that the long history of Nako's economic stability and religious prosperity becomes apparent. Scrutiny of the village's abundance of religious material evidence—comprising temple architecture, painting programs, and a now-neglected monastery—makes it plain that Nako indeed played host to a thriving and important Buddhist community in the western Himalayan region from the twelfth century onward.

* * *

At the heart of Nako's flourishing religious life are four temples located at the southwestern corner of the village (fig. 0.2). Two pairs of temples face one another, creating a plaza space between them. At the north end of the plaza is now a gathering hall and storage unit; the entrance and exit point for the compound is located at the plaza's southern end. According to conservation analysis, it is possible that the four mud-brick temples were built during or around the twelfth century.[3] Each of these temples has a complicated history of patronage and use, which is evident by the multiple painting programs in each temple. Moving in a clockwise direction inside the compound, one comes to the Dkar chung (Karchung [Little White]) Temple, which has a badly eroded painting program. Next to it is the sizable Lo tsā ba (Lotsawa [Translator]) Temple, with its elaborately painted maṇḍala murals of circa twelfth century. Immediately

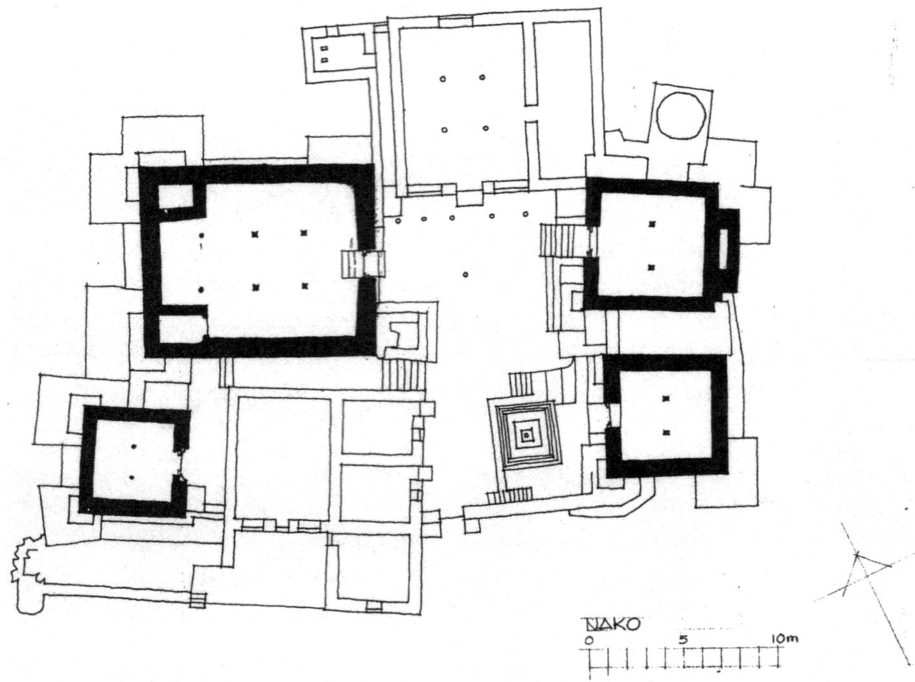

Figure 0.2. Plan of Nako's religious compound. The Gyapagpa Temple is at lower right. WHAV (architect John Harrison).

across from Lotsawa is the Gong ma (Gongma [Upper]) Temple, with a steep staircase leading into a richly painted interior dating to the circa twelfth century. Completing this clockwise circuit around the compound, one comes to the Gyapagpa Temple, with its circa late-sixteenth-century paintings.

This small 5.6 × 5.4 meter temple has had an unusually complex history (plate 2). Confusion over this temple extends even to its name, which is transliterated as Rgya 'phags pa and has no clear translation. Such uncertainty is perhaps oddly fitting, as this temple has assumed different identities—each layered upon the other—over the nine hundred years of its use. Initially, this temple was constructed in the twelfth century to serve one particular Buddhist community, and its interior walls furnished with a painted program suited to this community's use. In the sixteenth century, however, another Buddhist group claimed the temple, and the original murals were covered over with a new painting cycle.[4] Since then, this temple and its sixteenth-century iconographic program have been re-"visioned"—that is, reinterpreted but not repainted—by yet another religious community and subsumed within its religious framework and communal memory.

Despite the faded pigments and water damage, the paintings that adorn the walls of the Gyapagpa Temple contain critical information that has allowed me to reestablish this temple's sixteenth-century religious affiliation. Such a finding has been significantly helpful in the process of outlining the region's socioreligious history of the fifteenth and sixteenth centuries, which has remained rather opaque due to the dearth of textual and material sources directly addressing the area's religious and political status. Accordingly, the Gyapagpa Temple's sixteenth-century paintings constitute some of the most important and rare sources of historical documentation for this area. They provide the material evidence with which to create a more coherent—but by no means complete—picture of sixteenth-century Kinnaur, an otherwise little-understood period and understudied region, which is often eclipsed by two powerful political and religious centers: Ladakh to the north, and West Tibet (hereafter referred to by its Tibetan name, Mnga' ris [Ngari]) to the east.

As one of the first thorough analyses of post–fifteenth century visual culture in the western Himalayan region, this study provides insights into the style of the temple's paintings and addresses the larger cultural and political environment in which these paintings and the village of Nako operated during the sixteenth century. As such, I investigate the points of connection between Kinnaur and its surrounding principalities of North India, as well as to Buddhist political and religious centers of Ladakh and Tibet. These points of comparison serve to delineate the religious and political landscape of Kinnaur as well as the larger aesthetic environment to which it was responsive and with which it interacted. This book also allows us to study in greater detail a well-known, but only partly understood, regional painting tradition that has been cursorily written about since the 1930s but never fully analyzed. Consequently, this book provides much-needed analysis of the style's idiomatic expression, geographic spread, and chronological development.

Chapters

My study comprises five chapters that work in tandem to identify and analyze the Gyapagpa temple's rich artistic heritage as well as its complex religious history. The first chapter, "Nako's Sociopolitical History and Artistic Heritage," locates the village within the greater political, religious, and artistic environs of Kinnaur, the larger Spiti valley, and the greater political centers of North India and Tibet. The chapter is organized into two sections. In the first, I portray the political and artistic milieu of the Upper Kinnaur district, in which Nako is located. The village belongs, however, to a much larger cultural zone that stretches into what

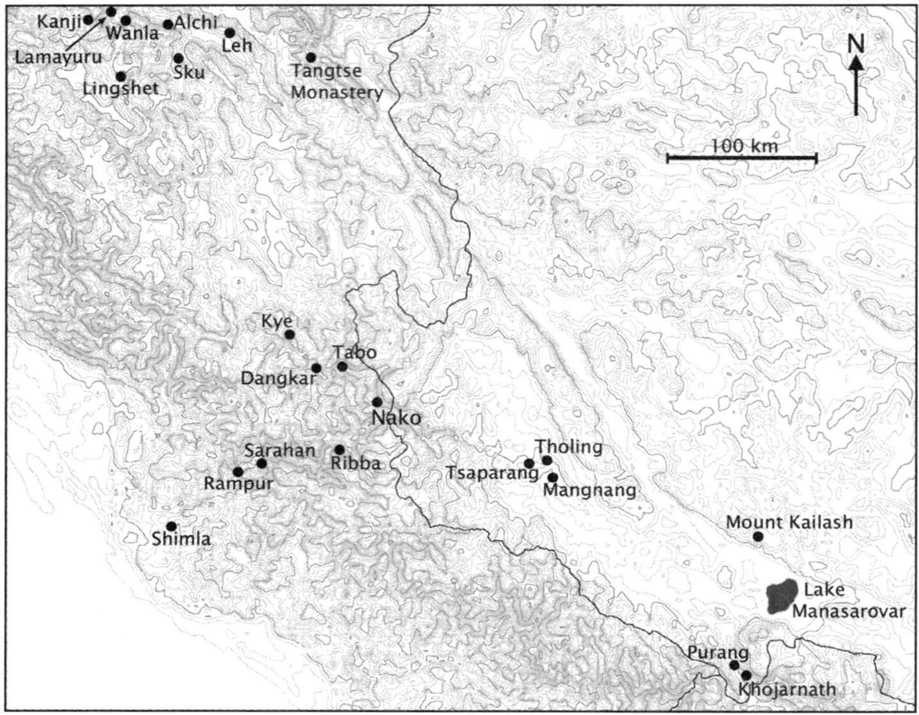

Figure 0.3. Map of Ladakh, Kinnaur, and Ngari.

is now Ngari (fig. 0.3). The modern political boundaries between India and Tibet make it nearly impossible for a foreign researcher to conduct fieldwork in the contested western border zone, over which China and India fought a war in 1962.[5] Although the political boundaries are now heavily policed, it should be remembered that Kinnaur was at various times from the tenth to seventeenth centuries subsumed within Ngari's kingdoms, such as that of the fifteenth-century Guge kingdom. Despite the enforced division of modern-day boundaries, there is considerable evidence of artistic and cultural continuity between what are now two different political zones (fig. 0.3).

The second part of the chapter focuses on Nako's religious history and artistic heritage, based primarily on the extant material evidence located in the village and also on local knowledge of Nako's various temples. The last component of this section specifically concentrates on the Gyapagpa temple, providing more detailed information about the temple's architectural structure and its paintings.

Chapter 2, "Forgetting to Remember: Gyapagpa Temple's Shifting Identity," analyzes the various and often divergent ways in which the academic community and the local village faithful have interpreted the temple's iconographic and inscriptional material. Based on previously little analyzed inscriptional and iconographic evidence, I offer a new interpretation of the temple's painted program, one that reestablishes its forgotten sixteenth-century sectarian affiliation with the 'Bri gung (Drigung) school of the Bka' brgyud (Kagyu) tradition of Tibetan Buddhism. The restoration of this temple's sixteenth-century sectarian affiliation is based on two critical pieces of iconographic information. The first, located above the temple door, is a female figure astride a white horse. An inscription beneath the horse identifies the rider as A phyi chos kyi sgron ma (Achi Chokyi Dronma), the protectress of the Drigung sect. The second iconographic clue comes from the lineage of monastics painted on three of the temple's four walls. The lineage begins with an inscribed portrait of 'Jig rten mgon po (Jigten Gonpo), the founder of the Drigung sect. With its iconography elucidated, the Gyapagpa Temple becomes the earliest material evidence of Drigung religious activity in Kinnaur and significantly contributes to reshaping our understanding of religious activity in the region.

This chapter also examines the discrepancy between the current reception of these murals and their original meaning based on the sixteenth-century iconographic program. The images were initially shaped and defined by one set of religious beliefs but have since been appropriated and re-visioned by another, that of the 'Brug pa bka' brgyud (Drukpa Kagyu) tradition. The chapter investigates the slippage between past religious affiliation and present-day practice, as well as between scholarly definitions and lived experiences of Buddhist art, in order to deepen current understandings of the multivalency of religious images within Tibetan Buddhist contexts. I position this phenomenon—of the appropriation and resignification of these late medieval paintings—within a larger theoretical context informed by ideas of the plurality of reception. Like the indeterminate text that is resolved only by the reader, the meaning of the religious image is brought to completion by the observer. Consequently, the reception of the image can mean different things based on the observers' "horizons of expectation," to use Hans Robert Jauss's concept.[6] The most compelling instance of Nako's dynamic reception of these paintings is the village's systematic forgetting of the original sixteenth-century meaning of these paintings in order that the village might establish new meaning to the murals' old signs. As I have interpreted it, this re-visioning process reflected the village's shift in religious identity. In this case, collective forgetfulness contributes to the formation of cultural identity.[7]

The third chapter, "Mapping Drigung Activity in Nako and the Western Himalaya," provides a larger context for understanding the Gyapagpa Temple's Drigung affiliation. Initially, this temple appears to be an isolated instance of Drigung activity within a largely Dge lugs (Gelug) and Drukpa Kagyu environment. However, by penetrating the layers of devotional history—in the form of primary and secondary sources as well as material evidence—for Kinnaur and the greater western Himalayan region, it becomes evident that a little-known, but critically important Drigung revival occurred in this and the surrounding areas during the sixteenth century. Moreover, the presence of several undocumented Drigung temples on the Tibetan side of the western Himalayan border helps to underscore the hypothesis that Nako was likely a part of what was once a larger interconnected network of Drigung communities.[8]

Having contextualized this temple's content and subject matter within the sociopolitical milieu of the broader western Himalaya, I turn to the question of style. Chapter 4, "Gyapagpa Temple's Painting Style and Its Antecedents," is organized in two parts. The first is dedicated to a thorough formal analysis of the sixteenth-century murals in order to define the painting style used at the Gyapagpa Temple. Ultimately, this chapter proposes that Nako's sixteenth-century painting style was a variant of a regional style originating in the Guge kingdom of Ngari in the fifteenth century. It is the second part of this chapter in which I outline the contours of this larger style, which is a frequently mentioned, if sorely underanalyzed painting tradition.

In this section I draw a distinction between a courtly mode of painting followed by a regional idiomatic expression of this style. The courtly style was initially commissioned under royal patronage of the newly formed Guge kingdom (fifteenth through seventeenth centuries) of Ngari at its cosmopolitan centers of Tsaparang and Tholing. The fifteenth and sixteenth century paintings of the Golden Temple in Tabo, located west of Tsaparang in the Spiti region, are also executed in what I have termed the courtly idiom of the larger Ngari style. The second phase, "regional idioms," encompasses the numerous stylistic variations that developed outside the religious and political centers of the Guge kingdom. I document the temporal, geographic, and stylistic range of this wider artistic movement, which I argue extended from Ngari, through Kinnaur, and into the upper Spiti valley. In so doing, I chart in an abbreviated manner this style's idiomatic developments and relative chronology—thereby documenting a cohesive corpus of visual forms operative from the fifteenth to sixteenth centuries and reflective of the region's aesthetic and political developments.[9]

The last part of this chapter addresses the significance of this style as it was used at a site such as Nako, which was peripheral to the metropolitan center of the Guge kingdom in Ngari. By the time the style was employed at Nako, it was divorced from its original semiotic referent, necessarily altering its valence. Thus, I suggest that patrons and villagers would not have associated the style with an ideological message of dynastic emulation as would have been the case in the fifteenth century;

rather, sixteenth-century viewers from the village of Nako likely would have had loose associations of this painting style with its royal and cultural antecedents at places like Tsaparang, Tholing, and nearby Tabo. Given that the Drigung sect was a struggling minority in the sixteenth century, it is understandable that the patrons of this new Drigung painting program at Nako's Gyapagpa Temple sought to use a style that at once communicated legitimacy but also linked the paintings and this temple to powerful cultural and political centers of the day.

This analysis provides the basis for the material found in chapter 5, "Origin and Meaning of a Revival Painting Style." I first explain how this courtly painting tradition is a renascent style by revealing the ways in which it revived many formal aspects of the eleventh- and twelfth-century painting style that had been patronized by the famous and successful Pu hrang–Guge (Purang) dynasty of Ngari. I go on to suggest that by emulating the earlier painting style, the fifteenth-century patrons and artists purposefully created a visual linkage between them and their eleventh-century counterpart. That intended visual resonance, I argue, communicated a greater ideological message of ancestral and political continuity and heritage. The significance of this revival style is further underscored when its sociopolitical context is considered; the style was fashioned and used after West Tibet had been subject to foreign rule. In the thirteenth and fourteenth centuries, Ngari, as well as the rest of Tibet, fell under the Mongol Yuan administrative rule.[10] Through its art, the Guge kingdom of the fifteenth century sought to fashion itself as the continuation of the august lineage of rulers of the eleventh century. This association with the eleventh-century kingdom of West Tibet is not arbitrary. These royal patrons were responsible for refining Tibetan Buddhist practice. They funded major translation projects of Kashmiri texts into Tibetan, as well as hosted important tantric monastic figures such as Atiśa, who resided at the royal center of Tholing at the behest of Ye shes 'Od (Yeshe Od). Buddhist practice and art patronage during the tenth and eleventh centuries marks a high point in West Tibetan history. That the fifteenth-century Guge kingdom emulates this eleventh-century kingdom is, I argue, an intended and carefully orchestrated association. This hypothesis of revival and renaissance is also supported through textual evidence, in particular the royal chronicle of the fifteenth-century Guge kingdom.

Methodology

The insights of these five chapters relate to three primary areas of investigation: art history, which includes analysis of style, iconography, and inscriptions; ethnography; and religious history. These lines of inquiry provide the foundation for what is simultaneously a formalist and contextualist investigation of the Gyapagpa Temple. By formalist, I mean that this book rigorously and systematically outlines the formal elements of not only the Gyapagpa Temple paintings, but related murals. This formalist analysis allows me to articulate and define a specific style, and substyles, in operation during the fifteenth and sixteenth centuries in this western Himalayan region. From this formal examination, my analysis moves outward to consider the greater sociopolitical environs that helped to catalyze the creation of these paintings. The contextualist approach to this study provides a social history for the temple,[11] and more specifically for its sixteenth-century murals, which allows me to bring into focus a web of interrelated issues among art, politics, economics, and religion that affected the production and function, as well as reception of these wall paintings both synchronically and diachronically.

What is distinctive about my methodology, at least within the context of western Himalayan or Tibetan art historical studies, is its emphasis on *both* the historical function and current understanding of the paintings. This approach is not intended to determine a thread of continuity in the way in which these images are understood from the past to the present. Rather, my interest in the present-day perception is to reveal the way in which the community engages these images and the meanings they construe from this painting program—which, as chapter 2 will reveal, is at odds with the sixteenth-century iconographic program illustrated on the temple walls. This approach highlights the instability of the iconographic form, which in studies of Tibetan Buddhism is too often considered to be a closed meaning system without fluctuation. What this study exposes are the multiple functions and shifting perceptions of the iconographic form. Another goal of this methodological approach is to serve as a corrective to Western projections on Tibetan Buddhist art, which are teeming with Orientalist agendas that have reified both the anonymous artist and the meditative, enlightenment-driven beholder.[12] Few observers of Tibetan art, such as those from Nako village, use these images as meditative supports (*rten*) integral to certain Buddhist practices. Rather, the community largely responds to these images as religiously potent objects imbued with power.

This twofold temporal focus, historical and contemporary, necessarily requires an interdisciplinary method that employs, in a limited fashion, ethnographic and anthropologic practices. Through interviews with the villagers—at their homes, in restaurants, and in temples—I gained firsthand information about how the village faithful related and responded to the temple. This information has been especially useful in altering the interpretative lens from my viewpoint as art historian to the viewpoint of the Tibetan practitioner visiting and using this temple. By incorporating the perspectives of the adherents and users of the temple, however, I am aware that I run the risk of presenting the so-called indigenous perspective.[13] Although this is potentially risky water to navigate, presenting the perspective of the contemporary village faithful allows one to consider how human agency necessarily affects viewing and reception practices. As Ronald Inden has discussed, "far from embodying simple, unchanging essences, all agents are relatively complex and shifting. They make and remake one another through a dialectic process in changing situations."[14] Although his comments relate to the ways people may be agents in the process of re/constructing images and history, in this case of India, his insights resonate with one of this book's basic points: that there is an organic relationship and developing dialogue between community and religious art object, resulting in an object's changing meaning and function over time. By documenting the ways in which contemporary Nako society responds to these images, we gain deeper insight into the multitude of meanings and uses of these religious images, which are still a functional part of the devotional community's life. This is an especially important goal in the study of western Himalayan and Tibetan art, which has largely been concerned with questions of chronology, style, and iconography. The community's interpretation and use of these religious art objects, thus far, has not been fully examined in any art historical study of this region.[15] This ethnographic method allows one to consider how this temple was folded within the village's changing meaning systems and devotional practices, thereby producing more nuanced insights about the intricate relationship between devotee and religious object within the western Himalayan Buddhist context.

The methodological approach employed in chapter 1 primarily relies on fieldwork and ethnography, although I also survey textual accounts, in particular the royal chronicles of the two neighboring kingdoms of Ladakh and Guge. Together these resources and methods of analysis allow me to suture together a socioreligious history of Kinnaur and its larger environment.

In chapter 2 I apply methodological approaches relevant to the distinct objectives of the chapter's sections. The first section draws on iconographic and inscriptional analyses as well as interpretation of written historic sources, dependent on both secondary and primary texts. The second section employs ethnographic documentation and theoretical inquiry pertaining to communal reception of these images at certain historic moments. This interdisciplinary approach helps to expand the current methods of analysis used in the field of western Himalayan art history. The more dynamic model of inquiry used in chapter 2 challenges the investigator to come to terms with the often contradictory aspects of images and to see them not as reified, static objects, but as developing, changing phenomena to which there are a variety of responses and histories. As Richard Davis writes, "In recounting diverse adventures of Indian images, I portray them as fundamentally social beings whose identities are not fixed once and for all at the moment of fabrication, but are repeatedly made and remade through interactions with humans."[16] Such an idea is particularly relevant when dealing with iconography and religious imagery, the meanings of which are often thought to be inflexible. Thus chapter 2 demonstrates that the relationship between the iconographic form and its meaning, at least at the Gyapagpa Temple, is not always prescriptive.

Chapter 3 is largely a history of Drigung activity in the western Himalaya. Examination of royal chronicles of both Ladakhi and Guge (Ngari) kingdoms, surviving visual materials, and secondary sources allows me to sketch a broader political and religious context in which I can situate the Gyapagpa Temple paintings and Nako's sixteenth-century Drigung community. Such positioning is of paramount importance given that these paintings are currently the only extant material evidence of Drigung activity in and around the Kinnaur region of northwest India. What now appears to be an island of Drigung activity amid a sea of Gelug and Kagyu practitioners was not always the case. This history explicates the ways in which Nako's Gyapagpa Temple worked within a much larger Drigung network extending from Ngari, into Kinnaur, and up to Ladakh during the fifteenth and sixteenth centuries.

Stylistic analysis of in situ material in India's western Himalaya and China's Tibetan Autonomous Region forms the basis of my insights for chapters 4 and 5. This traditional formalist approach to visual analysis defines for the reader the essential characteristics of two painting idioms of a single regional style. In so doing I am able to provide an initial description of the Gyapagpa paintings and offer an in-depth comparative analysis of the Gyapagpa murals with the larger stylistic set to which they belong. Through this two-part examination I gauge the rough parameters of the larger style's chronology and idiom, thereby situating the Gyapagpa painting program more precisely within its greater artistic milieu. This method of rigorous formal analysis also bears on chapter 5, where I outline the defining characteristics of the earlier eleventh-century painting style upon which the later fifteenth through sixteenth century paintings are based.

Objectives

This project and its interdisciplinary methodology offer multiple lines of inquiry and methods of analysis for the field of South Asian art history. In particular, I hope that this study will join a handful of others dedicated to the incisive documentation and holistic analysis of monuments—as opposed to isolated, individual objects—from India's Himalayan zone. Such comprehensive investigations of in situ material will help to develop a new trend in the study of art from this region, one that moves away from art-market and aesthetic values that have controlled much of the scholarship to date.[17] The production of prodigious catalogs of Himalayan art based on private or museum collections is symptomatic of this traditional approach that focuses on objects isolated from their original contexts. This monograph, therefore, joins the handful of others dedicated to studying the art of India's northwestern Himalayan region in situ. More broadly, this project contributes to an interdisciplinary discourse that addresses the ways that exchange, appropriation, reuse, and revision of objects affect reception and function over time. Scholars of both South and East Asian material have been helpful in terms of identifying appropriate methodological practices for scholarship addressing the dynamic and ever-changing reception and meaning of religious art objects.[18]

Although my study addresses issues germane to the greater discipline of art history, such as appropriation, reuse, ideology, as well as reception and identity formation, I also make efforts to preserve some of the issues unique to this specific cultural and geographic context: a small Tibetan Buddhist village located at 3,600 meters—or almost 12,000 feet—in the semiarid western Himalaya. I do this, in large part, by documenting and including the voices of the people who use this temple and the larger religious compound of which the Gyapagpa Temple is apart. One very notable local perspective relates to the creation story of the Gyapagpa Temple, which—according to the villagers of Nako—was created by deities. Perspectives such as this, which are necessarily grounded in the local community's sensibility and shared history, are integral to my exploration of this temple's paintings, which are still used, responded to, interacted with, and worshipped. By emphasizing the mural's contemporary lived context, as well as local perspectives on the origination of the religious objects, I hope to provide a narrative that responds to the vitality and endurance of these Buddhist art objects. It is also a narrative that privileges the voice of those who use these objects. In most art historical writing on Tibetan and Himalayan visual material, objects are stripped of this layer of meaningful context, and discussed almost exclusively in terms of iconography, chronology, and style. My scholarship moves toward opening these overly determined discussions in order to gain fuller and more complicated understandings of the dynamic functions and meanings of Buddhist art over time.

Studying these objects in situ, within their original geographic environs, also benefits traditional art historical lines of inquiry, such as style and chronology of style. When provenance is secured, one can ask pointed questions about circulation and diffusion of style alongside issues of the relationship among various artistic centers throughout this area of the western Himalaya. For works that have been divorced from their original contexts, especially after the implementation of antiquities' laws, such discussions relating to geography are inherently limited because provenance is obscured or uncertain. This, of course, is a problem for much of the western Himalayan art historical world.

Lastly, this book, which places at the center of its analysis paintings of modest quality in a community on the periphery of courtly and cosmopolitan life, helps us to reconsider so-called canonized material. This book is very much a story about an overlooked temple set within a marginalized region of India. Yet what this microhistory reveals is how such a site, when thoroughly documented and investigated, yields useful insights into the complex, overlapping, and nebulous networks of meaning, re/use, and reception at a single site over time. In this case, these paintings reveal the richly complex social, religious, and political environments of the western Himalaya during the late medieval period, but also the present day.

1
Nako's Sociopolitical History and Artistic Heritage

The western Himalayan region is situated in the most extreme mountainous landscape in the world, claiming such mountain ranges as Ladakh, Zangskar, and the Great Himalaya. Despite the demands of this high-altitude, semiarid environment, village life in the western Himalaya has long existed and is less isolated than one might think. Villages are linked to one another via intricate trade and pilgrimage routes, which have allowed for the exchange of various commodities and the sharing of religious images, texts, and teachings over centuries.[1] Even now, during the summer months, many of these old routes still serve as primary thoroughfares and trade corridors. It is within this geographic context and along these paths that this book is situated.

Kinnaur

Poised at the lower end of the Spiti valley, approximately 3,637 meters (11,932 feet) above sea level, is the village of Nako. This once-prosperous settlement, which boasts eight functioning temples, is set within the district of Khu nu (Kinnaur), one of the twelve administrative districts of Himachal Pradesh formed in 1960. Since the 1962 Sino-Indian Border Conflict—when China invaded India's Himalayan border regions and claimed them as part of Tibet, and therefore Chinese territory—travel to this region of Kinnaur has been restricted. Only with an Inner Line permit is one allowed to visit places that lie between Jangi and Sumdo (see

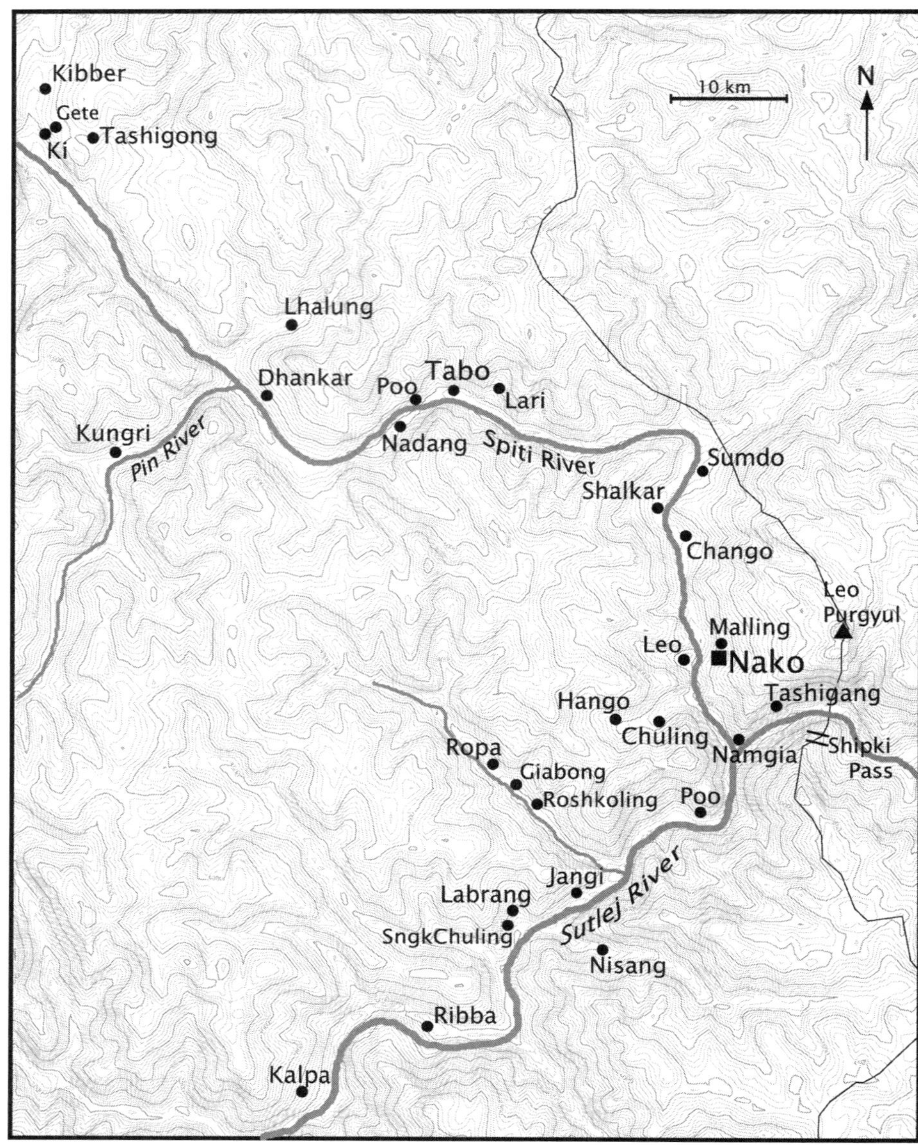

Figure 1.1. Map of villages researched in Kinnaur and Spiti.

fig. 1.1). It is this stretch of approximately eighty kilometers that is known as the Upper Kinnaur region, which is less an official or administrative term than it is a descriptive one.

Today, two routes take the traveler to Upper Kinnaur. One of these requires travel through Lahaul, over the Kunzum Pass, and into Spiti.[2] The other is through Shimla, the capital of Himachal Pradesh, along National Highway 22, which follows the Sutlej River. As Nako is not located directly on the Sutlej, a link road of seven kilometers connects Nako to the highway. Traveling by jeep from Shimla, it generally takes two days to reach Nako, although it can be done in a harrowing single day's jeep ride. The village is set high on the side of a mountain well above the Sutlej River. As Jogishwar Singh explains, "The Satlug valley is the largest valley in the district but is steep and does not lend itself to much settlement or cultivation along its banks. Hence the villages are mostly situated at heights above the river."[3] Behind Nako, one can glimpse the sharp peak of the highest mountain in Kinnaur—Leo Purgyal, at 6,791 meters.

Upon arriving in the Upper Kinnaur district, it becomes evident that this area is geographically and culturally quite different from the lush environs of the lower region. From the lower region came a great deal of the materials for commercial trade with Tibet, such as deodar wood and indigo.[4] As semiarid Upper Kinnaur is within the "monsoon shadow," its soil is friable and water scarce. The villages manage to subsist on the cultivation of peas and potatoes, as well as apple orchards planted in the lower climes. Given the challenges of high-altitude agriculture, trade is very important in this part of Kinnaur.[5] The villages of this upper district of Kinnaur consistently traded with their eastern and northern neighbors, Tibet and Ladakh.

Although the modern-day boundaries of Kinnaur are clearly delineated, this was not always the case.[6] Moreover, it seems that the names Khu nu or Kinnaur were not consistently in circulation. Deborah Klimburg-Salter makes the point that early texts, such as the eleventh-century biography of Rin chen bzang po (Rinchen Zangpo), do not include the place name of Kinnaur or Khu nu.[7] By the fifteenth century, however, Khu nu is specifically mentioned in the *Mnga' ris rgyal rabs*.[8] Indeed, Khu nu is mentioned in other post–fifteenth century texts or documents, indicating that the name had come into use by the fifteenth century, if not slightly earlier. Other secondary sources indicate that the name Khu nu was used around the seventeenth and nineteenth centuries. For instance, Giuseppe Tucci uses "Kinnaur" in his translation of the travel itinerary of Stag tshang ras pa (Tagtsang Repa), also known as O rgyan pa ngag dbang rgya mtsho (Ogyanpa Ngawang Gyatso) (1574–1651), a seventeenth-century Buddhist monastic and pilgrim. The colophon states that the text was sponsored by the king of Ladakh at the time, Seng ge rnam rgyal (Senge Namgyal), which would date the text to about the seventeenth century, contemporaneous with the monk's life.[9] Lastly, a nineteenth-century pilgrimage text featuring the Kailash region mentions Kinnaur with regard to a 'Bri gung (Drigung) monastery operative in the thirteenth century.[10]

None of these texts, however, provides specific information about the location of the Kinnaur region. It is likely that the boundaries of Kinnaur shifted and were redrawn over time. For instance, Klimburg-Salter mentions that Tucci identifies the area "south of the Sutlej and eastward to Charang" as Kinnaur.[11] Such a region would be much smaller than the current boundaries and would not include Nako. What complicates things further is that while Kinnaur is mentioned in several of these historical contexts, Nako is not.[12] Given the dearth of textual documentation for Kinnaur, and Nako in particular, it is useful to think of Upper Kinnaur and Nako as part of a larger cultural zone that included Spiti in the west and Mnga' ris (Ngari) in the east. The material evidence in Nako and throughout the Spiti valley and its side valleys (the Hango, Pin, and Lingti valleys in particular), as well as Ngari, suggest that there was a rich and consistent flow of Buddhist transactions within this extended area.

Political Profile

Politically, Kinnaur's structure is difficult to identify. Up until the sixteenth century there is no evidence of state formation. Until this point, the small settlements of Kinnaur are thought to have ruled themselves, creating a network of fiefdoms throughout the Kinnaur region.[13] As Singh states, "It is quite likely that villages existed under some sort of system of governance without there having been a state as we understand the term."[14] Although Kinnaur, and its individually governed villages, Nako among them, were certainly connected to the powerful kingdoms of Ladakh and Guge through a network of pilgrimage and trade routes, as well as marriage alliances, the exact nature of Kinnaur's political relationship with these two powerful political entities during the late medieval period cannot be clearly determined. It is likely, though, that Nako, fell under, if even loosely, Guge rule, as did neighboring Spiti from the tenth through seventeenth centuries.[15] By the seventeenth century, a major shift unfolded in West Tibet's political structure; it fell under Central Tibetan rule. The fifth Dalai Lama campaign to unify all parts of Tibet under a centralized authority affected Guge and all of the Ngari area. The satellite, but important districts of Spiti and Kinnaur were split up under different political entities. Part of Kinnaur was subsumed within the Indian Bhashar rule, the reasons for which will be explained later.

Although the critical dearth of historical records leaves many questions about Kinnaur's political relationship to Guge, what is likely is that it, along with Ladakh, loomed large on Kinnaur's political horizon. From the fifteenth through the seventeenth centuries, Kinnaur was situated between two distinct political centers, that of Guge in the Ngari region and Ladakh, which lies north of Kinnaur. The resurgent Ngari suzerainty developed in the late fourteenth to early fifteenth centuries under the rule of Rnam rgyal lde (Namgyalde [born 1372]), which is discussed in more detail in chapter 5. His rulership at the end of the fourteenth century marks a particularly interesting period in Ngari's history because it ushers in a time of financial security and military strength. This productive period came after what can only be understood as a nebulous and undocumented period of rule in West Tibet from 1277 to 1372. The royal chronicle written in the fifteenth century says very little about this hundred-year period. In fact, a single paragraph is devoted to it, a paragraph without mention made to rulers' names or other particularities that this chronicle readily mentions elsewhere in the text. Rather than documenting occurrences, this paragraph of the chronicle relies heavily on metaphor to describe the "royal feats" of the kings and princes who "did not leave anything undone."[16] This section of the chronicle is at odds with what is otherwise a detailed account of royal family members' names, place names, patronage deed, and religious associations. Although little can be gleaned from the textual sources about this hundred-year period, it is an essential period for one to understand in order to appreciate the significance of the Guge kingdom and its art in the fifteenth and sixteenth centuries.

This relatively undocumented period directly corresponds to the period of foreign rule by the Mongols of the Yuan dynasty, which lasted for nearly a century (1271–1368). It should be noted that some scholars are hesitant to suggest that the Yuan dynasty had a direct effect in this western region—which was physically far removed from central Tibetan political orbits—because of a dearth of substantive evidence suggesting direct Yuan control.[17] As Roberto Vitali's critical reading of the *Mnga' ris rgyal rabs* reveals, the hundred-year interruption in West Tibet's suzerainty coincides with an escalation in Sakya, and therefore Yuan, control of Ngari. Moreover, based on a translation of documents from Zha lu (Shalu), a Sakya pa monastery in Central Tibet, Giuseppe Tucci also suggested that West Tibet was indeed under the control of the greater Yuan Empire during the fourteenth century.[18]

Fifteenth-century rulers such as Namgyalde, and subsequent rulers, carefully fashioned the newfangled Guge kingdom, through text and image, to reflect the values and patronage of the august sovereignty of the Pu hrang (Purang)–Guge kingdom of the eleventh century. This is made explicit by the very commission of the fifteenth-century chronicle, in which the latter kingdom depicts itself as a continuation of the earlier eleventh-century Purang-Guge kingdom.

While the Guge kingdom's presence was prominent in the western Himalayan region, Ladakh was another powerful kingdom in the fifteenth century that was very much part of Kinnaur's orbit. The kingdom of Ladakh to the northwest was a steadily growing empire that promoted Bka' brgyud (Kagyu) Buddhism, switching from Drigung in the late sixteenth century to 'Brug pa (Drukpa) in the early seventeenth.[19] Ladakh's strong association with Drigung Kagyu is of particular interest given that

Nako was home to a Drigung community in the sixteenth century. This may have fostered some direct interaction between the two areas. Politically, however, Ladakh threatened Guge, the political entity that likely controlled some of Kinnaur. The two kingdoms were at odds with one another during the late medieval periods, vying for political control and religious patronage. Ladakh invaded Ngari at several points during the sixteenth century. Eventually, by the seventeenth century, Central Tibet saw an opportunity to thwart Ladakh's presence and to bring West Tibet within its fold. The several-year struggle, commonly referred to as the Tibet-Ladakh-Mughal war (1679–84), brought success to Central Tibet, who had relied heavily on the support of the Indian Bashahr kingdom, the capital of which was located in Rampur, in the area now called "Lower Kinnaur."

The so-called Namgia Document, or Treaty, found by Tucci at the monastic site of Namgia located at the confluence of the Sutlej and Spiti rivers and approximately twenty kilometers southeast of Nako, narrates the political relationship at the end of the seventeenth century among four polities: Bashahr, Ladakh, Guge, and Central Tibet. This document reveals that once Ladakh gained power over Ngari, Central Tibet intervened.[20] After strategically garnering the support of the Indian hill kingdom of Bashahr, Central Tibet overtook Ladakh in the late seventeenth century. With Bashahr's defences in place, Ladakh was essentially surrounded on the east and west fronts, and was quick to accept defeat. As outlined in the Namgia Document, once Ladakh was overtaken, Central Tibet gained control of "upper Kinnaur," which was then "ceded to the Rāja of Bashahr who had cooperated with the Lhasa troops."[21] That Upper Kinnaur became the bargaining chip for negotiations between the Central Tibetan government and the Bashahr kingdom reveals the value of this region, which was rich with materials and trade routes. The rāja of Bhushahr understood that this upper region of Kinnaur was not simply a semiarid land of little agricultural potential, but that it served as the threshold of major commercial thoroughfares running between India and Tibet. This deal, therefore, was a financially prudent one on behalf of the Bashahr kingdom.

The question remains, however, what constituted "upper Kinnaur"? It may well have been the area now considered the Upper Kinnaur region—Jangi to Sumdo. If so, this would have included Nako, which would suggest that it was a tributary of the Guge kingdom in West Tibet. Thus, although Nako, and more broadly Kinnaur, may have been officially subsumed within the Guge kingdom, it is likely that it was not directly governed by Guge. Moreover, the boundaries of various regions, not just Kinnaur, and the alliances among the feudatories in the western Himalaya likely blurred and shifted over time, preventing any conclusive insights about Nako or Kinnaur's precise relationship with the West Tibetan kingdom.

As for Nako's—or even more broadly, Kinnaur's—political relationship with well-established Indian kingdoms, such as Brahmour (Chamba), it is too specious to suggest any concrete relationship. The areas of what are now east and west Himachal Pradesh were connected economically through trade. Chamba, as a well-defined Hindu kingdom by the sixteenth and well into the seventeenth century, offered little to Buddhist-centered Nako as a model of governance, religion, or even art. Chamba looked to Gangetic India for its political and artistic prototypes while Nako, and much of Kinnaur, looked to Tibet. Their discrete sociopolitical identification is borne out through the material and architectural evidence surrounding each community. Nako's seismically active and brittle terrain could never accommodate Chamba's stone temples, which were fashioned according to *Nāgra* prototypes; moreover, the meaning and association that such a lithic temple would communicate—Hindu India—would not reflect Nako's identity as a Tibetan Buddhist village. Subsequently, there are no immediate or obvious linkages between the areas except for what was likely an active trade corridor running between them into Tibet. Only with more detailed research in these northern reaches of India will we gain insight into such subtle, yet likely important, avenues of exchange.[22]

That Nako does not have any extant textual record, such as a royal chronicle, genealogy, or lengthy inscriptional record, nor is it ever mentioned explicitly in the fifteenth-century *Mnga' ris rgyal rabs* (*Ngari Gyalrab*), helps to buttress the point that Nako never assumed a powerful political position. Rather, the village seems to have resided at the margins, both physically and politically, of the major power centers controlling the region to which it belonged. This peripheral political position should not eclipse Nako's central religious role. Given the accumulation of Buddhist art and the numerous temples constructed in Nako from about the twelfth century onward, this village must have had a substantial body of patrons and enough wealth to uphold robust patronage practices. This would indicate that Nako may indeed have been an important node along pilgrimage and trade routes running through what was once considered the larger Ngari kingdom. Indeed, Nako's material evidence, such as inscriptions, temples, wall paintings, and sculptures provide a valuable historical record that provides insight into Nako's religious history and its potential connections to both Ladakh and Ngari.

Religious History

Tibetan Buddhism is the predominant religion practiced in Upper Kinnaur, although in some villages there is an intermixing of Hinduism and

Buddhism.[23] The village of Ropa is a good example of such religious syncretism. There, the primary village temple site is Tibetan Buddhist. According to its iconographic program, it seems that the temple was affiliated with the Rnying ma (Nyingma) tradition, yet in the village there is clearly Hindu activity as seen by the palanquin housed under a *maṇḍapa*.[24] The sign for it reads, "Jaya Durgā mātā Ropā serā valī," which can be roughly translated as "Hail Durgā mātā of Ropā, the one who rides the lion." Although this sign seems to indicate the existence of Hindu devotional practice, in particular reverence of a specific form of Durgā, it also points to the importance of the Hindi language in the area, as opposed to Tibetan. By the time one travels the fifty kilometers from Ropa to Nako, however, the cultural landscape has dramatically shifted. Tibetan Buddhism dominates but coexists with the worship of local mountain deities, such as Purgyal in Nako. Such religious syncretism between Buddhism and mountain deities is not unusual; one finds that local deities, especially mountain deities that are not part of the accepted Buddhist pantheon, are propitiated throughout the Tibetan cultural zone.[25]

Placing Nako within the larger context of the Spiti valley and Ngari, it is evident that this village was part of a thriving system of Buddhist sites from various sects over hundreds of years (fig. 1.1). Given the modern-day political boundaries and tensions, it was not possible for me to investigate temples freely on the Tibet side of the border. I did, however, travel via foot and jeep along paths connecting many of these villages in Kinnaur, Lahaul, Spiti, Zangskar, and Ladakh. I was particularly interested in locating other Drigung sites as well as painting programs that could be stylistically connected to the paintings of Nako's Gyapagpa Temple. Although there were no other Drigung temples, I was able to chart in a rough manner the artistic and religious landscape of the Spiti valley and its subvalleys. The following section briefly addresses some of these sites in order to provide an abbreviated understanding of the religious context and artistic environment surrounding Nako. The following analysis reveals this region's rich presence of Buddhist art with iconographic programs illustrating syncretic religious practice relating to Gelug, Kagyu, and Nyingma traditions.

Starting with Tashigang, a village that is a full day's walk southeast of Nako (fig. 1.1), there were two small temples that I was allowed to see, but could not photograph. The primary temple structure of this village was a *Tungyur* temple, which according to inscriptional evidence in the area can be transliterated as Dung 'gyur, a local term for this kind of temple.[26] This is a small temple used primarily to shelter a large prayer wheel, a cylindrical piece of metal, approximately 1.5 × 1.0 meters, upon the metal surface of which is generally embossed the same prayer numerous times:

Oṃ ma ṇi pad me hūṃ. Inside the metal casing are reams of paper printed with the same prayer. When the prayer wheel is spun in a clockwise direction, it is thought to release the prayers and wishes of wellbeing into the cosmos. Turning wheels like this, therefore, is thought to be beneficial for the world and especially meritorious for the practitioner who sets the wheel in motion. The walls of the Tashigang Tungyur were painted in a circa nineteenth-century style. Another, smaller temple was situated to the side and behind the Tungyur. This temple's paintings were also executed in a nineteenth-century style, with an iconographic program revealing Kagyu affiliation, although the exact sect could not be determined. The temple caretaker indicated that the village followed the Drukpa school of the Kagyu tradition.

Southwest of Nako, the Hango valley had two interesting villages: Hango and Chuling (fig. 1.1). Although this area is just over the pass from Ropa, the two temples at Hango did not reveal any stylistic or architectural similarities with Ropa. One temple was quite small and considered to be the temple of the village deity. Although the other temple was considerably larger, it was a modern-day concrete construction; its interior walls painted in vibrant, glossy colors, depicting Nyingma iconography. In contrast, the village of Chuling was home to a much older stone temple—the undressed stone architecture of which is notable as Tibetan Buddhist temples in this Upper Kinnaur region are more commonly built with unfired earth-brick laid over a rubble base.[27] Inside this single-story, rectangular building was a number of circa twelfth-century clay sculptures. The painting program in the temple was a virtual palimpsest of different periods. One could detect a twelfth-century layer as well as some fourteenth-century paintings, and all of these have been repainted to varying degrees. The religious affiliation was not clear from the iconography on the walls. As at Nako, this twelfth-century temple may have been a Bka' gdams (Kadam) site that was later converted to a different school, such as Drukpa of the Kagyu tradition.

Lying north of Nako is the rather large and prosperous village of Chango, with at least four functioning temples for a sizeable population of approximately twelve hundred. Of these, three painting programs reveal a combination of Kagyu and Nyingma iconography. The fourth temple's iconographic program was in such poor condition that it was impossible to discern any sectarian affiliation. The paintings at the three Kagyu/Nyingma temples were painted within a fifty-year period, beginning about the second quarter of the nineteenth century, and all shared a similar aesthetic of bright, colorful, and highly glossed paints (fig. 1.2).

The two villages of Tabo and Dankar, which are of paramount importance as religious and political centers of this region, are located northwest of Chango. In the village of Tabo one will find seven temples—six in

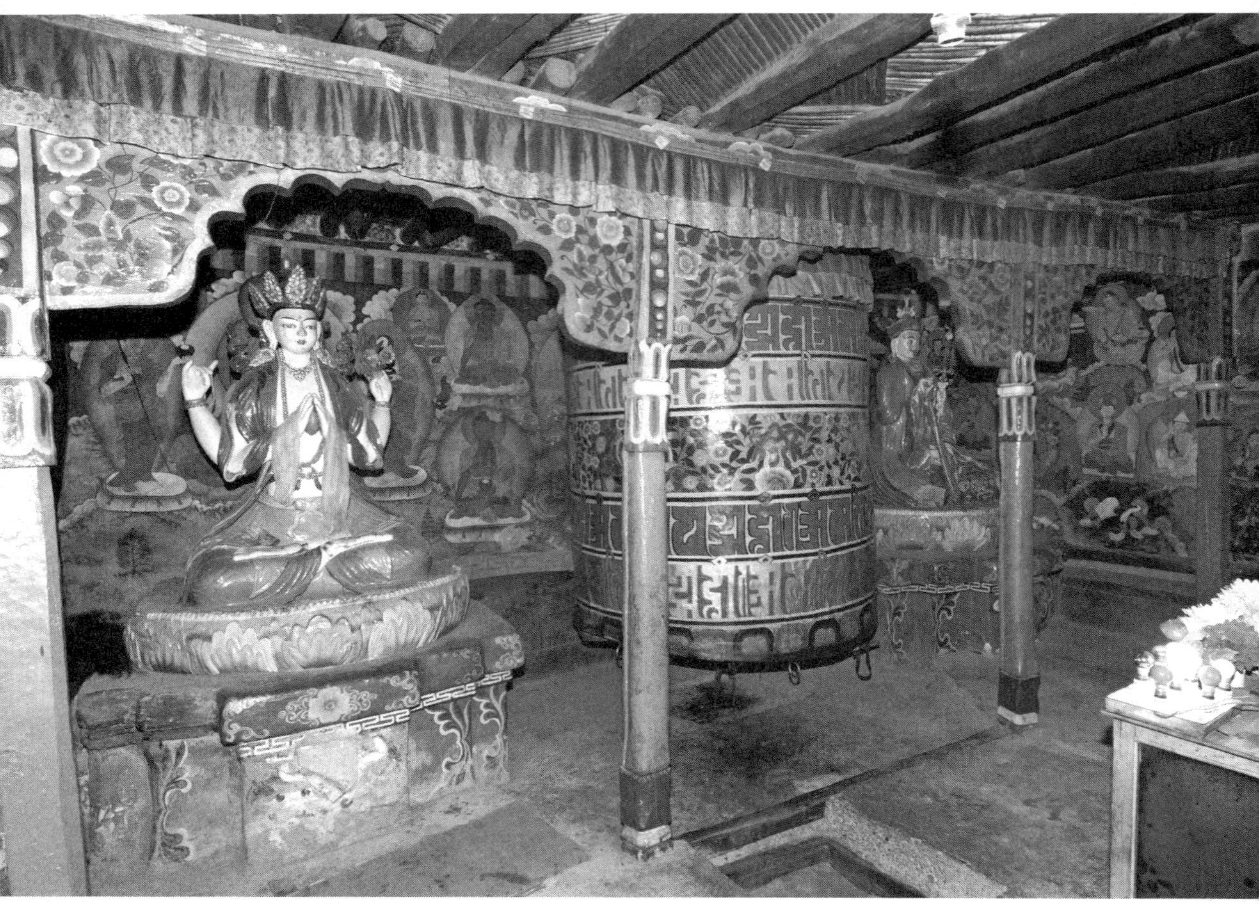

Figure 1.2. Inside Chango's Dung 'gyur (Tungyur) (Chango, Kinnaur Dist., H.P.).

the compound and one cave temple located on the hill north of the village. Five of these seven temples display clear Dge lugs (Gelug) iconography. The style of several of these temples can be dated to the sixteenth century and are directly related to the West Tibetan painting idiom of that time. As two of these temples pertain to the stylistic vocabulary used at the Gyapagpa Temple, they will be discussed in greater detail in chapter 4. Continuing up the road from Tabo one will find the village of Dankar (fig. 1.3) dramatically positioned high on the cliffs overlooking the Spiti River. Dankar, which was once the capital of the ruling family of Spiti during the late medieval period, has numerous temples.[28] Of the two temples I documented there, it was the Nangasan Temple that had a circa eighteenth-century painted program with what seemed to be iconographic elements of three different traditions: Kagyu, Nyingma, and Gelug. Gelug imagery was evident in the large portrait of the tradition's founder, Tsong kha pa, (Tsongkhapa) on the southwest wall. The presence of Dmag zor rgyal mo

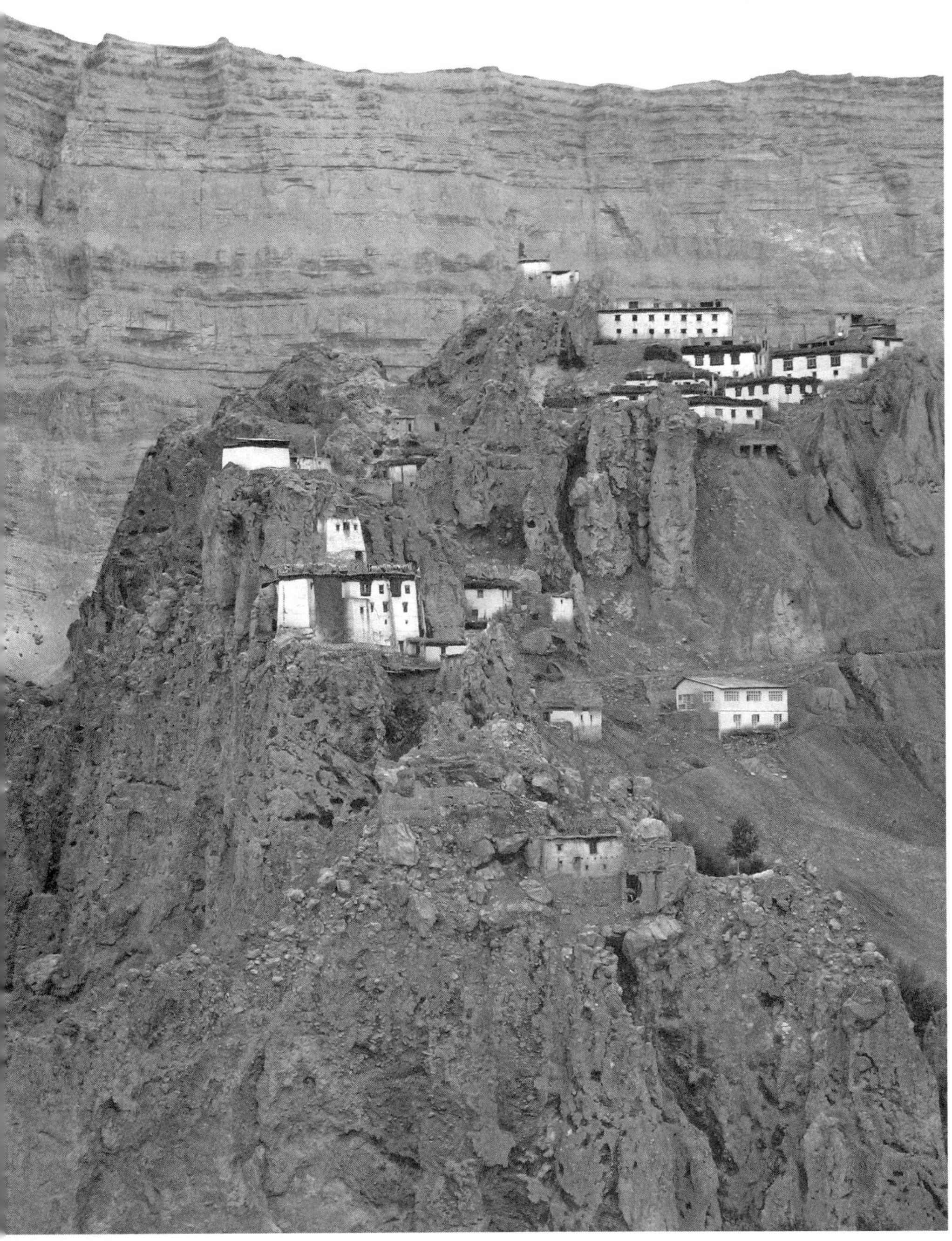

Figure 1.3. Village of Dankar (Lahaul Spiti Dist., H.P.). RNL.

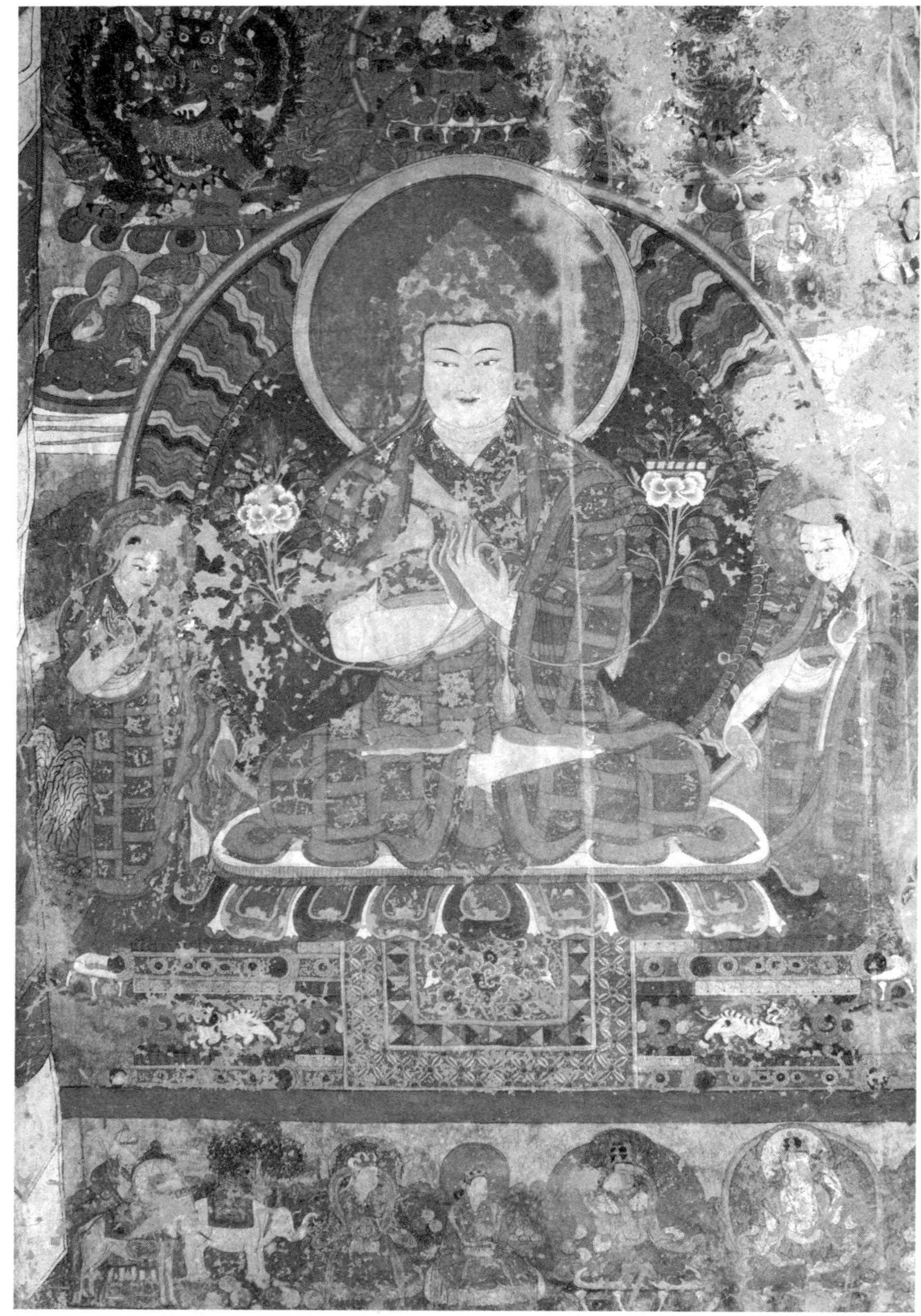

Figure 1.4. Dankar (Lahaul Spiti Dist., H.P.), Nangasan Temple, Tsongkapa, c. eighteenth century.

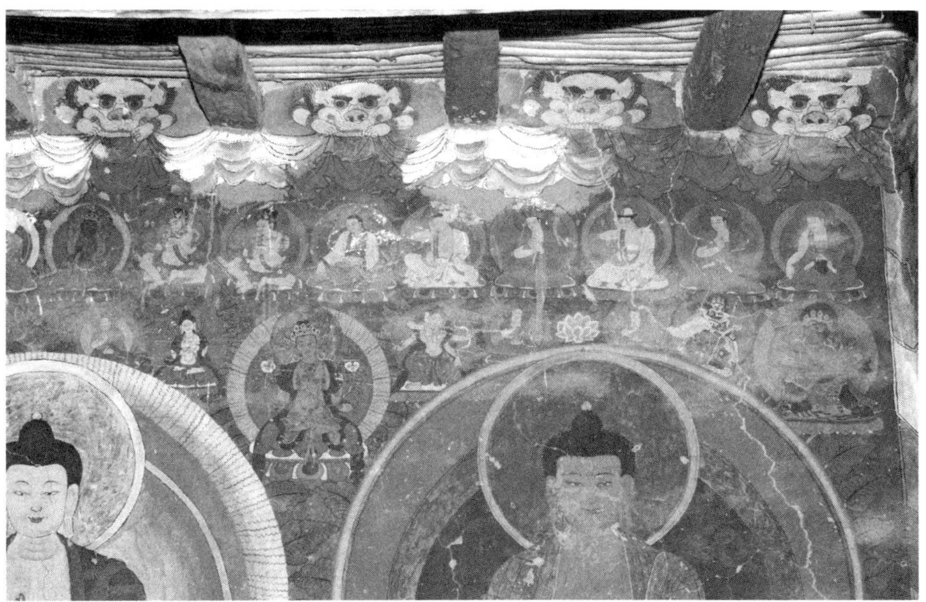

Figure 1.5. Dankar (Lahaul Spiti Dist., H.P.), Nangasan Temple, 'Brug pa (Drukpa) lineage, c. eighteenth century (Lahaul Spiti Dist., H.P.).

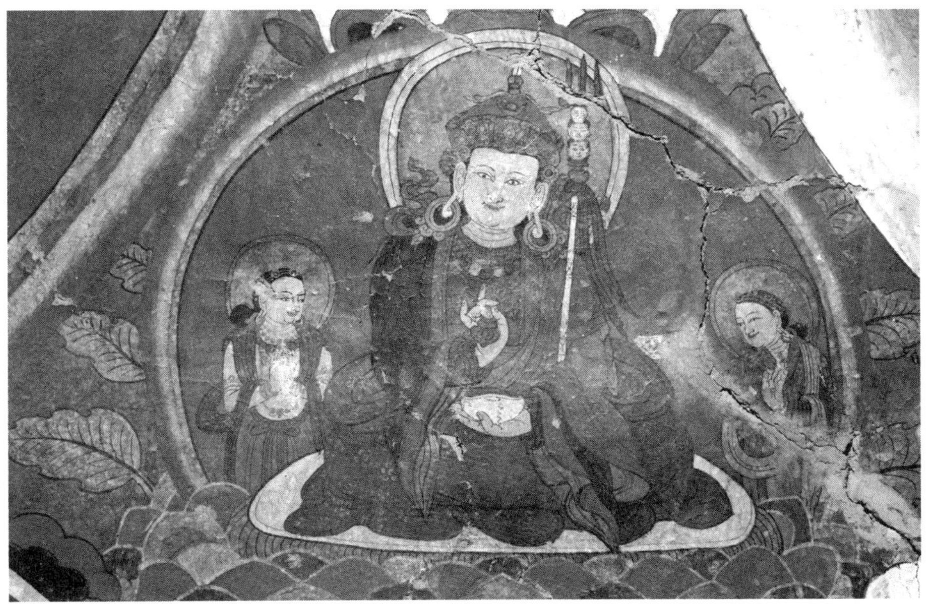

Figure 1.6. Dankar (Lahaul Spiti Dist., H.P.), Nangasan Temple, Guru Rimpoche, c. eighteenth century (Lahaul Spiti Dist., H.P.).

(Magzor Gyalmo) on the northeast wall, which is the entrance/exit for the temple (fig. 1.4), also confirmed Gelug affiliation. On the northwest wall, however, there is a painted lineage of the Drukpa school of the Kagyu tradition, replete with Vajradhara, mahāsiddhas, Marpa, and Mi la ras pa (Milarepa) (fig. 1.5). Tucked between two larger images on the southeast wall is a small image of Guru Rinpoche and his two wives (fig. 1.6). He is a venerated Buddhist saint, also known by his Sanskrit name, Padmasambhava, who is strongly associated with the Nyingma tradition.[29] This admixture of iconography raises questions about the possibility of regional religious pluralism or perhaps inclusivism. Although these issues are beyond the scope of this book, much pertaining to eighteenth-century religious practice in the area could be gleaned by analyzing the paintings and their iconographic information.[30]

Across from Dankar, on the south side of the river, is the small, but spectacular Pin valley, which had a Nyingma temple at Guling. The monastic community at Guling seems to have been a long-established one, although the religious architecture was newly constructed. Painted concrete structures, such as a temple and prayer hall could accommodate the roughly fifty monks in residence.[31] At the compound there was a smaller, older temple with soot-covered wall paintings making it impossible to determine their style or date.

Continuing up the Spiti valley there is the well-known Gelug monastery of Ki (Kye), and north of this is the village of Kibber that sits at over 4,000 meters (fig. 1.1). There were approximately five temples in this fairly small village, one of which was painted in a circa eighteenth-century style. In terms of its iconography, this is another example of a mixture of Gelug figures with Arhats, the thirty-six Buddhas, and a rather prominent image of Guru Rimpoche (fig. 1.7). The image of Guru Rimpoche amid Gelug iconography in any other context may be confusing, but in this area of the western Himalaya, this much beloved historical figure, who traveled throughout this region, is frequently incorporated into the iconographic programs of temples despite differing sectarian associations. This was the last site I was able to visit in the Spiti valley, as the road over the Kunzum Pass was blocked by glacial melt.

This cursory review of some of the Buddhist temples in the Spiti valley reveals that the region was rich with religious activity and densely populated with villages, each financially stable enough to commission several temples, all with elaborate painting programs in varying styles. Many of these mural cycles have been repainted, which for the art historian is a great loss but generally indicates that these temples are still a vital part of the villages' religious lives. Certainly, this repainting raises the question of whether the religious affiliation of the temples altered over time. In some temples, such as at Dankar, the addition of Gelug imagery was deliberate

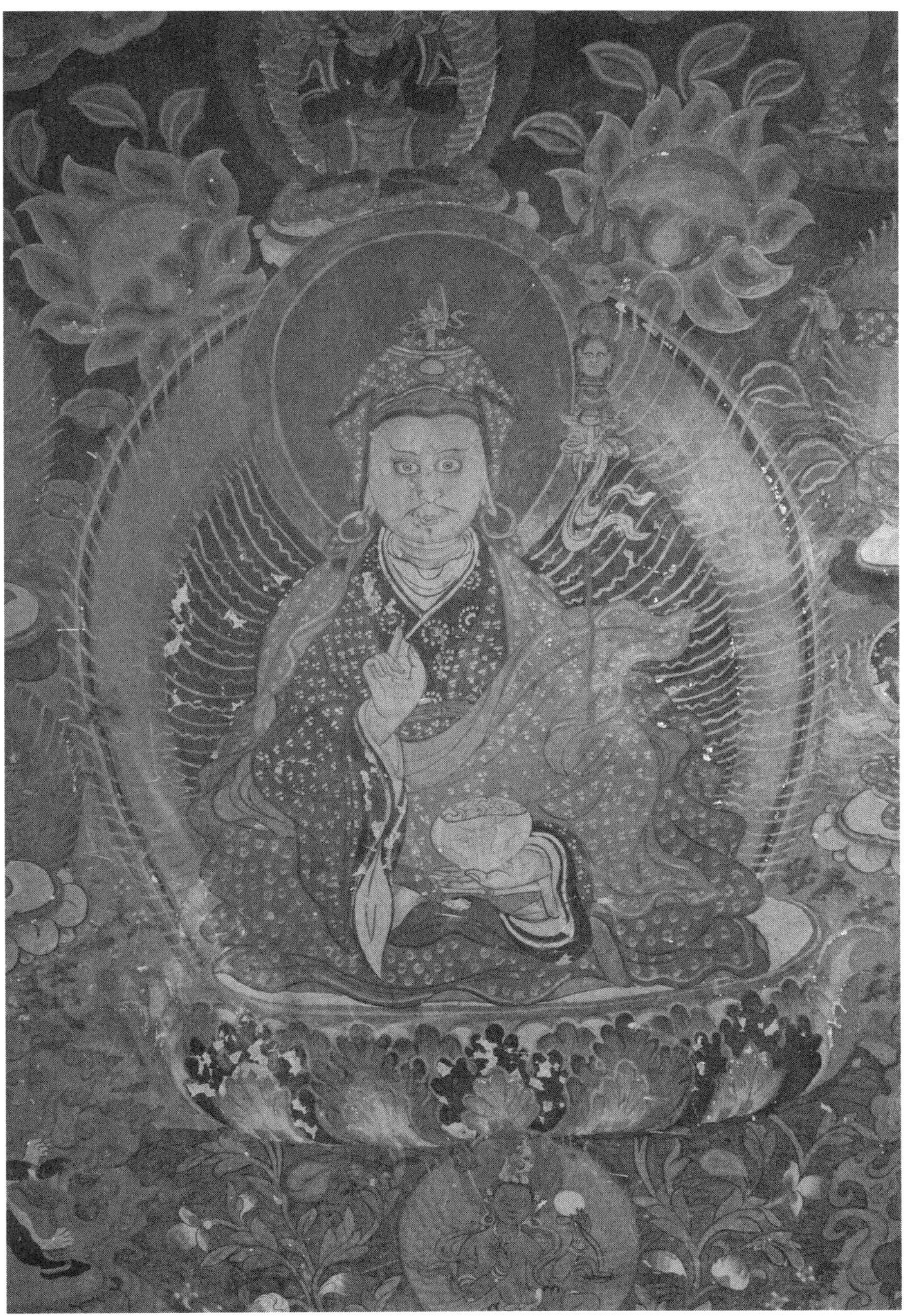

Figure 1.7. Kibber (Lahaul Spiti Dist., H.P.), temple with Guru Rimpoche wall painting, c. eighteenth century.

and intended to alter the temple's original religious affiliation. Frequently, Gelug and Kagyu iconography was further supplemented with images of Guru Rimpoche, which would indicate an awareness of, if not association with, the Nyingma tradition. These pastiche-like iconographic programs would seem to indicate a larger trend toward religious syncretism in this area.[32] These layered iconographic programs represent a spectrum of diverse Tibetan Buddhist traditions that currently exist in the Spiti valley and its subvalleys. In terms of styles of painting, there was less continuity or stylistic connection than I had hoped to find among these various painting programs. It seems that only Tabo's post-fifteenth-century painting programs resonated with those of Nako's Gyapagpa temple.

Within this larger context of the Spiti valley, Nako was intricately connected to what seems to have been a well-established tradition of temple patronage and religious activity. These villages of the Spiti valley were also part of a long pilgrimage circuit moving east and west. Nako was very likely an important node on that pilgrimage path. According to oral tradition and a written record on rock inscriptions found above Nako, the village was originally known as Gnas sgo, literally meaning "pilgrimage door."[33] Located at the cusp of the Tibetan plateau and the Spiti valley, Nako may have functioned as a threshold for pilgrims moving both eastward to Tibet's venerated Mount Kailash or westward to important monastic sites at Tabo, Kye, or even into the area of Swat in the Hindu Kush. In the eleventh century it is likely that pilgrims traveled these same paths to Kashmir and Swat, which were then hubs of Buddhist learning. Indeed, Kashmir was of critical importance to Ngari during the second diffusion of Buddhism.[34] Such a route could have gone through the Kinnaur region, and perhaps even through Nako itself. The limited scholarship on Kinnaur pilgrimage routes, however, has not yet revealed that Nako was a named node on such circuits. For instance, Tucci makes note of pilgrimage routes running between Ngari and the Swat valley to Uḍḍiyāna, the birthplace of Guru Rimpoche. Tucci reconstructed these pilgrimage routes running east and west based on Tibetan texts outlining the itineraries of three pilgrims, Rgod tshang pa (Gotsangpa; early 1200s), his disciple, O rgyan pa (Ogyanpa; 1230–93),[35] and the previously mentioned Stag tshang ras pa (Tagtsang Repa), also known as O rgyan pa ngag dbang rgya mtsho (Orgyanpa Ngawang Gyatso), the founder of Hemis monastery in Ladakh (1574–1651).[36] Although Kinnaur is mentioned, none of these texts explicitly references Nako; speculatively, the village may have been known by a different name in the thirteenth and sixteenth centuries.

The part of the text dedicated to Gotsangpa's travels during the thirteenth century suggests that he traveled from Kailash to Tholing and into Spiti on his way to Uḍḍiyāna:[37]

[He] went without hesitation through the big rivers. . . . Then having crossed the whole country of Zhang Zhung [Ngari] he went to Spiti, where, above Bi lcogs, he met the great Siddha K'a rag pa who was unrivalled in the meditation of the rDsogs c'en system.[38]

Tucci tentatively locates Bi lcogs (Bichog) in the Lipak valley, which he says is near Nako, but it is located within the Pin valley, at least eighty kilometers west of Nako.[39] Thus, the pilgrim traveled the northern route into Spiti and Lahaul, which undoubtedly went through Kinnaur and perhaps into Nako or close to it. Furthermore, the mention of Kha rag pa (Kharepa), the ascetic famous for his mastery of Rdsogs chen (Dzogchen), is also an important detail. He is, in fact, one of three ascetics with whom Gotsangpa meets while in the Kinnaur/Spiti region, which underscores the existence of a well-developed ascetic life in this region.

It is only in the later seventeenth-century pilgrimage text that Kinnaur is specifically mentioned. The path discussed in this later text takes the pilgrim Tagtsang Repa south of Nako along the Indus and eventually into Kangra. In Tucci's translation,

He then reaches K'yun lun and after five days he halts at the bottom of the Sarang la. Having crossed this pass, he enters the narrow valley of Ku nu and through rNam rgyal, Pu, Sa, he arrives after two days at So rang and then sets out to K'yags; in five days he reaches Su ge t'an and after three days more Dsva la mu khe.[40]

Tucci explained that these texts are challenging because many of the place names no longer correlate to the names of villages known today. Still, he hazards guesses for some of the places mentioned in the previous quotation, such as rNam rgyal as the village located at the bottom of Shipki Pass or Pu as Poo, which is approximately twenty-five kilometers south of Nako. Sa, Tucci suggests is Sasu, which is located between Poo and Kanam. Lastly, So rang, according to Tucci is Sarahan. It would seem, given the places noted on the pilgrimage path, that it runs a southerly route along the Indus, bypassing Nako completely.[41]

The point of discussing these pilgrimage paths and textual evidence is to highlight the fact that Nako was located within an active network of pilgrimage routes running from east to west. Furthermore, the districts of Kinnaur and Spiti were punctuated by the spiritual presence of important yogis, which again supports the idea that this region was a center for Buddhist practice, a fact already supported by the built record of the region. Although these texts focus on the westward movement of pilgrims, the "door of pilgrimage" undoubtedly swung eastward to Tibet: specifically to Mount Kailash. Though there are no pilgrimage texts that discuss this, it is likely that the Drigung followers, from Zangskar and Ladakh traveled east to Kailash, a region once dominated by the Drigung tradition.

They, too, may well have gone through or near Nako on these routes to the sacred mountain.

Commercial Context

Nako was part of a larger network of religious sites that were and remain active within the Spiti valley from the eleventh century onward. These same routes through Kinnaur and Spiti, along which there were scores of temples, most likely had a dual purpose as pilgrim paths and commercial corridors. Nako was poised at an important religious and commercial crossroads, which may be why such a small village has an abundance of temples. These temples suggest prodigious patronage practices that necessarily were dependent on economic prosperity.

Generally, trade coming from Ngari along well-established trade routes, dotted with several Buddhist temples, consisted of both luxury and conventional goods such as gold, *pashm* (pashmina wool), borax, and salt.[42] Singh has charted the various routes used by Upper Kinnaur tradesmen traveling to Ngari.[43] Although Nako was not specifically included in Singh's list of villages, it would fall within the area he designates as the Hangrang Pargana, "villages in the lower valley of the Spiti river."[44] In fact, it seems that tradesmen of Nako would have easily traveled along east–west routes alongside other tradesmen from the villages of Poo, Chango, and Khab.[45] This commercial and religious interaction was vibrant, even as early as the tenth century. Klimburg-Salter writes:

> [T]he kings of western Tibet were able to construct an efficient international trade network which allowed them to export precious metals mined in their territory, particularly Guge. This network certainly depended, in part, on the small monasteries established throughout the kingdom and located at strategic points along the trade routes.[46]

Commerce moving from the west to the east included Indian spices (ginger and turmeric, in particular), dye agents such as indigo, deodar wood, sea buckthorn berries, and apricots.[47] In the sixteenth century Nako was also at the nexus of centuries-old trade routes and pilgrimage paths moving north and south.[48] These routes were protected in the late seventeenth century by the previously discussed Namgia treaty, which the Busharh kingdom of Kinnaur came to govern. The Busharh capital was in Rampur, one of the important trading posts for the circuit running among Kinnaur, Ladakh, and Tibet. As Singh writes, "This treaty remained in force down to 1962 when the border with Tibet was closed as a result of the Sino-Indian conflict of that year."[49] This history of the region's political structure, religious affiliations, and commercial connections form a backdrop against which Nako and its religious compound, which includes the specific temple that is the focus of this monograph, can be further explored.

Nako and Its Temples

Of the seven temples in Nako, four are in the village's religious compound, while the other three are scattered throughout the village. I will begin with the Guru Rimpoche Temple, which is situated near Nako's small lake.[50] The plan of this temple is unlike any of the others in that it is organized around a large stone that, according to local legend, bears a foot imprint of the temple's namesake, Guru Rimpoche.[51] This stone supports a rather wide and tall weight-bearing column positioned at the center of the building. Halfway up the column is a niche with a sculpture of Guru Rimpoche.

The four walls surrounding the main column and niche are badly damaged and its paintings only partially visible. The surviving portions of the painting programs indicate that this was once a finely decorated temple with paintings executed in a style associated with and derived from Central Tibet, which was popular in all reaches of the Tibetan cultural zone during the twelfth through fourteenth centuries. This style and its many idioms were once known collectively as the Inner Asian International Style.[52] These paintings are important for the sectarian information that they provide. On the east and south walls there is a lineage of what look to be Kagyu monastic figures, based on their distinctive red hats. This set of lineage portraits is thought to be the "earliest evidence we have for a Kagyu presence at Nako."[53] Unfortunately, the specific school of Kagyu cannot be determined despite several inscribed portraits and the presence of a rather lengthy inscription located on the south wall near the door. All of the temple's inscriptional evidence has been translated by Kurtis Tropper of the University of Vienna.[54] None of the inscriptions, however, provides information about the specific school, patron, or date of the paintings.

The next two temples, though they are not located near each other, are discussed together because they are both Tungyur temples and can be roughly dated to the same period, circa mid-nineteenth century. The first of these temples is located near the Guru Rimpoche Temple; the second, referred to in the village as "Upper Tungyur," is located a bit to the northeast, essentially above the other. The first, referred to simply as the Tungyur Temple, is cared for by an elderly Nako resident, Kunchok Ngodrub, and his family, who are also responsible for maintaining the small shrine in what is now the defunct monastery on the hill above the

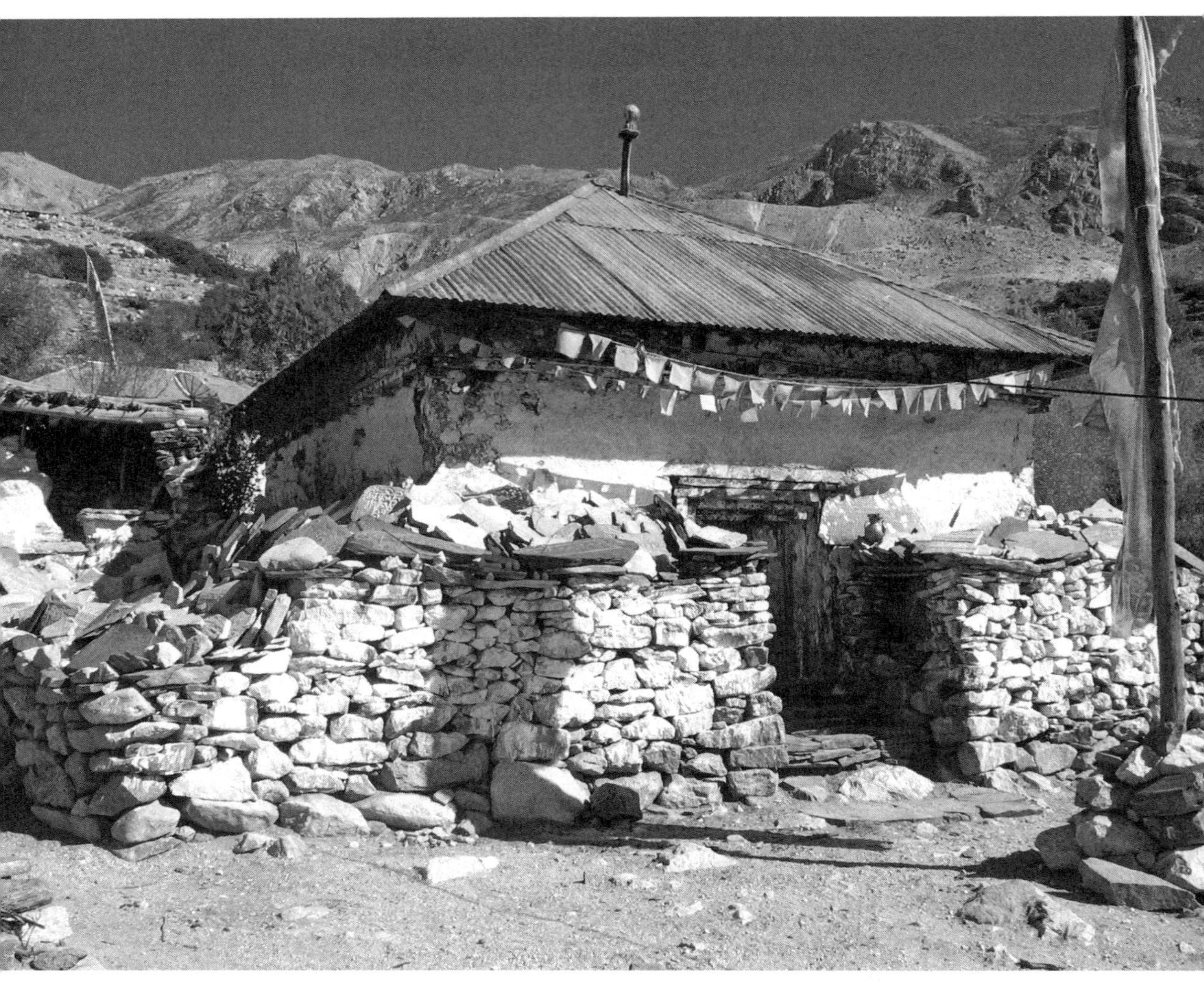

Figure 1.8. Nako (Kinnaur Dist., H.P.), Upper Tungyur Temple,
c. nineteenth century. MRK.

village.[55] Both temples are constructed according to square plans and currently have pitched roofs made of corrugated tin (fig. 1.8).[56] Their interiors
are similarly organized, with the rear third of each temple taken up with
a large prayer wheel flanked by two heavily painted wooden sculptures.
Distinctive wooden arches painted with floral patterns frame the section
with the wheel and sculptures (fig. 1.9). Both temples have a fair amount
of wall painting though the condition is quite poor due to the accumulation of soot, a common problem for Tibetan Buddhist temples caused
by smoke from incense and butter lamps. The painting program at each
temple includes an elaborate depiction of the Drukpa lineage of the Kagyu

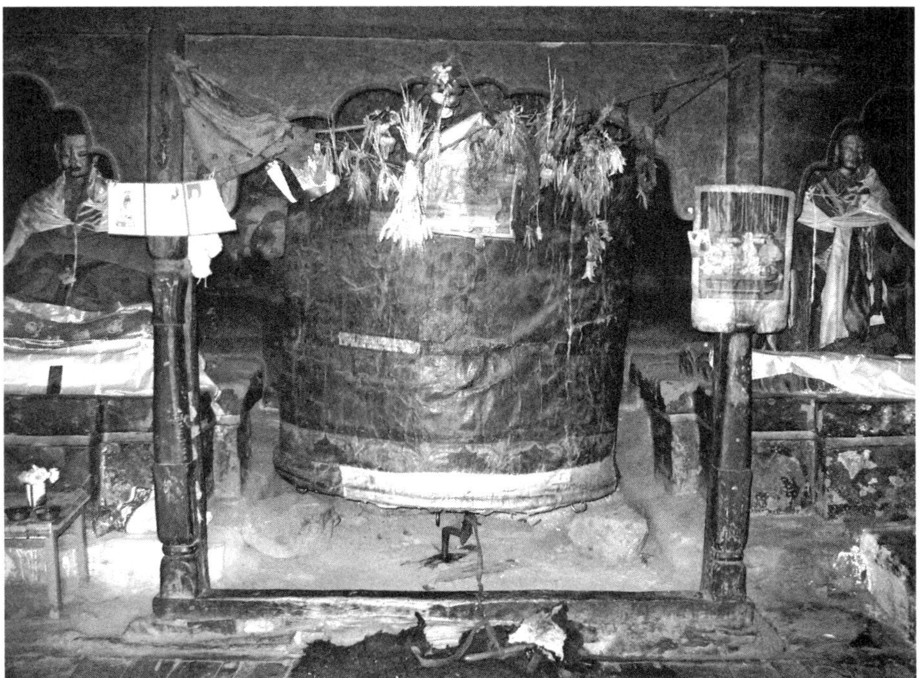

Figure 1.9. Nako (Kinnaur Dist., H.P.), Upper Tungyur Temple: interior with prayer wheel.

tradition. Each temple has a fairly lengthy inscription by the threshold, although the inscription at the Upper Tungyur is in considerably better shape and provides useful information about the patron.

Whereas little is known about the foundations of the other temples in Nako, these two temples and their patrons are mentioned in the village's oral tradition. In an interview with caretaker Kunchok Ngodrub, he discussed who commissioned these temples and when.[57] During our interview, which took place inside the Tungyur temple, a woman named Ani Kuntsog spontaneously joined our conversation, answering many of the questions that Kunchok could not. She was a song-singer, one of the few people in the village who transmits local history through song. One of her songs celebrated the patron of the temples, Lobsang Chodak, who was thought to be an incarnation of Chenrizig, the bodhisattva of compassion.[58] Although Lobsang Chodak's exact dates are not known, it is thought that he lived sometime in the mid-nineteenth century.[59] He was part of a wealthy family in Nako that owned many fields. He married a Ladakhi woman, which is of interest because it demonstrates the marital alliances between these two different regions of the Tibetan cultural zone. Lobsang Chodak patronized the two Tungyur temples in Nako, but also several in other villages, including Malling, Chango, and Dankar, all of which were supposedly constructed under his patronage. After documenting and analyzing all five of these temples it became evident that all were built according to the same architectural plan and style. The original iconographic programs of the temples, however, do not survive at Dankar or Chango.[60]

Religious Compound

At the southwestern corner of Nako is the temple compound, a grouping of four single-story temples of unfired earth-brick construction.[61] Typical of early temple construction in the Tibetan cultural zone, the walls are slightly battered and windowless.[62] Although little of the temple architecture has been altered over the years, save for the addition of rubble buttresses, the area immediately surrounding the compound has changed radically in the last century. According to A. H. Francke, in the early 1900s there were monastic cells directly outside the compound: "Four large temple halls are still standing and form a kind of court. South-east of them, there are many ruins of other buildings, probably the cells of monks. There are also plenty of more or less ruined *mchod-rten* (stupas)."[63] Unfortunately, none of these cells, even as ruins, has survived.[64] The space they must have occupied, immediately surrounding the southeast of the compound, has been leveled and left as an open area, as can be seen from the site plan (fig. 1.10). This open area is now used for religious ceremonies because the plaza within the compound can no longer accommodate the growing number of devotees. To the northeast and southeast of the compound there is a little path and a rather new prayer-wheel shrine or Tungyur, made of concrete.[65]

Within the compound itself, each temple is constructed according to either a square or rectangular plan, which varies considerably in size. Two groups of two temples face one another creating a plazalike space between them (See fig. 1.10). The two oldest of these four temples—T2 the Upper Temple (Gong ma [Gongma]) and T1 the Translator Temple (Lo tsā ba [Lotsawa])—are opposite one another, although not on the same elevation. On the north side of the compound is the Upper Temple, which must be named to describe its elevation, in that it is up, or above the others. Facing the Upper Temple is the Translator Temple, presumably named after the famous monk Rinchen Zangpo (958–1055), who collected and translated Sanskrit Buddhist texts from Kashmir under the sponsorship of the royal family of the Purang-Guge kingdom from the eleventh century. According to tradition, he established numerous temples in the western Himalayan region under the patronage of the Purang-Guge king, Ye shes 'Od (Yeshe Od). Nako's Translator Temple may be one of his

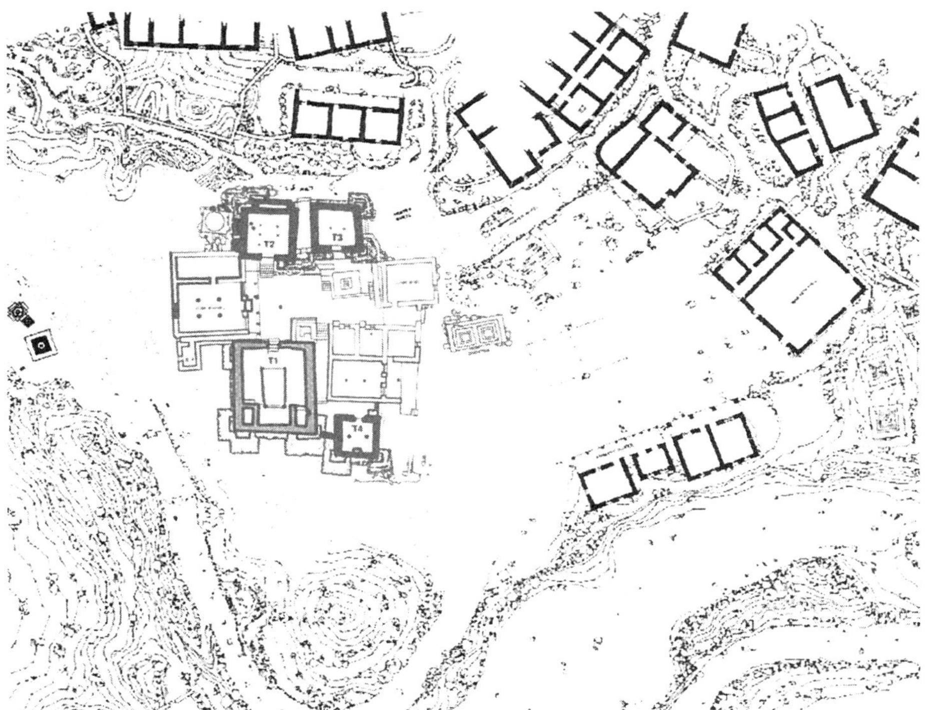

Figure 1.10. Site plan of Nako with temple compound. WHAV.

namesake temples, but there is no evidence to substantiate the local claim. Despite the lack of inscriptional or textual evidence, Francke documents the temple accordingly: "This great monastery is believed to have been founded by Lo-tsa-ba Rin-chen-bzang-po, in the days of king Ye-shes-'od of Guge, c. 1025 A.D., and I am convinced that this assertion is right. Here we are certainly on ancient ground."[66]

The painting programs of these two temples are largely executed in a twelfth-century style.[67] Of the two temples, the Translator Temple has had the most repainting. The twelfth-century paintings are often lauded as innovative in terms of Buddhist iconography, as art historian Christian Luczanits writes: "[A]t Nako fully developed maṇḍalas with gates and fire circle are represented as part of a temple's decoration for the first time in the area, and probably in the whole of the Tibetan cultural region."[68] In terms of religious affiliation, it is likely that the original iconographic programs of these twelfth-century temples expressed Bka' gdams (Kadam) subject matter. Kadam was one of the earliest Tibetan Buddhist schools to develop and had many followers in the Ngari region.[69]

The third temple of the compound is known as the Little White Temple, or Dkar chung (Karchung; noted as T4 on site plan), and is slightly set back from the others. The date of this temple's foundation is less certain, although the working hypothesis is that it, too, originated in the twelfth century.[70] The paintings, which are in very poor condition, are not from the same early period. The sections of wall paintings that do exist can be roughly placed in the late sixteenth to early seventeenth centuries.[71] The iconography, unlike that of the other two temples, reflects standard, widely known Buddhist themes, such as a thousand-armed Avalokiteśvara and Amitābha in his Pure Land. It is thought that this temple was also dedicated to the local mountain deity, Purgyal. As a result, the White Temple provides a useful example of the syncretism that occurs between Buddhism and local belief traditions. The fourth temple of this group is the Gyapagpa Temple, noted as T3 on the site plan (fig. 1.10).

Gyapagpa Temple

This rather small, single-cell temple (5.6 × 5.7 meters) is often given short shrift by scholars (fig. 1.11). It sits next to the Upper Temple on roughly the same elevation, although immediately in front of the Gyapagpa is situated a large stupa, one of two stupas in the compound. Compared to its twelfth-century neighboring temples' painting programs, executed in a rich palette and accented in gold impasto, the painting cycle at the Gyapagpa Temple is faded, badly damaged, and relatively unimpressive. Yet these paintings contain critical information about Nako's religious history, as well as insights into a well-known, if only partly understood, regional painting tradition.

Gyapagpa Temple is the only one within the compound with a complete, albeit damaged, post-fifteenth-century painting program conceived and executed as part of a single stylistic and iconographic plan. The Translator and Little White Temples have at least two—and up to four—painting phases reflecting different periods, styles, and iconography.[72] Taken as a whole, the painting programs in the four compound temples constitute a valuable range of stylistic and iconographic developments, allowing analysis of patterns of religious and aesthetic change over the centuries.

While the Gyapagpa Temple's painting program is later than fifteenth century, its foundation is thought to date to an earlier century (see introduction), as pieces of an earlier painting program can be seen in several places throughout the temple. These patches of the older painting layer are not large enough to yield stylistic information, but they confirm that the temple structure is older than the sixteenth century and may well date to the twelfth century. As Stephen Rickerby, the main conservationist for this temple explains, "The stratigraphic characteristics of the concealed schemes [at the Gyapagpa and Dkar chung Temples] clearly resemble

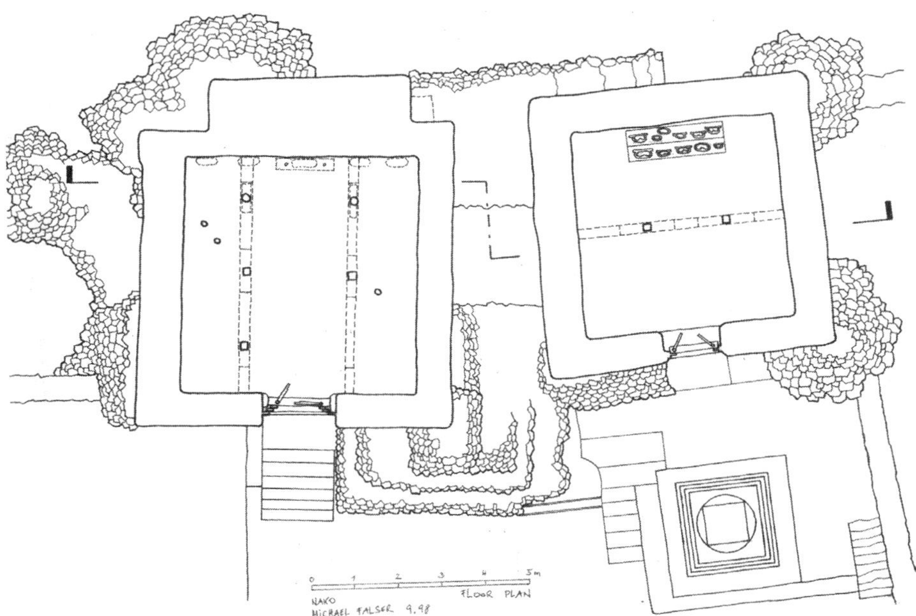

Figure 1.11. Nako, plans of Upper Temple on left and the Gyapagpa Temple on right with stūpa in front. WHAV.

those of the 12th-century paintings in the two main temples."[73] Thus, the current hypothesis is that this temple is coeval with the others in the compound.

Unlike the descriptive names for the other three temples in the compound, this temple's appellation is fairly enigmatic and does not have a direct translation. Further, its name has changed over the course of the last one hundred years or so. Francke refers to the temple as Lha khang gong ma, or Upper Temple, which, as has already been discussed, is the name of another temple in the compound.[74] It is worth noting, however, that both of these temples, which are situated side by side, are at a higher elevation than the other two temples they face. Indeed, each of these temples requires one to climb a set of steep stairs in order to gain entry.

By the time Tucci conducted fieldwork in Nako in the early 1930s, his informants called the temple Rgya dpag pahi lha khang (Gyapagpe Lhakhang), which is closer in sound to the name currently used, although transliterated differently.[75] Klimburg-Salter suggests that the name, depending on its transliteration, could link the temple to a now obsolete religious practice dedicated to Ārya Avalokiteśvara: "This deity appears to belong exclusively to an early phase of Buddhism in Kinnaur, thus suggesting that this temple may also belong to the founding period of the Sacred Compound in the 12th century."[76] Klimburg-Salter does not,

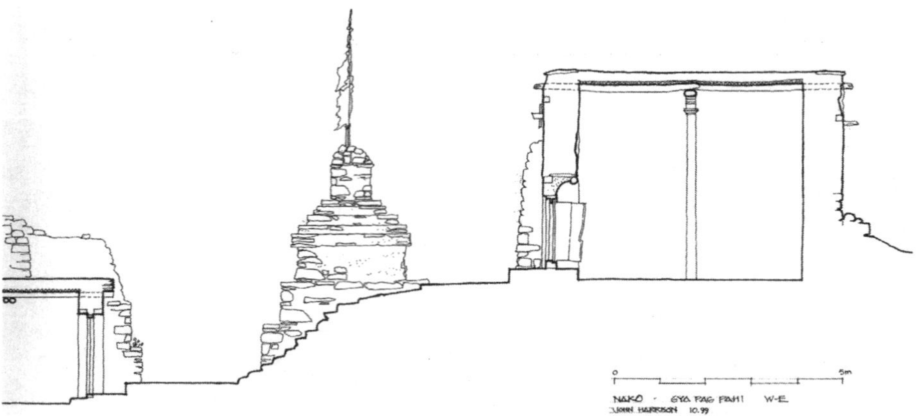

Figure 1.12. Section of the Gyapagpa Temple and stūpa. WHAV.

however, provide an etymological explanation of how this specific trans-literation of the temple's name relates to the four-armed manifestation of Ārya Avalokiteśvara. In 2004 Luczanits offered another translation of the temple's name: "the temple of wide proportions." This translation is un-doubtedly based on the current romanization of the temple's name. *Rgya* can be translated as "wide," but also as "vast" and "extensive." There is not, however, a word that could be translated to mean "proportions."

The villagers today call the temple Gyamagma. In several interviews, when asked about the difference in the names, Nako residents indicated that there was no great difference. In fact, the pronunciations were inter-changeable. And as for the meaning of this temple's unique name, none of the people with whom I spoke provided a meaning or translation of the temple's name. Although most temple names are descriptive, such as the Golden Temple or White Temple, and others are named for a particular person, this rather enigmatic name defies clear identification. This lack of a direct correlative meaning for the temple's name, I should add, seems to be more intriguing to Western scholars, as no one with whom I spoke in the village found this particularly bothersome.

Another unique aspect of this temple is its proximity to a *Mchod rten* (chorten), which is positioned directly in front of the Gyapagpa Temple (fig. 1.12). Leaving the temple, the devotee faces the chorten, only four feet away. The placement of this chorten is far from arbitrary. I posit that this reliquary must have some direct relationship to the temple or to the lineage of practitioners of the temple. It is tempting to think that the chorten may in fact contain the remains of a teacher from the Drigung sect with which this temple is associated, but this is pure speculation.

What Nako's abundant material evidence suggests is that this vil-lage has continued to be an important religious hub within the Tibetan

Buddhist world from the twelfth century onward. Despite its artistic and religious activity, this village has escaped significant mention in primary textual sources. Without textual documentation, the art historian must rely on the extant material evidence to suture together Nako's religious history and artistic heritage. As close analysis of the Gyapagpa Temple will reveal, its iconographic program is evidence of what has become a forgotten religious history at Nako.

2

Forgetting to Remember

Gyapagpa Temple's Shifting Identity

Tibetan Buddhism often places a strong emphasis on memory. Supernatural powers of recollection, for example, are among the great
abilities acquired through enlightenment; the saṃsāric state, by contrast,
can be described as amnesic.[1] In artistic contexts, this ideal of perfect
recollection has often found visual expression in the form of maṇḍalas,
iconographic compositions of highly orchestrated constellations of deities housed within precisely rendered geometric forms. Another visual
tool used to catalyze a more pragmatic level of mnemic engagement[2]
is the illustrated lineages of Buddhist teachers who have mastered and
taught Vajrayāna practices. Wall paintings such as the ones found at
the Gyapagpa Temple include painted lineages that are carefully and
deliberately used to communicate the veracity and heritage of a specific teaching and lineage. This lineage works in concert with the larger
iconographic program including deities, Buddhas, and bodhisattvas, all
identified with accompanying inscriptions. But what happens when these
carefully crafted identities—both divine and human—are forgotten? In
this chapter I look at precisely this problem.

In order to understand better the ways in which the meaning of this
temple's wall paintings has been transformed through a process of adap-
tation and forgetfulness over time, I examine the scholarly record, local
knowledge among Nako's village faithful, and the iconographic and inscriptional material at the temple. This investigation yields three distinct
interpretations of the temple and its iconographic program: the scant
Western academic record, the current reception of the village faithful,

and lastly my interpretation, based on inscriptional and iconographic analyses. Although they are at times divergent, the combination of these three viewpoints provides a deeper understanding of the complex ways in which this temple's imagery has been reused and re-visioned over time. These insights have allowed me to reestablish Nako's forgotten sixteenth-century religious affiliation, which bears significantly on contouring the rather vague religious history of the region.

The findings of this chapter contribute to a dialogue concerning the ways that iconography can be a dynamic system of meaning that is not only in flux, but polysemic, which counters the more traditional notion of iconography as a static or fixed symbol. Although these images certainly were intended to help preserve the memory of a specific Tibetan Buddhist affiliation, the reality is that these iconographic forms now function within a different meaning system. Such a mutation of meaning raises a particular tension between the Buddhist canonical ideal of the perfection of memory versus actual, "on the ground" practice tinged, in this case, by a kind of amnesia.[3] Nako's forgetfulness regarding its religious past is not a unique situation for the Tibetan cultural zone. There are many places within Tibetan Buddhist contexts, and more generally in South and East Asia, in which the intended meaning of an iconographic form has morphed and changed over time. Scholars are beginning to see these complex narratives of mutating iconography as valuable case studies that reveal much about the multifaceted, even messy, world of Buddhist imagery and iconography. As with this temple's history, it reveals the complex relationship among religious practitioner, image, and Buddhist practice.

Scholarship on the Gyapagpa Temple

Although the temple was founded in the twelfth century, remarkably little has been written about it. Most regrettable is the absence of any Tibetan historical documentation about the temple, its patrons, or sectarian affiliation. This is the fate of many Tibetan Buddhist monasteries, but there are sometimes substantial inscriptions painted on interior walls of temples that provide pieces of information about a temple's history. This temple and the other three temples of Nako's religious compound are without such founding inscriptions. The little that has been written about this temple has been generated in the last hundred years by four scholars, all of whom focus on limited iconographic details.[4] German missionary August Herman Francke brought to light the little-known Tibetan cultural zone of northwest India with his 1914 publication, *Antiquities of Indian Tibet*. Francke discusses Nako's several temples paying particular attention to the religious compound. He proposes that

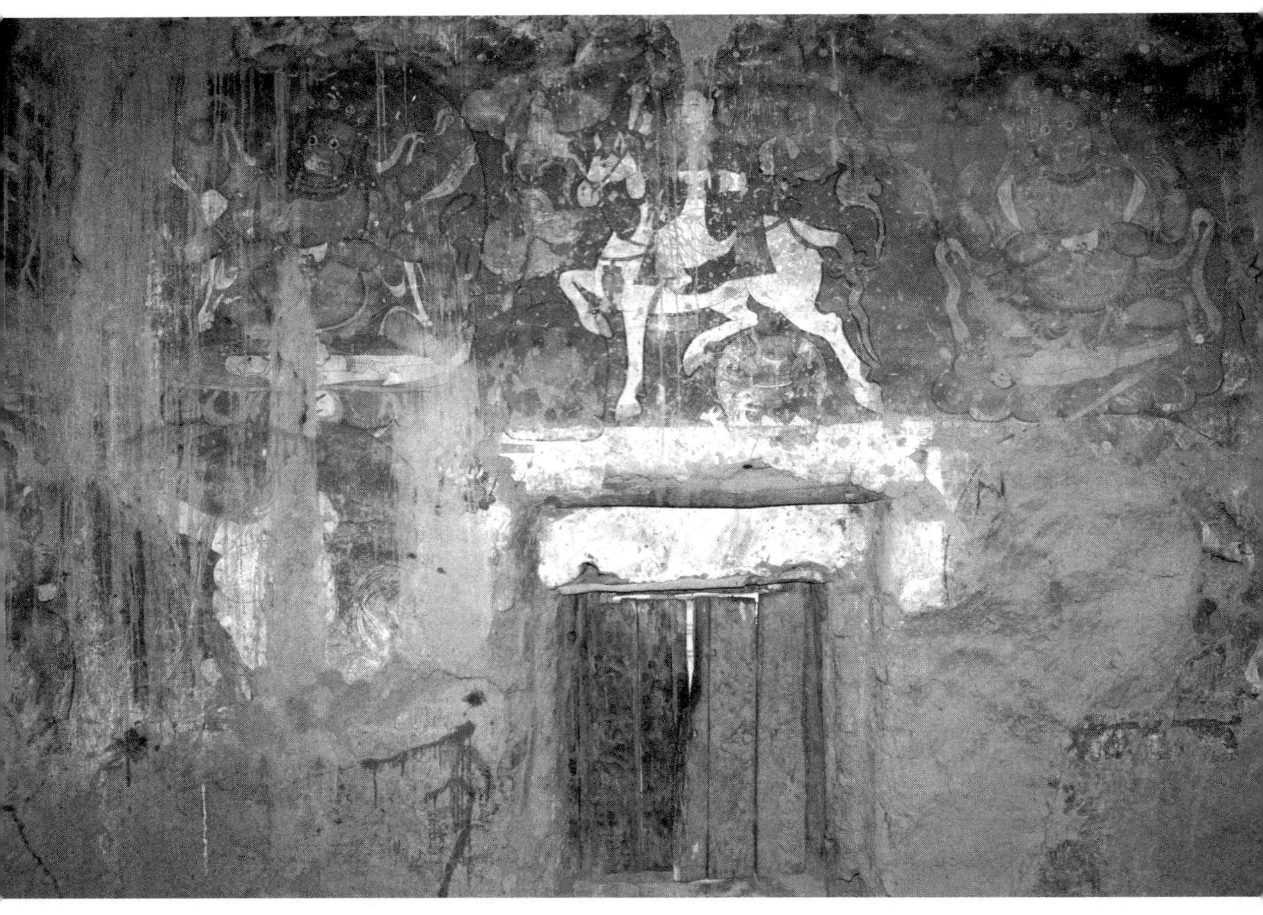

Figure 2.1. Gyapagpa Temple, west wall: Achi on white horse.

the Gyapagpa Temple, as well as the other temples of the compound, is part of a larger 'Brug pa (Drukpa) monastic complex at Nako.[5] His formal analysis of the Gyapagpa Temple's painting program is limited to a cursory discussion of some iconographic elements. The image that is most compelling to Francke is featured on the west wall, above the door of the temple (fig. 2.1); Francke identifies the protector deity as Ge sar (Gesar), the legendary hero of Tibetan folklore.[6] He writes, "Above the door, among other tutelary deities, there is a large fresco of King Gesar riding on a white rKyang (wild ass). At Nako he is called gLing sing chen rgyal po, 'Great Lion King of gLing.'"[7] As is true of his assessment of the temple's religious affiliation, he does not provide any definitive supporting evidence for his identification of this particular figure.

Giuseppe Tucci's scholarship followed Francke's lead. In 1935 Tucci published a volume featuring the temples of Ngari, in which he briefly mentions Nako's Gyapagpa Temple. Tucci's usual attention to detail and keen interest in iconography and inscriptions are absent in his assessment of this temple, leading him to endorse Francke's misidentification of the protector figure as Gesar and of the temple itself as a Drukpa site. He concluded, "It does not contain anything noteworthy with the exception of some frescoes. Above the door [is] the figure of Gesar the king of Gling, the hero of the Tibetan epic."[8]

In Laxman Thakur's 1996 article about Nako's monastic complex, he, too, posits that "Above the door has been painted a figure of Ge sar, a popular character of Tibetan epic who is considered the king of gLing."[9] He goes on to make an important identification of an inscribed monk portrait that reads 'Jig rten mgon po (Jigten Gonpo). Although Thakur recognized this person as the historic founder of the 'Bri gung (Drigung) school of the Bka' brgyud (Kagyu) tradition in Tibetan Buddhism, he did not clarify what it might mean to have such a portrait featured in this temple.[10]

In a 2003 article Deborah Klimburg-Salter cautiously mentions the Gesar attribution, but does not otherwise discuss the temple's iconographic or sectarian associations. Her primary interest is in the temple's enigmatic name and spelling. As discussed in chapter 1, Klimburg-Salter suggests that the temple's name may be associated with a standing four-armed manifestation of Ārya Avalokiteśvara.[11]

Communal Responses to the Temple

The temple under discussion is still a functioning religious site within the Nako community. Ritual activity at the Gyapagpa Temple was evident when villagers, most of whom were older women, made regular offerings of prayers, prostrations, and butter lamps. Upon leaving the temple, villagers would then circumambulate the stūpa, placed only four feet away from the entrance. These simple ritualized gestures were part of the maintenance practices for the temple's religious life, as well as ways for these women to undertake meritorious activities that could be readily woven into their everyday lives. In 2004 and 2005, I interviewed many of the villagers who visited the temple in order to gain a better sense of their understandings and uses of the Gyapagpa Temple. In all cases, formal interviews evolved into larger group discussions with family members and friends contributing their reflections. This resulted in lively conversations about this temple and the villagers' relationships to it.

One of the first people with whom I had extended conversations about this temple was a nun named Ani Samten Wangmo, a young woman who lives eight months of the year in a nunnery well outside of Nako because there is currently no functioning nunnery in or around the immediate area of Nako. She returns to Nako during the spring and summer to help her family plant and harvest crops.[12] We met at her family's home to discuss the Gyapagpa Temple and its iconographic program.[13] One afternoon, while drinking butter tea and watching the resident artist repaint some of her family's clay statues, I asked her if she knew the identity of the main figure who rode a horse, painted above the door on the west wall. She immediately answered that it was Gesar, king of Ling, and her mother nodded in agreement. I mentioned to Ani Samten Wangmo that underneath the horse was an inscription and wrote down for her what was inscribed under the horse: "A c*xx*s kyi sgron ma la na mo." Though a small part of the inscription was damaged, it was clear that the whole inscription was to be translated as "praise to Achi cho kyi dron ma." She looked fairly surprised and asked, "But this is the guardian deity of Drigung, no?" Her question was a critical one, for it revealed her awareness of the protectress commonly known as Achi and her link to the Drigung school of the Kagyu tradition. Excitedly I nodded yes and waited for her to respond with more information, but she did not. She and her mother simply and kindly explained that the figure was in fact Gesar, no matter what the inscription read. Ani Samten Wangmo also impressed upon me the importance of Gesar for the people of Nako; this epic hero took on the role of a protector deity in the village. As for the inscription, they offered no possible interpretation or reason for its appearance. The inscription was not treated like evidence; it was entirely disregarded. What was important for them to communicate was the horse rider's identity as Gesar and the temple's association with Drukpa despite what inscriptional or iconographic information may indicate. Wanting to understand if Gesar has a special relationship to Drukpa, I inquired, but the mother and daughter did not confirm this. Instead, they underscored how significant Gesar was to Nako. I then asked if there were ever a point in Nako's history when this temple might have been Drigung. She and her mother adamantly affirmed Nako's unchanging Drukpa association.

Ani Samten Wangmo and her mother were not the only people in the village who identified the horse-mounted protector figure as Gesar. This became quite evident while I was at a local eatery where some people from the village came in the evening to drink tea, play cards, and gossip. I spoke with the proprietor of the restaurant, Moni, and several of her customers about the temple.[14] They reflected upon the temple's name and its ritual function, and all agreed that it had always been a Drukpa temple and the protector figure was Gesar. That Gesar, a legendary folk hero would have been converted into a temple protector, based on his position over the door, is a bit unusual. Certainly, Gesar is a protector of the Dharma and of his people of Ling.[15] He is not, however, a deity, yet he has at times been deified, as is evident by the temple devoted to Gesar in Lhasa. Nonetheless, there were no other instances of Gesar being used as the temple protector in or around Nako.

While I did not discuss the inscription under the horse figure with most villagers, I did probe a bit more into the villagers' ideas about the temple's religious identity. Might it have changed over the years it has been in use? After some discussion it became apparent that no one could remember it having been anything else. As far as they were concerned, it was always Drukpa. The comments made in another interview provided some insight into why people were resistant to thinking about this temple's changing religious affiliation. In talking with Kunchok Ngodrub, caretaker of the first Tungyur temple and a member of one of Nako's more noble families, he explained that this temple, along with the other three temples of the compound, was created in a single night by a Buddha.[16] As for when this miraculous event might have taken place, Kunchok simply said a very long time ago. This divine creation story for Gyapagpa Temple and the religious compound in general is of interest because it is part of a ubiquitous trope in South Asia and Tibet.[17] One will find that temples (and stūpas) are often self-emanating or built by deities or rulers who are said to have divine origins; these buildings, therefore, are not man-made.[18] It is likely that this temple's divine creation is one reason villagers did not feel comfortable with discussing the possibility of the temple's alternating religious affiliations. Moreover, there was no living memory among the community members with whom I spoke of the temple having been anything other than Drukpa.

There was however, one person from the village who did suggest that the Gyapagpa Temple's religious affiliation had altered over time. Tenzin (also known as Lama ji, a combination of Tibetan and Hindi meaning "honorable teacher"), was a middle-aged man who once studied as a monk, but was now a lay practitioner who was the caretaker of the four temples in the religious compound. Given Tenzin's monastic training, and therefore his higher level of literacy, we went to the temple together to read several of the inscriptions found within the painted program. He was rather surprised to see that the inscribed lineage of six monastic figures did not reveal a correlation with the Drukpa Kagyu tradition, which is what the current Nako community follows. Our conversation then turned to the horse figure over the door and its accompanying inscription. He read the name out loud several times, shook his head, and simply said that this was Gesar. That the inscribed name did not correspond to his, and the villagers', shared perception of this deity's identity was not problematic, though perhaps momentarily confusing to Tenzin. He did propose at one point that the temple might have been aligned with another tradition at some earlier period in Nako's history, which may account for the reason why the inscription identified the horse rider as being someone other than Gesar. His suggestion that the temple may have changed religious affiliations over time stood in sharp contrast to the majority of the villagers with whom I spoke. Tenzin's unusual insight may be due to his education and to his interaction with Western preservation and art historical teams that have come to work on Nako since it was included on the World Monument Fund's list of one hundred most endangered sites in 2002.[19] As the temple caretaker for the four oldest temples at Nako, Tenzin serves as the main conduit between Western research teams and the village. He has had access to academic information about the construction and preservation of these four temples as well as their iconography. While Tenzin suggested that there may have been a point when the temple functioned under a different religious affiliation, he was careful to say that the temple was now Drukpa and the protector figure Gesar.

The findings of this ethnographic survey reveal complex and faceted interactions between the religious viewer and the image or icon—issues that are often overlooked in scholarly writing about Buddhist art and iconography. By highlighting this gray and murky area regarding unstable meanings and resignification of images I hope to underscore the complexity of viewing practices at Nako and allude to them within the larger Tibetan Buddhist context. There is not necessarily a one-to-one correspondence between iconography or inscriptions and meaning. Furthermore, the changes in reception of iconography speak to larger issues regarding communal identity formation and reformation over the hundreds of years during which this temple and its images have been in use. These issues, as well as the striking similarity between the villagers' interpretation of the temple and that of the aforementioned scholarly record, will be discussed at the conclusion of this chapter.

Revealing the Sixteenth-Century Iconographic Program

Based on my analysis of the temple's iconographic and inscriptional evidence, an alternate interpretation emerges, one that differs considerably from that of the scholarly record and the villagers' perspectives. In systematically documenting, translating, and analyzing the inscriptions and iconography of this temple, I point to two critical pieces of evidence that prove this temple's Drigung affiliation, not Drukpa as both the local and scholarly communities have suggested. Though both schools are part of the larger tradition of Kagyu, they focus on different deities and teachings, and ultimately have had very different sociopolitical histories. One example of this is the fact that the Drigung school never flourished in the way that Drukpa did after the fifteenth century in West Tibet.[20] Consequently, there is a dearth of Drigung material evidence, both artistic and textual from West Tibet and surrounding areas including Khu nu (Kinnaur). Gyapagpa Temple's painting program, therefore, becomes the first material evidence of Drigung activity in the Kinnaur region.[21] As such, these paintings become critical historical documents substantiating Drigung activity in the sixteenth century in an area and at a time better known for its Drukpa Kagyu and Dge lugs pa (Gelug) affiliations.

The first piece of evidence that aligns this temple with the Drigung tradition is the identity of the protector figure located on the west wall, who by now the reader knows as Gesar (fig. 2.1). When the standard iconographic form for Gesar is compared with the actual painting, however, it is evident that this figure on the west wall is not Gesar. Gesar's typical iconography depicts him clothed in metal armor, appropriate for a warrior who is protecting the Buddhist teachings, and wears boots and a helmet festooned with colorful flags.[22] He rides a white wild donkey, while holding in his left hand a bowl of jewels and in his right, a weapon such as a spear or dagger. The figure painted on the west wall of the Gyapagpa Temple is quite different, most strikingly in that this figure is female. She wears Tibetan boots and dress—not armor—and sits astride a horse and carries different ritual objects in her hands (plate 3). Furthermore, positioned directly under the belly of the horse on which she rides is a partially obscured inscription that reads, "A cxxs kyi sgron ma la na mo," the deity commonly known as "Achi," and who the Drigung school uses as its protector (fig. 2.2).[23] Without having been able to locate other sixteenth-century imagery of Achi, and due to the general dearth of visual evidence for her, I have looked to textual descriptions of Achi.[24] The image at Nako closely resembles a description of her found in one of the many Drigung devotional texts dedicated to this protector deity. What follows is a description of Achi based on a late-twentieth-century devotional text. The point of highlighting this excerpt is not to suggest that there is a direct correspondence between this later text and the sixteenth-century painting. Rather, my chief interest in the text is to demonstrate some continued resonances in form and iconography.

> A phyi has a white colored body, red cheeks, and a slightly wrathful expression. [She] wears a conch shell turban and jewels on her head. [She] has a plaited topknot of long hair . . . and a crown of assembled silken ribbons. On [her] body [she] wears robes of silk. [Her] right hand strongly sounds the *damaru,* the nature of emptiness, . . . [her] left hand carrying, at her heart, a skull cup filled with demon-blood [for her] compassionate consumption. [Her] two legs in a wrathful stance are astride an exceedingly fast [yet] graceful thoroughbred bluish-grey [in color] which extensively wanders the four continents at noon and midnight.[25]

Much of this late-twentieth-century description agrees with the iconography of the sixteenth-century temple mural, though there are some clear

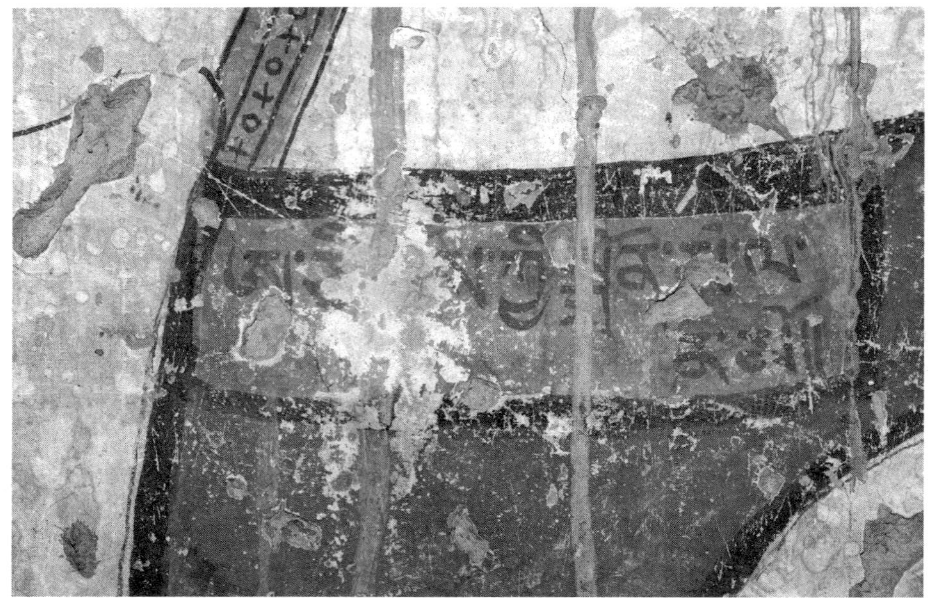

Figure 2.2. Gyapagpa Temple, west wall: inscription identifying the protectress, A cxxs kyi sgron ma la na mo (Achi).

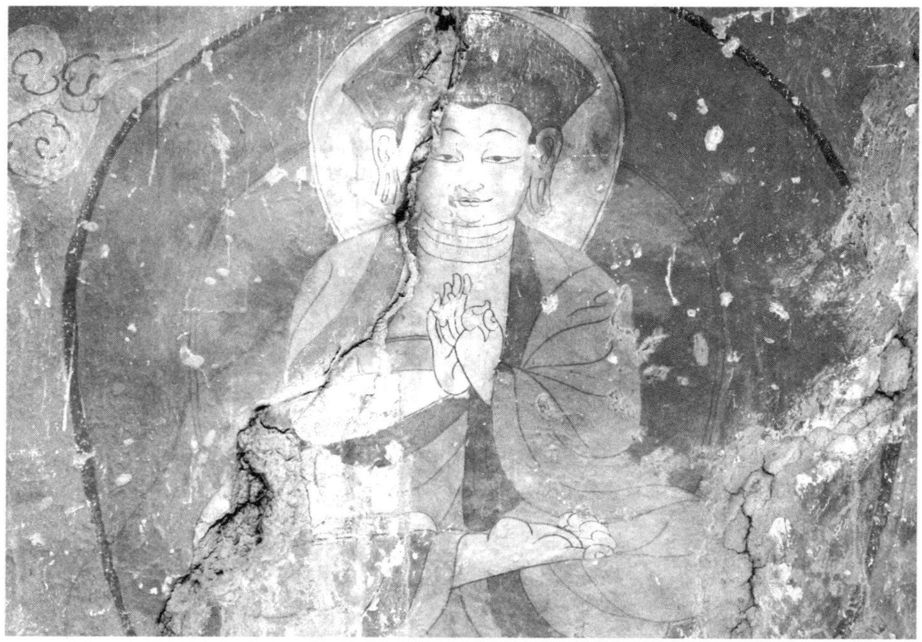

Figure 2.3. Gyapagpa Temple, north wall: 'Jig rten mgon po (Jigten Gonpo).

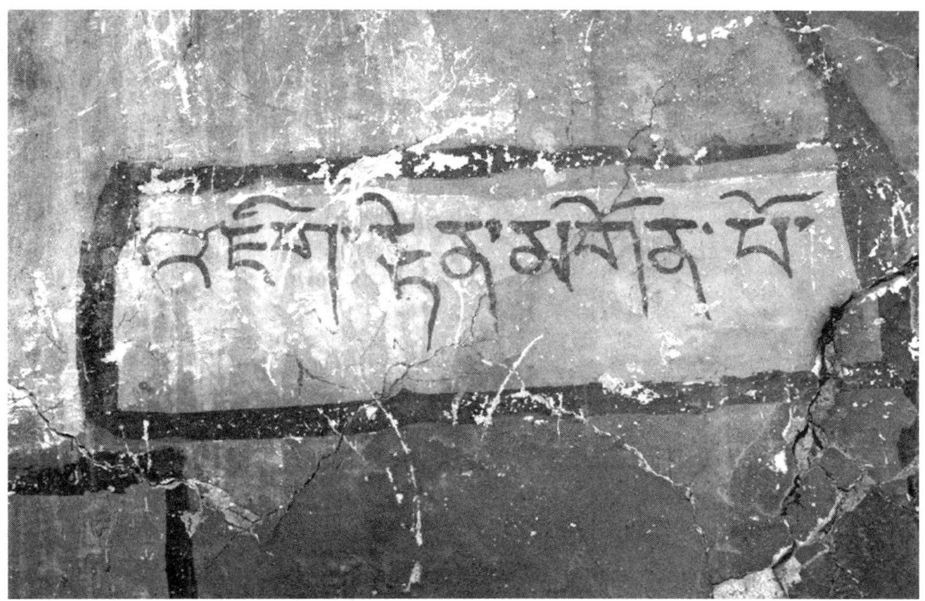

Figure 2.4. Gyapagpa Temple, north wall: Jigten Gonpo's identifying inscription.

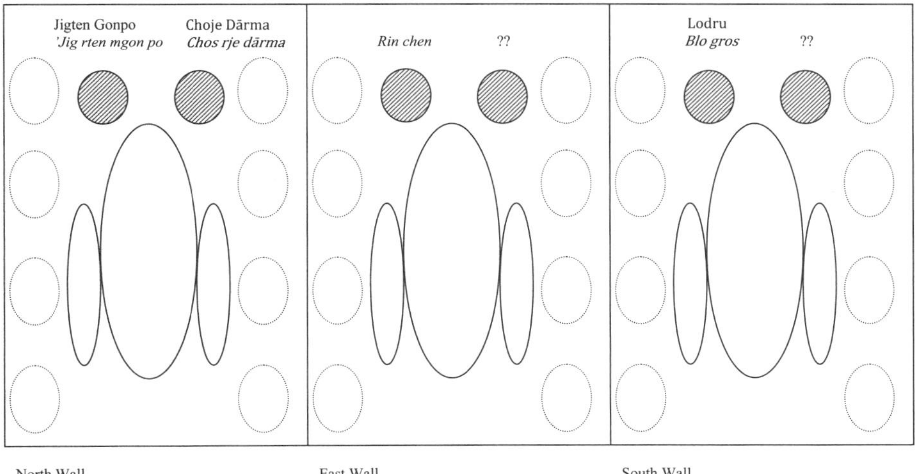

Figure 2.5. Schematic drawing of 'Bri gung (Drigung) lineage on north, east, and south walls of the Gyapagpa Temple. Where multiple versions of a name appear, the top name is a phonetic Tibetan spelling; below it is an italicized transliteration of the inscription. Shaded areas indicate Drigung lineage portraits.

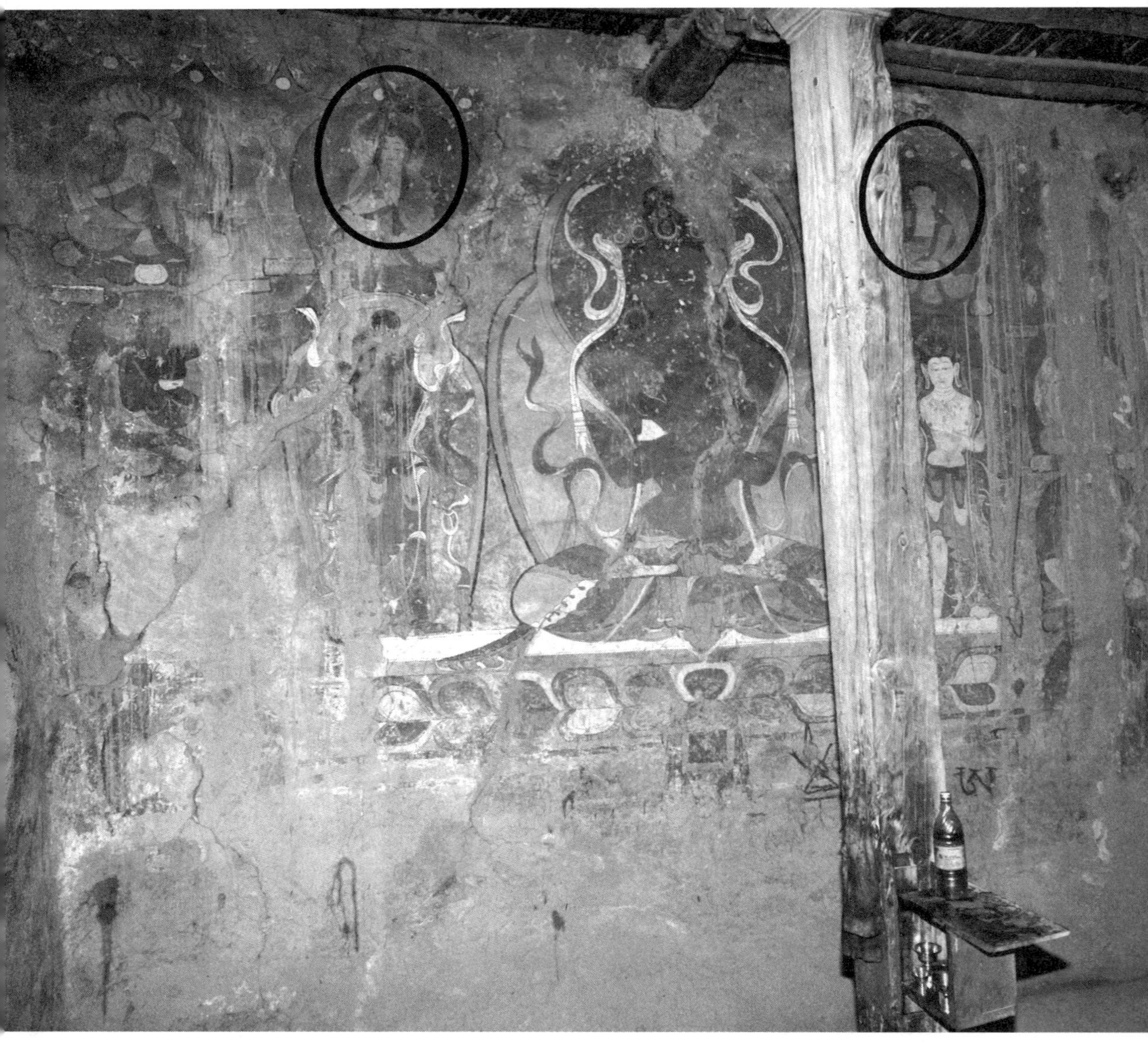

Figure 2.6. Gyapagpa Temple, north wall: lineage portraits circled.

discrepancies such as the color of her horse. The continuity of forms can be seen in her complexion, hairstyle, ritual implements, and posture.[26] This iconographic resonance combined with the inscription found under the horse solidifies her identity. There can be no mistaking this figure for any other; she is Achi, the protectress who steadfastly protects Drigung teachings and adherents. As such, she is appropriately positioned above the threshold, that liminal space between mundane and sacred worlds, which requires safeguarding.[27]

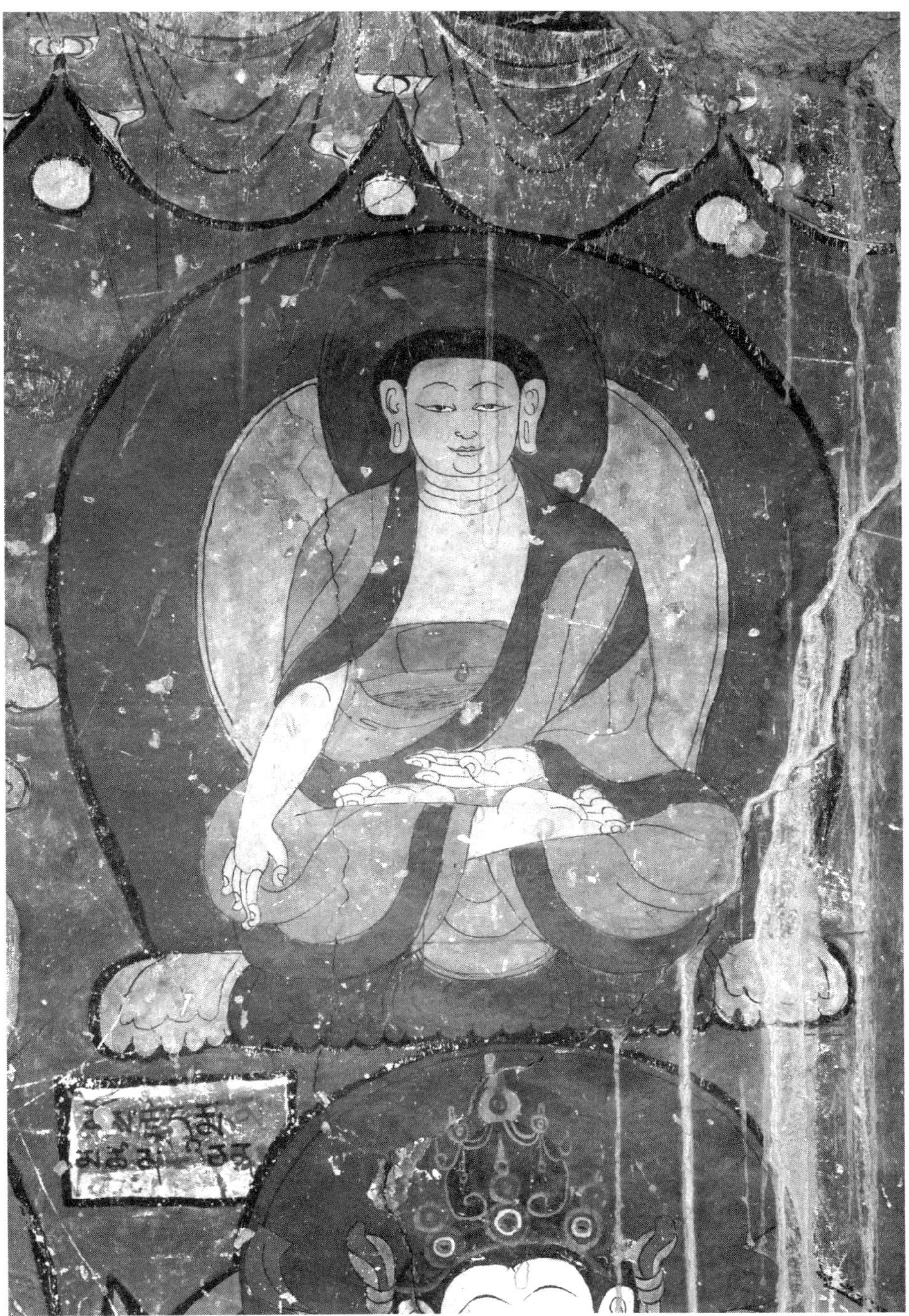

Figure 2.7. Gyapagpa Temple, north wall: Chos rje dārma (Choje Dārma).

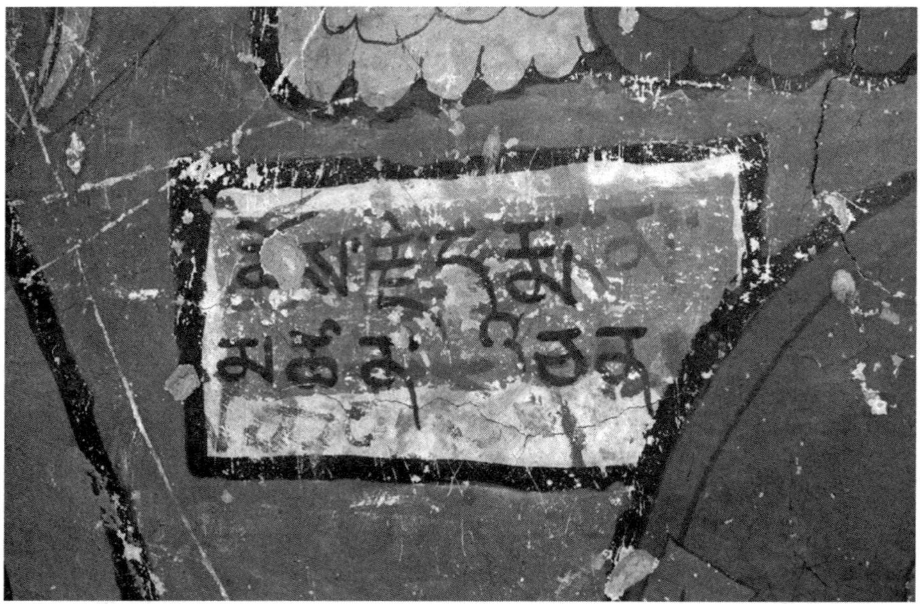

Figure 2.8. Gyapagpa Temple, north wall: Choje Dārma's identifying inscription.

Another important piece of inscriptional evidence further supports my claim that this is a Drigung temple. The inscribed image of Jigten Gonpo, the twelfth-century founder of the Drigung school, whom Thakur briefly mentioned in his 1996 article, is located on the temple's north wall (figs. 2.3 and 2.4). This portrait and its accompanying inscription are part of a larger group of portraits featuring six teachers, which had escaped the notice of scholars. The north, east, and south walls each display two portraits, roughly the same size and situated at the same height and position on the wall (fig. 2.5).[28] These portraits, based on formulaic portrait types, were executed without individualized characteristics. The only marks of their identities are their names written below their figural representations; of the six, only three figures have well preserved identifying inscriptions. Another has a partially intact inscription, and the remaining two inscriptions have not survived.

In an analysis of horizontal lineage presentations in Tibetan paintings, David Jackson explains that for the "Tantric traditions" it is common to have the earliest teacher positioned to the proper right of the other lineage members and to the right of the "Tantric Original Guru," Vajradhara.[29] Indeed, this is precisely the case in the Gyapagpa Temple, where Jigten Gonpo is situated on the north wall, to the proper right of the other lineage members and above Vajradhara's proper right shoulder (fig. 2.6).[30] In the expected second position, to Jigten Gonpo's proper left,

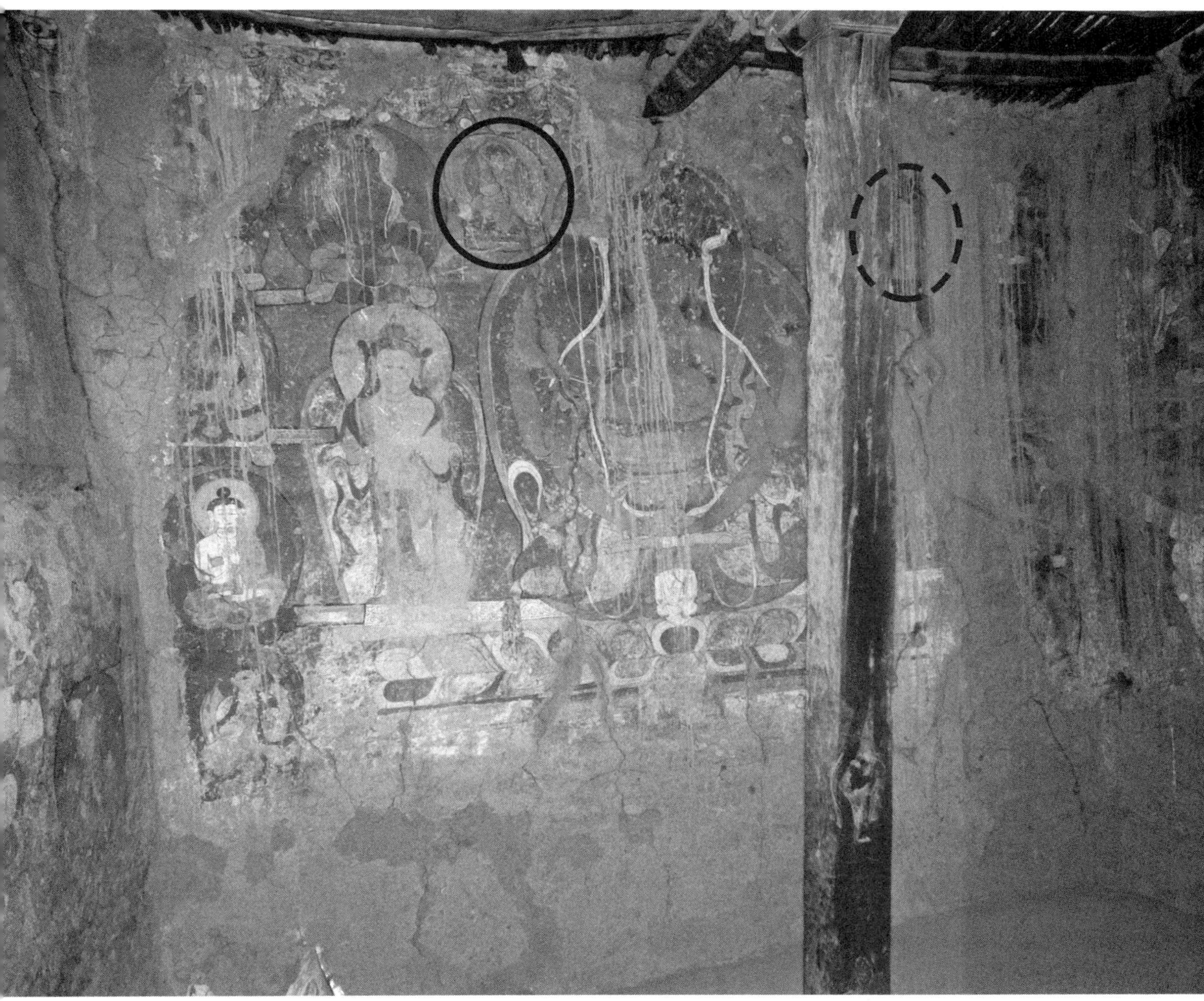

Figure 2.9. Gyapagpa Temple, south wall: lineage portraits circled.

is a figure with the inscription that reads "Chos rje dārma mtshan can" (figs. 2.7 and 2.8). It should be noted that this inscription bears considerable underpainting, but both layers can be read to communicate the same name, though with a slight spelling variation. The underlying inscription does not include a long A and thus reads "Chos rje darma," unlike the final version, which reads "Chos rje dārma" (Choje Dārma). The third and fourth members of the lineage are located on the east wall (plate 4). Only part of one of their inscriptions survives, under the third figure, and reads simply "Rin chen . . . [illegible]." Completing this clockwise circuit, the south wall features the last two lineage members (fig. 2.9).

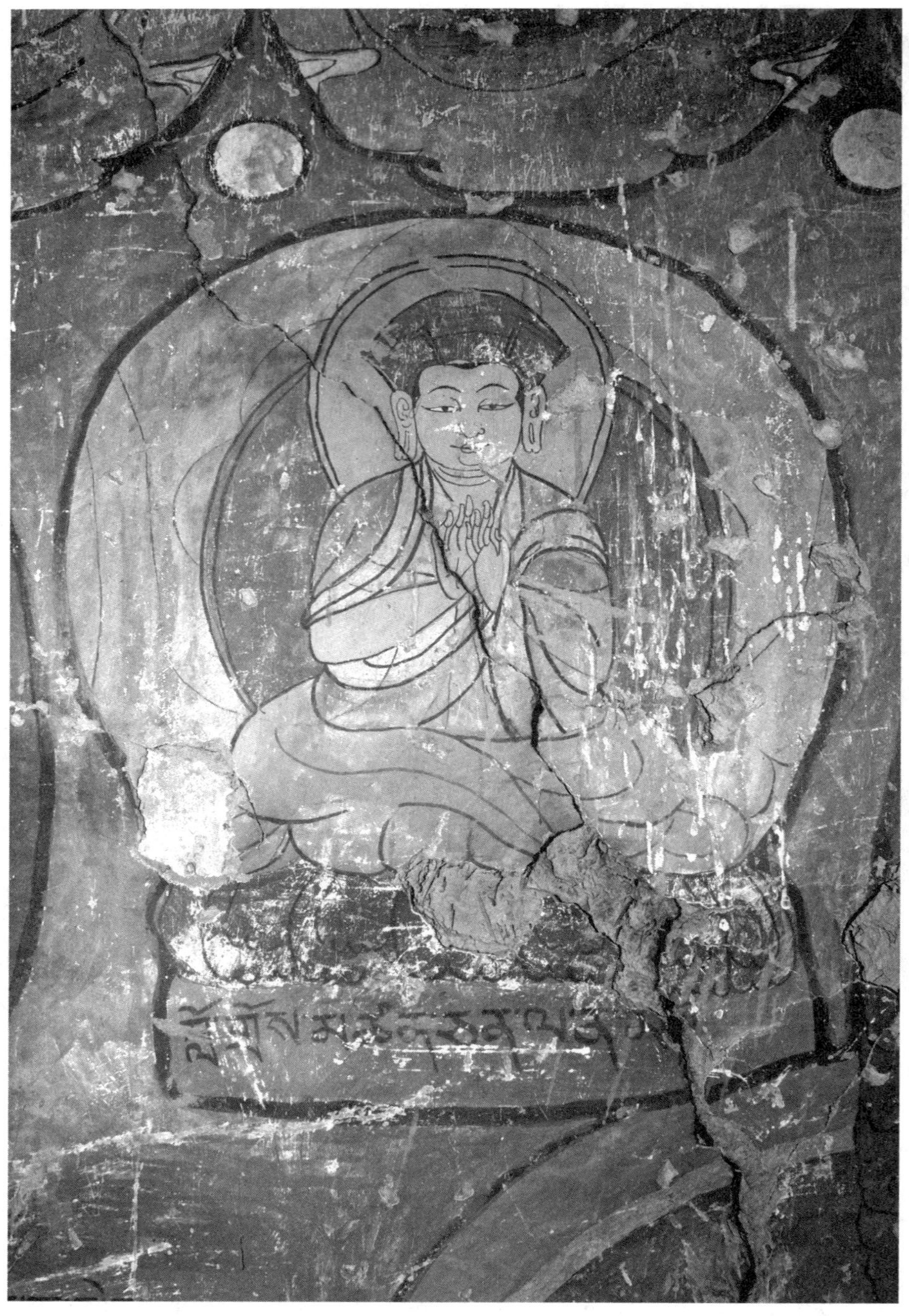

Figure 2.10. Gyapagpa Temple, south wall: fifth lineage portrait.

Fortunately, the fifth figure's inscription clearly reads, "Blo gros mtshan can la na mo" (fig. 2.10), but the final portrait and its inscription are beyond legibility. While these six portraits comprise a Drigung lineage, given Jigten Gonpo's presence in the initial position, the exact lineage is not yet known.

The lineage currently functions for the village community more as a symbolic motif—emblematic of an authentic, religiously valued space—than as an index of a specific religious affiliation. For the current village faithful, recollection of the actual identities of these Drigung lineage members is not critical for practical purposes. In fact, forgetting these identities, and seeing them as signs of general religious authority, is most beneficial in their process of forming a new religious identity.[31] The villagers of Nako, despite the iconographic information, understand this temple and its paintings to be part of the Drukpa school of the Kagyu tradition. For the art historian, however, the loss of this lineage's specificity is significant. There is very little known about Drigung practice in the Kinnaur region. The dearth of extant Drigung material evidence in this area underscores the uniqueness of the Gyapagpa Temple's iconographic program, and its usefulness in piecing together aspects of Kinnaur's history. It is, therefore, a crucial historical document to the historian in helping to remember a forgotten Drigung past at Nako.[32]

Gyapagpa Temple's Complete Iconographic Program

Although the presence of both Achi and Jigten Gonpo—the protector and founder of Drigung—are clear indicators of this temple's Drigung association, there are other iconographic features within this painting program that suggest Drigung affiliation. More interestingly, however, the iconographic information on these walls provides insight into the manner in which this small Drigung community fashioned itself as a well-developed and authentic tradition.

West Wall

The west wall, which serves as the entrance and exit point for the temple, contains all the wrathful imagery of the temple's iconographic program. The main protector is positioned over the door, which is the highest and most central part of the west wall's composition. Here, the protector deity Achi, who is surrounded by three female figures, is painted in relatively saturated colors (fig. 2.11). Each retinue figure is identified with an inscription: "Dkar mo," "Rdor rje chen mo," and "Re ma . . . [illegible] i" (figs. 2.12 and 2.13). To the right of this constellation of female protector

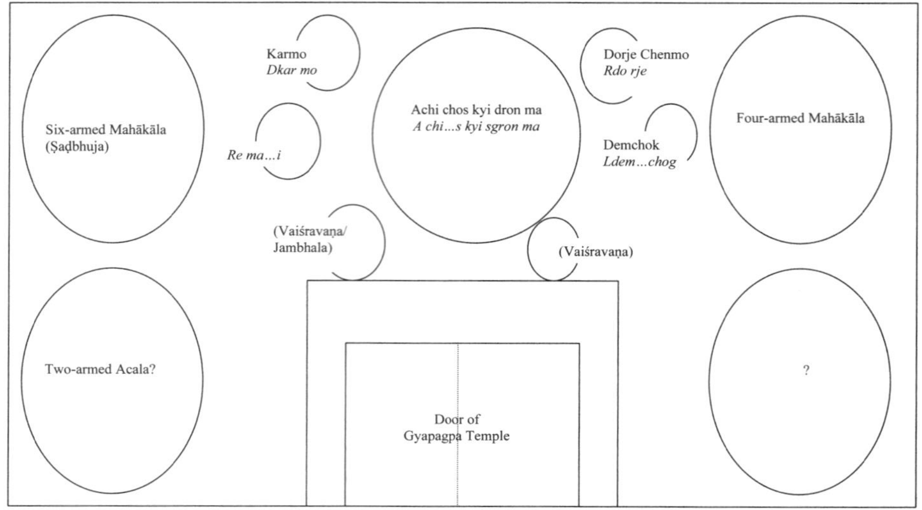

Figure 2.11. Schematic drawing of west wall. Where multiple versions of a name appear, the top name is a phonetic Tibetan spelling; below it is an italicized transliteration of the inscription. Where there is no inscription for a figure, the Sanskrit name is used.

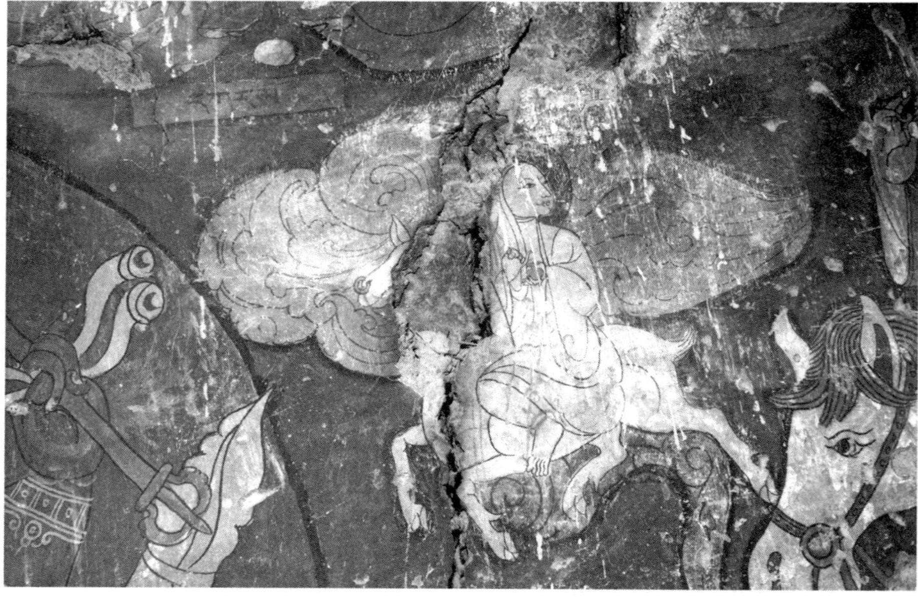

Figure 2.12. Gyapagpa Temple, west wall: Achi attendant, Dkar mo (Karmo).

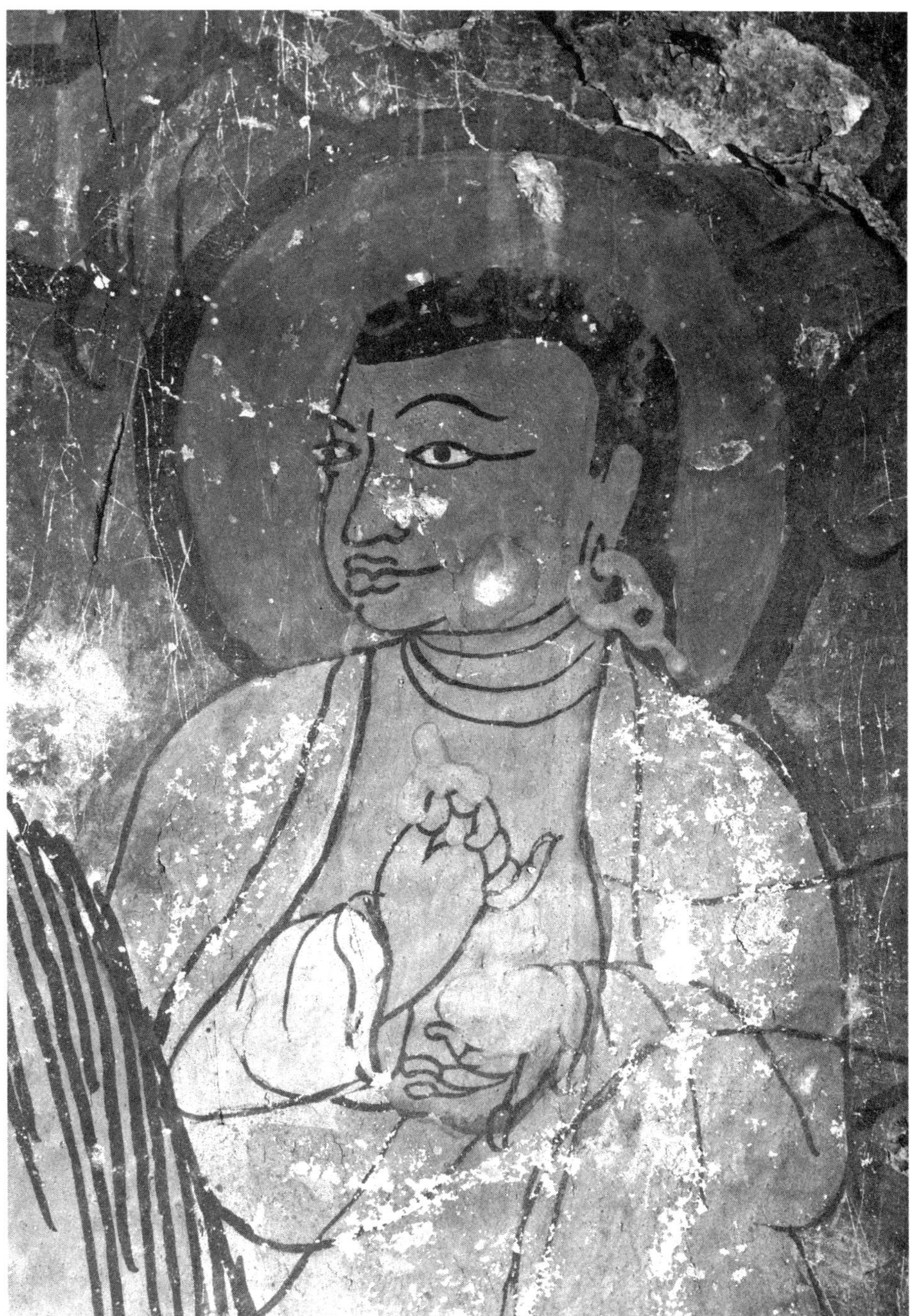

Figure 2.13. Gyapagpa Temple, west wall: Achi attendant,
Rdor rje chen mo (Dorje Chenmo).

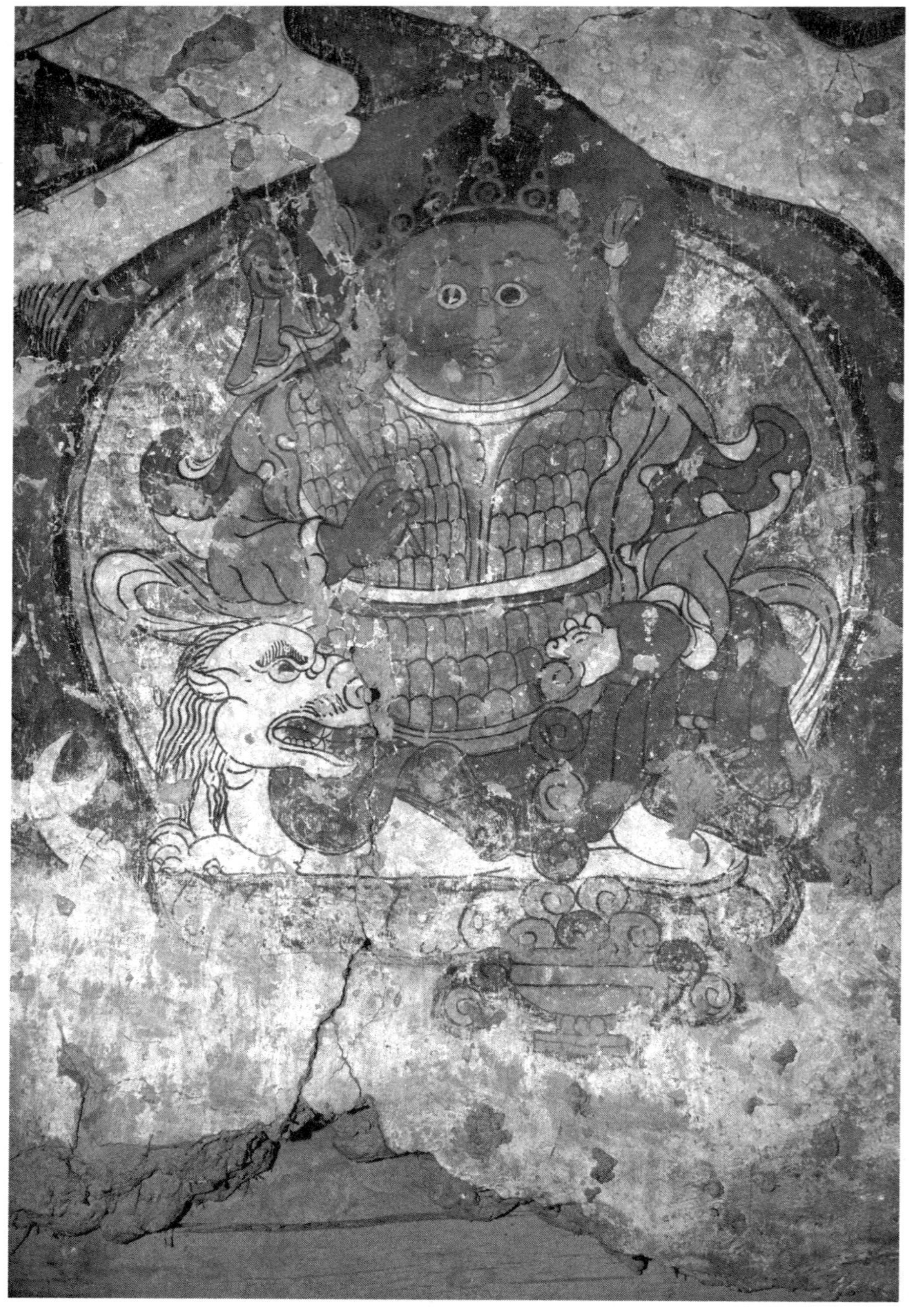

Figure 2.14. Gyapagpa Temple, west wall: Vaiśravaṇa on lion.

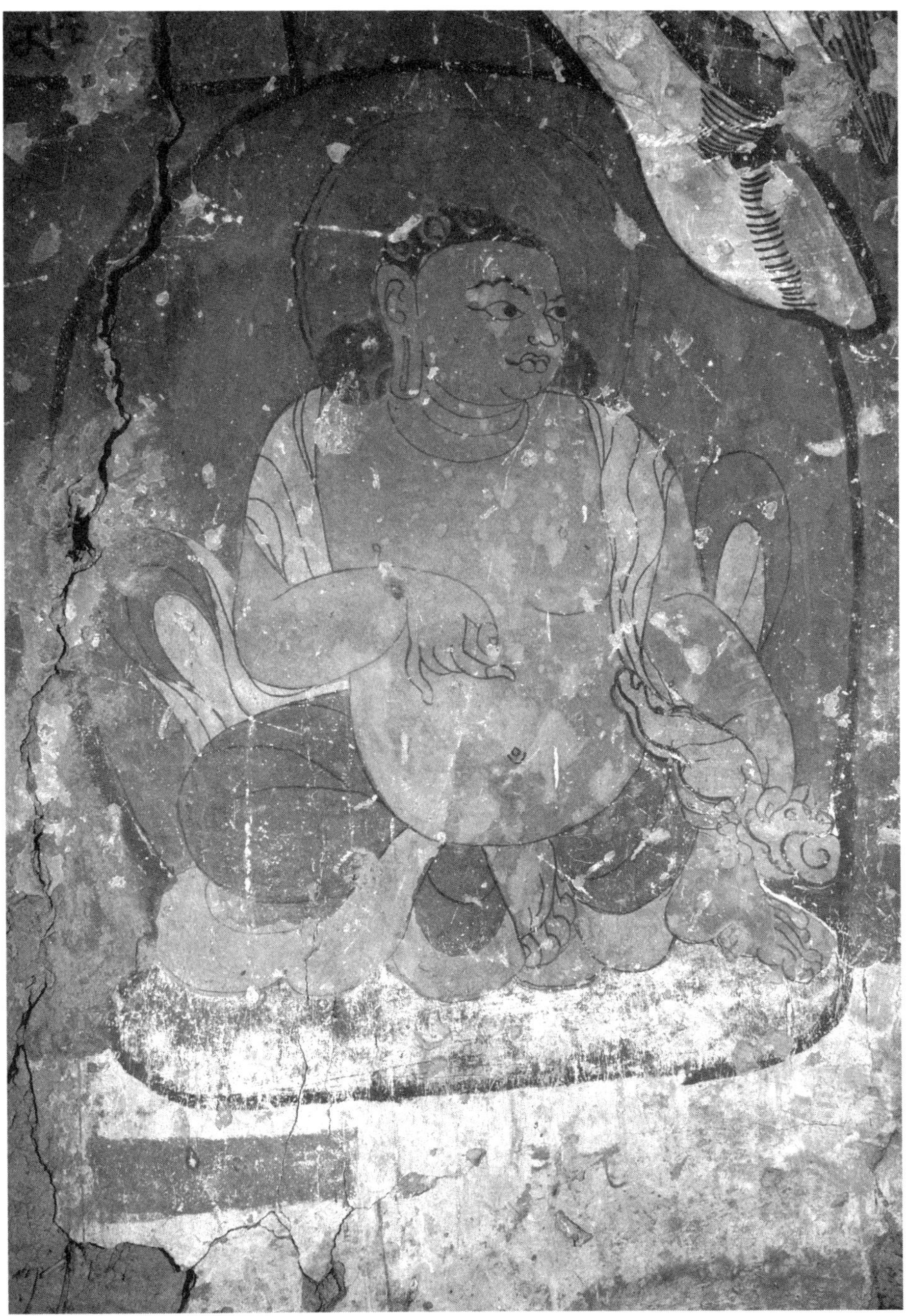

Figure 2.15. Gyapagpa Temple, west wall: Golden Vaiśravaṇa (Jambhala).

deities is a small image of a two-armed male figure embracing his female consort. The pair is appropriately inscribed "Ldem . . . [illegible] chog." Despite water damage to the inscription, it is clear that the inscription is meant to identify Cakrasaṃvara (Tibetan: Dem chog), a significant deity for the Drigung school.[33] Further to the right of the embracing figures of Cakrasaṃvara and Vajrayoginī are two large protector deities, one placed directly above the other (see fig. 2.1). Four-armed Mahākāla, who is the protector of the Cakrasaṃvara Tantric teachings, is situated above another wrathful protector deity too damaged to identify (plate 5). These two wrathful deities are matched on the left side of the wall by images of a six-armed Mahākāla, also known as Ṣaḍbhuja, and possibly a two-armed Acala (plate 6).

Immediately below the Achi figure, and above the lintel of the door, are painted two manifestations of the deity Vaiśravaṇa (Tibetan: Rnam thos sras [Namtose]), a guardian who protects the Buddhist teachings and is also the deity of wealth (fig. 2.14).[34] In one painting he is depicted in his protector manifestation clad in military armor and boots. Looking directly out at the viewer with large bulging eyes, he sits astride a white snow lion. In the other painting, he appears as the benefactor, who sits cross-legged and bare-chested, and holds the jewel-disgorging mongoose by its neck (fig. 2.15). His left hand holds up a victory banner, which in this case is emblematic of Vaiśravaṇa's victorious defeat of all obstacles along the Buddhist path.

The west wall's constellation of protector deities is quite familiar within Drigung settings, but is not limited to them. As there are so few Drigung sites with extant fifteenth- through seventeenth-century wall paintings in Tibet and its extending cultural zones, it is only possible to compare this iconographic program to thirteenth- and fourteenth-century Drigung sites in Ladakh, an area once rich with Drigung activity. According to Christian Luczanits, Drigung iconography in the thirteenth and fourteenth centuries reveals an emphasis on Cakrasaṃvara, Vajrayoginī, Acala, and Mahākāla; all of these protector deities are present on the west wall of Gyapagpa Temple.[35] What we see at Gyapagpa Temple, therefore, is an extension of this same grouping of wrathful deities that was prevalent several centuries before.

North Wall

The other three walls are organized in a straightforward manner, each depicting a centrally positioned Buddhist figure flanked by an attendant on each side. Arranged around this grouping of three figures are smaller, subsidiary figures. On the north wall, Vajradhara, the root guru for the Tantric Buddhist tradition, is positioned at the center of the composition.

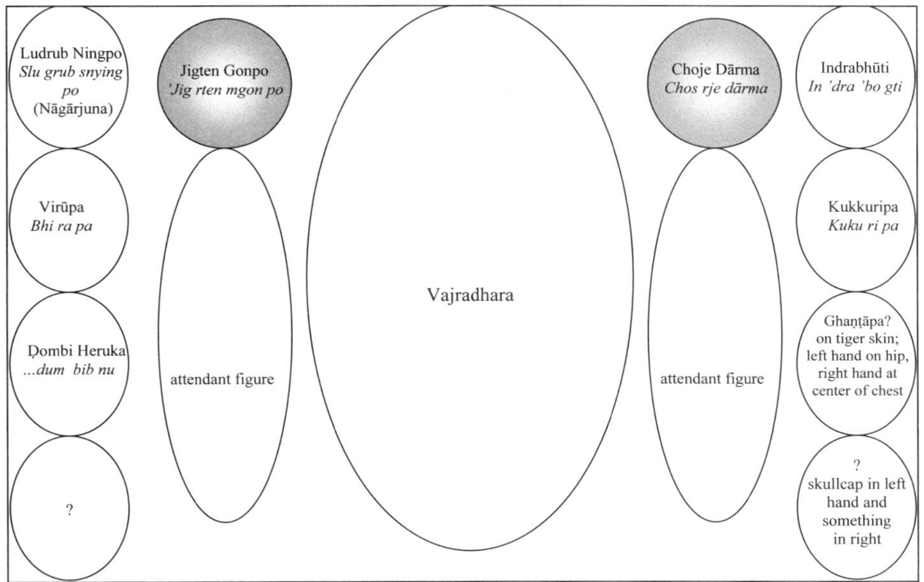

Figure 2.16. Schematic drawing of north wall with Mahāsiddhas. Where multiple versions of a name appear, the top name is a phonetic Tibetan spelling; below it is an italicized transliteration of the inscription. Sanskrit is in parentheses. Where there is no inscription for a figure, only the Sanskrit name is used. Shaded areas indicate Drigung lineage portraits.

Deep blue in color, he sits with his legs crossed and his arms drawn up to his chest and crossed at the wrists. His left hand holds a bell and his right, a *vajra*. He is attended by two bodhisattvas, one blue and the other white. Directly above each attendant figure is a portrait of a monastic figure, with Jigten Gonpo, the founder of the Drigung lineage, above the left attendant. To the right is positioned the second lineage member, Choje Dārma (fig. 2.16). Framing this central group of figures—the main deity, attendants, and two lineage members—are two columns comprising four figures each. Together, these constitute a group of eight mahāsiddhas, spiritually accomplished adepts.

Five of these eight mahāsiddha figures are easily identifiable based on their iconography and accompanying inscriptions. At the top of the left column is a seated figure dressed in monastic robes, hands positioned in the teaching mudrā and head protected by a snake-hood. His inscription reads, "slu grub snying po," which is Old Nāgārjuna; this refers to the Indian monk-scholar who was one of the founders of the Madhyamaka school and is generally included in gatherings of eight mahāsiddhas (figs. 2.17 and 2.18).[36]

Below Nāgārjuna are a number of identifiable mahāsiddha figures. The first is the corpulent figure of Virūpa, who sits on a tiger skin (only

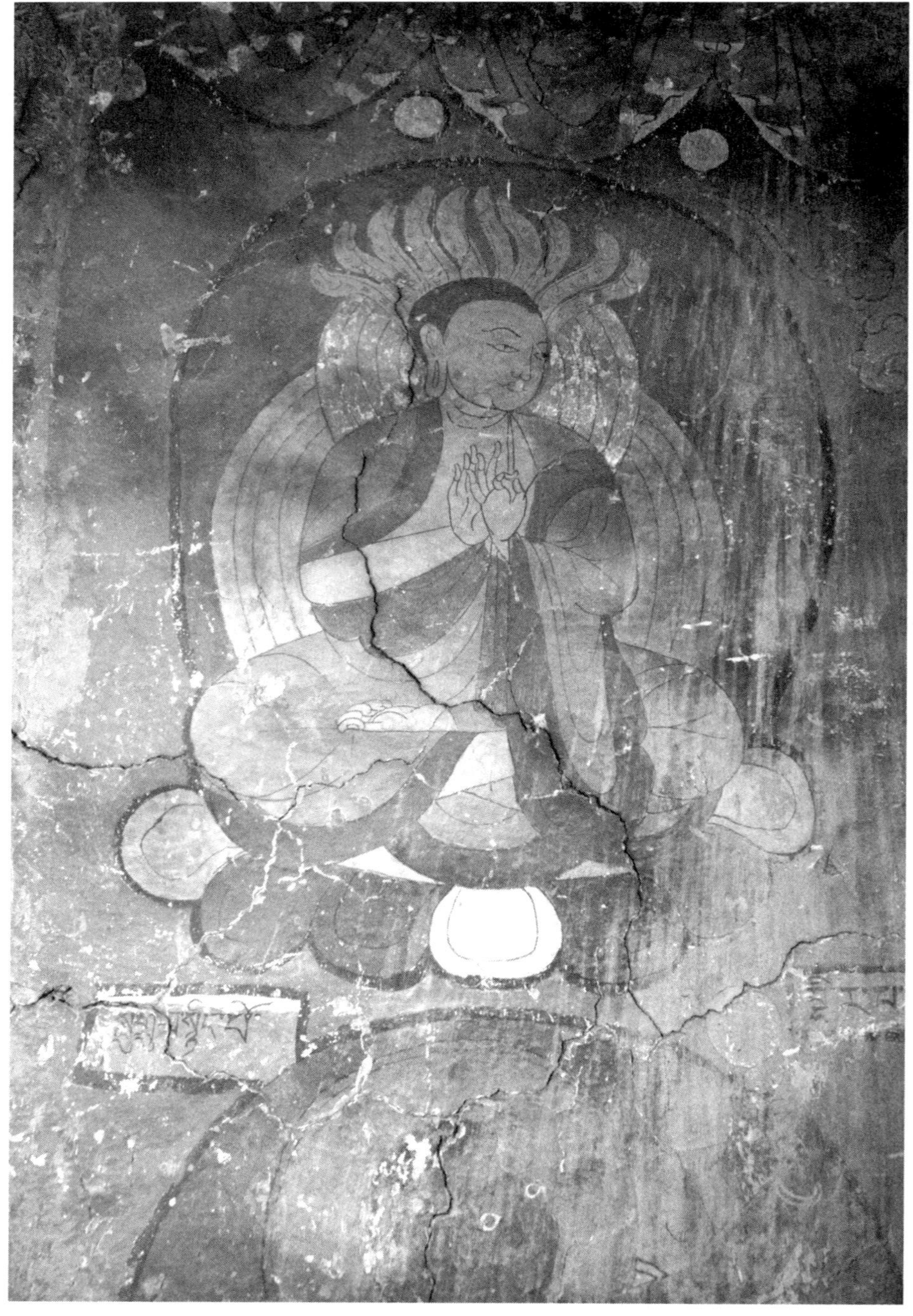

Figure 2.17. Gyapagpa Temple, north wall: Old Nāgārjuna portrait.

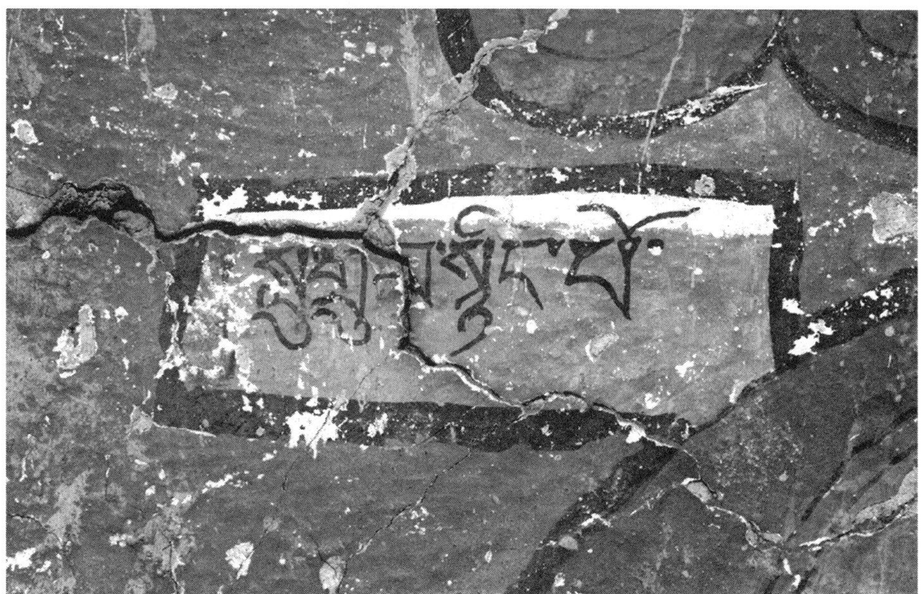

Figure 2.18. Gyapagpa Temple, north wall: Old Nāgārjuna's identifying inscription (Slu grub snying po).

partially seen on the right side) and points his left hand to the sun (fig. 2.19). Close to his raised left arm is an inscription that reads "bhi ra pa," a phonetic spelling of the Sanskrit name, Virūpa.[37]

Below Virūpa sits a vague outline of Ḍombi Heruka, the mahāsiddha who rides a pregnant tigress and sometimes holds a skullcap and snake. Only marginal elements of this badly damaged image are recognizable: the face and raised arm of the mahāsiddha, and the striped tail and head of the tigress.[38] A faint inscription located to the right of the figure reads, "[illegible] dum bib nu . . . [illegible]." This is likely a Tibetan transliteration of the Sanskrit name Ḍombi Heruka.

Below Ḍombi Heruka is the fourth and last mahāsiddha of this column. While his outlines are clearly visible, his attribute is nearly completely destroyed. He sits with his head angled down toward his left shoulder. His right hand is positioned at the center of his chest; his left elbow rests on his left knee, with the forearm raised. He holds something in his left hand, but it cannot be determined with certainty, and thus, this figure remains unidentified.

Starting at the top of the right column is Indrabhūti, the Indian king who renounced his worldly possessions to take up the life of an ascetic, who is clearly identified by the inscription reading "In 'dra 'bo gti," which is a phonetic Tibetan rendering of this Sanskrit name (fig. 2.20).[39] His facial features and other details are covered by a thick layer of mud

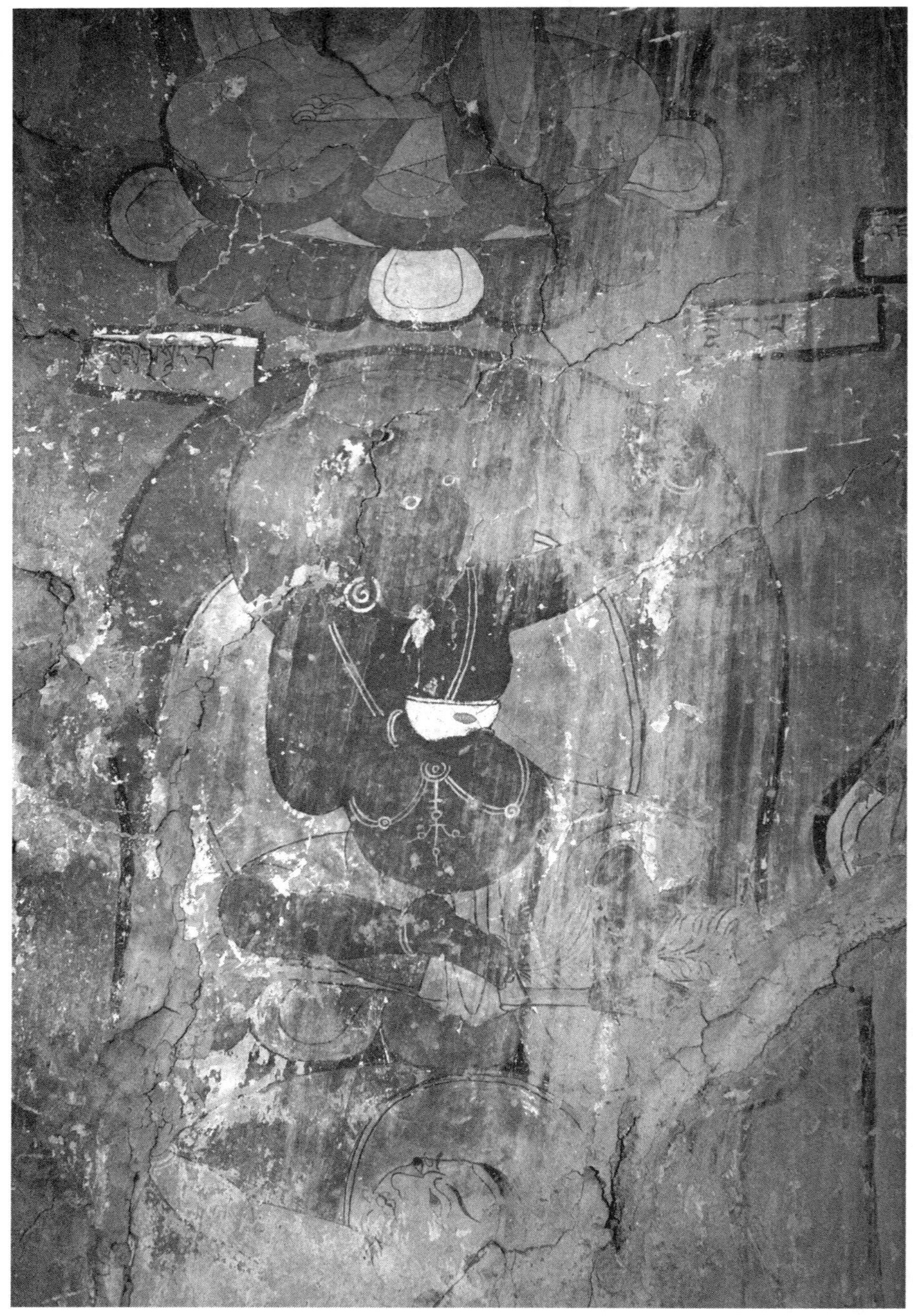

Figure 2.19. Gyapagpa Temple, north wall: Mahāsiddha Virūpa.

Figure 2.20. Gyapagpa Temple, north wall: Mahāsiddha Indrabhūti inscription.

that runs the length of the wall. Beneath this figure is that of Kukkuripa ("Kuku ri pa"), the mahāsiddha who is famously accompanied by a mangy dog who later reveals herself to Kukkuripa as a *ḍākinī*. Though the majority of the image is nearly destroyed, the telltale visual signs remain, such as the white tail and hind legs of the dog who sits on Kukkuripa's lap (fig. 2.21). His inscription is also clearly legible—although notably written in white, not black, paint.[40]

Identifying the third and fourth figures in this column proves quite challenging. In both cases their inscribed labels are completely destroyed, as are their attributes. The figure immediately below Kukkuripa is rendered sitting on a tiger skin with his left hand on his hip. Water damage has obliterated most of the details, except for his posture and the bottom edge of what may be a ritual bell he holds in his left hand. If this is a bell, this figure may be Ghaṇṭāpa (Tibetan: Dril bu). The last figure of the column holds a skullcap in his proper right hand and something beyond recognition in his left. With such limited visual information it is impossible to determine the figure's identity.

East Wall

Poised at the center of the east wall is the image of Śākyamuni Buddha in what would certainly be his "earth-touching" mudrā if the water damage had not so badly obscured the proper right portion of the Buddha's body

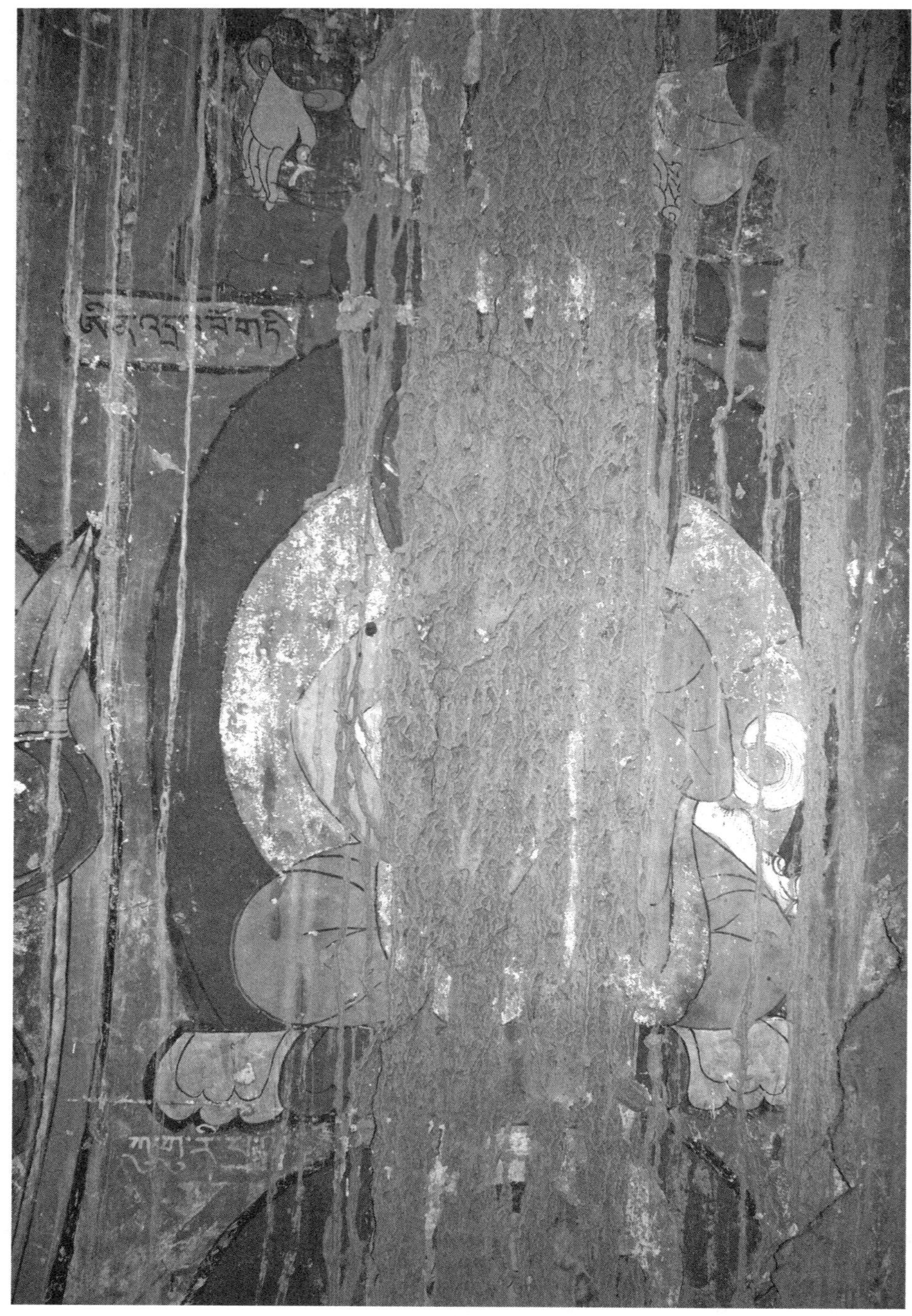

Figure 2.21. Gyapagpa Temple, east wall: Mahāsiddha Kukkuripa.

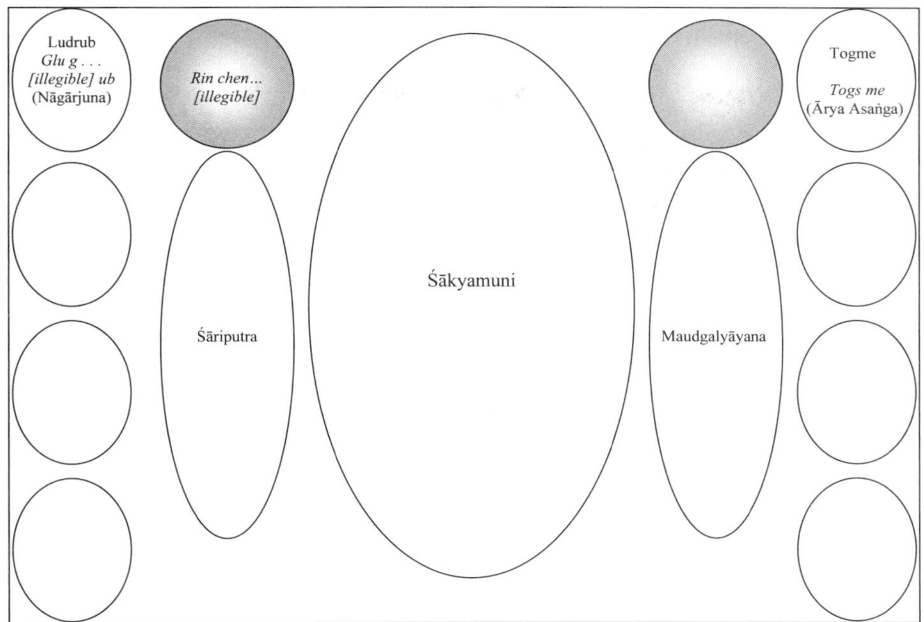

Figure 2.22. Schematic drawing of east wall with "Six Ornaments and Two Supreme Ones" (Tibetan: Rgyan drug mchog gnyis). Where multiple versions of a name appear, the top name is a phonetic Tibetan spelling; below it is an italicized transliteration of the inscription, followed by Sanskrit in parentheses. Where there is no inscription for a figure, only the Sanskrit name is used. Shaded areas indicate Drigung lineage portraits.

(fig. 2.22; plate 4). He sits on a regal lotus-petaled thronebase with an elaborate throne-back composed of *makaras* with scrolling, decorative tails. On either side of him would be two monastic attendant figures, but only the one to the Buddha's proper left survives. From this image it is clear that the monastic attendant figure holds a begging bowl in his right hand and a staff in his left; these two symbols respectively symbolize renunciation and meditation on Emptiness.[41] His two monastic attendants are no doubt meant to be his disciples, Śāriputra and Maudgalyāyana. As on the north wall, a small, seated figure is located above each of the attendants. These are the third and fourth members of the Drigung lineage.

Flanking this assembly of five figures—Buddha, two attendants, and two lineage members—are two columns, one on each side, with four figures each. Nearly all the inscriptional evidence from this wall is damaged beyond legibility. Only two inscriptions remain; each identifies the top monastic figure from the columns of robed figures flanking the Buddha. On the top left a monastic figure holds his hands in the teaching mudrā, and his head is covered by a snake-hood (plate 7). The inscription reads, "Glu g . . . [illegible] ub," the phonetic rendering of Klu

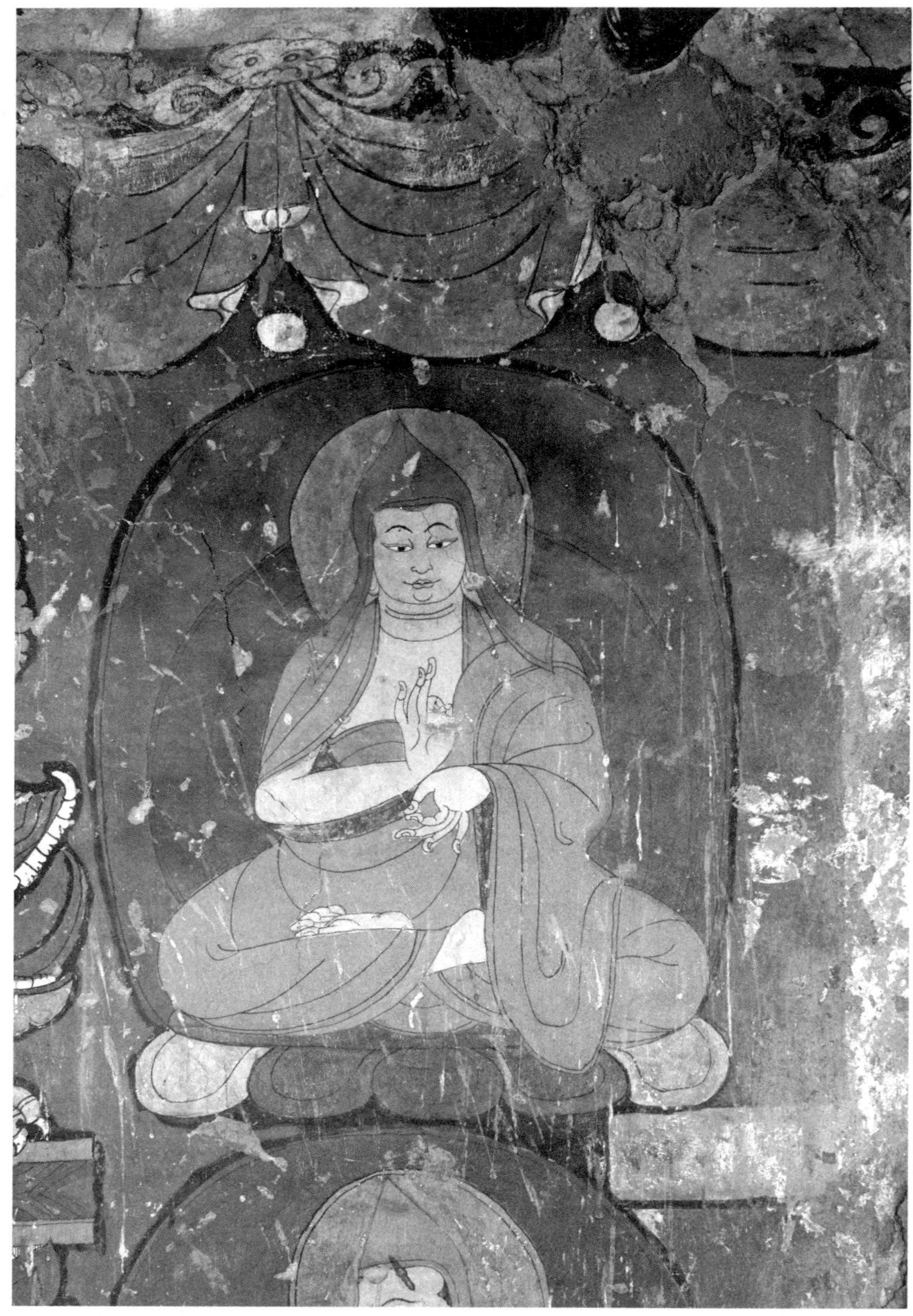

Figure 2.23. Gyapagpa Temple, east wall: Thogs med (Ārya Asaṅga) portrait.

sgrub, the historical figure known in Sanskrit as Nāgārjuna, who is in a similar position on the north wall. At the top of the right column is a portrait inscribed, "Togs me" (fig. 2.23), a phonetic rendering of Thogs med (Togme [Sanskrit: Ārya Asaṅga]), the founder of the "Mind-Only" or Citta-mātra school of Buddhism. Togme's identification helps to determine the identification of this second Nāgārjuna, who must be none other than the founder of the Madhyamaka school. These two figures are often depicted in concert with six other figures: Asaṅga, Vasubandu, Dignāga, Dharmakīrti, Guṇaprabha, and Śākyaprabha. The complete group of eight is known as the Six Ornaments and Two Supreme Ones (Tibetan: Rgyan drug mchog gnyis [Gyandrug chogni]) and is considered to be the group of thinkers and practitioners who developed the "Commentary" tradition of Mahāyāna Buddhism, of which Vajrayāna is a part. The iconographic program of this wall is not specifically associated with any one Buddhist tradition, but is simply a visual message associating Vajrayāna practice with the larger, well-established Mahāyāna school. As such, the image is a fairly ubiquitous one employed by all Tibetan Buddhist schools.

South Wall

Identifying the deities of the south wall proved more difficult than the other three walls. Confusion was due in part to Francke's and then Tucci's misidentification of the central deity. Francke initially identified the central figure as "Thse dpag med (Amitāyus), probably in his capacity of medicine Buddha (sman bla) surrounded by his eight followers."[42] Approximately twenty years later, Tucci identified the central figure as "Amitāyus with other gods of medicine."[43] Although there are four-armed forms of Amitāyus associated with the Medicine Buddha, none of them exactly matches the image featured on the south wall.[44] At Nako, this deity holds a text in its upper-left hand; the upper-right hand holds a scepter, or *dorje*. The lower two arms cradle a vase or water pot topped by leaves. Although the ritual implements of the text and scepter are not associated with Amitāyus, they are strongly associated with a female deity of wisdom known in Sanskrit as Prajñāpāramitā (Tibetan: Yum chen mo). Indeed, there are iconographic depictions of Prajñāpāramitā with four arms: in her upper-right hand she wields a *dorje,* in her upper-left a book, and her two lower hands hold a water pot in the *dhyāna* mudrā.[45] The water pot seen in standard Prajñāpāramitā's iconography usually does not have foliage coming out of the top, as is seen in the Nako painting.

This central figure's identification as Prajñāpāramitā is further supported by other iconographic evidence, in particular the presence of three

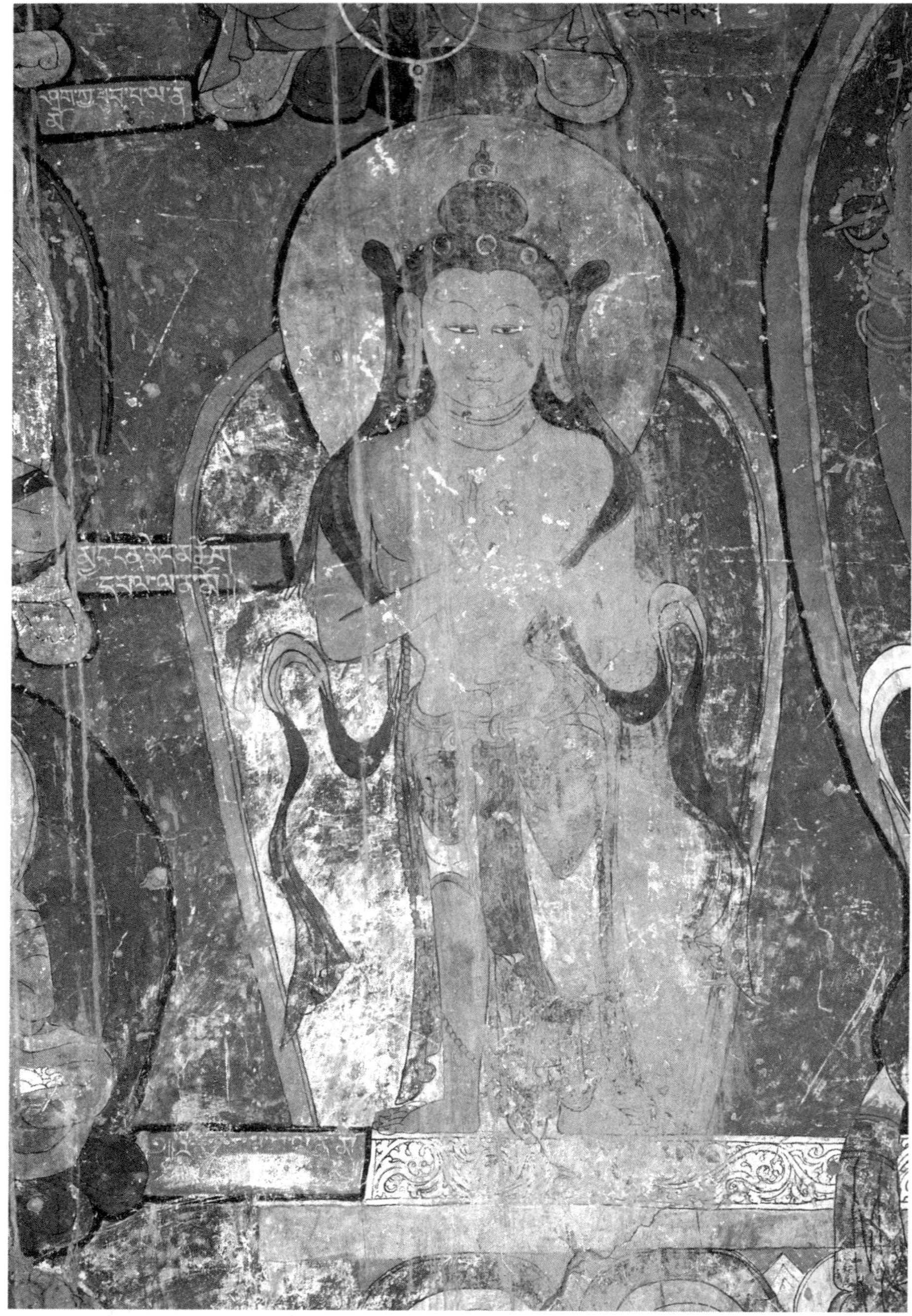

Figure 2.24. Gyapagpa Temple, south wall: Maitreya attendant.

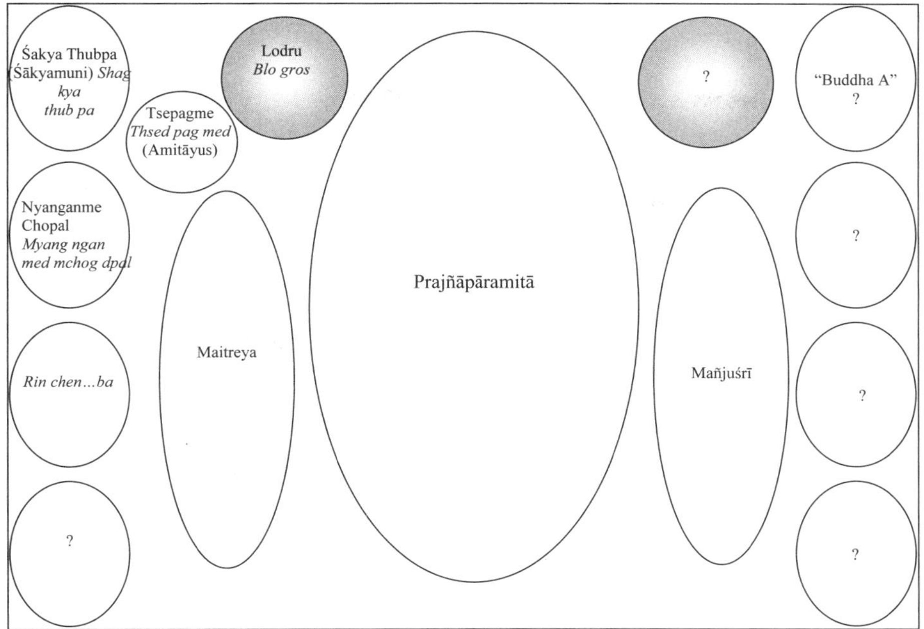

Figure 2.25. Schematic drawing of south wall. Where multiple versions of a name appear, the top name is a phonetic Tibetan spelling; below it is an italicized transliteration of the inscription, followed by Sanskrit in parentheses. Where there is no inscription for a figure, only the Sanskrit name is used. Shaded areas indicate Drigung lineage portraits.

Figure 2.26. Gyapagpa Temple, south wall: inscription for one of the eight Medicine Buddhas (Myang ngan med mchog dpal).

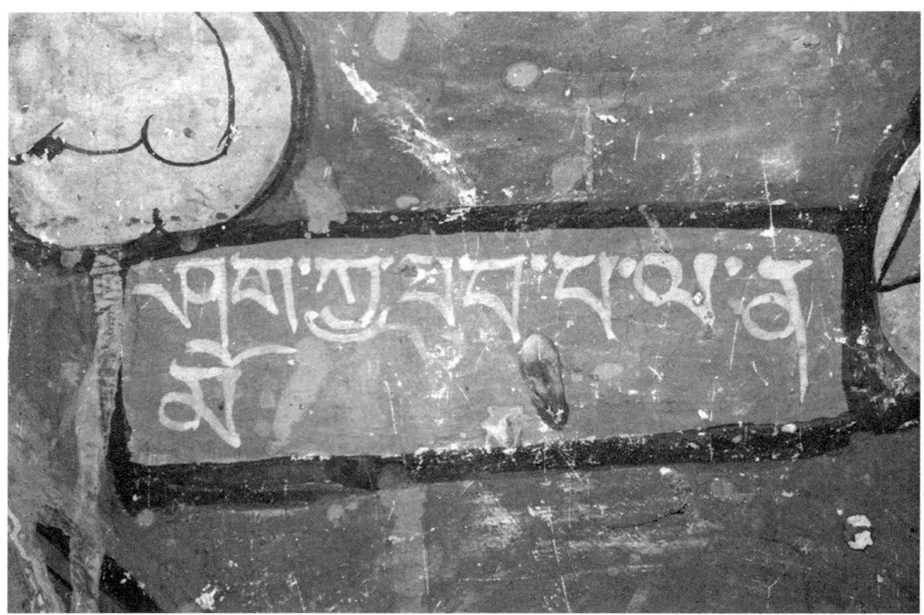

Figure 2.27. Gyapagpa Temple, south wall: inscription reads,
"Shag kya thub pa la na mo."

figures. The first two are attendant figures positioned on either side of her pedestal—figures that until now have not been given specific identities. Upon close examination, it is clear that the attendant on Prajñāpāramitā's proper right is Maitreya, the Buddha of the future. Nearly indiscernible is the small vase containing the elixir of immortality, painted in gold against a red background, which rests on a lotus flower at approximately the same height as the attendant figure's left shoulder (fig. 2.24). Such an attribute, which is emblematic of immortality, is Maitreya's primary identifying iconographic feature. The other attendant figure, yellow in color, is badly damaged, but his attribute is still detectable. Emerging from the worn red paint is a faded image of a golden sword. This attribute confirms the attendant figure's identity as Mañjuśrī, the bodhisattva of wisdom. Both of these figures are considered male wisdom deities and are often associated with Prajñāparamitā.[46] Lastly, the presence of Amitāyus (inscription reads: Tshed pag med), who is painted to the proper right of the central deity (plate 8), and next to one of the lineage members, also supports the main deity's identification as Prajñāpāramitā because this is the Buddha family to which she belongs.

Surrounding this central figure are two columns of four Buddhas (see fig. 2.25). Each of these eight Buddhas is variously colored and holds a different mudrā. Originally, these seated Buddha figures were all inscribed, but only two inscriptions have survived. One clearly reads, "Myang ngan med mchog dpal la na mo," who is one of the Eight Medicine Buddhas (fig. 2.26). Another reads, "Shag kya thub pa," which is a phonetic rendering of Śākyamuni, who is the historical Buddha, but can also be subsumed with this grouping of eight Medicine Buddhas (fig. 2.27). These two inscriptions, along with the colors and mudrās of the Buddhas, help to confirm that this grouping of eight Buddhas is indeed meant to be the eight Medicine Buddhas. This iconographic arrangement of Buddhas surrounding the deity of wisdom, Prajñāpāramitā, creates an abbreviated Medicine Buddha maṇḍala. While Bhaiśajyaguru (Tibetan: Sangye men lha) can often reside at the center of this maṇḍala, it is not uncommon for Prajñāpāramitā to occupy the central position in Medicine Buddha maṇḍalas.[47]

Conclusion

Painted within the small space of the Gyapagpa Temple is an iconographic program that communicates Drigung's relationship to the Mahāyāna tradition and, more specifically, esoteric practice. Upon entering the temple space the viewer is first met with the image of Śākyamuni, the historical Buddha, and the eight adepts who developed various aspects of Mahāyāna thought. On either side of the viewer are the north and south walls with larger-than-life images of Vajradhara and Prajñāpāramitā, respectively. The presence and relationship of these two—the Tantric root Guru faces the mother of all Buddhas, who is the personification of wisdom itself— clearly suggests the esoteric association of this temple and its patrons. Directly behind the viewer is the west wall, where one would exit the temple; the wall is painted with at least five protective deities, Achi being the centrally positioned and most important of these figures.

Although Achi's presence is critical in determining this temple's sixteenth-century Drigung affiliation, the portrait of Drigung's founder is perhaps even more telling. As previously mentioned, Jigten Gonpo commences the lineage of monastic teachers, who are all painted along the upper portion of each of the north, east, and south walls. Not only is the small scale of these portraits noticeable, but so is the abbreviated nature of the lineage itself. Commencing with Jigten Gonpo, the lineage avoids including the earliest and most seminal figures associated with the Kagyu lineage, such as Tilopa, Naropa, Marpa, and Milarepa, from whom all the sub-schools of Kagyu developed. Thus, the patrons chose not to follow convention and begin the lineage with celebrated Indian and Tibetan ascetics, which would have easily served to legitimate the lineage under investigation.[48] As I have interpreted it, by limiting the lineage to this particular subgrouping of the Drigung school practiced in Nako, the patrons were highlighting this small grouping of what were presumably well known teachers from the area, as opposed to the larger Kagyu tradition. The placement of the Drigung lineage within the larger composition, however, underscores the patrons' larger concern for establishing a strong sense of lineage and legitimacy. Placed along the uppermost section of the walls' compositions, this lineage, articulated on a small scale, is visually enveloped by the other bulwarks of the Buddhist tradition.

Although the constellation of deities, siddhas, and lineage holders displayed on these four walls unquestionably aligns this temple with the Drigung school, the erstwhile Drigung association is nowhere evident among the living Nako community. This temple's transition from one Buddhist school to another—from Drigung to Drukpa, which eventually became the dominant form of Buddhist practice in the area—is not without precedence. There have been documented incidences to show that this sort of appropriation of one site and its ensuing resignification is not new in Tibetan cultural zones or South Asia in general.[49] What remains puzzling about this temple, however, is the phantom presence of the heroic figure, Gesar, who notably is not part of the pantheon of deities specifically connected to the Drukpa school. Why, then, would his presence be evoked by the Drukpa community at Nako?

The response to this question adds yet one more layer to this narrative of appropriation and "accretion of meaning."[50] The Gesar appellation for the protector deity in question was first reported, and may have been promoted, by the missionary-scholar August Hermann Francke, the first Westerner to document this temple in the early 1900s. Francke's misidentification of this image may have been driven by his personal fascination with Gesar, an interest that led him to document an oral version of the epic hero's story and eventually to translate it from Ladakhi into English in the early 1900s, the very period when he was working in Nako.[51] Francke's preoccupation with Gesar—a horse-riding epic hero—may have led him to the assumption that the Gyapagpa Temple's horse-mounted figure was Gesar. It is tempting, then, to presume that Francke passed on this misidentification to the villagers. Such an explanation is problematic, however, because it renders the villagers without agency, or at the least very impressionable, when it comes to interpreting their own religious and iconographic imagery. A possibility that cannot be discounted, therefore, is that the villagers informed Francke of the protector figure's identity. It is possible that the village faithful assigned the meaning of Gesar to the protector figure after the Drigung connection died out. Of course, there remain questions about when this transition of meaning may have happened. Furthermore, it is conspicuous that Gesar does not feature prominently as a protector figure in any of the other temples in Nako or other temples I surveyed in the region, making Franke's claim and Nako's rather idiosyncratic use of the figure doubly intriguing.

Despite the obfuscating layers of meaning and interpretation, it is clear that the existing iconographic program and inscriptional evidence found on the walls of the temple are incidental to the community's current reception of the images. In fact, the inscriptions are especially extraneous, as literacy in Nako remains quite low.[52] Within this largely illiterate environment, the text does not serve to anchor the denoted meaning.[53] For practical purposes, it matters little that the inscriptions associate these images with the Drigung school of the Kagyu tradition. The villagers perceive the Gyapagpa Temple to be part of the larger Drukpa landscape of Nako; and they make offerings to the temple with this understanding. This dissonant relationship between word and image highlights the lack of semiotic value of the word in present-day Nako, and perhaps in the past as well. Although the words may be seen, they may not be read, and they do not play an instrumental role in the village's present construction of the images' meanings. In fact, even when the inscriptions are read, as Tenzin the temple caretaker had done, the written information does not change the meaning of the villagers' current perceptions.

As the Nako example shows, over time there can be shifts in meaning and perception of these larger-than-life wall paintings. Initially shaped and defined by one set of religious beliefs, that of the Drigung school, these images have since been re-visioned within another period and sociopolitical context. That the villagers of Nako did not repaint these temple walls to illustrate their adherence to a different Buddhist practice is telling. Instead, the Drukpa community at Nako folded the existing paintings within a different meaning system, giving new life to these old signs. Thus, in this case the plurality of these images' reception is based on a slow *re*signification process caused by gradual shifts in the viewers' devotional context. The appropriation of this temple, therefore, does not symbolize a hostile, or even a calculated, takeover, as is often associated with the idea of image appropriation.[54] I speculate that the potency of this religious site was recognized and responded to by a community that eventually replaced the Drigung adherents. This shift in the religious affiliation marked a change in the cultural context at Nako, which caused a re-viewing of these old images.

Although theories of reception and models of appropriation help to deepen our understanding of how the Gyapagpa Temple paintings were an integral part of a complex network of meaning that developed over the centuries they were in use, there are lingering questions regarding the religious and political contexts that provided fertile ground for the patronage and creation of these images in the late sixteenth century. The next chapter seeks to provide rough contours for a portrait of the patron(s) who commissioned Drigung iconographic program at the Gyapagpa Temple in Nako. To do this, I address the institutional affiliations and political forces at work in Nako and its surrounding areas. Of particular relevance in the next chapter is the role of the Drigung school and its presence in Nako, Kinnaur, and beyond.

3
Mapping Drigung Activity at Nako and in the Western Himalaya

The task of tracing Nako's 'Bri gung (Drigung) religious history has been a challenging one in large part because there is no documented religious history for Nako and no known inscriptions that provide substantive political and religious information. Given the paucity of such textual and inscriptional information at Nako, the artistic remains become that much more crucial in piecing together Nako's devotional history. Although research on Nako's early painting programs of circa twelfth century have been studied and published, the material of the late medieval period has been neglected. This body of work, and in particular the Gyapagpa sixteenth-century painting program, is of crucial significance in piecing together what has otherwise remained an opaque religious history for Nako and the surrounding region of Kinnaur.

As the last chapter established, the murals at Nako's Gyapagpa Temple unequivocally align the temple with the Drigung community of the larger Bka' brgyud (Kagyu) tradition. One of the most revealing pieces of information from this temple's iconographic program was the six-person lineage painted on three of its four walls. While this has been useful in establishing the temple's sixteenth-century religious affiliation, many other questions linger. For instance, who are these lineage members and what lineage, exactly, is being referenced? A survey of various texts listing Drigung abbot lineages has not yielded correspondences with the particular combination of names, or partial names, depicted in Gyapagpa Temple.[1] Furthermore, I have consulted several scholars of West Tibetan and Drigung history from India and Tibet, but none has been able to identify the lineage depicted.[2] The inability to identify this six-member group as part of an established and recognized Drigung lineage raises the possibility that Nako's grouping represents a lesser known and little documented—Drigung lineage, specific to this area of Kinnaur. That there are no other temples in the region with Drigung iconography makes it impossible to verify that what we see at Nako is, in fact, a local lineage.

This dearth of *comparanda* was underscored during fieldwork in Kinnaur and Spiti, when I surveyed upwards of fifty temples—most of them in the Upper Kinnaur area—in an attempt to locate a single Drigung temple, but without success. Based on the lack of material evidence for Drigung activity in Kinnaur, we are left with an image of Nako as an isolated island of Drigung activity. I do not think that the extant material evidence, however, reveals the extent of Drigung activity during the sixteenth century. I suggest that despite the lack of material evidence, it is likely that Nako's Gyapagpa Temple was part of a now nearly forgotten Drigung revival movement of the sixteenth century, which generated a network of Drigung temples spanning the western Himalayan region. This hypothesis is based on the documented activity of a charismatic Drigung figure who traveled from Central to West Tibet and on to Ladakh in the mid-1500s in order to revive what was then a waning religious tradition.

In order to flesh out the historical and religious context of the temple's sixteenth-century painting program, and more specifically my thesis that this temple functioned as part of the late medieval Drigung revival in the western Himalaya, I first outline the general history of Drigung, and its activity in West Tibet and Ladakh. I then turn to the specific area of Kinnaur.

Early Period of Drigung Activity in the Western Himalaya

The political and religious history of the westernmost reaches of the Tibetan cultural zone during the fifteenth century and after is far from well understood. The history of Drigung in this region is even more obscure. The lack of critical understanding of this area's history—political and religious—has to do with its having been only intermittently studied from the early 1900s. Limited textual resources have also restricted our understanding. The academic works produced by Tibetan scholars Dkon mchog (Konchog) Gyatso and Guge Tsering Gyalpo, as well as Western scholars Luciano Petech and Roberto Vitali, have done a great deal to fill in significant gaps. Based on their pioneering works and recent work of a few other scholars, a modest outline of Drigung history is sketched in the following pages in order to elucidate, as much as possible, the Drigung environs of West Tibet, Ladakh, and especially Kinnaur from the twelfth through the sixteenth centuries.

The first Drigung monastery, 'Bri gung mthil (Drigung thil), was established in Central Tibet in 1179 by the school's founder, Jigten Gonpo.[3] After this seminal event, the newfangled tradition quickly spread to Mnga' ris (Ngari) by way of expeditions sanctioned by Jigten Gonpo. The first of these was organized in 1191 and the second in 1208.[4] One of the most successful of these expeditions took place in 1215, when one of Jigten Gonpo's disciples, known as Ghu ya sgang pa (Ghuyasangpa), was sent to Mount Kailash as the first 'Bri gung rdor 'dzin (Drigung Dordzin [head teacher]) in 1215. As a royally supported religious figure, Ghuyasangpa was given abundant resources with which to establish several monasteries during his twenty-five-year tenure in Ngari.[5] One of the most important monastic complexes was Gyang grags (Gyangdrag), located at the foot of Mount Kailash, which is still in operation today as a Drigung center.[6] Through the development of these monastic centers and the influx of Drigung hermits and monks to the Mount Kailash region, combined with continued political and financial support, the Drigung school became a dominant presence in Ngari and Ladakh by the mid-thirteenth century.[7]

Critically important to Drigung's dominance in West Tibet during this early period was the royal support it garnered from some of the western kingdoms, such as that of the Tise (Mount Kailash) area, in West Tibet. Roberto Vitali reminds us that the political situation in West Tibet was ripe for allowing this Central Tibetan tradition to take root there.[8] He writes, "Ensuring the survival of members of the 'Bri.gung.pa community necessitated the stable occupation of meditation places, but this was only possible when political conditions were suitable for the ri.pa-s to settle in sTod."[9] Indeed, Drigung followers and mountain-dwelling ascetics (*ri pa*) had a secure foundation and enjoyed royal support during the thirteenth century in West Tibet, especially before the Yuan-Sakya administration took root. For instance, under the thirteenth-century ruler, Grags pa lde (Dragpade), the Pu hrang–Guge (Purang) kingdom flourished and expanded, while Drigung sites were prodigiously supported.[10] Most noteworthy about this linkage between the Purang kingdom and the Drigung school under Dragpade is his kingdom's expansion into parts of Kinnaur in the late thirteenth century. According to the fifteenth-century *Mnga' ris rgyal rabs*: "He extended the boundaries of his kingdom to Kumaon (lost to Ya rtse), parts of Garhwal and the lands from Rong chung until the entrance to lower Khu nu."[11] Moreover, a nineteenth-century pilgrimage text notes Kinnaur as home to the Drigung Bsam gtan chos gling

(Samten Choling) monastery in the thirteenth century, which was directly connected to Mount Kailash's famous Gyadrag monastery.[12] The whereabouts of the Kinnaur-based Samten Choling monastery, noted in this nineteenth-century pilgrimage text, remain unknown, however.[13] It very likely has been habilitated for Dge lugs (Gelug) or 'Brug pa (Drukpa) use, as this must have been the case for the majority of other once-Drigung temples from that area and period. Consequently, there is no extant material evidence of this temple. These pieces of textual evidence from the fifteenth and nineteenth centuries provide some evidence, albeit sparse, that Kinnaur was historically related to the Purang-guge-Drigung orbit of the thirteenth century.

Northwest of Ngari, the Ladakhi kingdom had a considerable Drigung population, which was also established in the thirteenth to fourteenth centuries. In western Ladakh three still-functioning Drigung temples are thought to date back to this early period of Drigung activity: Lamayuru, Wanla, and Kanchi. The exact dates for a Drigung presence at these sites is still unclear. In the cases of Lamayuru and Wanla, these sites were established earlier than the thirteenth century and likely as a different religious tradition. It seems that once Drigung garnered royal support, sites such as these were appropriated and renovated for Drigung use. At Wanla, for instance, there is inscriptional evidence that identifies 'Bhag dar skyabs (Bagdar Kyab) as the main patron and obliquely mentions Drigung as the main religious affiliation at the temple.[14] Although questions remain about the extent of Bagdar Kyab's patronage and period of his reign, Kurt Tropper suggests—on the basis of inscriptional, epigraphic, and art historical evidence—that Bagdar Kyab very possibly patronized part of the Wanla religious complex, specifically the Sumtsek, at the end of the thirteenth to early fourteenth century.[15] Despite the uncertainty of some of the factual details, these sites are of great import as they remain among the few continually functioning Drigung temples in the region.Perhaps the best known and earliest Drigung temple site in Ladakh is found east of Wanla in the village of Alchi. One of its most famous temples, known as the Sumtsek, is similar in type to Wanla's three-story temple. Based on internal inscriptional evidence and iconography, the temple has been dated to the early thirteenth century and affiliated with the Drigung school.[16] Unlike Wanla, Lamayuru, and Kanchi, this temple is no longer an active Drigung site. It has, in fact, been placed under the care of the nearby Gelug monastery.

There are a handful of lesser known, but incredibly valuable, Drigung sites in Zangskar, the neighboring region of Ladakh, which have been dated to circa late thirteenth to fourteenth century. For instance, the recent discovery of two Drigung temples in the Zangskari village of Lingshet, now a functioning Gelug site, demonstrates that Drigung activity in this area was more extensive than previously known.[17] In terms of religious history, the paintings at these two temples provide invaluable documentation of Drigung activity in an area where religious history before the fifteenth century was relatively unknown. As Martin Mills explains, "As part of the expansion of Gelukpa power, a variety of institutions in Ladakh and Zangskar (such as Karsha and P'ukt'al monasteries) were converted to the Gelukpa during the 1440s by Tsongkhapa's disciple, Changsems Sherabs Zangpo."[18] Since this massive conversion to Gelug, the original religious orientation of these and other sites in Ladakh has been lost. Indeed, at Lingshet, as Rob Linrothe explains, its Drigung past was completely erased.[19] This process of erasing and forgetting Lingshet's Drigung past was facilitated by boarding up and decommissioning the temples.[20] As discussed in the last chapter, this process of forgetting at Nako did not involve blatant practices of omissions, but rather revision. The paintings remained untouched, but were, I suggest, slowly revisioned; over time, they were interpreted differently from their intended meaning based on sixteenth-century iconographic evidence. Despite their differences, both sites are examples of active forgetting, a practice helpful in creating a new religious identity.

There is still a tremendous amount of documentation and analysis of these western Himalayan Drigung temples' iconography and style that needs to be conducted in order to understand better their chronological, stylistic, and religious relationships to one another.[21] Nonetheless, the raw material evidence strongly demonstrates a prominent Drigung following throughout Ladakh at this early point in Drigung's activity from the thirteenth and fourteenth centuries.

By the fourteenth century, however, the political and religious currents shifted in West Tibet. At the end of the thirteenth century, the Sakya branch of Tibetan Buddhism gained majority control of Tibet due to its political connection to China's Yuan dynasty, then the governing body over both Tibet and China.[22] Sakya's control of West Tibet began at the end of the thirteenth century, after the reign of the Guge king Dragpade, in approximately 1277–80. At that point, "Gu.ge passed under the Sa.kya. pa-s, who ruled locally by means of their Khab Gung."[23] By the fourteenth century, the Yuan court sanctioned governors to control various parts of Central and West Tibet.[24] What this foreign rule meant for Drigung prosperity in West Tibet is not immediately apparent. Some textual accounts indicate that despite Sakya's political sway in West Tibet and its subsequent religious dominance, the Drigung community remained active through the fourteenth century, although it did not flourish.[25]

As Drigung fell out of royal favor, its presence and power diminished significantly by the fifteenth century. In West Tibet and Ladakh, Drigung communities found it difficult to stay competitive with the florescence of the Gelug tradition. Nonetheless, the Drigung community was recognized as an important part of Guge's history in the fifteenth century, the period of their waning success. For instance, at the capital of the fifteenth-century Guge kingdom, Tsaparang, murals in its Red Temple illustrate historical portraits of kings and religious personages. Here, one can find an inscribed portrait of Jigten Gonpo, the founder of the Drigung school.[26] His inclusion amid this esteemed lineage of religious and political leaders of Tibet clearly indicates that there must have been a significant enough population of Drigung followers in the Guge kingdom, and specifically Tsaparang, to warrant the inclusion of Jigten Gonpo in the Red Temple's painting program. This further supports the hypothesis that although the Gelug tradition was favored, the Guge kingdom during the fifteenth century expressed recognition of and interest in several religious traditions and fostered an environment of religious inclusivity.[27]

Textual evidence from the *Mnga' ris rgyal rabs* corroborates the fact that the royal families of Guge were not exclusively devoted to the Gelug tradition.[28] According to Vitali, for instance, the Gelug abbot who authored the Guge royal chronicle, "found Sa skya pa and 'Bri gung pa exponents at the Gu ge court."[29] In other words, while one tradition may have been favored, several religious traditions were practiced simultaneously in a given region and even within the same court. Awareness of these other functioning religious traditions is important in creating an accurate picture of religious plurality in Ngari during the fifteenth century. Thus, while Drigung may not have flourished at this time, it was tolerated, if even limitedly supported. Thus, in the fifteenth century, Guge, and Ngari more generally, were not exclusively Gelug, though this tradition's prominence would grow over the next hundred years to then sharply escalate in the seventeenth century.

During the fifteenth and sixteenth centuries, Zangskari and Ladahi royal communities also favored the new Gelug tradition, which is evident by their patronage of lamas, as well as construction of temples and monasteries dedicated to the tradition.[30] Places such as Lingshet, which escape mention in chronicles, are useful for us to analyze in an effort to see the spread of the Gelug tradition and the impact it had on the Drigung community in the western Himalaya. It is thought that Byang sems shes rab bzang po (Changsem Sherab Zangpo [1395–1457])—the fifteenth-century disciple of Tsongkhapa, the founder of the Gelug tradition—established the Gelug monastery at Lingshet, as well as numerous others in Zangskar and beyond.[31]

Shared Gelug religious affiliation between Ladakh and West Tibet did not mollify mounting political hostilities between these two regions. In fact, in the mid-1400s the Ladakhi king Blo gros mc'og ldan (Lodru Chogdan; active mid-fifteenth century) attacked the Guge kingdom.[32]

Likely his attempt at expanding and strengthening the Ladakh kingdom was a response to the warring activity immediately surrounding Ladakh. Muslim forces took over Kashmir and Baltistan in the fifteenth century during a series of raids.[33] At this same time, one of these raids, led by sultan ul-Abidin (active 1420–70), penetrated as far as Guge territory of West Tibet.[34] Perhaps Lodru Chogdan thought that by taking Guge, already enfeebled by the Muslim invasion, he would have control of its multiple natural resources, which would help him bolster his kingdom against impending Muslim invasion. His rather clumsy raid against Guge, however, did not seem to have any lasting or even notable effect. Of course, Muslim forces did invade Ladakh again, this time under Jahangir Magre's supervision, but Ladakh held its own against these Muslim Kashmiri forces.[35] With their failed takeover of Guge and a successful defense against Muslim intruders, the fifteenth century in Ladakh proved to be a time of religious and political ferment.

The sixteenth century was no less demanding. Petech, consulting several sources, is able to piece together a story of recurrent Islamic raids and invasions in Ladakh. The most significant of which were led by Mīrzā Haidar, who was ruler of Kashmir.[36] At the end of this rather tumultuous sixteenth century is a period of relative peace under the ruler Bka shis rnam rgyal (Tashi Namgyal, active 1555–75). It is under him that the political and religious landscape of Ladakh stabilizes and even prospers. Indeed, it is because of Tashi Namgyal's patronage that Ladakh witnesses the second revival of Drigung activity (the first being in the thirteenth century).

Drigung Resurgence

One of the most important religious developments of the sixteenth century in West Tibet and Ladakh relates to the renewal of Drigung activity.[37] This rekindling of the Drigung community was due in large part to a religious figure known as Ldan ma kun dga' grags pa (Danma Kunga Dragpa), who traveled to Kailash from Central Tibet in the early 1500s. He, among hundreds of other Drigung monks, was sent to West Tibet by the sixteenth-lineage-holder of Drigung, Gyalwang Kunga Rinchen (r. 1475–1527), who lived at Drigung Thil, the main Drigung temple in Central Tibet. Danma was to guide this new infusion of monastic life in West Tibet, and as such was made abbot of the Gyangdrag monastery near Mount Kailash.[38] Once at Gyangdrag monastery, the first Drigung monastery established in West Tibet dating back to the early thirteenth century, Danma garnered the support of three different western Himalayan kingdoms: Guge, Purang, and Ladakh.[39] Apparently, the king of the Guge dynasty, 'Jig rten dbang p'yug (Jigten Wangchu), and the Purang king, Bsod nams rab brtan (Sonam Rabten), took Danma as their "fundamental teacher."[40] Once Ladakhi royals Bkra shis rnam rgyal (Tashi Namgyal) and Ts'e dbang rnam rgyal (Tsewang Namgyal) formally invited Danma to Ladakh, he left Gyangdrag monastery for Ladakh.[41] There, Danma Kunga Dragpa served as the Ladakhi king's root guru and was given permission and land to establish various Drigung monasteries, the most famous of which was named Sgang sngon bkra shi chos rdzong (Gangnon Tashi Chudzong), more commonly known as Phyi dbang (Piyang) monastery located twenty kilometers to the west of Leh, the capital of Ladakh.[42] The exact dates of the founding of this monastery are not known; but it is speculated that Danma established this royally supported Drigung temple in the 1550s.[43]

Although royal chronicles provide evidence of Danma's royal support, there is little other information to be gleaned. Without proper hagiographic sources, much of Ddanma's life and work remain vague. We do not know, for instance, what areas he traveled through on his way to Ladakh. It is tempting and not entirely fanciful to think that he may have traveled through Kinnaur on his way to Ladakh. Whether Danma Kunga Dragpa was active in Kinnaur, the region and specifically Nako benefited from this groundswell of Drigung patronage in the surrounding areas of West Tibet and Ladakh. That Danma's presence in Ngari and Ladakh in the sixteenth century directly coincides with the date of the Drigung painting program at Nako's Gyapagpa Temple is no small point. Undoubtedly, the temple and its paintings were products of and a testament to fervent Drigung activity in this western region of the Tibetan cultural zone in the sixteenth century.

While Nako's Gyapagpa Temple currently stands as a singular example of Drigung activity, such an example of isolated, unsupported religious activity is highly unlikely. Instead, I suggest that Nako's Gyapagpa Temple is evidence of what was a larger Drigung network of temples that emerged in the sixteenth century, which was a revitalization of the previously discussed thirteenth-century Drigung activity of the area. In reimagining Kinnaur's sixteenth-century Drigung history, the Gyapagpa Temple can be seen as a satellite temple that served as a conduit between Kinnaur and the larger, well-established Drigung community in West Tibet.

Historian Guge Tsering Gyalpo's insights bolster my position that Nako's Drigung temple related to a larger Drigung network. In discussing Nako's Gyapagpa Temple's iconographic program with Gyalpo in Lhasa in June 2006, he explained that on the other side of the Indian border, in the restricted Tibetan Autonomous Region, now heavily policed and accessible only to Tibetans, are several small temples with Drigung iconography. Although it was not possible for me to conduct fieldwork at these sites, and thus they remain largely undocumented, their presence needs to be acknowledged. While other questions about the dates of the temples' construction and their current uses linger, we must put them on hold until further research can be carried out in this restricted border zone. Once these temples can be documented and analyzed, they will likely provide tremendous insight into Drigung's religious history. For now, however, I suggest that they were part of both the thirteenth- and then sixteenth-century Drigung periods of lively activity that resulted in Drigung temples and artwork in West Tibet, Kinnaur, and Ladakh.[44]

With regard to Nako's temple there are some issues that still need to be addressed, such as who its potential patrons were. Without inscriptional evidence the patrons' identities remain uncertain; however, one can begin to think in broad terms about the patrons' status and motivation. One is left to infer, for instance, that although the patrons were supporting a rather small resurgent movement, they had enough money and enough of a presence in the community to repaint one of Nako's centrally located temples. Why did they choose to reuse this temple? Was it a way to impart an immediate sense of legitimacy to the likely fledgling Drigung community? By positioning their religious tradition at the heart of the community's religious life, this seems an intentional move to establish Drigung as a critical, perhaps even foundational, part of Nako's religious identity.

Drigung's Demise

Given the religious and political developments in West Tibet and Ladakh after the sixteenth century, it is likely that this Drigung resurgence was rather short-lived. At the least, Drigung presence faded into the background as tensions between the regions of Guge and Ladakh, as well as between the religious factions of Gelug and Drukpa, played out. For instance, in seeking to take control of Guge, Ladakhi troops once again invaded Guge; this time they attacked the capital of Tsaparang in the early seventeenth century. This event is mentioned in two contemporaneous sources, the Ladakhi chronicle and an account from Antonio de Andrade (1580–1634), a Portuguese Jesuit monk who was on a mission in Tsaparang at the time of the invasion.[45] Although there was never a complete overthrow of Guge power, this invasion resulted in ever increasing enmity between Ladakh and Guge, which depleted Guge's agricultural supplies and financial reserves.[46] Guge was in a vulnerable position against other attacks, of which there were several. Adding to these already fraught relationships was the growing antagonism between the early Gelug tradition, which was supported by the Guge kingdom, and the Drukpa population of the Guge area, which did not have the same royal patronage. For instance, in the early 1600s, when the king of Guge, K'ri bkra shis grags pa lde (Dri Tashi Dragpa), did not support Drukpa shrine rebuilding endeavors, friction between the Guge ruler and Drukpa populations worsened. One of the consequences of these diminished relations was that Drukpa monks from the Mount Kailash area looted various parts of the Guge kingdom.[47] Although the Ngari Drukpa population may not have been royally supported within Guge, they had Ladakhi royal patronage from 1624 to 1641.[48] Ladakh was a key player in supporting the Drukpa presence in Ngari and sent delegations to Drukpa monasteries in and around Mount Kailash bearing gifts of gold, silver, gems, and wool.[49] Of course, Ladakh's interest in patronizing Drukpa activity in Guge was not solely beneficent, but rather embedded with political motives: they wanted to maintain an active presence in the Guge kingdom.

At this time in the seventeenth century, the Ladakhi royal family also patronized the Drigung sect, although it was quickly dying out. As Petech writes, "We may add that the king was also a patron of K'ru sgo, the 'Bri-gung-pa monastery on the shore of the Manasarovar; but in his time the 'Bri-gung-pa of that zone fell into serious decay and their hermitages were almost deserted."[50] Of course, this region had once been a stronghold of Drigung activity in the thirteenth century, and was then reinvigorated in the sixteenth century by the presence of Danma, the charismatic Drigung monk. By the seventeenth century the Drigung population around Mount Kailash steadily diminished. The impact of the weakened condition on the peripheral Drigung communities, such as those in places like Kinnaur, is not immediately evident, but it is reasonable to speculate that as the heart of the Drigung community weakened, so did its ancillary sites.

Certainly, the Tibet-Ladakh-Mughul War in the late seventeenth century did not help the already tenuous political, religious, and financial situation in Ngari.[51] Although there was no single episode that sparked the fighting, there had been escalating tensions between Ladakh and Tibet over religious and trade issues.[52] As Petech explains, "This quarrel between the two sects [Drukpaof Ladakh and Gelug of Tibet] concerned above all the Dalai Lama, as the spiritual head of Tibet; but the resulting insecurity of the trade routes could not leave indifferent the Mongol king bsTan-ạdsin Dalas Khan, the temporal suzerain of Tibet."[53] There were also hostilities between Central Tibet and Bhutan, a kingdom that was strongly affiliated with the Drukpa school of the Kagyu tradition.[54] Moreover, Ladakh and Bhutan were allies.[55] Central Tibet, undoubtedly feeling threatened by two strategically located forces—one in the southeast, the other in the northwest—sought to minimize its risks by reclaiming the territory of Ngari from Ladakh.[56] They sent a garrison of troops to this distant region and were able to conquer it, but only with support of a critical ally. As Petech explains, Dga' ldan tshe dbang dpal bzang (Gadan Tsewang Palzang), the monk and commander of the army, needed alliances with Ngari's neighboring regions: "It was very important to him [Dga' ldan tshe dbang] to have some faithful allies on whom to rely in a country so distant from his base."[57] Thus, before attacking the Ladakhi presence in Ngari, Gadan Tsewang Palzang met with Kehari Singh, king of Bashahr, to secure his support. The Bashahr troops did not play a role in the initial battles with Ladakhi troops, but they were used later when Gadan Tsewang sought to invade Leh, Ladakh.[58] In return for Basharh's support, they received unfettered access to the trade routes between Kinnaur and Tibet. Petech explains, "Upon his [Gadan Tsewang Palzang's] arrival in the Kailasa-Manasarovar region he obtained, by personal interview, the armed help of Kehari Singh, Raja of Bashahr, in exchange for trade facilities."[59] This agreement essentially granted the people of Bashahr immunity from any taxes or interference. As the so-called Namgia Document (a treaty discovered by Tucci in a monastic site by the same name some twenty kilometers south of Nako [see chapter 1]) reads, "wherever they go upwards or downwards in that period of time, must not be molested even by a hair with taxes or anything of the sort."[60] This war and Central Tibet's increased presence in Ngari, which brought about even stronger Gelug affiliations, led to the complete dissolution of the Guge kingdom in the seventeenth century and contributed to the continued disintegration of Drigung communities.

All of the conditions that contributed to the demise of Drigung's once prosperous state in Ngari are difficult to determine, but certainly the increase in Gelug and Drukpa Kagyu supporters played a large role in redirecting patronage and practitioners. Further weakening Drigung presence in Ngari was the decreased support it received from its Central Tibetan political and monastic ceneters.[61] Clearly, these factors added to the steady decline of Drigung communities and their sites; it seems probable that there was no sudden termination of Drigung practice in the larger Spiti valley and Ngari. Rather, the Drigung likely assimilated into the more popular and well supported Drukpa Kagyu tradition over the seventeenth and eighteenth centuries.

As had happened at Nako, it is likely that the followers of the Drukpa Kagyu acquired temples that were neglected or virtually abandoned by the flagging Drigung communities in and around Kinnaur and West Tibet. It is the appropriation and redesignation of older Drigung sites that can account for the current paucity of material evidence in Kinnaur. Consequently, the task of dis-covering Drigung religious activity in Kinnaur and Ngari is made that much more difficult. While Nako's Gyapagpa Temple is presently the only material evidence for Drigung activity in Kinnaur, the textual evidence suggests that the temple was once part of a much larger Drigung community that spread from Ngari to Kinnaur, and into Ladakh in the sixteenth century.

Tracing Nako's devotional past allows us to gauge better when transitions in Nako's religious identity took place in the late medieval period, but there are still other important questions that have yet to be answered. The most critical of these pertains to the six-person Drigung lineage painted on the walls of the Gyapagpa Temple. That the lineage has no correlation to standard Drigung abbot lineages may suggest that this grouping of Drigung teachers was in fact locally based.

4

Gyapagpa Temple's Painting Style and Its Antecedents

Based on the insights of the last two chapters it is clear that the Gyapagpa Temple's sixteenth-century painting program was the result of a vital 'Bri gung (Drigung) resurgence that affected much of the western Himalayan region during the late medieval period. Given this temple's significant role in piecing together the region's religious history, a lingering question must be raised: How could this valuable historic document have gone underanalyzed for so long? The answer to this question is enmeshed within at least two interconnected issues regarding trends in South Asian, and specifically Tibetan, art historical scholarship. As for the first of these two issues, there has generally been a tendency to document, analyze, and publish Tibetan art from earlier rather than later periods. Much of Tibetan art history has focused on earlier material of the eleventh through fourteenth centuries.[1] Indeed, this is the case with the late sixteenth-century paintings at the Gyapagpa Temple, which were overshadowed by neighboring eleventh- and twelfth-century painting programs, both in the compound and in surrounding villages, such as Tabo. Antiquity was not always the deciding factor, however. It would seem that issues of connoisseurship also came into play when scholars neglected Gyapagpa's paintings. Likely, its now faded paintings with limited modeling and sometimes clumsily executed lines inspired scholars to look at other sites, with similarly dated murals, such as at the religious and political centers of Tabo, Tholing, and Tsaparang.

Continued analysis of the Gyapagpa paintings, now from the perspective of style, yields a number of insights about the larger style to which these paintings belong. Although the murals are not the lustrous and richly embellished paintings of their fifteenth- and sixteenth-century counterparts in Tholing, Tsaparang, and Tabo, they do indeed need to be considered in relation to these three sites as the Gyapagpa paintings share the same style and visual vocabulary. Careful visual analysis of Gyapagpa's murals reveals the ways in which motifs of this fifteenth-century West Tibetan courtly style have continued into the sixteenth century and in places well outside of Tsaparang, the capital of the Guge kingdom. In particular, this chapter will identify shared stylistic elements such as figural forms, including idiosyncratic renderings of chins and earlobes, drapery patterns, and a number of decorative motifs, such as crown and jewelry types. Through this close reading of the visual material, I suggest that the Gyapagpa murals are a regional idiom of a style that is better known for its courtly expression.

The first part of the chapter is dedicated to presenting a comprehensive visual analysis of the Gyapagpa paintings, examining composition, palette, figural type, dress, jewelry, and other leitmotifs. This analysis outlines the main characteristics of the style used at the Gyapagpa Temple. The second part of the chapter is devoted to a formal analysis of the court idiom with which I argue the Gyapagpa paintings are associated.[2] These two idiomatic expressions—courtly and regional—are grouped within what I refer to as the larger late medieval Ngari painting tradition, named for its temporal and geographic scope. In this section a two-part rigorous visual analysis serves several purposes. The first is to identify and define the core stylistic elements used at the Gyapagpa Temple painting program. I then consider the number of hands at work in the execution of this painting program, which is useful in understanding the program's subtle variations in figural forms and decorative motifs. The last objective of this analysis is to provide a working definition of the larger style, late medieval Ngari painting tradition, and two of its substyles. The goal is to set the groundwork for a more theoretical discussion of this style's meaning and function, issues that will be addressed in chapter 5.

STYLISTIC ANALYSIS OF GYAPAGPA'S MURALS

In this section I analyze the organization and composition of each of the walls, as well as examine several standard elements found within the paintings, specifically figural forms, clothing, and jewelry. My discussion of figural forms is divided between divine or enlightened figures—including deities (pacific and fierce) and Buddhas—and historical figures, such as lineage members, teachers, and mahāsiddhas (although the historicity of some could be contested). I have been able to identify basic stylistic features of these figural forms, such as clothing designs, bodily adornments, and other decorative motifs that unify the various parts of this painting program. As a result of this detailed analysis of figural forms and motifs, I am able to suggest that the majority of the program was executed at a single time in one, coherent style that was executed under one workshop with a primary painter who had one, if not two, assistants.

Composition

Without any suggestion of recession of space or plasticity of form, the murals have a decidedly flattened, two-dimensional composition. The outlined figural forms are painted parallel to the picture plane within compositions that emphasize linear organization. At the center of three of the four walls is a large, fully frontal, iconic image of a Buddhist deity, who sits cross-legged on a double lotus platform. Each of these iconic figures is flanked by attendants. Above each attendant figure is a small portrait of a monk sitting on a lotus cushion. Framing this central group of five figures—central deity, two attendants, and two portraits—is a pair of columns with four figures in each. The systematic arrangement of figures on these three walls makes the temple's overall program immediately accessible. The upper portion of each wall is adorned with a common decorative motif: a painted border replicating a festooned banner held at intermittent points in the mouths of mythical animals, creating a scalloped edge.

The west wall's composition differs slightly from the others for two related reasons. First, the surface space available for painting is dictated by the presence of the door. The paintings are arranged around this door in an upside-down-U arrangement. Second, as this wall holds the door to the temple, it marks the liminal space between the mundane and sacred worlds; consequently, the paintings feature an assortment of wrathful and protective deities rather than the pacific deities and historical figures featured on the other three walls. Despite the west wall's having a compositional arrangement that is significantly different from the temple's other three walls, all four walls follow a logical and well-planned composition, which was not substantially added to or changed over the years.

Although it is hard to determine how the age of and damage to the murals of this temple may have affected the original saturation and depth of color, it is evident that one consistent, albeit limited, palette was used throughout the temple. The primary colors featured are a maroon red, cantaloupe orange, slate blue, khaki brown, and light ivory. In general, color has not been modulated in these wall paintings. Rather, uniform applications of color were applied without mixing or gradations of hue. This is the case for all aspects of the paintings, including the background, which is painted in slate blue that is at no point altered to indicate depth of field or perspective. Saturated, unmodulated colors create a very flat picture plane, which is reinforced by thick black outlining of all compositional elements. While the composition is largely flat in terms of dimension, modeling, and color application, there is an unmistakable boldness and immediacy about these paintings, which make them visually compelling.

Divine Figures

Pacific Deities

Starting on the north wall, the image of Vajradhara is one of the best-preserved paintings in the temple and retains wonderful painterly details (plates 9 and 10; figs. 4.1 and 4.2). His face and body are rendered with controlled paint strokes and a subtle level of intricacy that are still vividly apparent, for instance, in the deity's face. Vajradhara's once well-delineated facial features still show hints of high arching eyebrows that frame double-lidded, bow-shaped eyes. The lower eyelid is subtly lined with a pale pink color to indicate the red inner rim of the lid. Below the small nose is a pursed mouth that is approximately the same width as the nose. His broad-shouldered torso narrows to a pinched waist. He sits cross-legged with his hips slightly raised on the proper right side suggesting a subtle shift in weight (fig. 4.1). His two hands, crossed at the wrists and held at chest level, delicately hold their respective implements: a bell and *dorje*. Looking closely at his left hand, the artist's sensitivity to form and detail are immediately evident. The artist's sweeping strokes define the fluid curves of the deity's thumb and forefinger. Each finger is exquisitely defined with a precisely drawn nail bed, cuticle line, and fleshy fingertip (plate 10). The deity's feet are rendered with the same attention to form and line; the toes are painted with slightly rounded tips, and each toe pad is emphasized with a double line. Perhaps most elegant is the way the second toe meets the big toe; it has a distinctive curve that gives a defining shape to the toe and nail bed.

Although Vajradhara's clothing is sparse, and primarily works to frame and punctuate the figure's well defined form, his type of dress, its design, and drapery pattern provide important stylistic information. Across his broad shoulders he wears a thin scarf that is red, beige, and white. This falls past his elbows, dips below his hips, and finally billows upward to split into two curling strands. His dhoti-like pants, which cling to his full thighs, are simply decorated with horizontal bands of varying width and color. In some sections the dhoti fabric is painted with scalloped edging and repeated loops. Close study of a small detail seen in figure 4.1 reveals that portions of the dhoti are painted to suggest a

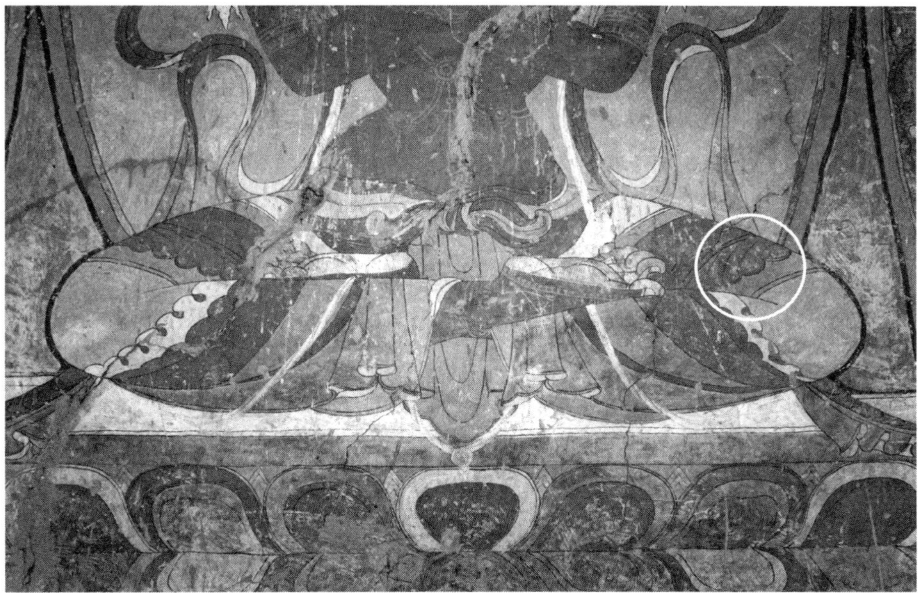

Figure 4.1. Gyapagpa Temple, north wall: detail of Vajradhara's drapery folds.

layering of materials. A thin, slate-blue piece of material is layered atop the cantaloupe-orange dhoti fabric. As it is painted, the blue material falls toward the inner thigh in a distinct pattern. Despite its subtlety, this detail is an important painterly effect that is given more attention in chapter 5.

Although clothing details are kept to a minimum, Vajradhara's jewelry is rather lavish. Much of the color is now faded, but the forms of the jewelry pieces—especially the crown, armbands, and necklaces—are still clearly discernible. One of the most distinctive pieces of jewelry painted in the temple is Vajradhara's five-pointed diadem, which is comprised of five teardrop-shaped plaques, each held within a foliate golden setting (fig. 4.2). The subtle detailing and soft gold hues that characterize this crown can also be found in the other pieces of Vajradhara's jewelry. This type of crown with teardrop-shaped plaques is used for many of the figures, such as the white attendant figure on the north wall and Amitāyus Buddha on the south wall. The difference, however, is that none of these other crowns is rendered with the same foliate setting.

The other pieces of Vajradhara's jewelry, in particular his gold bracelets and armlets, along with his anklets and foot chain, are painted to suggest a raised beading pattern. These pieces are punctuated with red gems that are secured within a setting that is further embellished with gold filigree work (see plate 10). Although miniature in form, this setting replicates the same basic pattern of the crown.

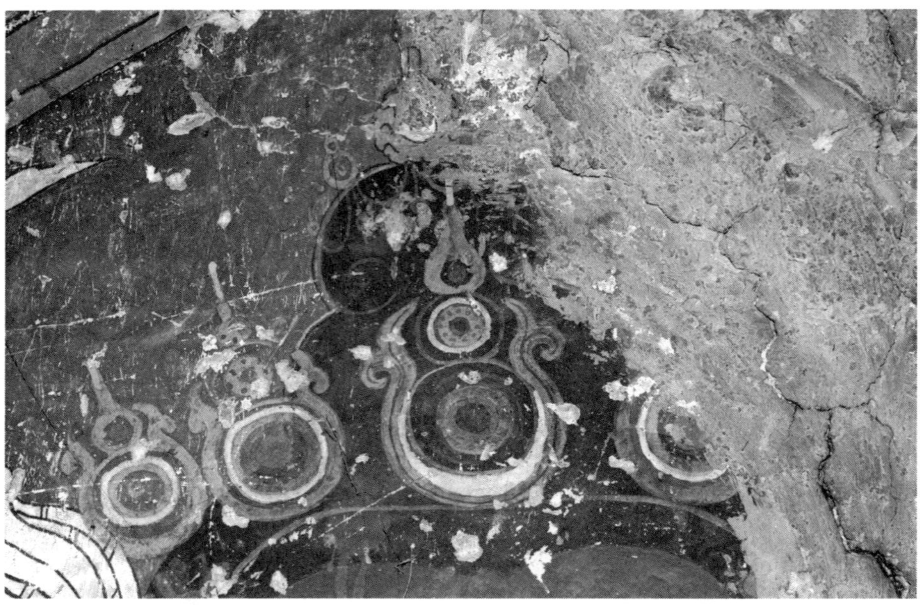

Figure 4.2. Gyapagpa Temple, north wall: detail of Vajradhara's crown.

Vajradhara wears two primary pieces of jewelry on his torso: one is a necklace, and the other a harness-like piece that is secured around the upper body. The first falls just below the throat, at the collarbone, and is rendered with what appear to be thin strands of gold with alternating red and blue stones. Between the swags of gold strands are short chains that have a small, three-part pendant at the end. This finely rendered necklace contrasts with the thicker, more substantial lines and designs of the harness that adorns the whole torso. The double-stranded chain of this harness has five large, beaded medallions. Hanging from these are the same pendant-like features found on the necklace, but here they are larger in size. In fact, one will notice that this three-part pendant appears throughout the jewelry motifs of this temple's paintings. A version of it is worn by the wrathful figures on the west wall.

Another piece of jewelry of note is the long, twisted strand of beads that cascades down Vajradhara's shoulders and past his hips, falling over his thighs and looping over his calves. Such long necklaces are also found on each attendant figure of the north and south walls. In each case, the necklace is nearly ankle length. This necklace is, I believe, a holdover from the eleventh- and twelfth-century West Tibetan or Khache Style that was based, in part, on Kashmiri prototypes. The exact jewelry type is seen in paintings from Tabo's 'Du khang (dukhang), for instance (see chapter 5).

Facing Vajradhara is the main deity on the south wall, who, despite confusing iconographic features, is Prajñāpāramitā. In comparing these

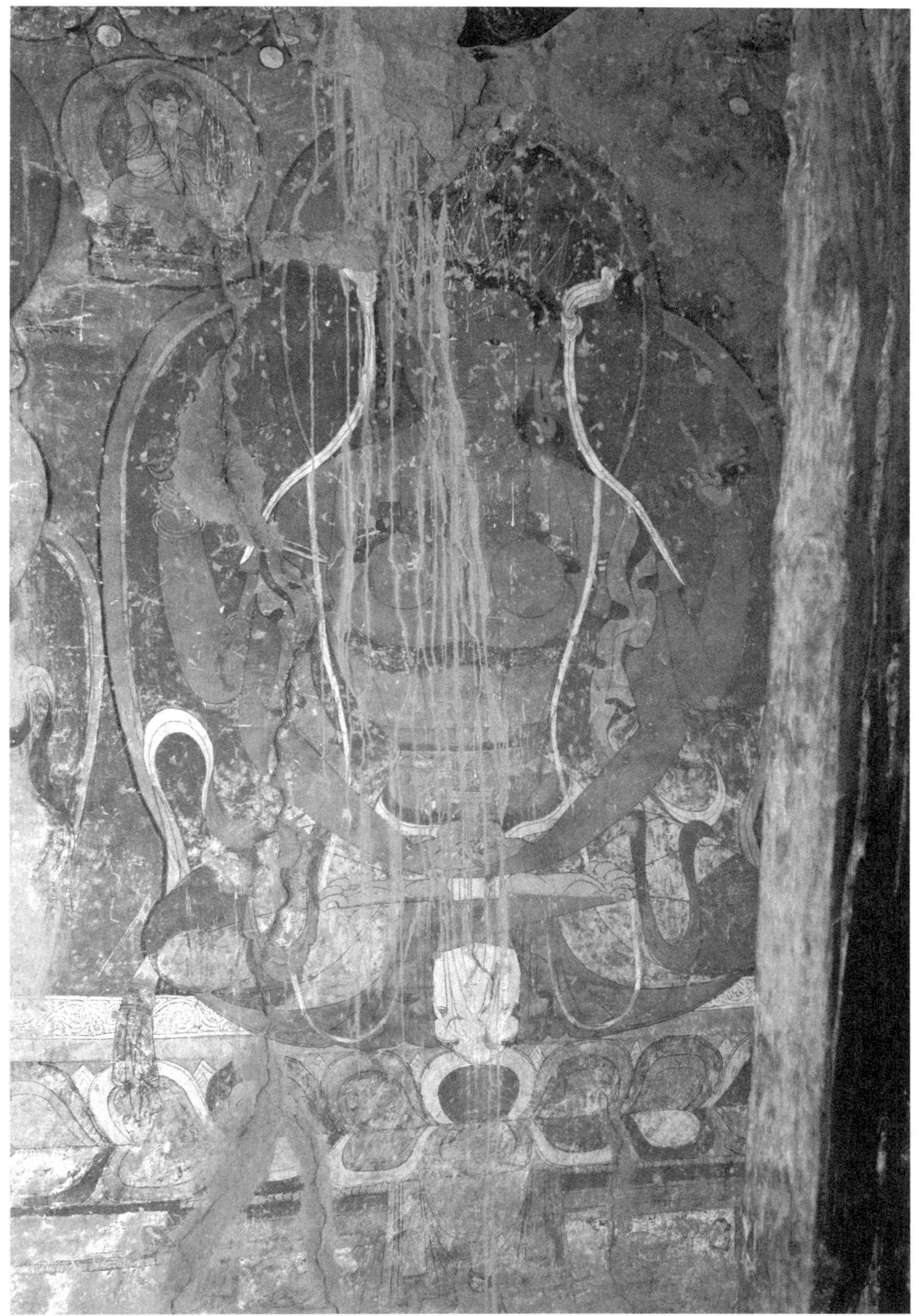

Figure 4.3. Gyapagpa Temple, south wall: Prajñāpāramitā.

two forms, we see that they share several important similarities, which can easily be seen from their sizes, positions, proportions, and in the details of the facial features (fig. 4.3). For instance, the proportions of the necks, shoulders, faces, and hips are nearly identical as are the pinched waists and slightly tilted hips. Each shares the same arching eyebrows and similarly rendered nose and mouth. While there are many shared elements, there are also some important, if minor, dissonances. One immediate disparity between the two main deities is the shape of their eyes and crowns. Prajñāpāramitā is painted with almond-shaped eyes, and her crown is comprised of five triangular plaques that are adorned with thin decorative chains from which hang pendants very similar in fashion to those featured on Vajradhara's jewelry (plate 11). The fact that a painting cycle may include a variety of eye shapes or crown types is not unusual, but rather points to the workshop's variety of forms.

Stylistic comparison reveals the strong similarity between the figural forms of Vajradhara and Prajñāpāramitā, and also elucidates differences between the ways in which these figural forms were painted. Consequently, close visual analysis raises questions and uncertainties about authorship and repainting. For instance, when comparing the quality of the painted line used for Prajñāpāramitā and Vajradhara, it is clear that the Vajradhara figure was executed with a practiced hand, whereas Prajñāpāramitā is executed in thin, unsteady lines. Moreover, the artist of the Vajradhara figure modulated, if sparingly, the width and curve of the line. This brushwork quality is discernible where Vajradhara's forearm and bicep meet. The line demarcating the forearm curves to suggest a subtle roundness of the forearm and then tapers off (plate 10). Further, part of the forearm slightly obscures the bicep, hinting at the layering of forms in space. The artist of the Prajñāpāramitā image does not have the same control over the brushwork; the outlining brushstrokes tend to be executed in an uneven hand, which creates a shaky line that often ends abruptly, as can be seen from the rendering of her hands, feet, and especially her breasts (figs. 4.3 and 4.4).

Such inexpert execution, which sharply contrasts with the rest of the painting in the temple, raises the question of whether this image was either painted by a less-experienced artist or was repainted, or re-outlined, at a later date—again by a less practiced hand. Based on the inequality of brushwork and the iconographic confusion surrounding this form of Prajñāpāramitā, which I address in chapter 2, I suggest that sections of the south wall underwent repainting by an artist who was not particularly skilled. The reasons for this minimal repainting and outlining only on the south wall are not readily apparent, however. As this is one of the more damaged walls in the temple, earlier refurbishing efforts may have been concentrated here.

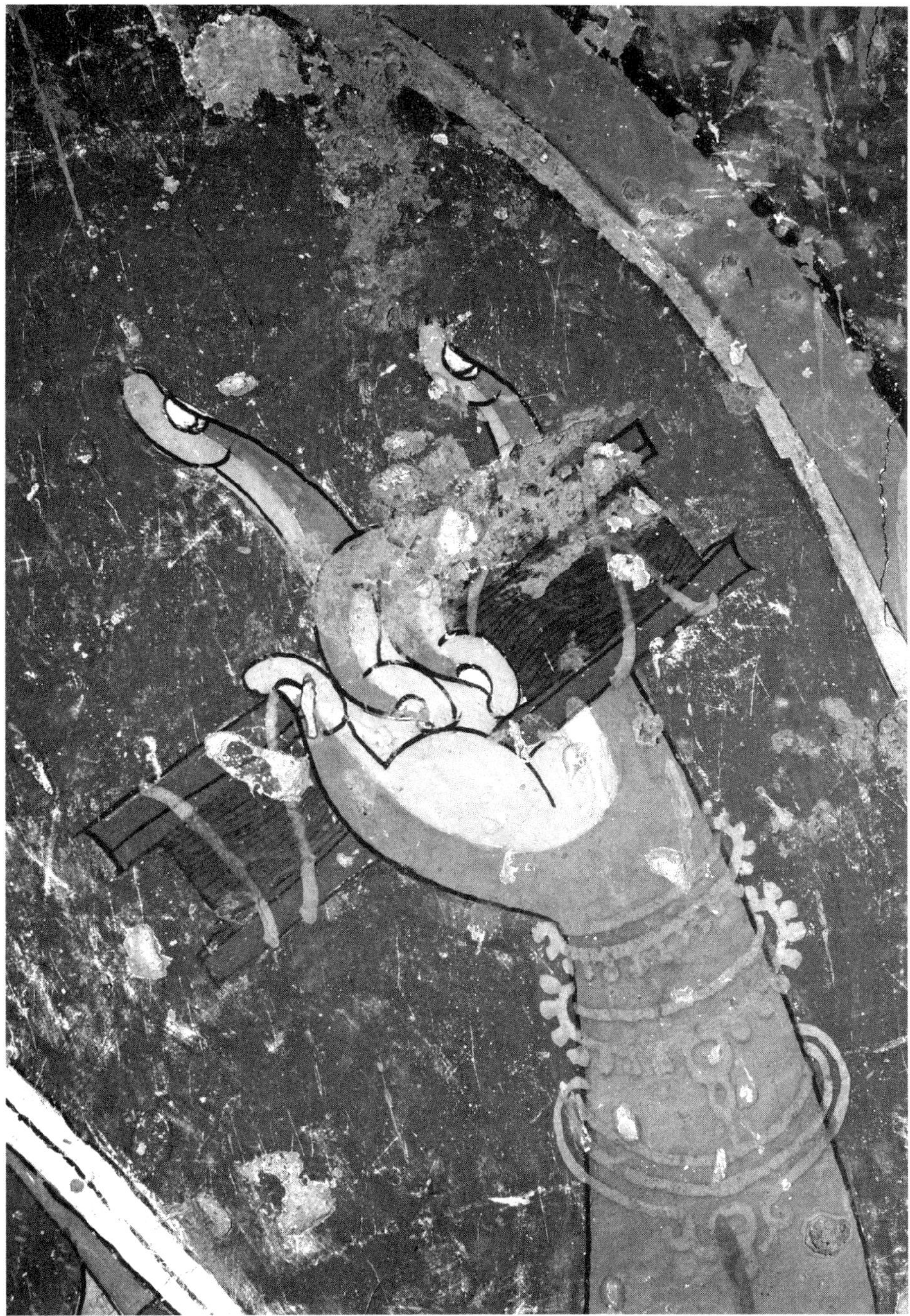

Figure 4.4. Gyapagpa Temple, south wall: Prajñāpāramitā's left hand holding Buddhist manuscript.

All of the semiwrathful and wrathful figures of this temple are painted on the west entry wall. The main protector, Achi, is placed at the center of the composition, above the doorway. As a typical semiwrathful figure, she sits on a horse while wearing Tibetan dress (*chuba*) and boots.[3] Over her white *chuba* that crosses at the front, she wears a red tunic trimmed in blue. There is no patterning on the material of her costume; folds and creases are defined in the simplest manner. In three-quarter profile, her face appears rather full and well delineated. Her elongated almond-shaped eyes, with the far eye protruding outward in an exaggerated fashion, are further defined by her strikingly rendered eye with the outer portion of the eyeball—the sclera that is usually painted white—painted in red, followed by a rim of white and then the black pupil (plate 12). Her long, well-articulated nose gives definition to her face, as does her softly rounded chin. A prominent, well-defined mouth painted in red contrasts dramatically with her otherwise very pale skin tone. The smaller retinue figures surrounding Achi, though less precisely painted, are also painted in three-quarter profile and share many of the same features such as rounded faces, long noses, full mouths, small pronounced chins and slightly protruding far eyes. This is especially the case for the figure identified as Karmo (fig. 2.12).

Two emanations of the semiwrathful deity Vaiśravaṇa (see chapter 2) are seated below Achi. These two figures are depicted in similar ways, though in different positions (figs. 2.14 and 2.15). Both have pronounced lips and noses. Their eyebrows are not painted as simple arches, as they are on most figures throughout the temple, but rather in a trilobed manner suggestive of a wiry and furrowed brow. Each figure wears a crown composed of golden teardrop-shaped plaques. This crown type is a more restrained version of Vajradhara's diadem and the type of crown seen on the attendant figures of the north wall and on Amitāyus, who is painted on the south wall.

Wrathful Deities

The only fierce deities painted in the temple are the four figures on either side of the main protectress, Achi. Of the four wrathful deities painted on this wall, only two, the four- and six-armed Mahākālas, have not been destroyed by water damage (plates 5 and 6) and can be carefully analyzed. What makes these deities particularly interesting and significantly different from the others in the temple is their modeling, which enhances their plasticity and volume. By painting these blue-toned forms with a darker blue at the edges and a lighter one toward the center of the forms, the artist successfully communicates the knotted muscle and corporality of these wrathful figures. With similarly robust figural forms, these two Mahākālas figures also share other similar detailing. Both have snarling, formidable countenances with bulging eyes and elaborate, flamelike eyebrows. Their noses are pushed up, giving the appearance of snouts. Their open mouths reveal sets of sharp teeth replete with fangs. Their jaws and necks are thick, and their shoulders broad.

These wrathful figures clearly represent a significant departure from the usual depiction of figural forms in the Gyapagpa Temple. It is the details of jewelry and other adornments that unquestionably connect these figures to the temple's larger painting program. Jewelry adorning these deities is quite similar in form to that worn by Vajradhara on the north wall. The bracelets and anklets are rendered in the same design, featuring a teardrop shape within a scrolling foliate setting. The torso harnesses are also similar in form, featuring the same three-part hanging medallion seen on Vajradhara's necklace and used as a decorative motif in Prajñāpāramitā's crown.

Buddha Figures

In total, there are ten Buddha figures painted in the Gyapagpa Temple. Arguably the most important of these is Śākyamuni, who is situated on the east wall, opposite the temple entrance. Although there is much damage to this Buddha image and to the east wall as a whole, there remain critical visual clues, including the eye shape as well as the form of the head and hairline. Unlike either the bow- or almond-shaped eyes that are so prominently used in this temple's painting program, this Buddha figure has a markedly different eye shape (fig. 4.5). The eyes are dramatically long, with heavy upper lids, above which are sharply arched eyebrows. Although different from the other eye shapes in the painting program, this form has an important precedent that will be discussed later in the chapter. The hair and head shape are also important details that help to determine the stylistic family to which this set of paintings belongs. Unlike the eyes, the head shape, which is defined in part by the prominent uṣṇīṣa, is quite similar to the other Buddha figures in the temple. The outer hairline creates a head profile that follows a long curve from the top of the head and tapers down to the midsection of the ear. This indigo-blue hair is then further defined by silhouetted hair curls that contour the outer hairline.

When examining the second largest Buddha figure in the temple—Amitāyus, who is identified by the adjoining Tibetan inscription as "tshed pag med"[4]—it becomes evident that it shares several formal elements with the Śākyamuni Buddha figure (plate 8). The most significant of these

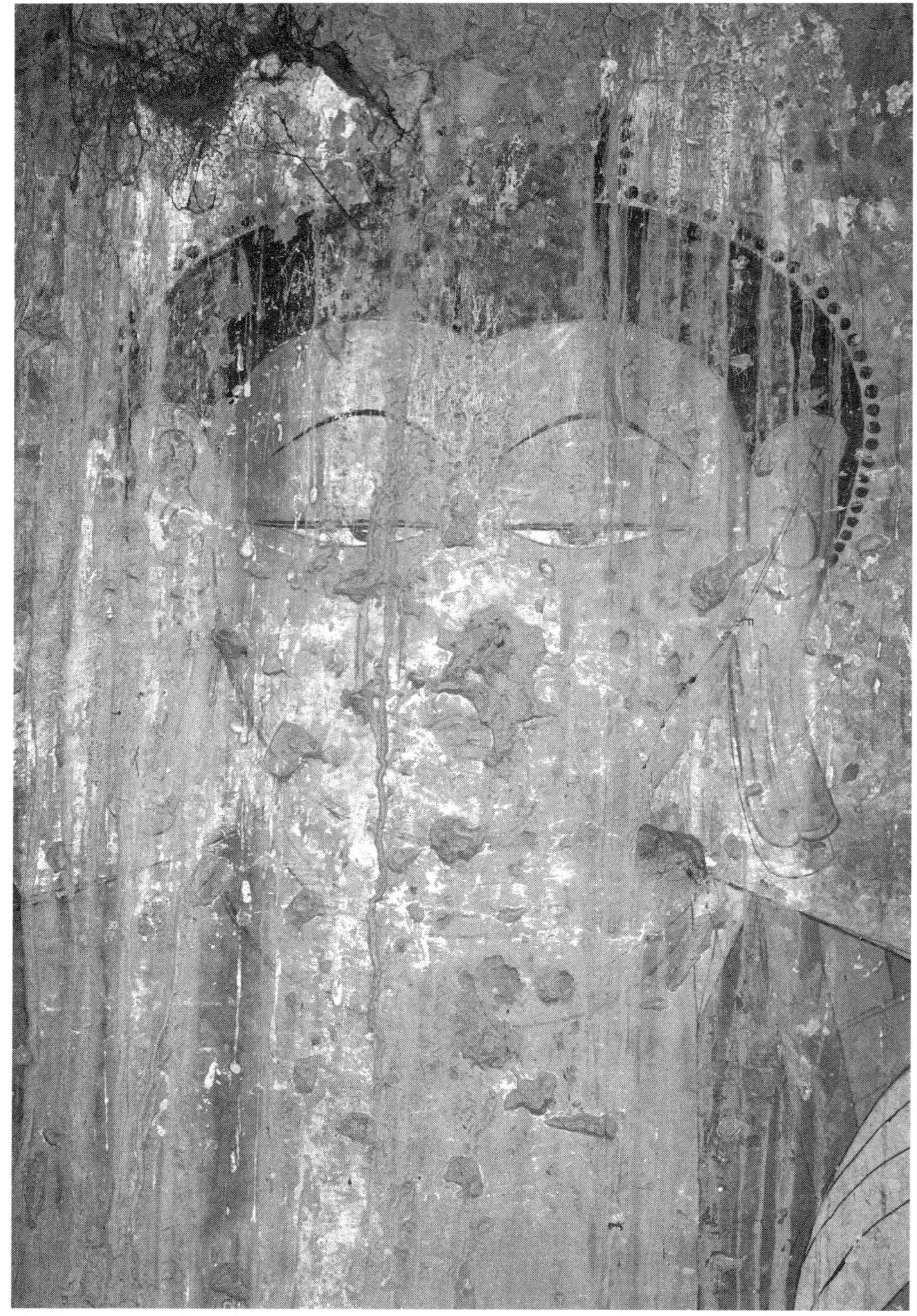

Figure 4.5. Gyapagpa Temple, east wall: Śākyamuni Buddha's head.

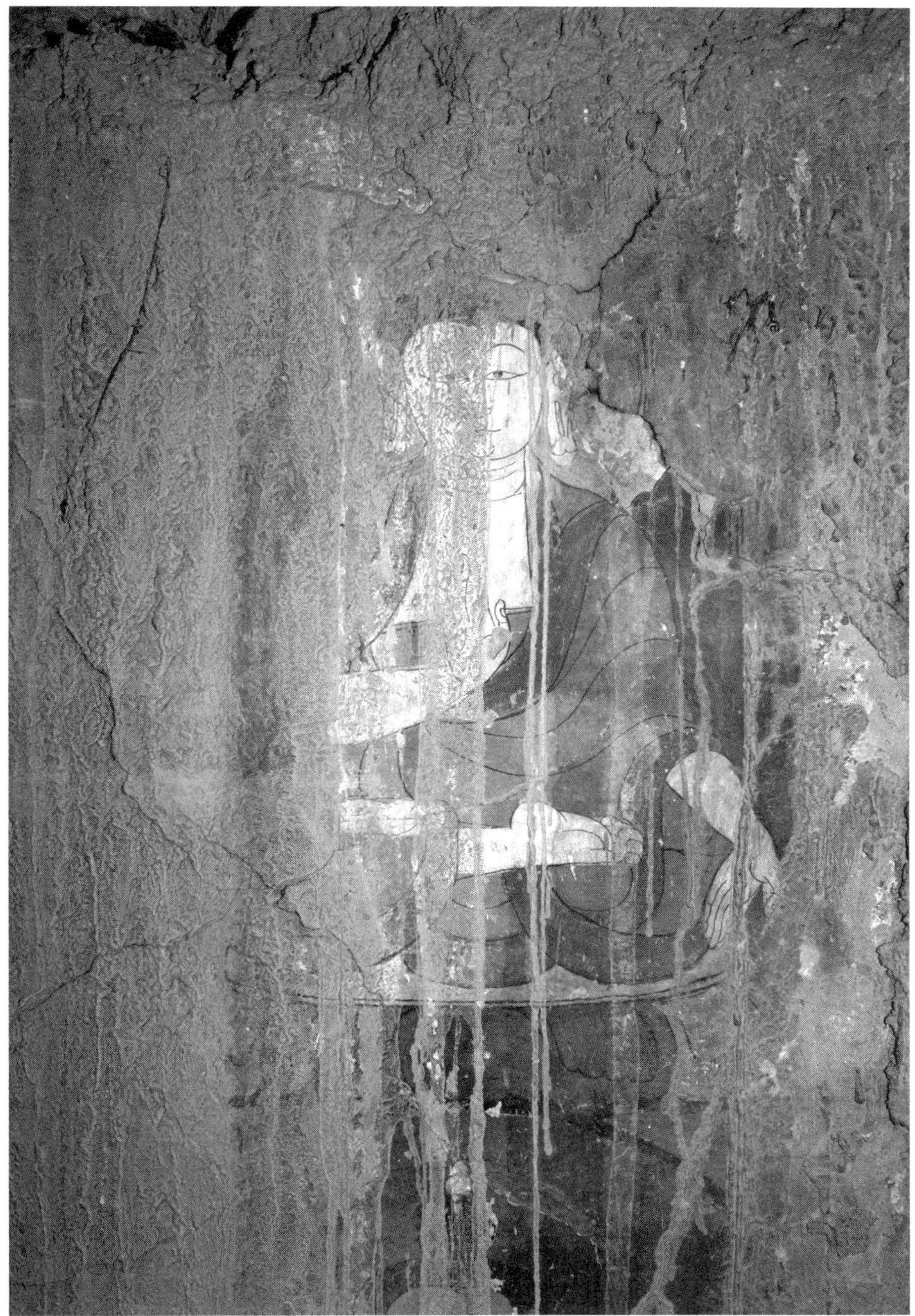

Figure 4.6. Gyapagpa Temple, south wall: "Buddha A."

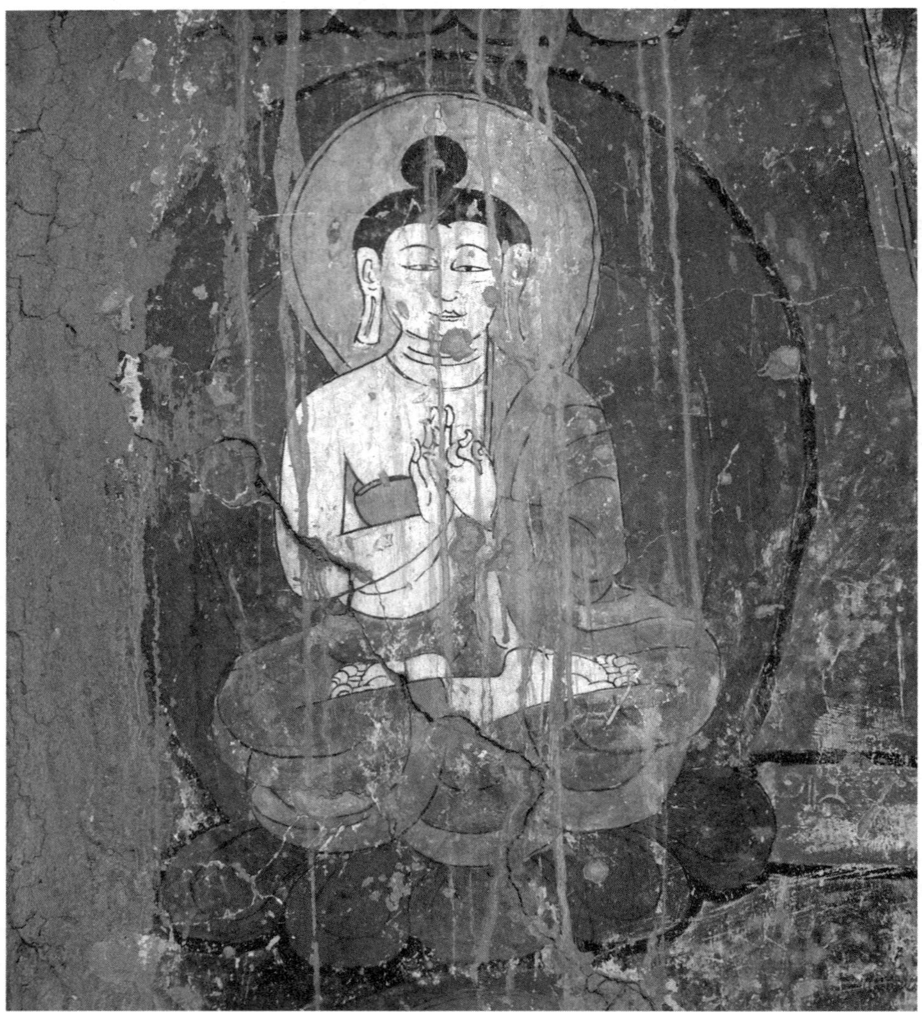

Figure 4.7. Gyapagpa Temple, south wall: "Buddha B."

similarities is their head shape. They each have an outer hairline that extends just past the ears and tapers down to the earlobe. This figure's eyes, however, are depicted in an almond shape as opposed to the long, flat-lidded type of eye painted on Śākyamuni. As Amitāyus wears just a dhoti and scarf, he is the only Buddha figure with an exposed upper body, allowing one to see that his broad chest narrows to a small waist.

The decorative motifs, such as ribbons and jewelry, connect Amitāyus to the rest of the temple's painting program. The white hair ribbons, with their simple horizontal patterning rendered in black, resemble the hair ribbons on the Vajradhara image on the north wall. Amitāyus's anklet features the foliate setting used on the Vajradhara image, whereas the bracelets and armbands are more simply fashioned—with only the pear-shaped plaque without any ornate setting.

The poor condition of the other eight Buddha figures makes it difficult to conduct a thorough examination. Nonetheless, certain patterns of display are discernible for this grouping of eight that is painted on the south wall in two columns, each with four Buddhas. They are based on a figural type, but these Buddha figures also exhibit a good deal of variation in their execution (figs. 4.6 and 4.7). Starting with the shape of their heads, they all have an outer hairline that extends past the top of the ears, as is seen in both the Śākyamuni and Amitāyus Buddhas. The hairline at their forehead is roughly consistent and includes a split widow's peak. While the eyes of the Buddhas are all painted with the same almond shape and their brows are rendered as softly curved arches, the earlobes are painted in different ways. Some Buddhas have a rounded lobe, others have a squared lobe (fig. 4.7) and others still have a small split at the base of the lobe (fig. 4.6), which we first see in the large Śākyamuni Buddha on the east wall (fig. 4.5). Another point of differentiation can be found in the neck and jawlines. "Buddha B" (fig. 4.7) is rendered with a gap between the neck and jawlines; "Buddha A" does not show this same opening and has a slightly more rounded face as a result (fig. 4.6). All the Buddhas wear a similar monastic robe style rendered in slightly different colors or with minor variations in the manner in which the robe falls.

I read these differences in dress and figural depiction as expected variations of a single workshop. More specifically, I suggest that the differences we see in the figural forms of the Buddha figures on the south wall may be due to the number at hands at work on these wall paintings. As I have analyzed these paintings, it seems probable that there were at least two artists at work. A close reading of Buddha A, located at the top of the right column (west corner of composition) of the south wall (fig. 4.6), helps to identify the different artists' contributions. While Buddha A is painted in roughly the same proportions and detailing as the other Buddhas on this wall, there are some subtle differences. In particular, the eyes, although rendered in an almond shape, are not executed with the same detail and confident hand as many of the others on this wall. The figure's proper left eye is larger and rounder than the right. Furthermore, both eyes are elongated and painted with upturned lines at the outer edges. Compared with other figures in the temple, this Buddha's characteristics seem to resonate with the manner in which at least two of the Drigung lineage figures were painted (two on the north wall [figs. 2.3 and 2.7]). The proper right eye of each of the lineage figures is painted a bit more narrowly than the proper left, suggesting an idiosyncrasy of a particular artist. Moreover, the proper right feet of 'Jig rten mgon po

(Jigten Gonpo; fig. 2.3) and Chos rje dārma (Choje Dārma; fig. 2.7) are rendered very similarly to Buddha A's feet, with thick soles and short toes. Given the similarities in the idiosyncratic ways in which the eyes and feet are executed for several of these figures, I suggest that we are looking at the hand of another artist, and one that may have been less experienced than the one responsible for the painting of Achi, Vajradhara, and Buddha figures on the west, north, and east walls, respectively.

Attendant Figures

The attendant figures on the north wall (figs. 4.8 and 4.9) share many of the same physical characteristics as Vajradhara. The faces of the white attendant and Vajradhara reveal striking formal resonances (plate 9 and fig. 4.10). Both have bow-shaped eyes that are double lidded, though the attendant figure's upper lid is outlined in a soft gray color. The arching eyebrows have the same contour and even the same thickness at the middle part of the eyebrow. The noses, lips, and chins also reveal strong parallels. The attendants' dhotis are fluid and layered in a similar fashion to the main figure's dress (fig. 4.8). The multicolored sashes that billow next to the white and blue attendants suggest buoyancy while also serving to frame the figures, as is the case with the Vajradhara figure (fig. 2.6). Although the crowns of the attendant figures vary in terms of the number of tines (the blue attendant has five, and the white, three), the general style of the crowns resonates with those already seen in the temple, especially on Vajradhara, Amitāyus, and Vaiśravaṇa.[5] Moreover, the attendants' jewelry echoes the same designs as those of Vajradhara: gold beading and simple bands adorned with teardrop-shaped medallions. These details, coupled with similarities in their physical forms and that of Vajradhara, make it evident that the two attendants were executed by the same workshop, and probably by the hand of the master painter of this temple.

Comparison between the white attendant of the north wall with the Maitreya attendant on the south wall, however, offers conspicuous differences between the two figures. These dissonances highlight the virtuosity of the artist of the north wall while the south wall's problematic condition becomes ever more evident. The most obvious discrepancy between the two figures lies in the proportions of the Maitreya attendant. The head and torso of the figure are much too large for its short pair of legs (fig. 2.24). Also, the hands of the figure are too small for the broad upper body. The white attendant on the north wall has hands that are nearly as long as the face and the feet. The legs of this same figure are nearly twice as long as the torso. By contrast, the Maitreya figure's legs are much shorter, making the figure appear relatively broad and squat. This may

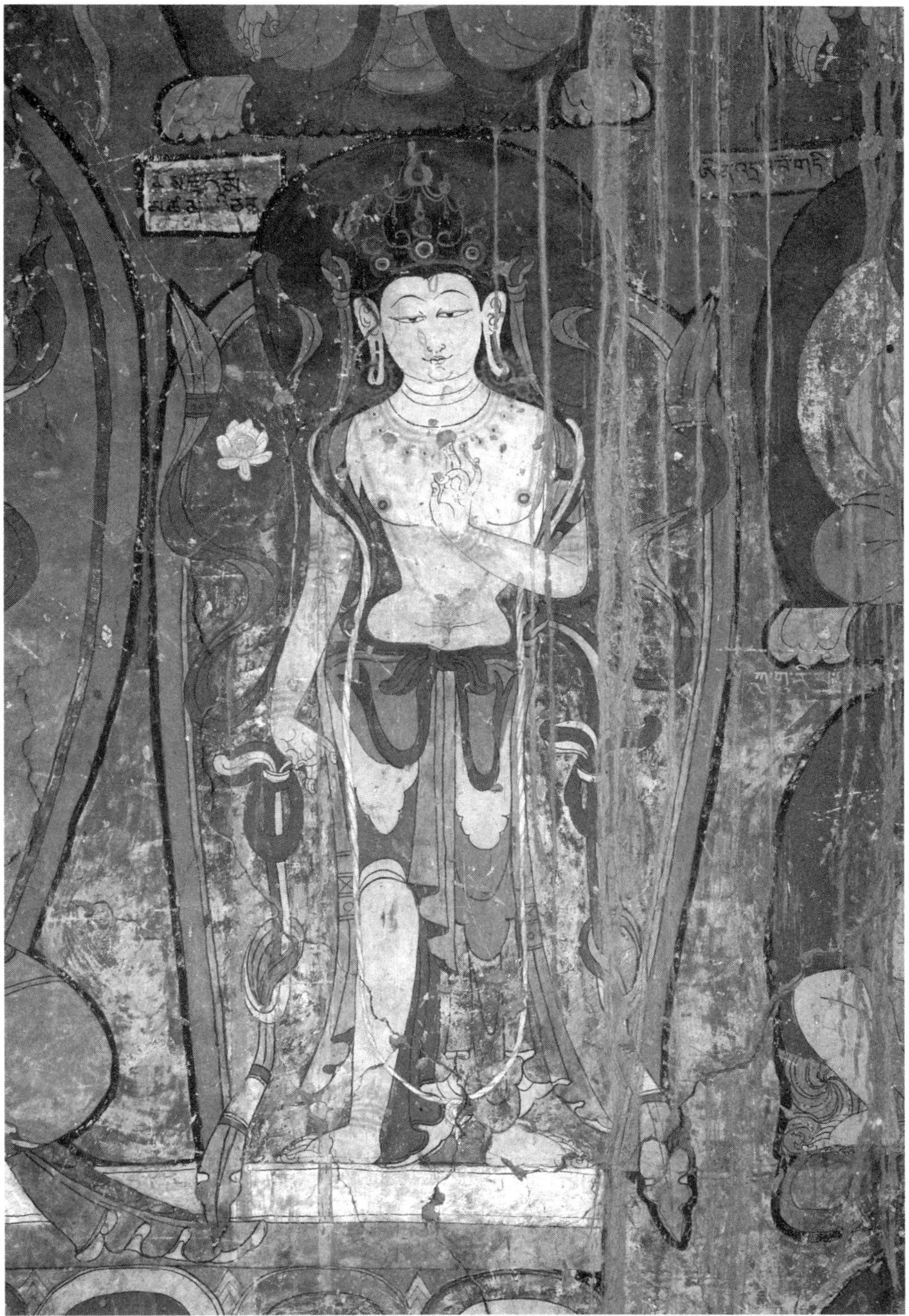

Figure 4.8. Gyapagpa Temple, north wall: white attendant to Vajradhara.

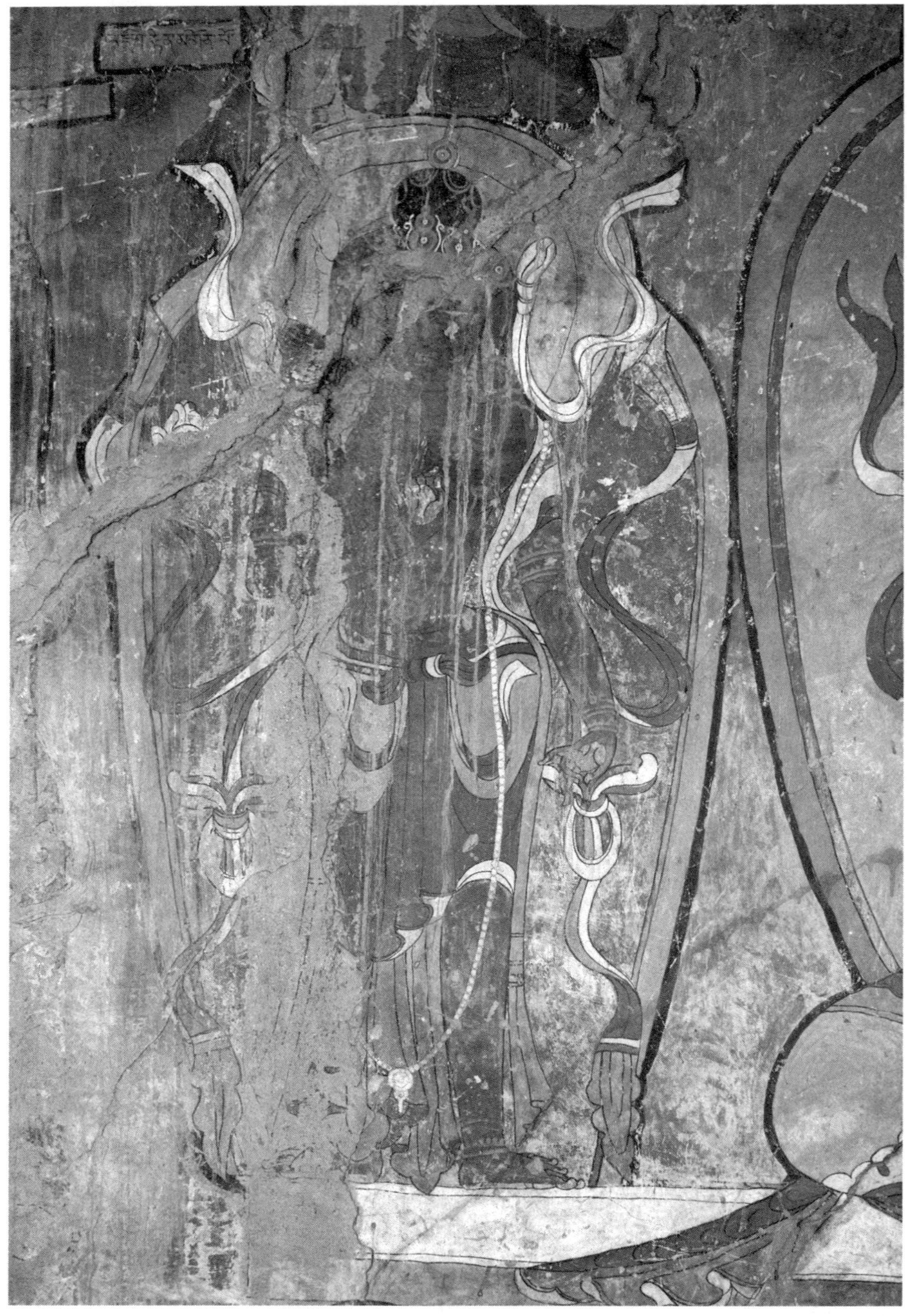

Figure 4.9. Gyapagpa Temple, north wall: blue attendant figure to Vajradhara.

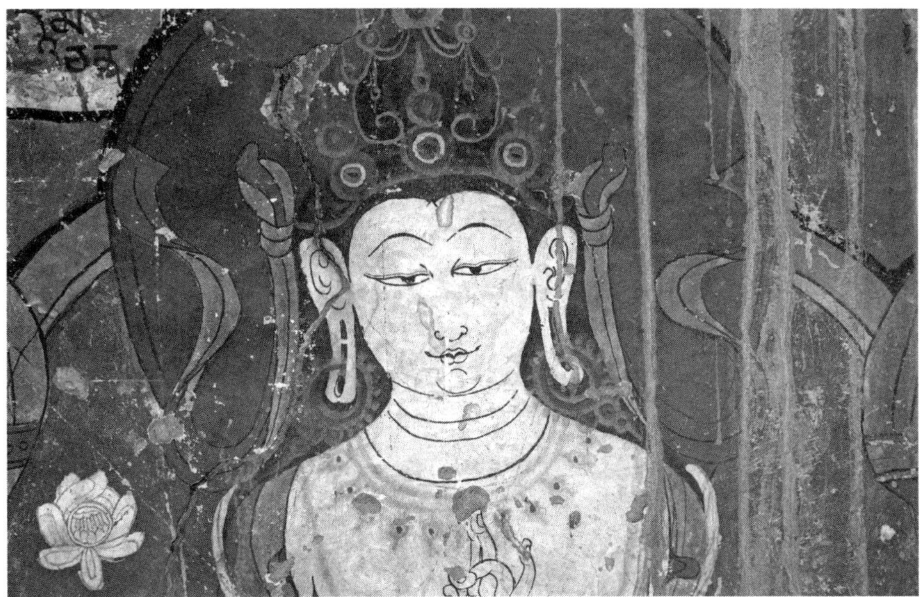

Figure 4.10. Gyapagpa Temple, north wall: white attendant face.

have had to do with accommodating the extra figure of Amitāyus, who sits directly over the attendant, within the composition. The proportions for the attendant figure should have been systematically recalibrated as opposed to simply making the legs shorter.[6]

Despite these strong differences, the attendants of the two walls are certainly of a similar type and have aspects that are quite comparable, such as their horizontal navel articulations and full hips. Their clothing, especially their colorful and tiered dhotis, is of the same design, as are the crown ribbons and even the crowns. Other stylistic resonances can be seen in shared jewelry motifs and nimbus articulation.

There is one other attendant figure of note. On the east wall, standing on Śākyamuni Buddha's left side, is a monastic figure who looks toward the Buddha and is rendered in three-quarter profile (fig. 4.11). He is paired with another monastic attendant, positioned to the Buddha's right side, but this attendant is barely visible. The surviving attendant's facial features are dramatically rendered with the far eye and eyebrow extending past the profile line. The eyes are long and almond shaped, and the brows too are animatedly painted with a small peak in the middle of them. The aquiline nose has a flared nostril, and the pronounced lips are full and well defined. A curved line indicates the chin, which also highlights the fleshiness of the cheeks. These distinctive features characterize many of the three-quarter profiles in this temple, especially the portraits of the eight commentators, known as the Two Supreme Ones and Six

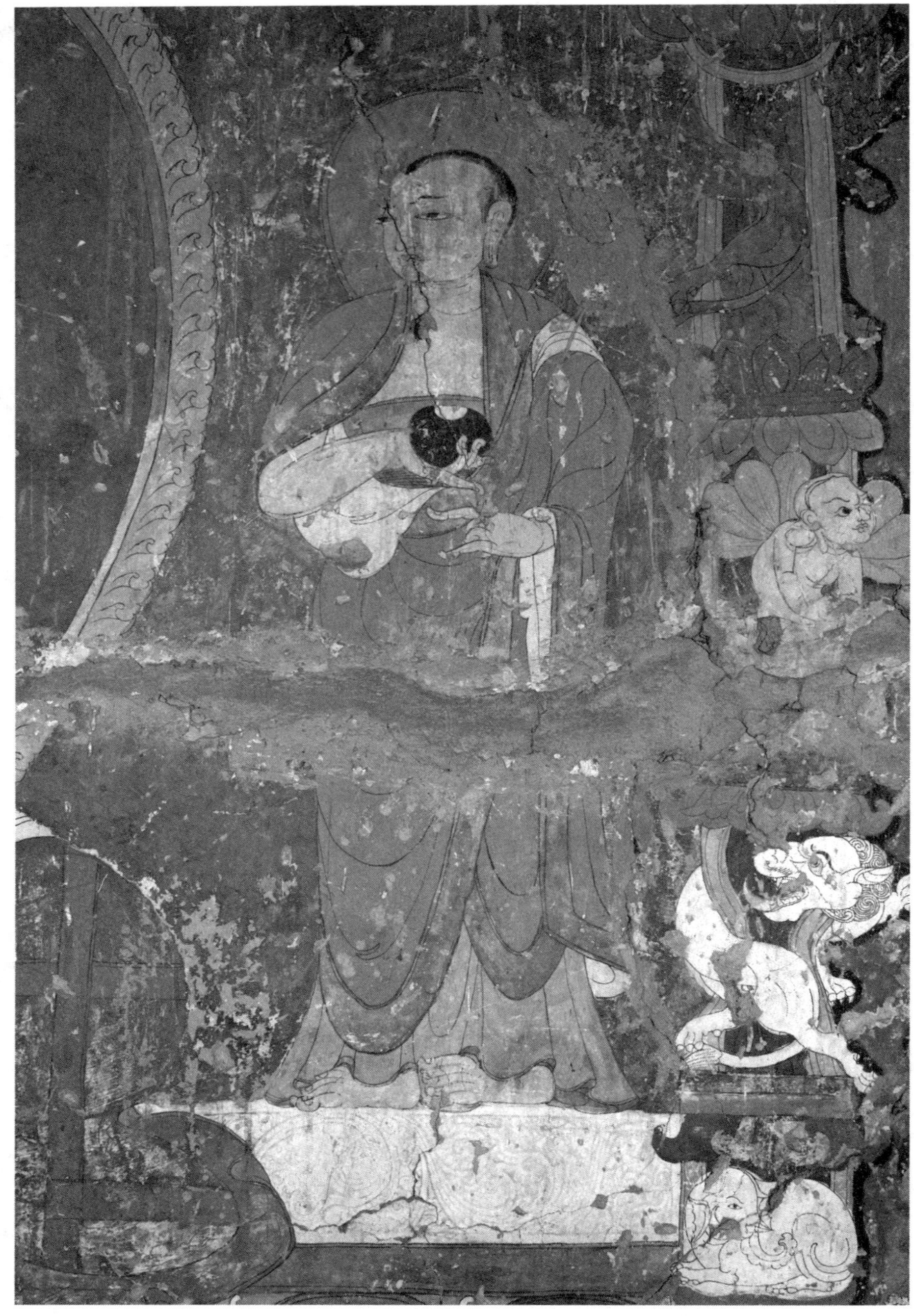

Figure 4.11. Gyapagpa Temple, east wall: monastic attendant figure.

Ornaments, who are also painted on the east wall (plate 13). These figures, as well as those on the west wall, in particular the figure of Achi and her entourage, and the image of Vaiśravaṇa in his manifestation as a benefactor, all share similar facial characteristics (figs. 2.12, 2.13, and 2.15; plate 12).

Historical Figures

Drigung Lineage Members

There are six historical figures, painted across three of the temple walls, which represent a lineage of Drigung teachers. Only four of these six lineage portraits, however, provide any valuable visual information; these four are found on the opposing north and south walls. When studied as a group, they clearly reveal that each portrait is based on a single type, which does not capture the verisimilitude of the historic personages represented. They share broad faces and wide jawlines, eyes with upturned outer lines, full mouths with indentations in the middle of the upper and lower lips, and lastly, monastic robes that cover both shoulders. As the iconographic significance of this lineage has already been addressed (see chapter 2), I will discuss the portraits out of order starting with one on the north wall inscribed "Chos rje dārma mtshan can" (fig. 2.7). It is this portrait that displays strong similarities with the previously discussed Buddha A from the south wall (see fig. 4.6). They both have fairly wide, square jawlines and large eyes with upturned outer edges. These same characteristics can be seen in three of the four Drigung lineage portraits, which suggests that they are not only of a type but were most likely executed by the same hand.

There is one Drigung portrait, however, that is not painted with the same features as the others (figs. 4.12 and 4.13). Located on the south wall on the right side, this portrait marks the last of the lineage. Unlike the others, this figure does not have the wide or square jaw or upturned almond-shaped eyes. Rather, he has a pursed mouth and bow-shaped eyes that are remarkably similar to those seen on another historical figure located on the east wall, Nāgārjuna (plate 7). Both of these figures, as will be discussed below, are evidence of the same brushwork and facial features.

Six Ornaments and Two Supreme Ones

On the east wall are eight figures, four in two columns located at either end of the composition. These figures represent a rather popular grouping of Indian pundits. The two columns feature figures that are quite resonant

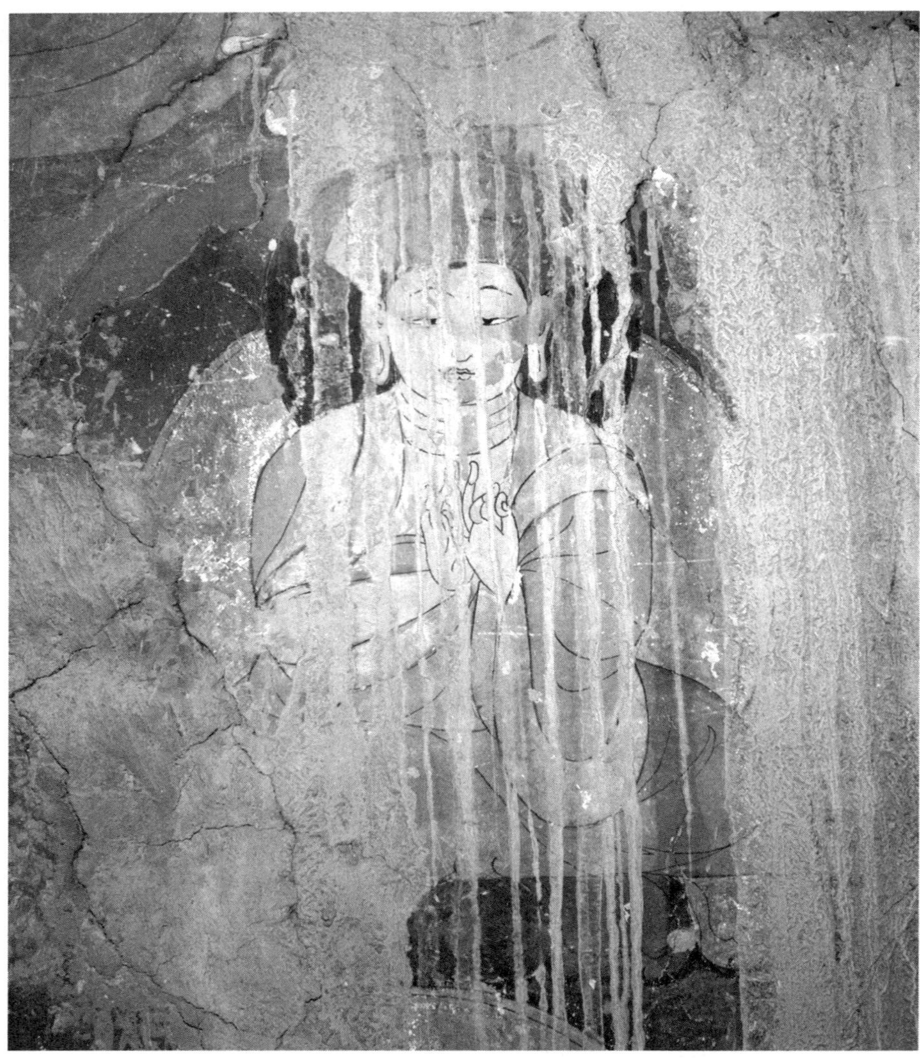

Figure 4.12. Gyapagpa Temple, south wall: sixth lineage portrait.

with one another: they are all framed within a red horseshoe-shaped nimbus, within which there is often another body nimbus (plate 13). Each figure is depicted in either a debating posture or teaching mudrā while sitting upon a simply fashioned lotus pedestal with alternately colored lotus petals. Each wears a pointed pundit hat and monastic robes that share the same cantaloupe and tan tones with a trim of blue, maroon, or green. Like the lineage members, these figures reveal so many similarities that they should be grouped as a figural type exhibiting only minor differences in the ways nostrils or earlobes are rendered. Six of the eight figures are painted in three-quarter profile; their faces are round with

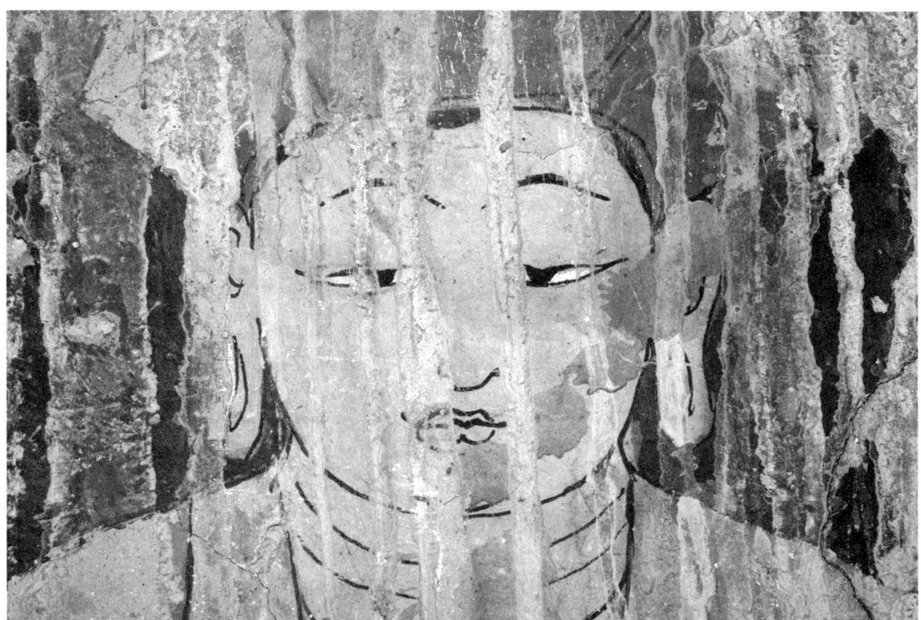

Figure 4.13. Gyapagpa Temple, south wall: close-up of the face of sixth lineage portrait.

full lips and pronounced far eyes. These facial features echo those of the other three-quarter profiles in the program, such as the monastic attendant to Śākyamuni Buddha and Mahāsiddha Nāgārjuna on the north wall (fig. 2.17). It should be noted that in closely studying these east-wall portraits, one can easily see significant underpainting (fig. 4.14). There is no difference, however, in the style of brushwork of the underpainting and final painting. Consequently, it is safe to posit that the artist of the underpainting is the same as that of the final painting.

While this grouping of eight figures is rendered in the same figural style, the topmost figure of each column is rendered in a slightly different form, which I suggest may be due to different artists' approaches. Analysis of the two forward-facing figures does not provide conclusive evidence regarding the number of artists working on this section, but does at least make one sensitive to the likely reality of different artists working on this program. The first of these two portraits that I will address is found at the top of the right-hand column, and has been identified as Thogs med (Togme; fig. 2.23). The manner in which this historical figure is articulated resonates with the overall stylistic approach of these wall paintings. Togme wears the same robes and hat type as the other figures, as well as sits on the same lotus cushion, and is generally quite similar to the other physical forms found on this wall. Comparing this figure with the others

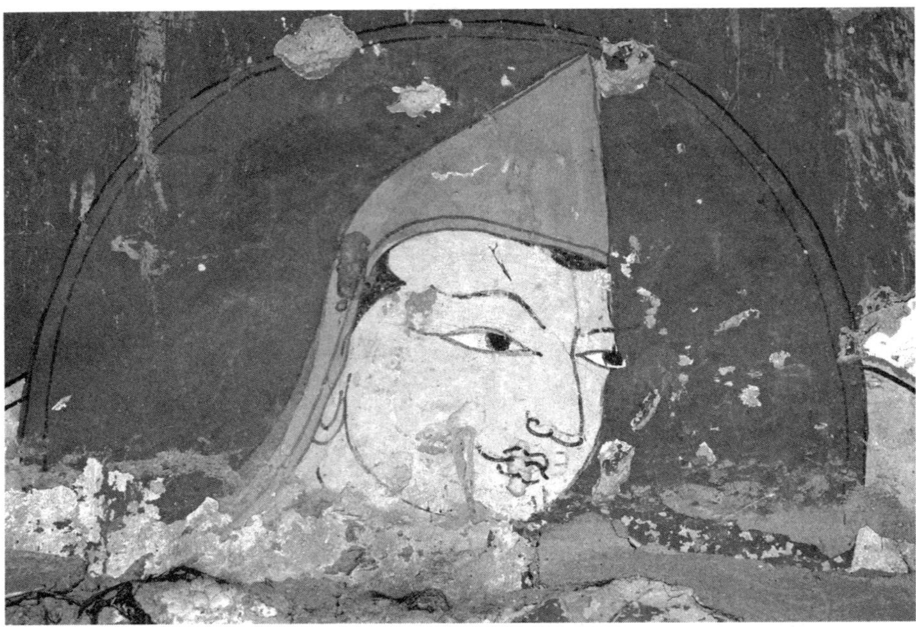

Figure 4.14. Gyapagpa Temple, east wall: detail of three-quarter profile of commentator ("Six Ornaments and Two Supreme Ones").

of the temple, one sees a resonance between it and the Drigung lineage paintings (figs. 2.3, 2.7, 2.10): the jaws are rather broad and square; the eyes turn up at the outer edges; and the eyebrows are thickly applied. In both this portrait and the Drigung lineage portraits, none of the lines is painted with the confidence or ease evident in many of the other figures in the temple. For instance, Togme's necklines are shaky and the neck itself slightly wide. I would suggest that this portrait was painted by the less exacting hand of the apprentice who worked on three of the Drigung lineage and Buddha A (fig. 4.6).

The second figure to be discussed is labeled "Glu g . . . [illegible] ub," the phonetic rendering of Klu sgrub (Sanskrit: Nāgārjuna), who is positioned on the flanking top-left column of the east wall (plate 7). With more petite facial features than those of the Togme figure, this image of Nāgārjuna is fashioned in a strikingly different manner. The jaw is less square and rendered in such a way that there is a gap between the neck and jawlines, a technique used with several of the Buddhas on the south wall. Pursed lips, small, articulated nose, and uniform neck lines are some of the aspects that differentiate this image from the fully frontal figure of Togme. In the previous section, parallels have been drawn between the east-wall figure of Nāgārjuna and the last of the Drigung lineage portraits positioned on the south wall. Their formal resonances can easily be seen in the shape of their eyebrows, eyes, noses, lips, and earlobes. These shared formal elements are not restricted to these two figures, but are also displayed on the white attendant figure on the north wall. Buddha B from the south wall also has several of these same features (fig. 4.7).

Mahāsiddhas

Another group of historical figures is that of the eight mahāsiddhas located on the north wall. All but two of these are in three-quarter profile. Each figure is surrounded by a large horseshoe-shaped red nimbus that contains the figure who is adorned with yet another head and body nimbus. Each mahāsiddha sits upon a lotus cushion, with downturned lotus petals that are alternately colored red, blue, and white. Thus, each figure's presentation with regard to profile, nimbus use, and color scheme follows the same pattern as the eight commentators (Six Ornaments and Two Supreme Ones) on the east wall.

Sections of the north wall are in such a state of disrepair that it will be possible to analyze only a few of the images. The best preserved of these is at the top of the left column, labeled Slu grub snying po (Ludrub Ningpo) or the Old Nāgārjuna (fig. 2.17). He sits with his body toward the viewer, but gazes to his left, giving a clear view of his strongly defined nose, rounded cheeks, and full mouth. This portrait bears a striking resemblance to several of the commentator portraits on the east wall, especially to fig. 4.14. Comparing the mahāsiddha with the commentator we see how their eyebrows share a distinctive arch and between their brows are painted the profile line of their strongly delineated noses. Their nostrils are marked by a C-shaped curve that has a tiny loop at the end of it. Their lips are shapely and full, and their visible earlobes are distinctly rounded. The artist responsible for these two portraits clearly used the same figural type for both; this makes sense because Nāgārjuna, while a mahāsiddha, was also known as a commentator. Using that logic, however, one may question why the other Nāgārjuna figure, on the east wall, does not adhere to the same figure type. This is due to Nāgārjuna being rendered in a fully frontal position on the east wall, not at a three-quarter angle.

Summation

The most defining features of the Gyapgapa paintings relate to the program's composition, figural forms, and decorative motifs. The program's composition is painted in a relatively limited palette of oranges, browns, blues, greens, and reds. As in most Tibetan Buddhist mural painting, the picture plane is shallow making the composition as a whole rather flat. The lack of dimension is further emphasized by unmodulated color use, lack of shading, as well as dark outlines of all the compositional elements. The second defining characteristic of the Gyapagpa painting style focuses on figural forms, of which there are a number of types. Despite the variety, there are several commonalities among them, as can be seen in the broad shoulders, narrow waists, and full hips. Exposed torsos of attendant figures, for instance, reveal distinct navel articulations with horizontal lines. The lines used to render the jaw and neck do not meet on many of the figures, which results in a rather distinctive gap between the jaw and neck. As for the main Buddha figure, and several of the diminutive Buddhas on the south wall, the earlobes are painted at an angle to reveal its width. The width and shape of the head for these figures is delineated by the outer hairline, which is rather wide and comes down to the earlobe. The inner hairline, above the face, often includes a split widow's peak.

Lastly, the decorative motifs, particularly of jewelry, give these paintings a flair, which can easily be seen in the elaborate crown types. The two crowns of Vajradhara and Prajñāpāramitā, for instance, while being quite different from one another, are wonderfully detailed in their presentation. The first features a medallion-like leitmotif, and the latter a pointed-plaque design with interconnected swags of bejeweled chains. Although they are not technically part of the crown's metalwork, there are silken ribbons tied to secure the crown in place. Other body adornments, such as harnesses, chokers, and armlets share design motifs, such as the teardrop-shaped settings for gems.

These stylistic elements help to define the visual vocabulary used in the painting program at the Gyapagpa Temple, although there are still questions that linger regarding the condition of the south wall. The main concern is if the south wall's repainting is significant enough that it disrupts the continuity of this style. In other words, one needs to ask if there are two instead of one painting program at the Gyapagpa Temple. The consistency of the south wall's composition, figural forms, color scheme, and decorative motifs, such as jewelry designs, indicate a strong stylistic connection with the existing painting program. Thus, I suggest on the basis of this close visual analysis that the murals were executed in one coherent style and by a single workshop, the artists of which were working within the conventions of a larger regional style. The strongest resonances between the Gyapagpa paintings and the larger regional style can be seen in the articulation of composition, figural forms, as well as some jewelry and decorative motifs. As will become evident in the following analysis, there are also a number of variations between what we see at Gyapagpa and the larger style. Such differences as palette, modeling, and some detailing will be addressed.

With a clearer understanding of the style used at the Gyapagpa Temple, I turn to the courtly idiom that served as its antecedent. Within the late medieval Ngari painting tradition I draw a distinction between courtly and regional idiomatic expressions.[7] In considering the cultural contexts that gave rise to these two idioms, it is useful to know that the style's original phase was commissioned under courtly patronage of the newly formed Guge kingdom of Ngari (Mnga' ris), and is referred to in this book as the "revival style" because of its calculated reuse of the eleventh-century Khache painting style.[8] The regional idioms that proceed from the revival style encompass numerous idiomatic variations that developed during the sixteenth century, outside of the royal and cosmopolitan centers, and likely without elite patronage.[9] These two classifications—courtly and regional—are part of the greater stylistic set, referred to herein as the late medieval Ngari painting tradition, named for its general temporal and geographic parameters. In particular, this label helps one to appreciate that although the style is strongly associated with the Guge kingdom of the Ngari region, it was not restricted to its use. Rather, we see the Ngari painting tradition circulated within the broader Ngari area, and even well beyond it.

The first objective of this section, therefore, is dedicated to defining the stylistic parameters of the courtly idiom, which, I argue, are epitomized by several sets of wall paintings from Tholing, Tsaparang, and Tabo. I refer to this group as the apogee, or high point, of this style's courtly expression. The second part of this section is a visual comparison illustrating the ways in which the Gyapagpa paintings share critical stylistic characteristics of this courtly idiom. Although Gyapagpa Temple paintings are not part of the courtly style, and not executed with the same level of refinement or high-quality materials as found in the courtly idiom, the artists of these paintings tapped into the same vocabulary of forms. Ultimately, I argue that the painting tradition found at Nako's Gyapagpa Temple is an integral part of the regional idiom, which was used in Ngari and related areas, such as Upper Kinnaur and Spiti, and Ngari. Visual analysis and comparison of both the courtly and regional idioms has allowed me to map, in a limited manner, this larger style's visual vocabulary, idiomatic expressions, temporal range, and geographic spread.

Problems with Defining the Style

A more comprehensive analysis of the scholarship on this style will be addressed in chapter 5, but here it is useful to look, if only cursorily, at some of the stylistic elements that define the style under discussion, as well as the persistent problems and misconceptions that limit scholarly understandings of this painting tradition. Giuseppe Tucci was the first to posit stylistic connections among the three sites of Tabo, Tholing, and Tsaparang. His treatment of what he calls the "Guge style" of the fifteenth through seventeenth centuries in his *Tibetan Painted Scrolls* is still the most extensive on the subject, despite the fact that it was written over sixty years ago. His analysis is primarily focused on a collection of individual scroll paintings, or *thangkas*. Tucci considers the medium of wall painting from these same sites in his *Indo-Tibetica* series, although Tucci never undertakes a careful analysis of both media and the questions of style that they raise.[10] Ultimately, while his initial comments on the late medieval painting styles of the Guge area served to identify and document this regional painting tradition, he never cataloged the distinguishing characteristics for this style. Rather than defining style, most of Tucci's comments on the various *thangkas* and wall paintings are focused on iconography.

Since the publication of Tucci's preliminary and seminal work, little has been done to define the chronological and geographic range of West Tibet's late medieval painting tradition. This dearth of thorough visual analysis and comparison has led to misunderstandings and assumptions that have been perpetuated over decades. Repeated points of confusion relate to the interrelated issues of the style's idiomatic expressions, regional scope, and chronology. For instance, Laxman Thakur compares the Vairocana figure from Tabo's Golden Temple to Tholing's Prajñāpāramitā located in the White Temple. Thakur writes the following:

> A closer study of the two murals suggests that the same artist did the paintings both at Tabo and at Tholing. Especially the broad shoulders, the thinning down of lines at the level of the navel, the arrangement of scarfs over the shoulders, the design of ear-rings, lotus thrones, the method of depicting the lions and elephants below the lotus-thrones and two dark blue auras encircled by a flaming design are some common characteristics of these murals.[11]

Certainly Thakur's recognition of the similarities between the two temples is well founded, as there are critical likenesses in the stylistic idiom as evidenced by shared motifs and compositional elements. Moreover, there are strong iconographic connections between these two temples. His assertion, however, that the painting programs were executed by the same artist requires much more analysis and comparison. Moreover, photographs for each of these two figures should be provided.

Another common problem one encounters when working with this material is the rather amorphous parameters of the style. Temples with painting programs that share some stylistic resonances also betray significant differences—Ladakh's Spituk and Basgo Temples, as well as Zangskar's Phuktal, have been included in this style.[12] While I am not arguing that these sets of paintings from Ladakh and Zangskar stand firmly outside the late medieval Ngari painting tradition, I am suggesting that at this point, more careful analysis and articulation of substyles is needed before we suggest that they are part of the same tradition. Art historians of this period and region would be well served to find ways of studying and documenting this material in relation to models of hybridity. What we see in Ladakh's Basgo Maitreya temple, for instance, may have been informed by two styles that were then brought together into a hybrid formation. This is likely the case for some of these outlying temple painting programs of the late medieval period. Ultimately, these painting programs are working with multiple stylistic currents and it is neither easy nor accurate to categorize them as definitively belonging to one painting tradition.

A contentious and often misunderstood aspect of this painting tradition is its chronology. None of these temples has yet been dated through internal evidence. Tsaparang's Red Temple is the only one of the sites painted in the courtly idiom that has a working date based on a textual account, but that account was not contemporaneous with the activities chronicled therein. One must take into consideration, therefore, that the Tibetan text in which this temple is mentioned, *Vaiḍūrya ser po bai ser,* commonly known as the *Bai ser,* was written in the seventeenth century, nearly two hundred years after the temple's supposed construction and decoration.[13] Nonetheless, it is the only Tibetan resource that provides a relative date and patron for Tsaparang's Red Temple, which allows us to build a rough chronology around it. I say "relative date" because the text does not specifically mention a year, but rather the king during whose reign the temple and its paintings were commissioned. A preliminary translation of the text reads, "The accomplished queen of Blo bzang rab brtan [Lobsang Rabtan] constructed the Red Temple, which possessed thirty pillars and the images of the Buddha, Maitreya, the protecting lords of the three [Bodhisattva] families, Tsong kha pa's [Tsongkapa's] disciples, also the supports for Body, Speech, and Mind."[14] This has left some question about when this royal couple actually reigned. Tucci, who first translated portions of the *Bai ser,* wrote the following:

> He [Sangs rgya mts'o (Sang Gyatso)] tells us, in fact, that the temples of Tsaparang were rebuilt, enlarged, and embellished in the time of Blo bzang rab brtan [Lobsang Rabtan]; his wife built the "red temple"; since that king was a contemporary of Ngag dbang grags pa [Ngawang Dragpa] and thus a pupil of Tsong Kha pa (1357–1419) it follows that the temple goes back to the first half of the fifteenth century.[15]

Since Tucci's work, several other scholars have suggested dates for Lobsang Rabtan and the Red Temple at Tsaparang. In 1980, Luciano Petech revisited accepted dates for King Lobsang Rabtan and posited a later date for the king based on the dates of two other historical figures, one of whom was Lobsang Rabtan's son. Petech convincingly concludes that Lobsang Rabtan must have lived closer to the end of the fifteenth century, and not the first half of it as Tucci proposed.[16] In 1996, based on his reading of the *Bai ser* and other texts, Roberto Vitali corroborated Tucci's finding that Tsaparang's Red Temple was built by the wife of the Guge king Lobsang Rabtan, whom Vitali also postulates ruled in the latter part of the fifteenth century.[17] In the same year, Michael Henss cited Tucci's 1949 article to substantiate his own claim that the Red Temple should be dated to 1470–80.[18] Nowhere in Tucci's "Tibetan Notes," article, however, does he provide such a specific date. The dating of Tsaparang's Red Temple is obviously of critical importance as it provides a chronological benchmark for this artistic period. Given Petech's and Vitali's respective research, the date in question could safely be considered to be the last quarter of the fifteenth century.

Apogee of the Courtly Idiom: Tholing, Tsaparang, and Tabo

Although an unabridged analysis of all the post-fifteenth-century painting programs from the sites of Tabo, Tholing, Tsaparang, and beyond is much needed, such an endeavor is beyond the scope of this chapter and book. Rather, I will first take on the more manageable, but equally significant, task of defining the apogee of this courtly idiom.[19] By paying particular attention to Tsaparang's and Tholing's dukhang temples, also known as the Red Temples, and Tabo's Golden Temple, I identify stylistic elements that characterize the courtly idiom of this style, such as compositional layout, figural forms, and decorative motifs of jewelry and textiles. Compositionally, the wall paintings are divided into units featuring a central deity positioned on a throne and who is surrounded, in many cases, by the deity's extended entourage. The deities generally have a lithesome appearance with broad shoulders; long, curved torsos; and tapered waists slightly raised on one side or the other. The navel articulation on these figures is one of the hallmarks of this style. Other distinctive physical features apparent on the deity figures are the double widow's peaks, small noses, and an incomplete jawline. Their long yet narrow eyes are framed by wide, arching eyebrows. The Buddha figures share in these same facial features and jawline, although they also display a number of other distinctive characteristics. The profile of their heads is fairly rounded and wide, extending past the ear, but tapers down at the lobe. The small, rounded topknot sits high on the head. Lastly, their earlobes are rendered at an angle to show their thickness. At all of the sites there is the shared use of decorative motifs such as abundant scrolling filigree work, crown types, necklaces, textile designs, as well as clothing styles. All of these formal elements are depicted at the three temples I am construing as the high-water mark of this courtly idiom.

One may take issue with what I call the apogee of this style.[20] How, for instance, have I determined that the three temples from Tabo, Tholing, and Tsaparang are representative of the style's high point? Without textual evidence, inscriptional or otherwise, to provide a clear chronology, I use stylistic analysis and comparison to establish the temporal contours of this material. Moreover, I approach this material with an assumption that the more detailed painting found at Tholing's Red Temple is the oldest of the group as it faithfully tries to replicate the eleventh-century Khache antecedents that were the original source of inspiration for this fifteenth-century painting style. Moreover, I presume that since these three sites—Tholing, Tsaparang, and Tabo—enjoyed a long history of royal patronage, it was likely that the fifteenth- to sixteenth-century painting programs at these same sites were also the result of royal patronage. We know that to be the case, for instance, at Tsaparang's Red Temple. Thus, my working hypothesis is that the height of the style occurred at its earliest stage when it was royally patronized in the last half of the 1400s at sites such as Tsaparang and Tholing. Tabo's Golden Temple falls a bit later and can be dated to the early sixteenth century.

When the painting programs of these three sites are compared to other painting programs executed in similar styles, such as Tabo's cave temple and the Gyapagpa Temple, I am able to discern a larger regional idiom, which is used at sites that are not necessarily royally patronized by the Guge court. I also suggest that these other painting programs are later in the chronological development and bring us to the later part of the sixteenth century. Through the following visual comparison, it will become evident that some formal aspects of the style changed with later generations of workshops and artists. With these subsequent generations of artists, I argue, there was a gradual "morphological disassociation," or *formenspaltung*, from the height of the style to its later usage.[21] This "form splitting" happened over a period of approximately one hundred years. While maintaining some of the characteristic features that define the style, the painting style developed in such a way that the line and palette became more simplified and abbreviated. Thus, in my presentation of the Ngari style of the late medieval period, this style moves from being intricate and finely delineated with gradations of color and sensitively applied modeling, as seen at Tholing's Red Temple, to a more pared down and simplified style with an emphasis on unmodulated fields of color and a reliance on line to provide contour. Consequently, by the time this style was employed on the walls of the Gyapagpa Temple in the late sixteenth century, it had split from its original referent and had become a regional, as opposed to exclusive courtly or revival, style. Nonetheless, there are telltale stylistic signs that connect the Gyapagpa paintings to the courtly idiom of the fifteenth century.

Overall Composition

The wall paintings at all three of these temples are divided into units featuring a specific deity sitting on an elaborate throne and surrounded by his or her entourage. Although the number of units on each wall varies depending on the temple, the arrangement of the figures is quite similar among these three sites. Moreover, the specific decorative elements used within these arrangements—such as the lotus pedestals, thronebases, pillar capitals, and nimbus detailing—is strikingly similar. For instance, figure 4.15 from Tholing's Red Temple shows the main figure—in this case it is Vajrasattva—with his entourage of deities. Vajrasattva is seated on an ornately decorated throne that is topped with a garuḍa figure on either side of whom is a nāgarāja. On each side of Vajrasattva stands a bodhisattva attendant. Enveloping this trinity of figures are rows of diminutive deity figures, each painted on his or her lotus pedestal that is encircled within a medallion formed by flowering vines (fig. 4.16). A similar constellation of deities is also found at Tabo. In figure 4.17, from Tabo's Golden Temple, the image of Vairocana is seated within an elaborate throne.[22] Bodhisattva attendants are painted as small, floating figures above each shoulder. Four tathāgatas hover nearby, and four gatekeepers are situated below Vairocana's throne; under them are eight offering goddesses. The remaining twenty deities, each on his or her lotus pedestal, fill the sides of the composition. Tabo's composition is slightly more compact, but it is arranged, as are the paintings from the Red Temples at Tsaparang and Tholing, according to the deity's full maṇḍala. In this case it comprises thirty-seven deities, which includes the central deity, Vairocana.

The thronebases at the Red Temples of Tsaparang and Tholing, as well as the Golden Temple at Tabo, are also similarly rendered. Generally, a filigreed moon-disk is set upon a lotus pedestal, which has both up- and downturned lotus petals that are often multicolored and variously decorated with scalloped or smooth edges. The lotus pedestal rests upon a large foundation that is divided into two and sometimes three levels with stepped basements and molding with upturned corners. Such architectural details, however, do not exist in Tibetan religious or vernacular architecture, which primarily consists of battered mud-brick construction.[23] These images, therefore, are referencing not Tibetan, but Indian, antecedents as they replicate—in varying degrees—north Indian

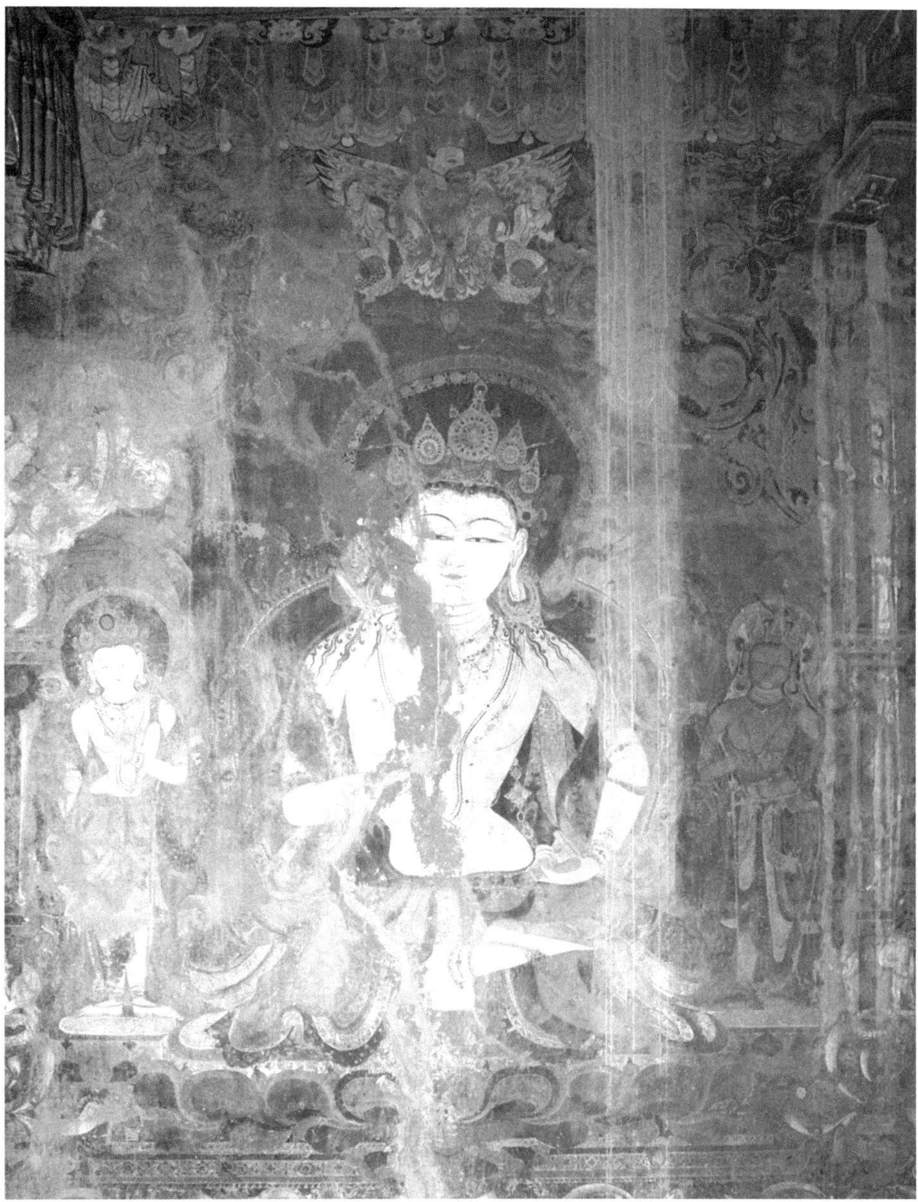

Figure 4.15. Tholing (West Tibet), Red Temple, north wall of apse: Vajrasattva, c. fifteenth century. WHAV JP93 424.

and perhaps even Kashmiri architectural sequences of basement moldings as they are represented in stelae from the Pala period. Art historian Claudine Bautze-Picron has discussed the ways in which these architectural motifs were incorporated into Tibetan painting from the twelfth to the fourteenth centuries. Certainly, as this material evidence from West Tibet suggests, the tradition of representing thronebases in such ways

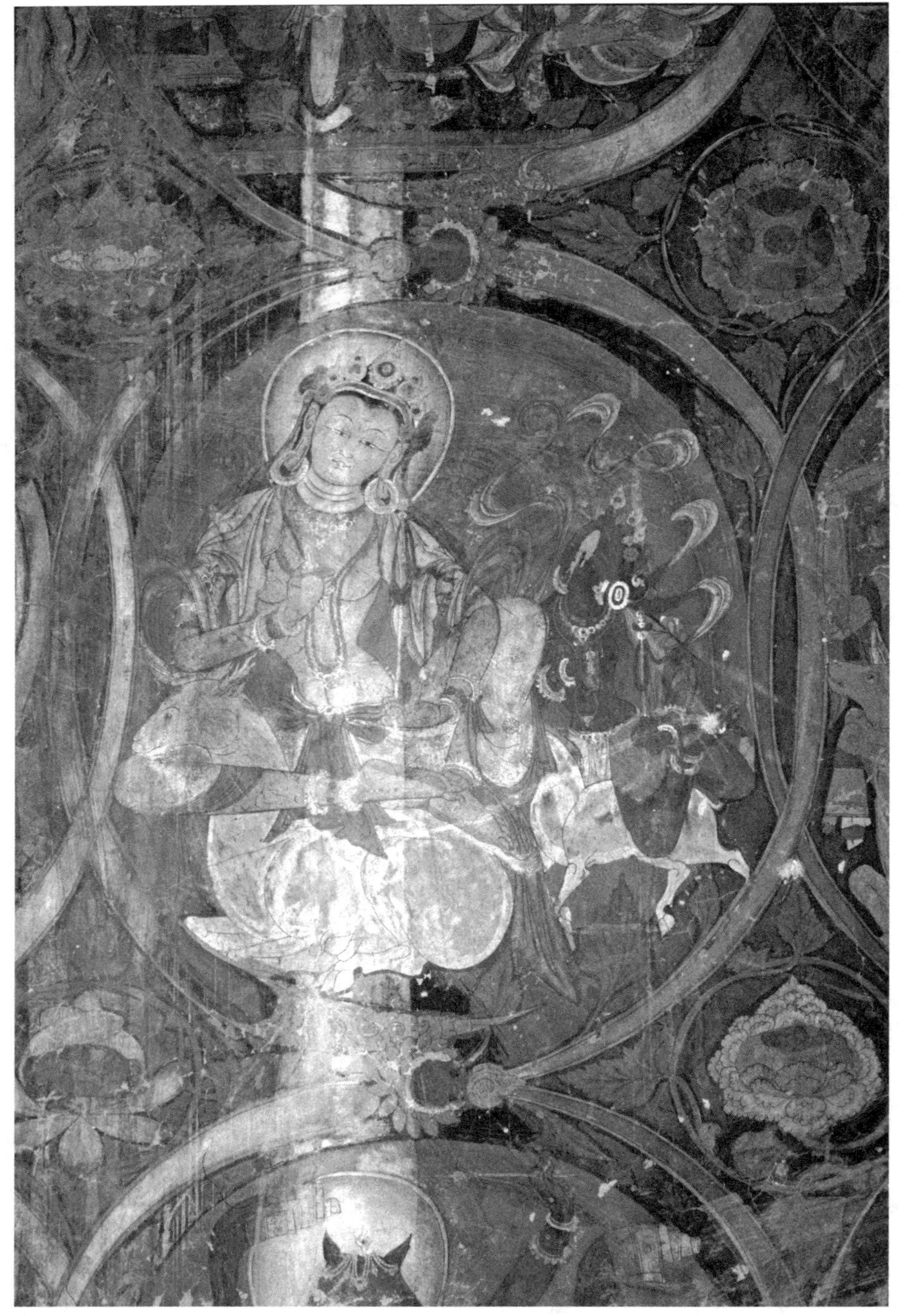

Figure 4.16. Tholing (West Tibet), Red Temple, north wall of apse: blue subsidiary deity surrounded by flowering vines, c. fifteenth century. WHAV JP93 481.

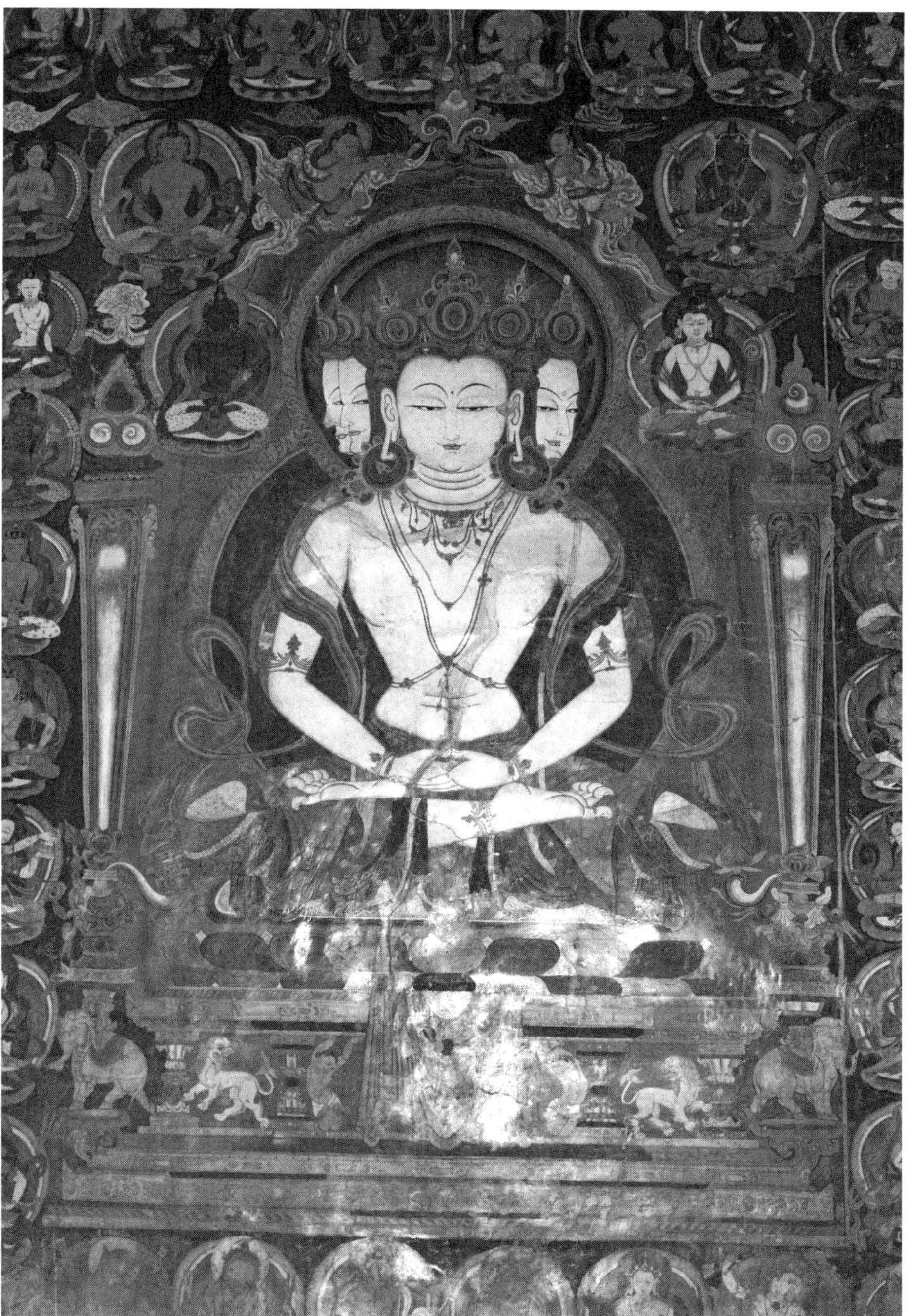

Figure 4.17. Tabo (Lahaul Spiti Dist., H.P.) Golden Temple: Vairocana, c. early sixteenth century.

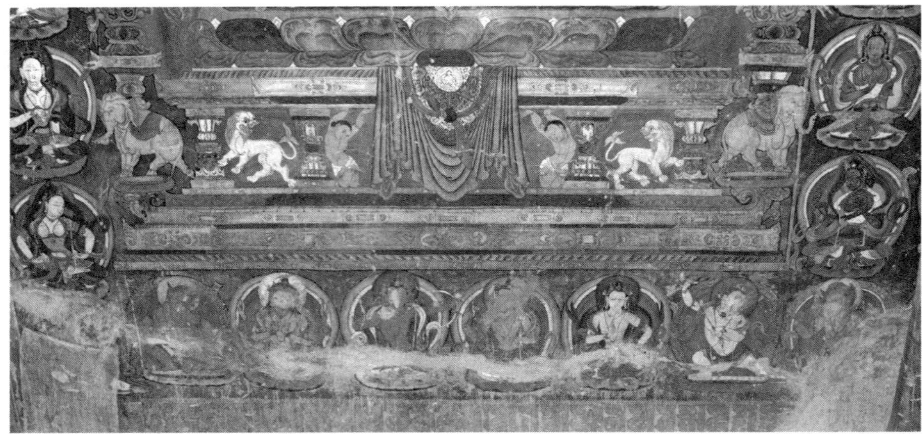

Figure 4.18. Tabo (Lahaul Spiti Dist., H.P.), Golden Temple: architectural structure of Vairocana's thronebase, c. early sixteenth century.

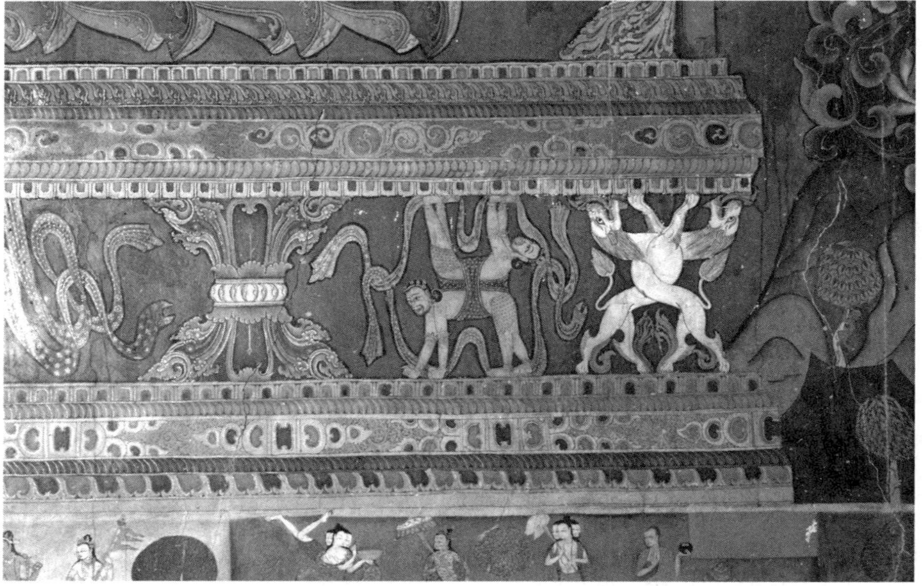

Figure 4.19. Tsaparang (West Tibet), Red Temple: detail of thronebase, c. fifteenth century. RNL.

carried on well after the fourteenth century.[24] Unique to the Ngari painting tradition, however, are the decorative forms that appear between the basement levels. Between basement levels are sometimes found groups of fantastically addorsed or twisted figures, human and animal, striking a number of contorted poses (figs. 4.18, 4.19, and 4.20). Very likely, this ornamental feature was adopted from the decorative programs of the

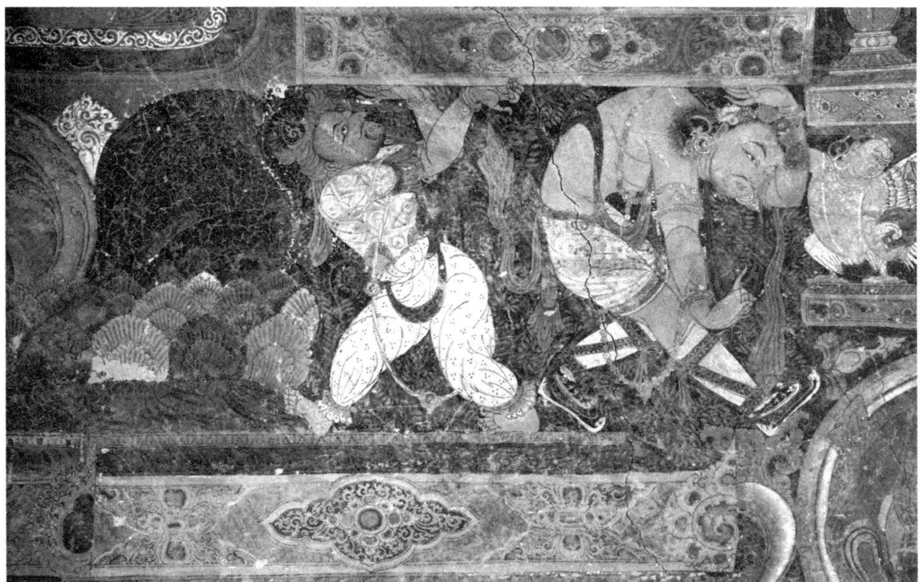

Figure 4.20. Tholing (West Tibet), Red Temple: detail of thronebase,
c. fifteenth century. WHAV JP93 586.

eleventh- and twelfth-century wall paintings of West Tibet, such as at the
painted caves in Dungkar. That these figures were incorporated into the
late-fifteenth-century style of West Tibet is an index of the later artists'
awareness of their artistic and aesthetic heritage.

Upon these elaborate thronebases are equally detailed thronebacks.
At Tholing and Tsaparang, *makaras* or other fantastic creatures balance
themselves atop ornate pillars as their long, foliate tails swirl upward to
create the top of the throneback (fig. 4.21). The degree to which these
thronebacks are decorated varies even within a temple. At Tabo's Golden
Temple, for instance, the majority of thronebacks are relatively simple in
their design. However, the throneback for the main figure of Śākyamuni
is exceptional in its intricate detailing.

The painting program at all three temples features the main deity sitting within this elaborate throne setting and against a backdrop of intricate filigree work composed of a light red hue applied to a background of
darker red (fig. 4.22). The deity's head and body nimbi are rendered with
stylized flames and more filigree work. The ornamentation of the deities'
thrones and nimbi are fairly ubiquitous at all three sites. Although there
are some minor differences among the detail work at these three sites—
such as the amount of filigree used, the way in which the apex of the
throneback is rendered, or the types of composite animals used as pillar
capitals—the main decorative schema is strikingly resonant among them.

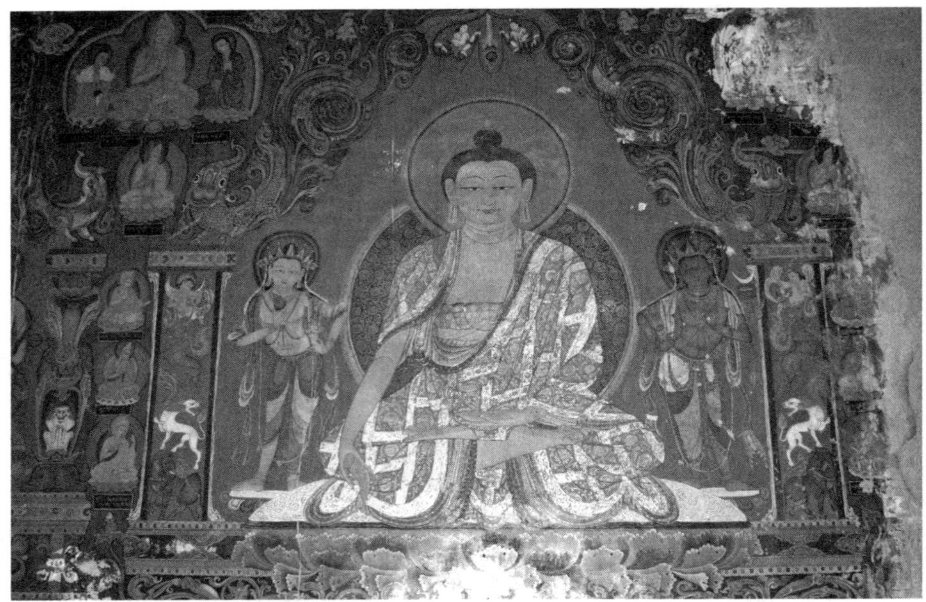

Figure 4.21. Tsaparang (West Tibet), Red Temple: Śākyamuni Buddha,
c. fifteenth century. RNL.

It is worth noting that the filigree decorative motif, seen in abundance
at the murals of Tabo, Tholing and Tsaparang, is a decorative flourish that
several scholars have pinpointed, among other details, as a significant stylistic element proving that the fifteenth-century Guge painting tradition is
a permutation of the Newar-based painting style.[25] In chapter 5 I explain
the origins of the fifteenth-century West Tibetan painting style; here I will
simply say that this style was not originally developed as a permutation of
the widely circulating Newar or Beri style and substyles. The presence of
the ubiquitous filigree decorative flourish, although likely introduced to
both Central and West Tibet through Newar paintings and artists, is not,
in and of itself, strong enough evidence to suggest that that these Ngari
paintings of the fifteenth century are rendered in the Newar style. Rather,
I think it is important to recognize that decorative motifs were adopted
and recirculated within numerous styles. During the fifteenth century,
West Tibet's Guge kingdom had contact with the royal and religious centers of Mustang.[26] This relationship is significant here in so far as it reveals
possible centers for neighboring Newar-based artistic activity. Newar
painting styles are well documented in the late medieval wall paintings of
Mustang, as can be seen in the painting program of the Great Maitreya
Temple, which undoubtedly employed Newar-trained artists to execute
the wall paintings.[27] The filigree scrolling work is also a decorative painting technique used in Central Tibet at Gyantse's fifteenth-century (1430s)

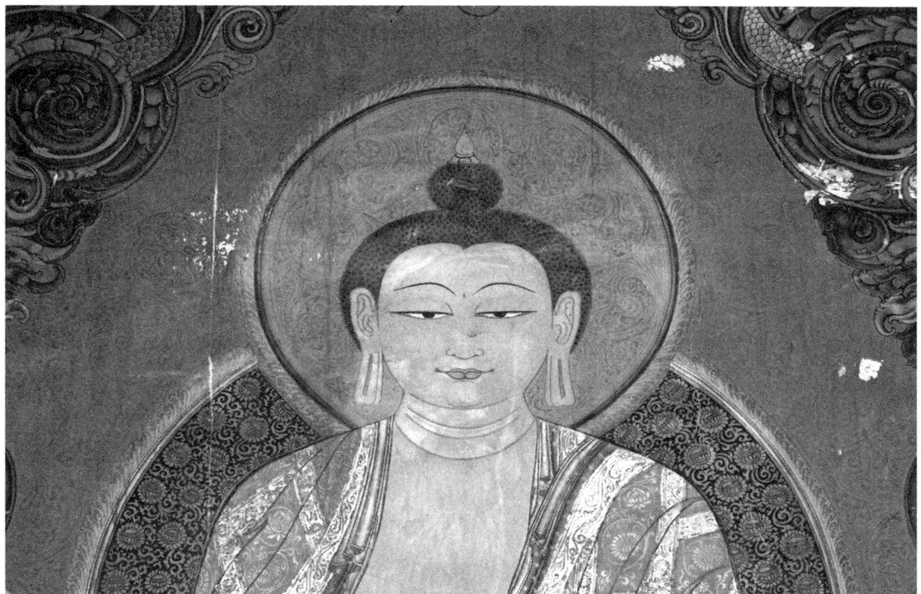

Figure 4.22. Tsaparang (West Tibet), Red Temple: Buddha head,
c. fifteenth century. MRK.

Kumbum Stūpa and in the fourteenth-century wall paintings at Shalu's lower circumambulation hall. As I interpret it, the presence of Newar-derived details, such as the filigree work, in the Ngari painting style is an example of motif borrowing. That this decorative flourish is in circulation in Ngari is indicative of its widespread use. The Ngari fifteenth-century painters incorporated Newar-based visual elements, among others, into their growing visual vocabulary; this, however, should not be confused with a wholesale adoption of a style. Consequently, the late medieval Ngari painting tradition should remain discrete from the Beri/Newar tradition.

Deity Figures

Nearly all the pacific deities featured in these three temples share similar physical forms (respective of male or female deities), proportions, and attention to detail, seen in the articulation of fingers and modeling. Deity figures are painted in fully frontal and cross-legged positions, wearing dhotis painted with intricate patterning. These figures are painted with prominent, well-defined shoulders and long torsos that narrow to small waists. The pinched waists of most deity figures accentuate the hips, which are slightly pronounced on one side as to give the impression of a subtle shift in weight (fig. 4.23; plates 14 and 15). Each of these deity

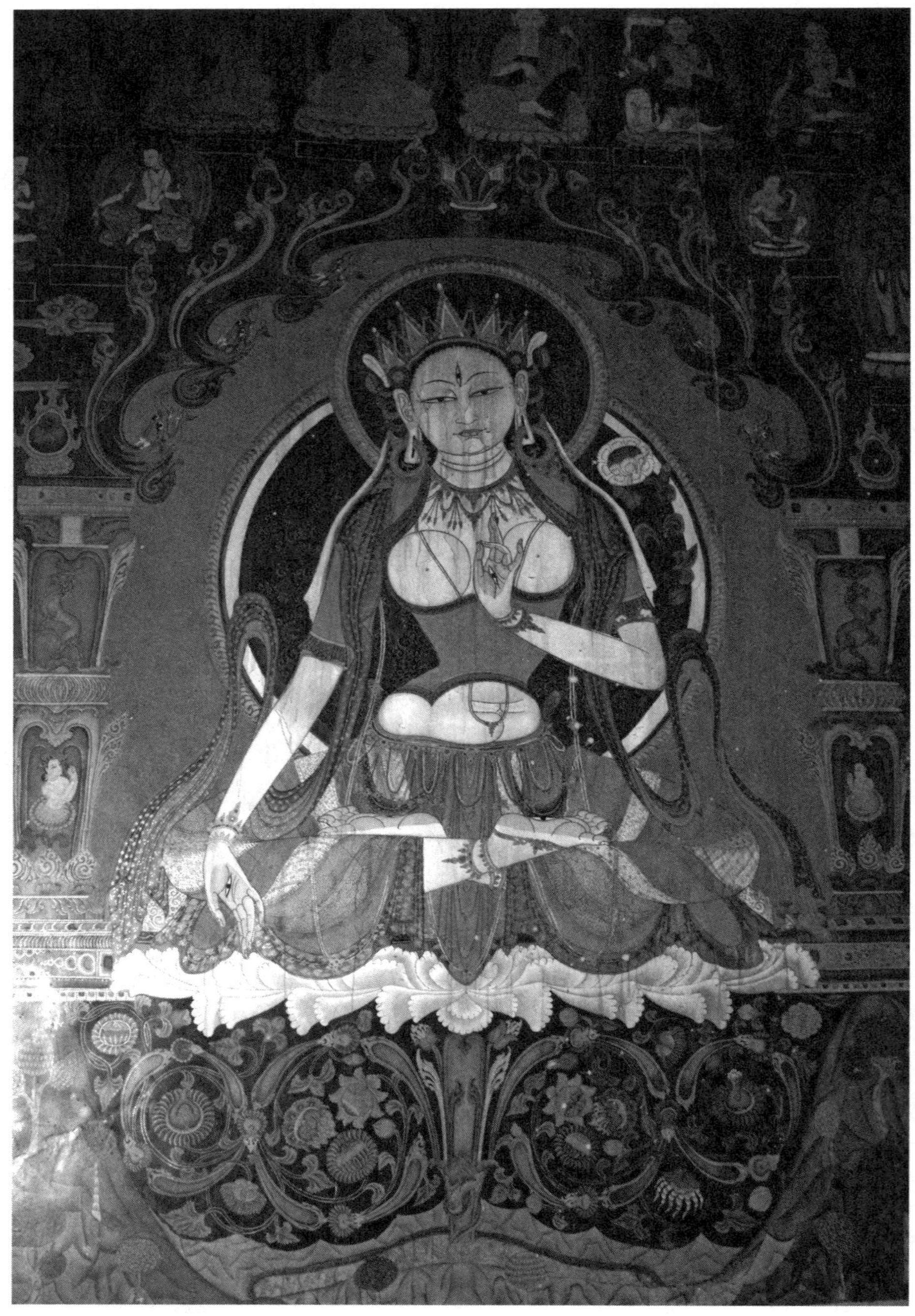

Figure 4.23. Tsaparang (West Tibet), Red Temple: White Tara,
c. fifteenth century. RNL.

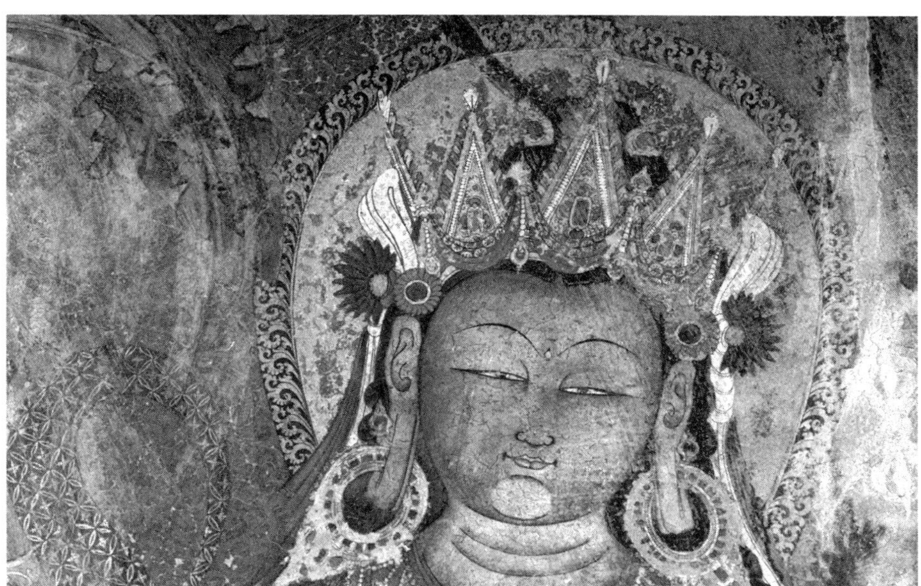

Figure 4.24. Tholing (West Tibet), Red Temple: face of bodhisattva Vajrapani, c. fifteenth century. WHAV JP93 55.4.

figures displays a navel marking of horizontal and vertical lines, which is unique to the western Tibetan area and for which there are clear antecedents dating to the eleventh-century Khache Style (figs. 4.23 and 4.25). The rendering of these figures' hands adroitly illustrates the ways in which the artists of these different programs observed intricate detailing. Long slender fingers with thin, curled tips appear boneless as they effortlessly flex and fold into contorted positions while holding ritual objects. What adds to the dynamic quality of these physical forms is the manner in which they are modeled. Many of the figures in these temples display some degree of modeling. In plate 15, as well as in figures 4.24 and 4.25, one can see that it is readily used to accentuate the deity's arms, chest, and stomach. This technique helps to create the illusion of the figure's plasticity and volume.

Some of the more distinctive qualities of this style can be seen in the rendering of the heads and faces of these figures (figs. 4.24 and 4.26). Most of the figures have a double widow's peak at the center of the hairline. Eyes, painted in an almond shape or with a straight upper lid, are often slightly modeled. Expansive, arched eyebrows frame these dramatically narrow eyes. The rest of the facial features, such as the small nose, red mouth, and chin demarcations are rendered with fine line work. For instance, at times the lower lip has a mark in the middle of it to suggest that two small lobes form the lower lip, as seen in Tsaparang's Red Temple (fig. 4.22). Although there is some differentiation in the way the lips are

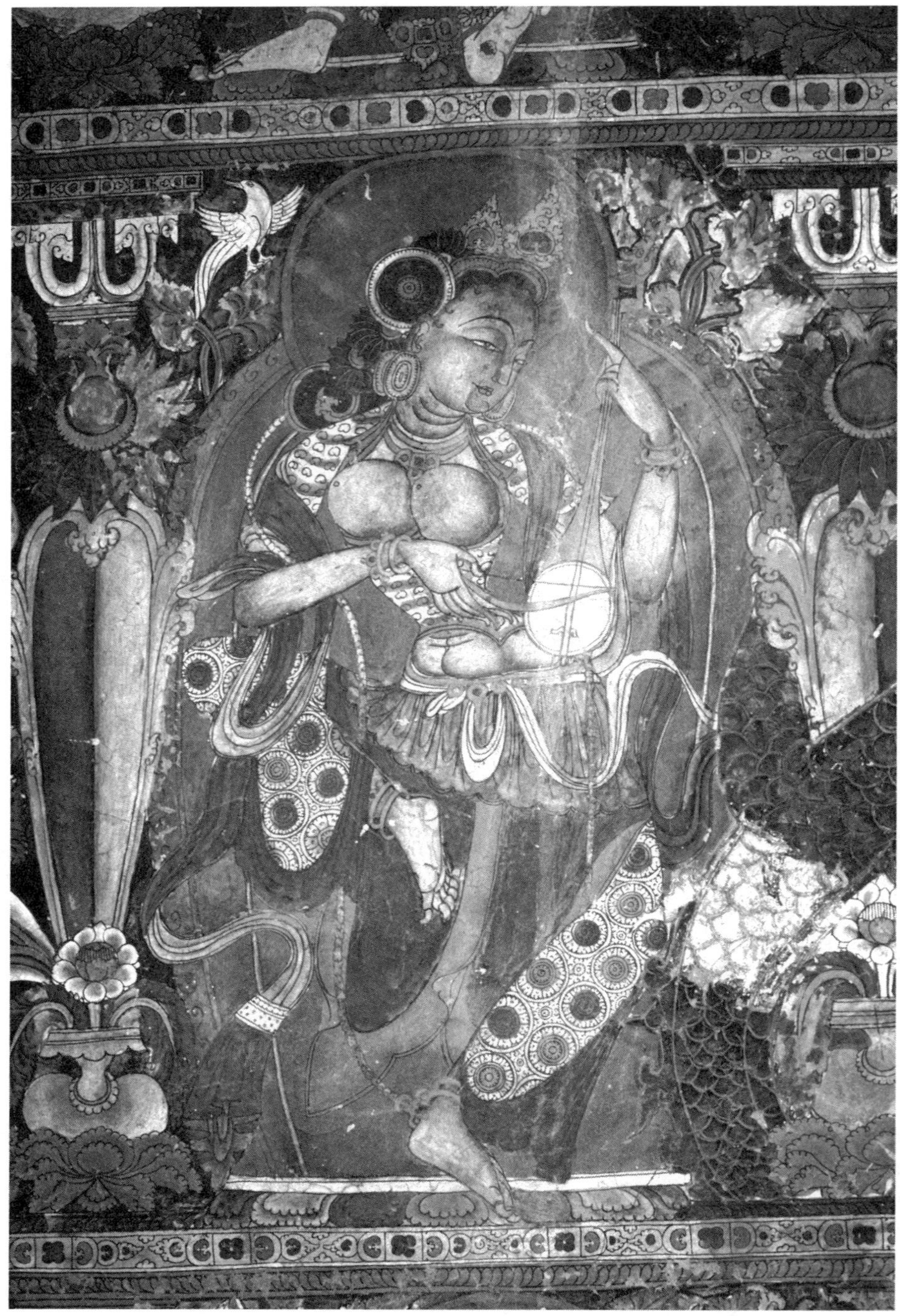

Figure 4.25. Tholing (West Tibet), Red Temple: offering deity, fifteenth century.
WHAV JP93 438.

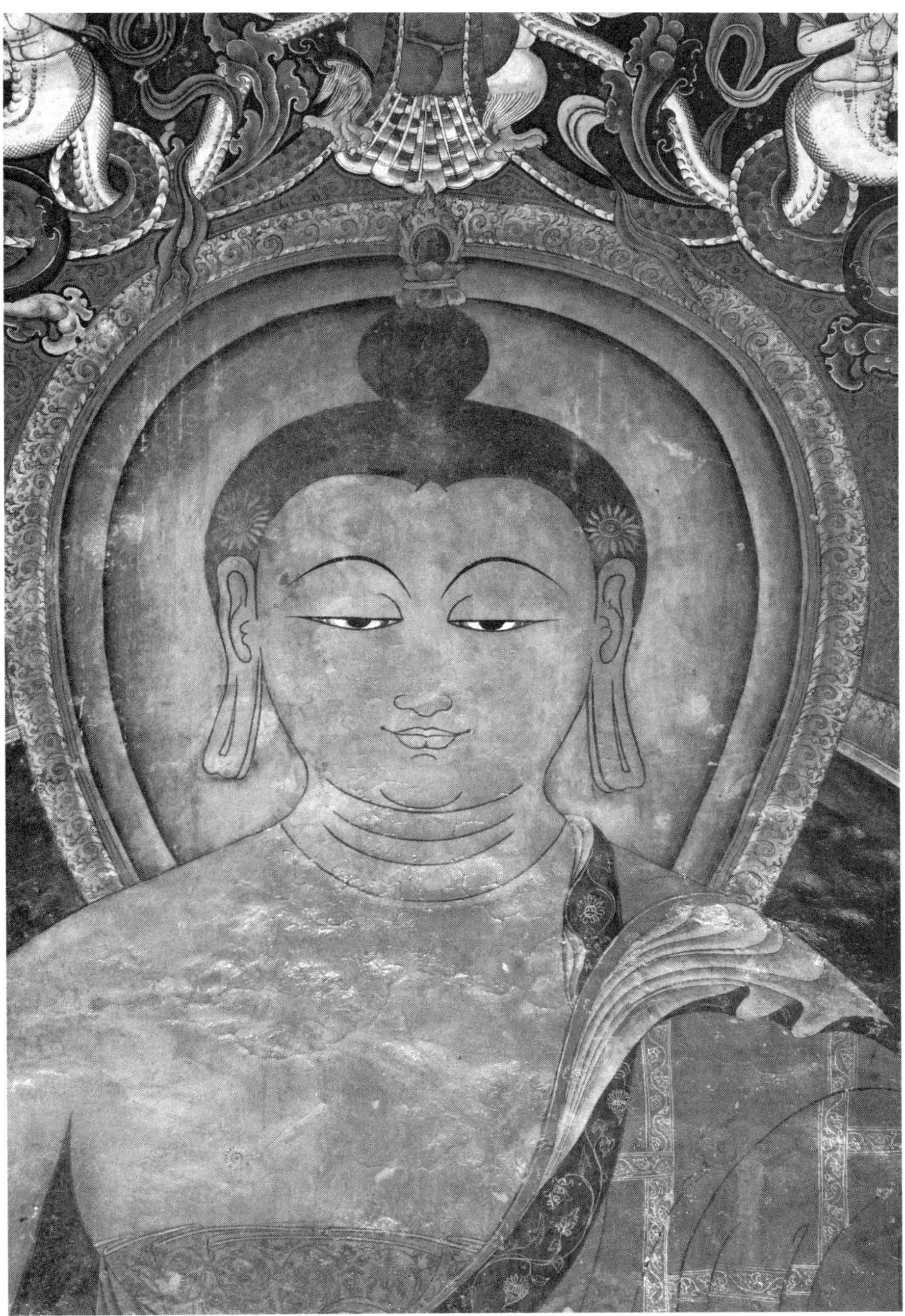

Figure 4.26. Tabo, (Lahaul Spiti Dist., H.P.) Golden Temple: Śākyamuni Buddha head, c. early sixteenth century.

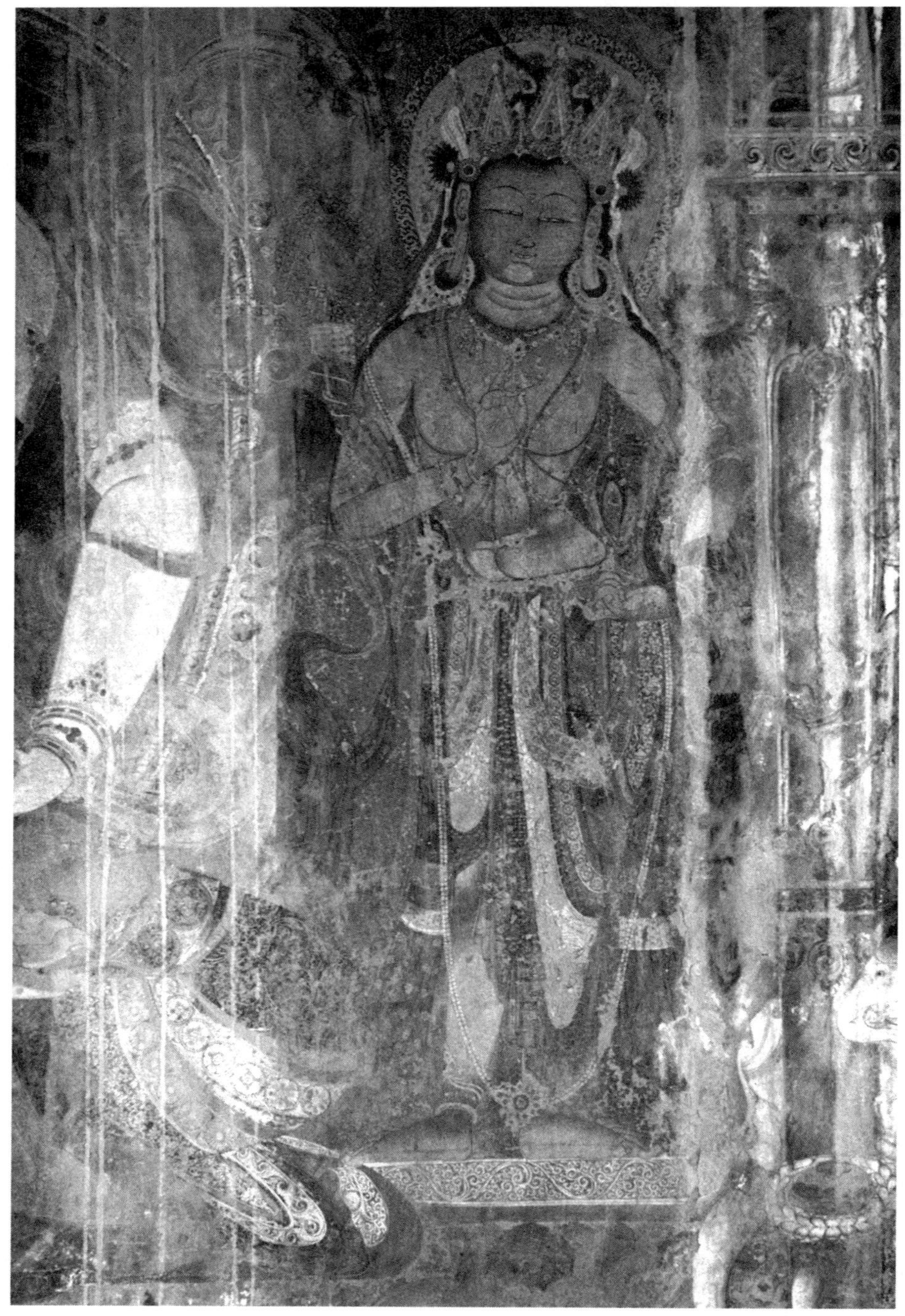

Figure 4.27. Tholing (West Tibet), Red Temple: bodhisattva Vajrapani figure,
c. fifteenth century. WHAV JH93 551.

rendered from image to image, they each display slight indentations at the corners of the mouth.

The shapes of the deities' faces are quite similar to one another in that most of these figures have a jawline that does not connect with the sides of their necks. This incomplete jawline is seen on the blue attendant figure to Vajrasattva at Tholing's Red Temple (figs. 4.24 and 4.27). The full face of the figure is suggested through a combined use of line and shadow; where the hard line stops, shading and modeling are employed to suggest the contours of the rounded jaw. This painterly approach creates a greater sense of dimension and volume for the face, neck, and jaw. Later in this style's development, modeling is not used and only the hard lines are painted. As such, there is generally a little gap left between the jaw and necklines as is the case in the painted programs at Tabo's cave and the Gyapagpa Temple. It can also be seen, however, in the earlier Tsaparang Temple (fig. 4.22). This anatomical detail, in both its fully realized and abbreviated forms, is a telltale sign of this revival style.

Buddhas

The primary and subsidiary Buddha figures featured at these three temples are executed in varying degrees of detail, though they all share similar characteristics and features.[28] Both large and small Buddha figures, for instance, are rendered with a distinctive head shape. Starting at the top of the head, the uṣṇīṣa is quite small and round, and is situated at the crown of the head. From here, the profile of the head curves down to meet the midsection of the ear, giving the head a rounded shape characteristic of this style. Like the pacific deities, the large and small Buddhas have a split widow's peak, straight upper eyelids, small, subtlety defined noses, pursed mouths, and jawlines that do not meet the line of the neck (figs. 4.22 and 4.26; plate 16). The Buddhas also have distinctive earlobes that flare out slightly to show their thickness.[29] It should be noted that the subsidiary Buddha figures at both Tsaparang and Tabo are executed in a slightly more abbreviated fashion than at Tholing. This seems to be the general trend: Tholing's paintings were painstakingly rendered with extensive detailing, patterning, and shading. The wall paintings at Tholing and Tabo, while of the same idiom, often reveal that the artists did not work in the same full-blown detail, but employed abbreviations in modeling or brushwork. These variations demonstrate that while the late medieval wall paintings of these three sites work within the same idiom, as seen in the their shared figural types—with similar head and eye shapes, facial features, and body proportions—different workshops were in circulation.

Although the physical forms of the Buddha figures are all quite similar, there is tremendous variation in the depiction of monastic robes. The large Buddha figures are clad in voluminous monastic robes articulated with patchwork detailing or embroidery patterns. Figures 4.21, 4.22, and 4.26, and plate 16, reveal some disparities in the drapery style of the robes. While both garments follow the same color pattern: a rust-colored robe with golden lines, pinkish coloring for the lining, and blue or green for the trim, the styling of the robes is not the same. The main difference is that the Tsaparang Buddha is painted with his proper right shoulder covered while the Tabo figure is rendered with his right shoulder completely bare. The Tabo image also has a few extra folding or drapery details that the Tsaparang Buddhas do not. For instance, on the proper left side, the monastic robe folds over the shoulder to reveal the pink interior of the garment. At the elbow of this same side is a triangular cascade of material that creates a colorful patch of blue, pink, red, and gold. Such flourishes are noticeably absent on the robes of the Tsaparang Buddhas. I interpret these variations as indicative of particular inclinations of different workshops/artists.

Historical Figures

Both Tholing's and Tsaparang's Red Temples have numerous historical personages and religious figures depicted in them, many of which are identified by accompanying inscriptions. These two sites, therefore, are storehouses of valuable information regarding West Tibetan dress, textile, and jewelry history.[30] Despite the wealth of historical information preserved on the walls of these temples, in terms of inscriptions and identified historical figures, this material remains unanalyzed.[31] While this visual evidence should be fully analyzed, my treatment of this data must necessarily remain focused on the issue of style. In terms of the historical figures depicted, there tend to be both religious and royal figures portrayed in either the more prevalent three-quarter profile or in a fully frontal position. Those painted in a frontal position generally seem to be religious teachers, such as Atiśa, or royal personages, such as Srong btsan sgam po (Songtsen Gampo), as is the case in Tsaparang's Red Temple (fig. 4.28). The majority of monastic figures are painted in three-quarter profile, with their far eye and brow projecting outward, breaking the profile line. The eye closer to the viewer is depicted in a long, almond shape, although there are instances also of bow-shaped eyes. Lips are full, while chins are fairly rounded, and jawlines clearly delineated. At Tsaparang, the faces and arms of these religious figures tend to be modeled, whereas at Tabo they are not. At both temples, the religious figures are depicted in mustard- or maroon-colored robes trimmed in a complementary color of green, blue, or sometimes orange. They wear pointed yellow hats that are meant to signal their association with the Gelug order. One of the

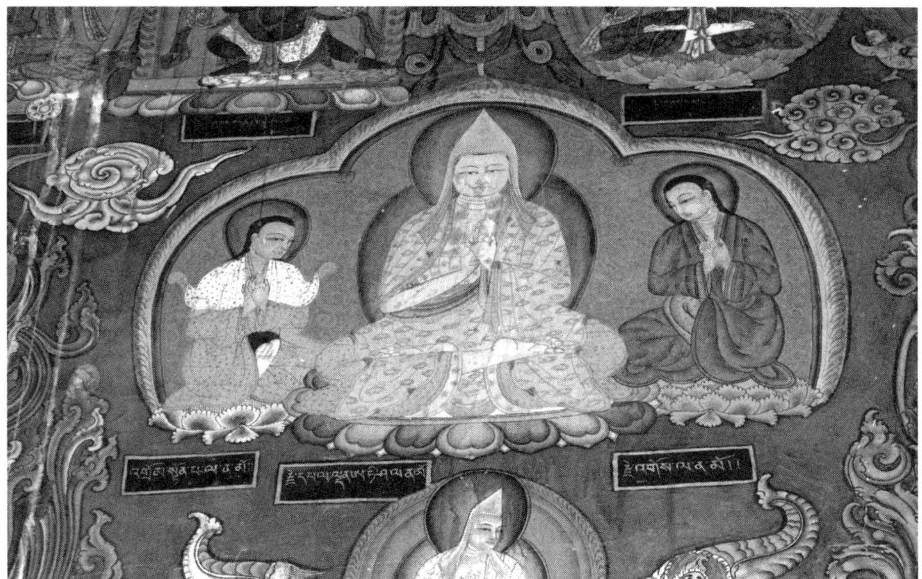

Figure 4.28. Tsaparang (West Tibet), Red Temple: Atiśa historical portrait, c. fifteenth century. MRK.

more characteristic features of this style is the hairline of monastic figures. Generally, while many wear the pundit hat that covers much of the head, a patch of closely cropped hair peeks out from under the hat at the forehead and temple.

Bodhisattva Attendants

There is tremendous variation in the articulation of the bodhisattva attendants at Tholing, Tsaparang, and Tabo. Among these different forms, there are several strong unifying features such as broad shoulders, attenuated waists, full hips, particular navel articulation, modeled bodies, delicately rendered fingers, and elaborately rendered crowns, textiles, and jewelry. Figures 4.27 and 4.29 illustrate bodhisattva attendants from Tholing and Tsaparang, respectively, which display similar body types, stances, and decorative motifs. There are, however, appreciable difference between these two figures as can be seen in the modeling, jewelry details, and body proportions. The painting from Tholing (fig. 4.27) represents a more detailed and better-proportioned figure that is exquisitely modeled to create a lithe, dimensional figure with the illusion of plasticity. While the Tsaparang figure is unquestionably painted in the same style, it is not of the same skill level—as can be seen by the lack of detailing around the nimbus and in the textile work. Furthermore, the proportions of the upper body are slightly thicker and longer, making the Tsaparang attendant a

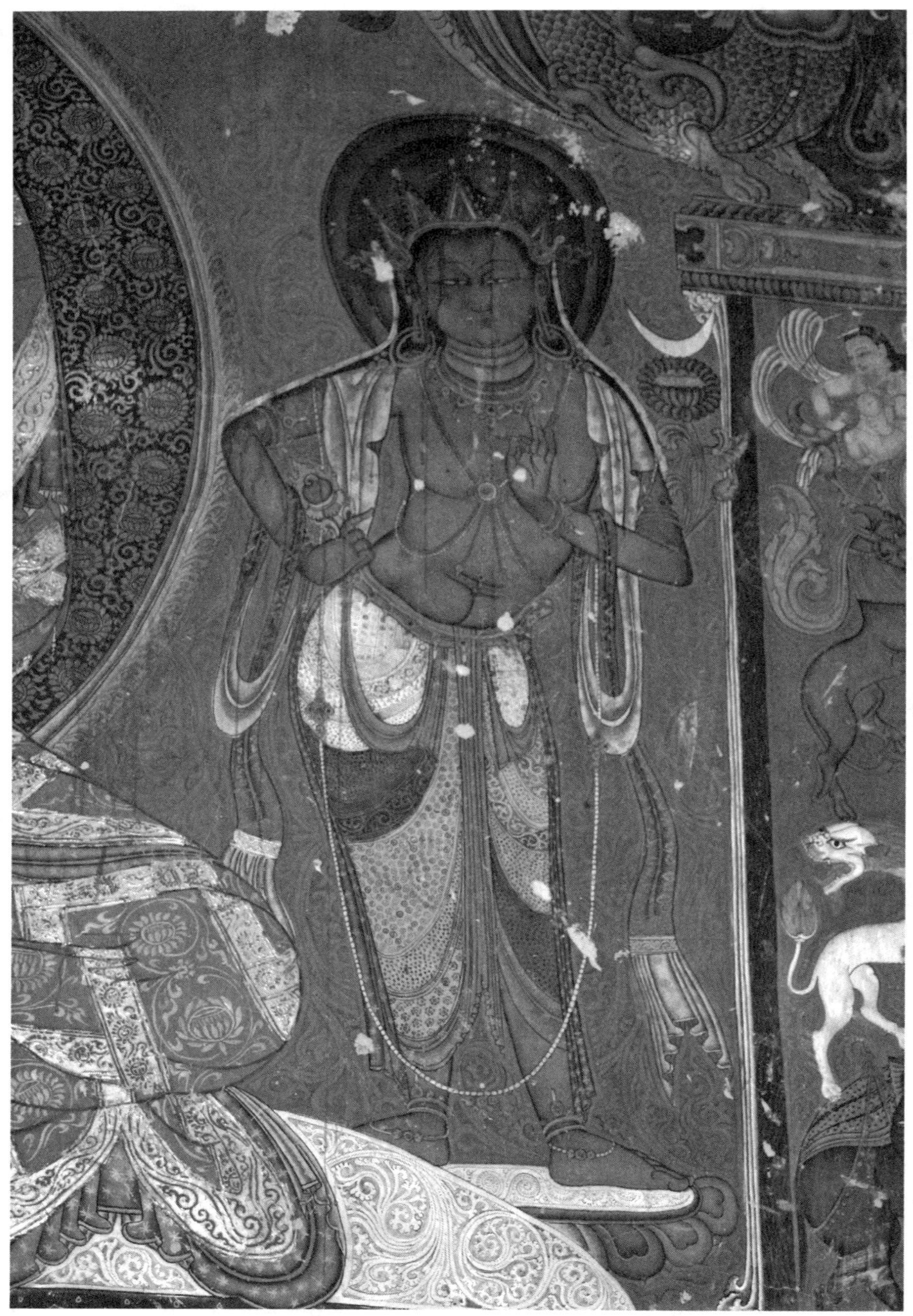

Figure 4.29. Tsaparang (West Tibet), Red Temple: green attendant figure, c. fifteenth century. MRK.

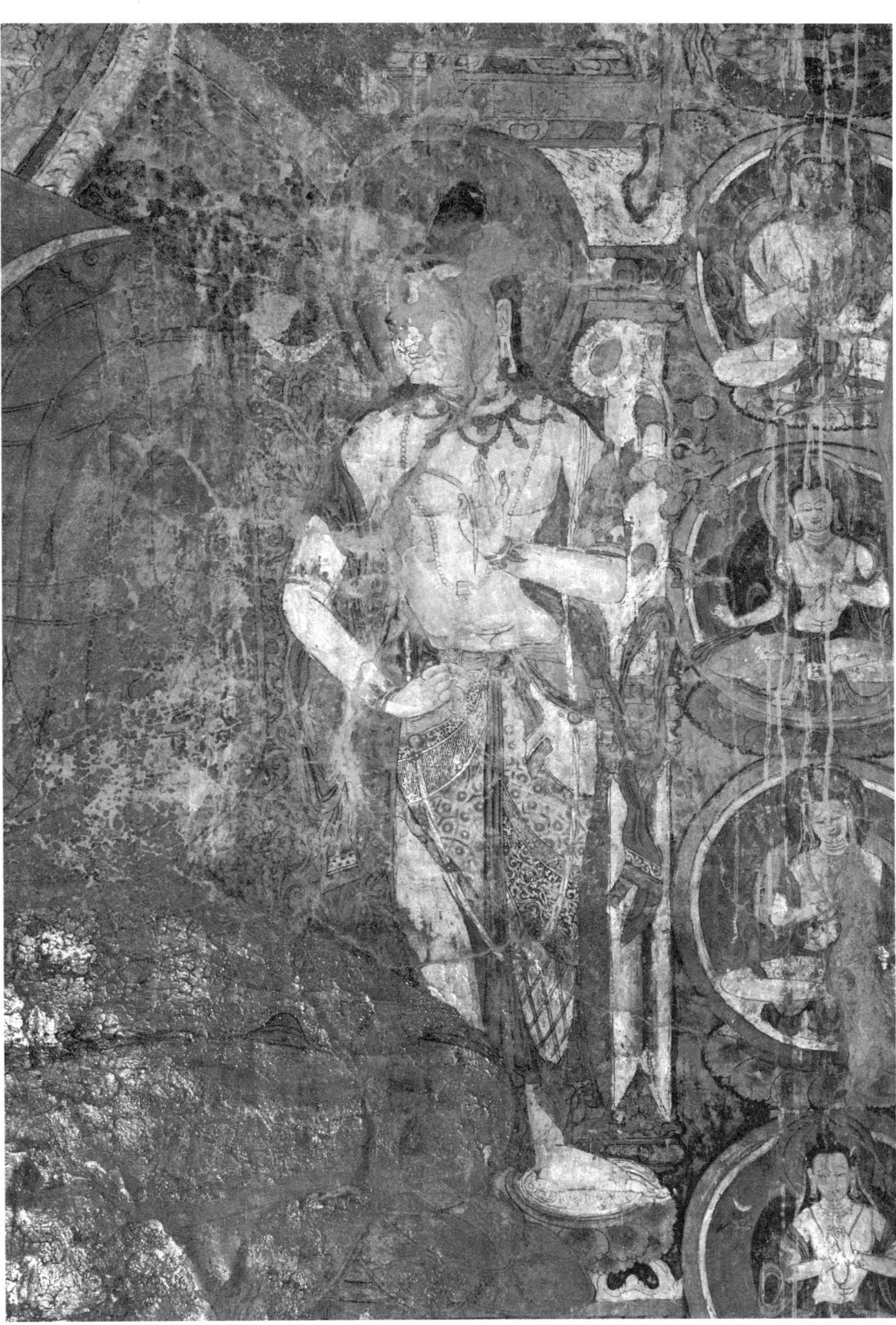

Figure 4.30. Tabo (Lahaul Spiti Dist., H.P.), Golden Temple: attendant to Medicine Buddha, c. early sixteenth century.

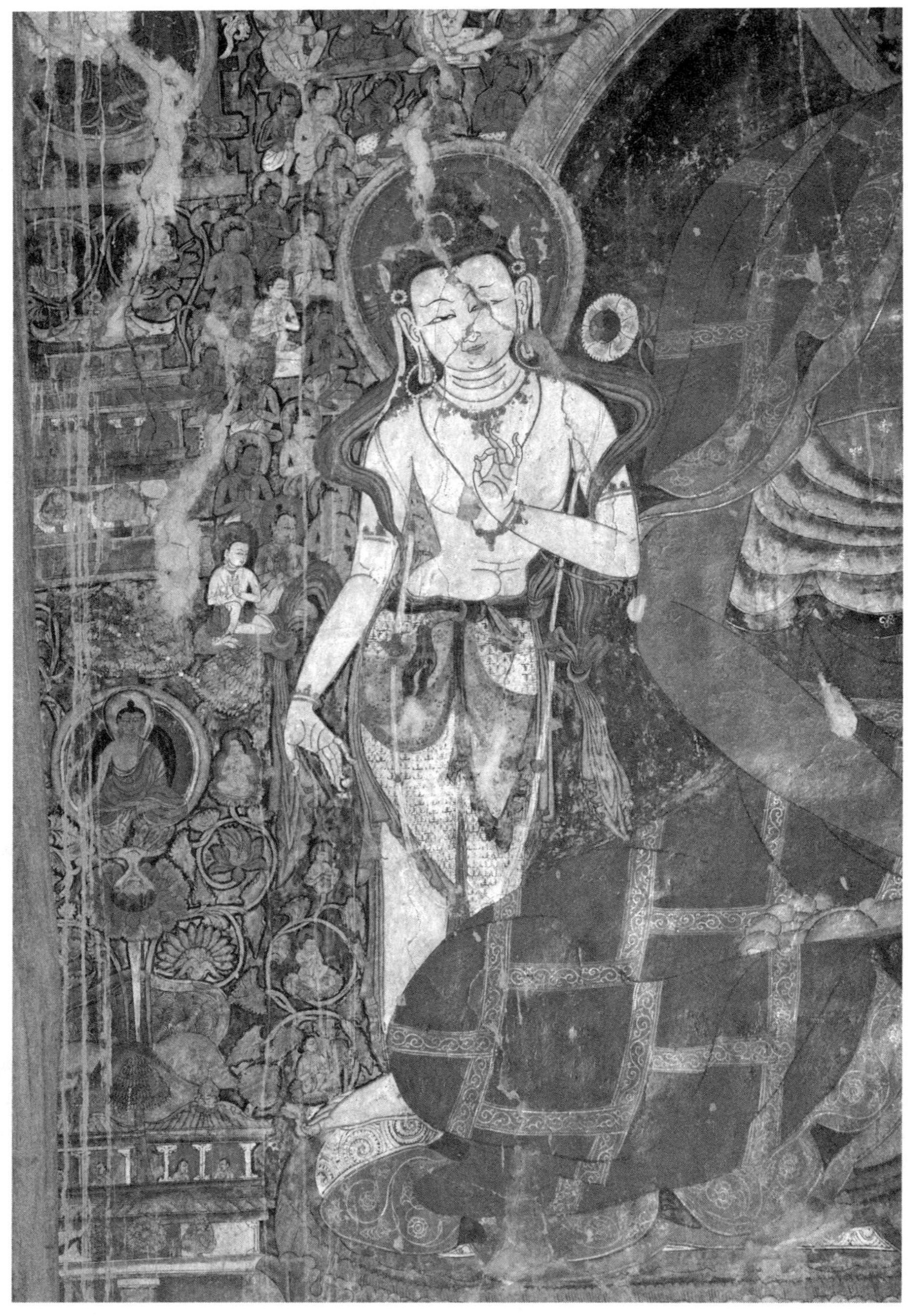

Figure 4.31. Tabo (Lahaul Spiti Dist., H.P.), Golden Temple: attendant to Amitābha, c. early sixteenth century.

little stiffer in its appearance. The fact that these two attendant figures are painted in the same style, but not executed with the same proportion or level of detail, is an important distinction that will be addressed with the Gyapagpa paintings.

At Tabo's Golden Temple there are fewer bodhisattva attendant figures. In fact, bodhisattva attendant figures are only used for the Medicine Buddha and Amitābha on the south wall (figs. 4.30 and 4.31). Although these figures are not as well preserved as those in Tsaparang or Tholing, one can still glean a significant amount of information from them. The attendant featured in figure 4.30 is one of two attendants flanking the Medicine Buddha. Here, the figure shares many of the same characteristics as the attendants from Tholing and Tsaparang (figs. 4.27 and 4.29), as can be seen in the navel articulation, pinched waist, pectoral definition, dhoti design, and fluttering sashes. Figure 4.31, also from Tabo, represents a slightly different bodhisattva type in that it is not dramatically modeled and his facial features, especially the bow-shaped eyes and upturned eyebrows, are not like the other figures'. Yet this figure shares important formal characteristics of the style—as can be seen in the textile designs, navel articulation, pinched waist, and body posture.

Monastic Attendants

Only in a few instances are there monastic attendant figures, who accompany either the historical Buddha or other historical figures, such as Tsong kha pa (Tsongkapa) in the case in Tholing's Red Temple.[32] The best photographic evidence of these monastic attendants comes from Tabo's Golden Temple (fig. 4.32). At both Tholing and Tabo, the monastic attendants are rendered in three-quarter profile with a shaved head and distinctive hairline, and are clad in monastic robes that fall to their ankles. These monastic attendants share many of the same features as the historical figures previously discussed in this chapter; the far eye and brow project slightly from the face, while the eye closer to the viewer is long and almond shaped. The nose is sharply delineated and the lips full. At Tabo, the neck and upper chest of the figure are modeled. Also important to note is the flared earlobe with the distinctive line indicating the width of the ear, a hallmark of the style as has been previously discussed.

Detailing: Textiles, Crowns, and Jewelry

One of the most distinctive traits of this style is the detailing of the clothing and jewelry. Dhotis are rendered in a fantastic range of textile patterns and colors. Such specific articulation of detail is not simply an aesthetic choice. Rather, the way in which these textiles are painted, to suggest

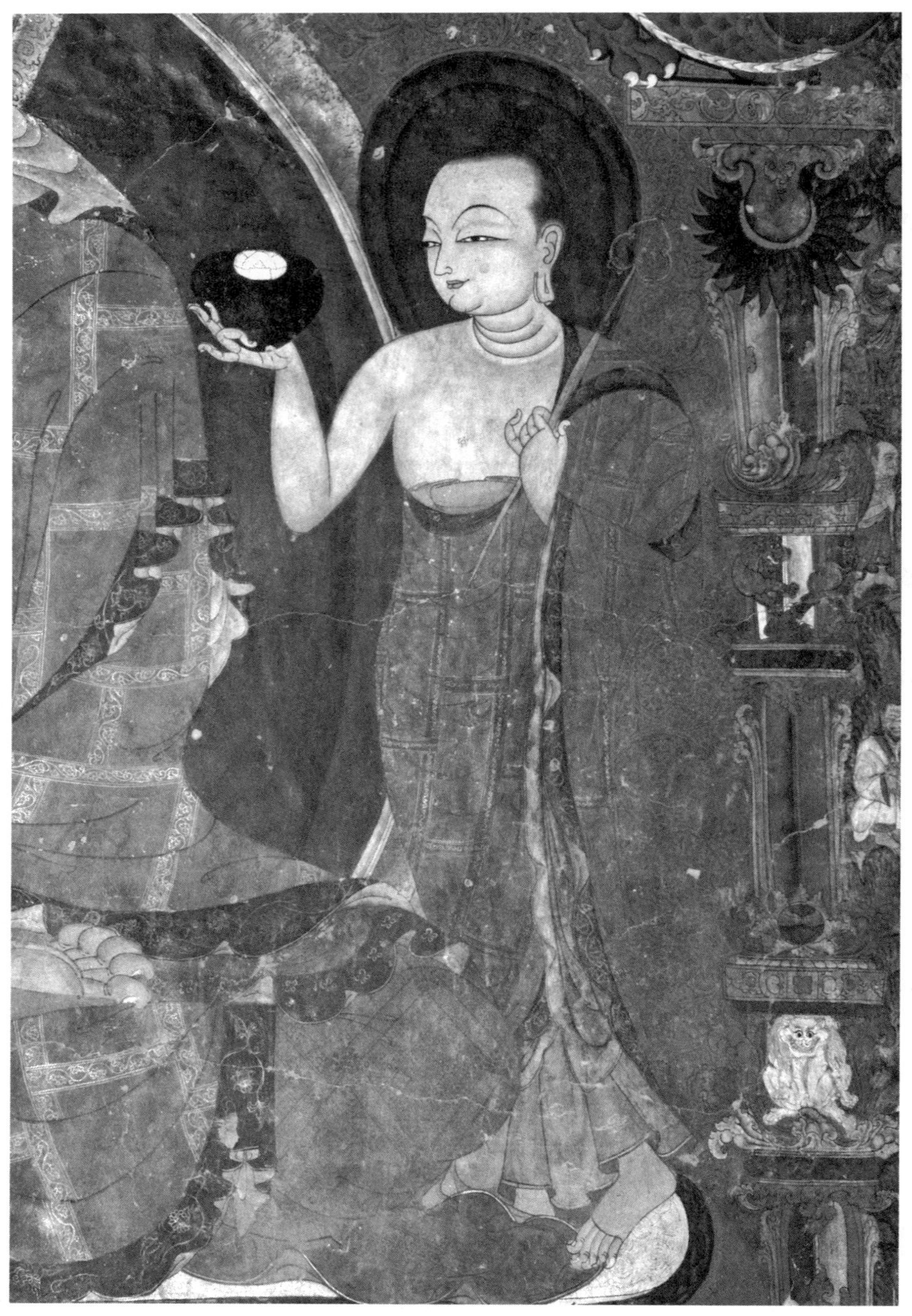

Figure 4.32. Tabo (Lahaul Spiti Dist., H.P.), Golden Temple: monastic attendant, c. early sixteenth century.

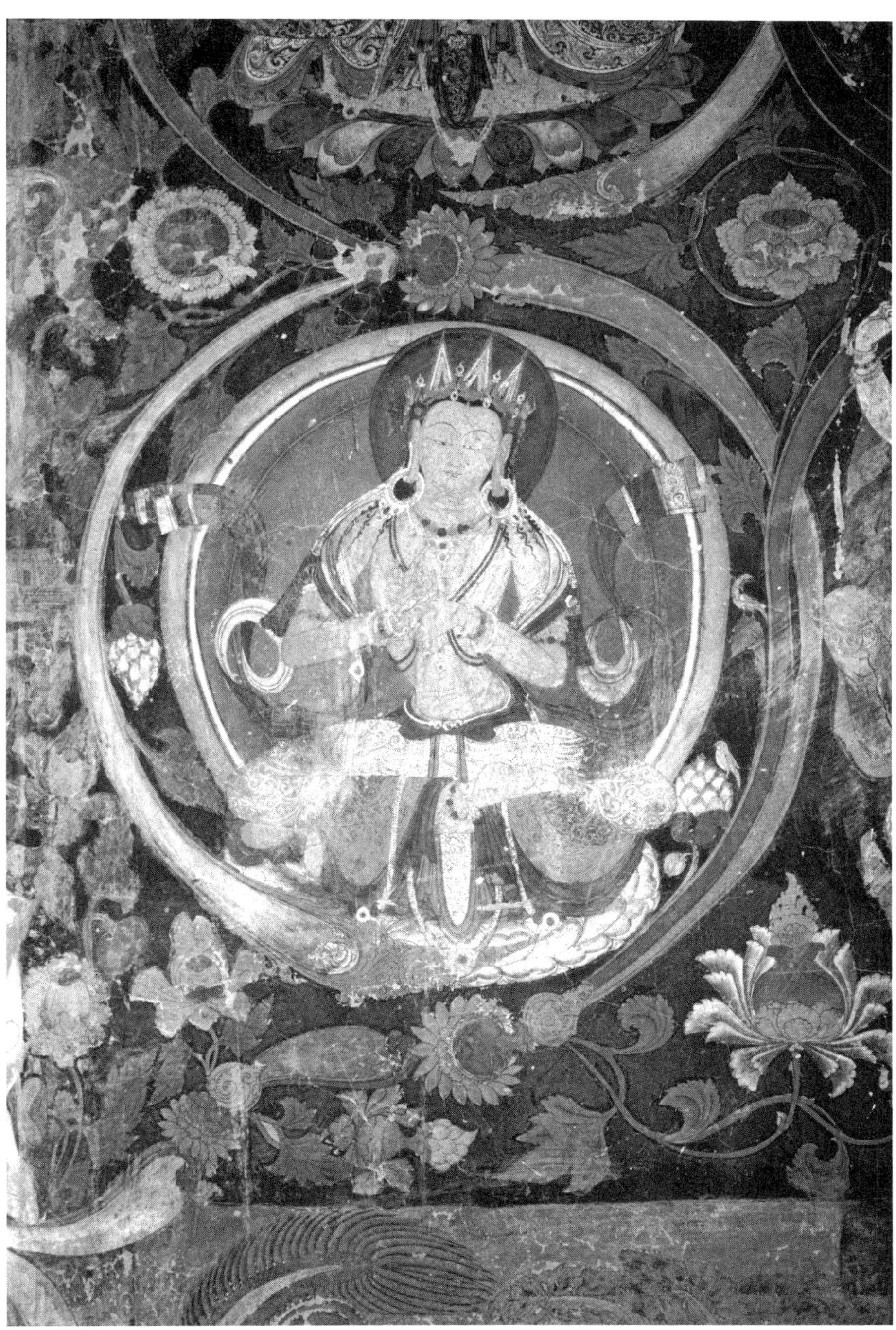

Figure 4.33. Tholing (West Tibet), Red Temple: subsidiary bodhisattva,
c. fifteenth century. WHAV JP93 426.

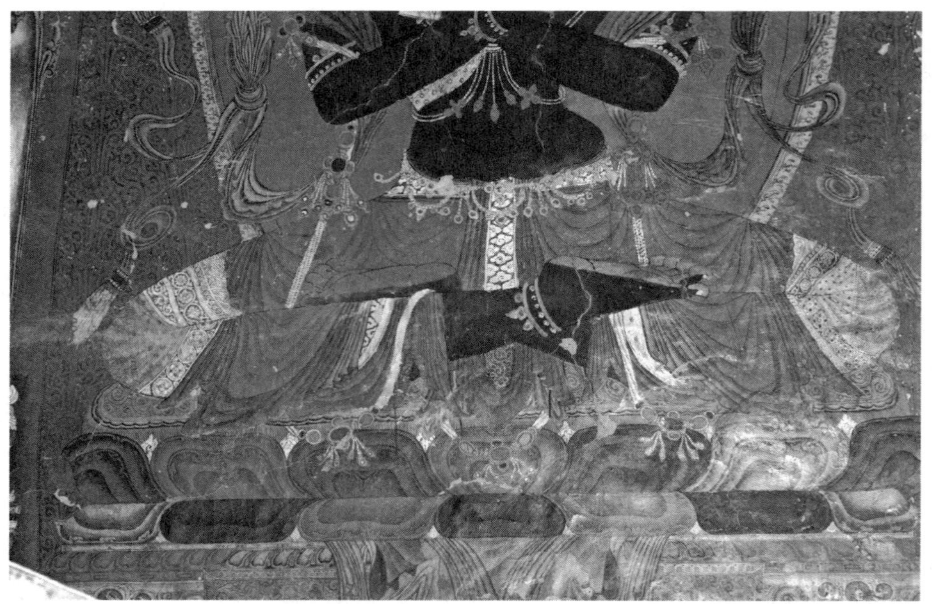

Figure 4.34. Tabo (Lahaul Spiti Dist., H.P.), Golden Temple: Vajradhara's dhoti, c. early sixteenth century.

specific dye and weaving techniques, necessarily carries with it meanings and cultural associations that are discussed at length in chapter 5. The complexity and specificity of the textile renderings, as seen at Tholing's Red Temple (figs. 4.27 and 4.33), is rather short-lived. In fig. 4.33 the deity wears a multicolored textile with detailed patterning featuring flying phoenixes at the hips, which then morphs into a scrolling foliate pattern. The attendant figures' dhotis from Tsaparang (fig. 4.29), Tholing (fig. 4.27), and Tabo (figs. 4.30 and 4.31) are good examples of the ways in which the paintings captured various dye techniques, such as the reverse dye method—seen specifically in figure 4.29 in the blue and red section of the garment that covers the attendant's knee and shin.[33] The drapery folds and textile patterns of the dhoti, especially for the subsidiary deities at Tsaparang and Tabo, are painted in less painstaking detail. Generally, these figures wear a simplified dhoti that is rendered in two or three colors. The Tabo example in figure 4.34, while still detailed in some places, has a limited palette. By the time this style is used at Tabo's cave temple (fig. 4.35) or at Nako's Gyapagpa Temple, there is considerable abbreviation and reduction in details such as textile designs, palette, and drapery patterns.

There is a wide range of jewelry motifs and bodily adornments featured in the paintings at Tholing, Tsaparang, and Tabo. For instance, the crowns are generally of three types: pointed plaques, rounded medallions

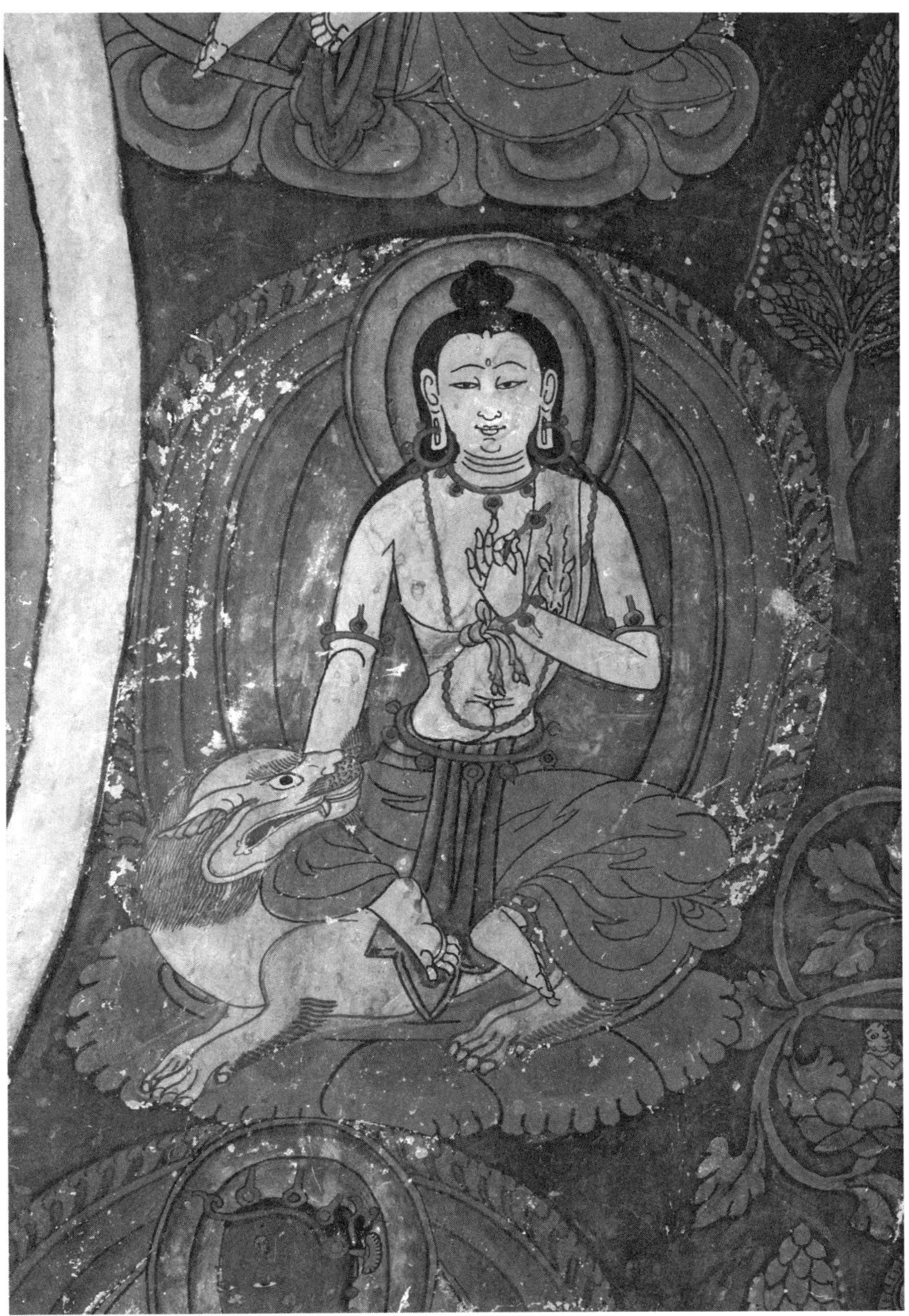

Figure 4.35. Tabo (Lahaul Spiti Dist., H.P.), Cave Temple: subsidiary deity,
c. late sixteenth century.

topped with finals, and cross-shaped tines. There seems to be an endless variation of designs for armbands, anklets, necklaces, and torso-chains from these three sites, but there is one consistent jewelry motif: the shin-length beaded necklace. This motif is carried over from Kashmiri aesthetics that had been widely used in the eleventh-century paintings of the western Himalaya.[34] While this is a repeated decorative motif seen on almost all figures, it is particularly noticeable on the attendant figures.

This visual analysis of these three temples helps to identify some of the defining features that appear not only in the apogee of the style, but throughout the wider painting tradition of the late medieval period. This analysis has also shown that while Tholing's and Tsaparang's Red Temples and Tabo's Golden Temple are strongly connected stylistically, they exhibit differences in decorative motifs, modeling techniques, and levels of intricacy, which suggest that these three painting programs were each executed by different workshops or group of artists. These variances in the courtly style of the Ngari painting tradition also help to demonstrate the style's range and scope. Awareness of different workshops and variances in the style contributes to documenting the richness and diversity of this style.

The Gyapagpa Program, Part of a Regional Idiom

Although the aforementioned characteristics define the height of the courtly idiom, many of these traits are also part of the visual vocabulary used in the larger late medieval Ngari painting tradition. I turn now to the wall paintings from Nako's Gyapagpa Temple, which I argue are a regional idiom of the Ngari painting tradition. To demonstrate their stylistic connection to the revival style or courtly idiom, I will analyze figural types, decorative motifs, and garment and textile designs. The point of this comparison is not to argue that the Gyapagpa paintings are part of the courtly idiom, but simply to reveal that the Gyapagpa paintings share the same vocabulary of forms that constitute the larger stylistic set to which both the courtly and regional idioms belong. In directly comparing a regional to courtly idiom, one first notices the dissonance between the idioms, as seen in the differences in palette, detail work, painterly lines, and materials. It is these points of difference with which I start the comparison.

The palette at the Gyapagpa Temple is considerably lighter and uses colors—such as orange, cream, and mustard yellow—that are not readily found at the sites of Tabo, Tholing or Tsaparang. These other sites favor a darker palette, dominant in reds, blues, and greens. Part of the difference in palettes can also be attributed to how much the paintings at Gyapagpa Temple have faded. Certainly the deities and lineage figures were all painted with red and blue nimbi against what was originally a dark blue background that has now faded to a slate blue. Given that the Gyapagpa paintings have suffered much more water damage than the other three sites, one wonders if there was not a closer match in the color saturation and the luster of paint, which has now been lost.

A more discernable difference between the Gyapagpa paintings and those of the courtly idiom is the level of detail. While the three other sites have intricately detailed textile patterning, jewelry motifs, and throne designs, the level of detail in corresponding elements at the Gyapagpa Temple is considerably less. None of the textiles in the Gyapagpa Temple, for instance, have elaborate patterns of flying phoenixes or replicate the effects of reverse-dye technique, both of which are found at the other three temples. Rather, the fabric and textiles are simply painted in two or three colors with little more than a few lines painted to indicate wrinkles and the fall of the fabric. The rich patterning and display of complex dye methods is missing entirely from the Gyapagpa program. We see this difference quite explicitly when looking at Vajradhara's dhoti from the Gyapagpa Temple (fig. 4.1). Although there is no patterning or textile work rendered, the dhoti's drapery and folding pattern bears a striking resemblance to the dhoti pattern of the Vajradhara figure at Tabo's Golden Temple (fig. 4.34). In particular there is one drapery effect that is used on both of these figures, which I briefly mentioned earlier in this chapter. The painter has created the illusion of a layer of fabric—blue with a red underside—falling toward the inner thigh and creating a subtle cascade of folds and color. This effect is not rendered at Tholing or Tsaparang. Although it is a small detail, it is worth noting such similarities between Nako and Tabo, as the latter was surely the primary source of inspiration for the Nako artists.

Another detail that is decidedly lacking at the Gyapagpa painting program is the foliate patterning. This decorative flourish—prominent at Tabo, Tsaparang, and Tholing in the nimbi, thronebacks, and lotus pedestals—is used sparingly at the Gyapagpa Temple, where it is only apparent in black-and-white coloring on lotus pedestals. This is especially apparent on the supporting platform for Prajñāpāramitā and her attendants (fig 2.24). This black-on-white foliate patterning is slightly different from the more subtle coloring of the foliate patterning used in the other temples, where one would more commonly find a dark blue–on–lighter blue or red-on-red color combination. These monochromatic foliate patterns evoke the image of damask weaves. The grisaille-like design is something else, however. While it is depicted at Tholing, Tsaparang, and Tabo temples, one sees it used sparingly (fig. 4.21). At Tholing, for instance, one noticed that this grisaille-like foliate patterning is used for a table at which one of the royal assembly scenes takes place.[35] As this table is used in a specifically royal context at Tholing, it raises the question of whether the black and white grisaille-like foliate patterning is meant to represent a royal or luxury good, perhaps such as ivory. This may, in fact, be the intended meaning of its use at Nako, as a platform made of luxury goods.

Lack of detailing is also seen in the figural depictions of the Gyapagpa Temple. None of the figures, except the wrathful deities on the west wall, is modeled in any way, giving a rather flat and one-dimensional effect. Moreover, some of the physical forms of the figures featured in the Gyapagpa Temple are quite different from the body types at the other temples. This is most evident with the lineage and monastic portraits, especially those rendered in a forward-facing position. Figures 2.7, 2.10, 2.23, and 4.13 feature figures that are quite similar to one another though not to the typical monk portrait type of the other three temples, where modeling and three-quarter positions are favored. The figures at the Gyapagpa Temple are painted in broad strokes, flat color, and without any modeling. Their facial features—such as the eyes, lips, and chin—are painted large and without subtle definition.

What these differences highlight is the breadth of this style. As the style moves from a courtly to regional expression, there is a discernible trend toward simplifying the formal elements of line and color. Consequently, the detailing is reduced, the figural forms flatter, and the palette less rich, modulated, and graduated.

Although these disparities are important to consider, ultimately, there are many more similarities than differences between the Gyapagpa paintings and the stylistic elements that constitute the courtly idiom. The examination of primary deities and attendant figures, as well as jewelry motifs and drapery patterns, reveals that the paintings of Gyapagpa Temple share the same stylistic vocabulary of the courtly idiom. As the basic characteristics of the courtly idiom were cited earlier in this chapter, I will simply list the shared elements between the Gyapagpa Temple and the courtly idiom. The pacific deities are rendered with broad shoulders, long torsos, and small waists, with one hip slightly elevated. They have a navel that is painted with a combination of horizontal and vertical lines. These figures generally have rather petite facial features with small noses and an incomplete jawline. The Buddha figures have other shared features—such as the long, narrow eyes and arching eyebrows. They have a double or split widow's peak and a rather rounded head shape, the silhouette of which extends past the ears and tapers at the lobes. This silhouette line creates a distinctive head shape. Also, the Buddha figures' angled earlobes impart a sense of dimension. Lastly, there is a considerable number of shared decorative features—for instance, they have three

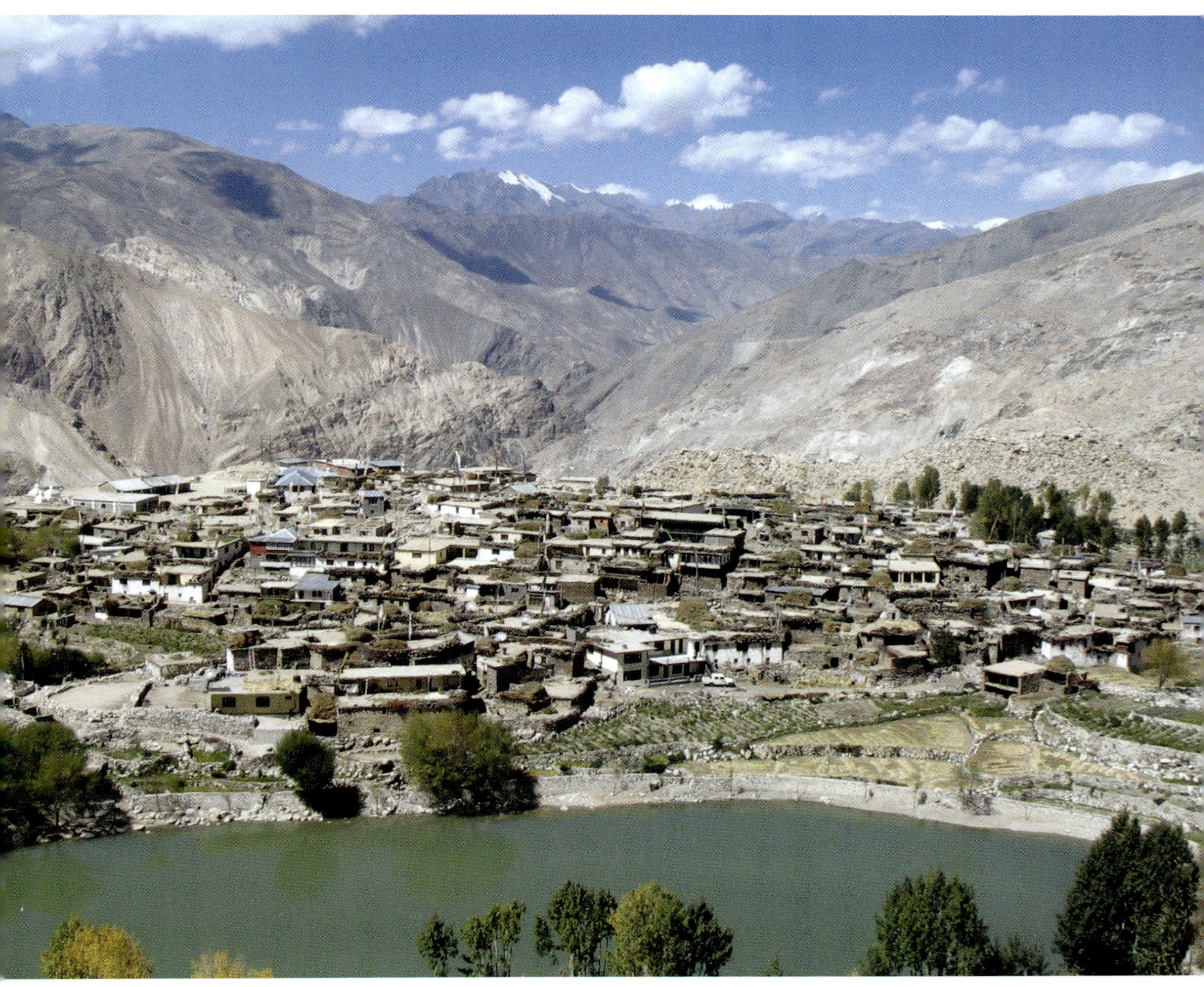

Plate 1. Nako Village with a view of the lake. MRK.

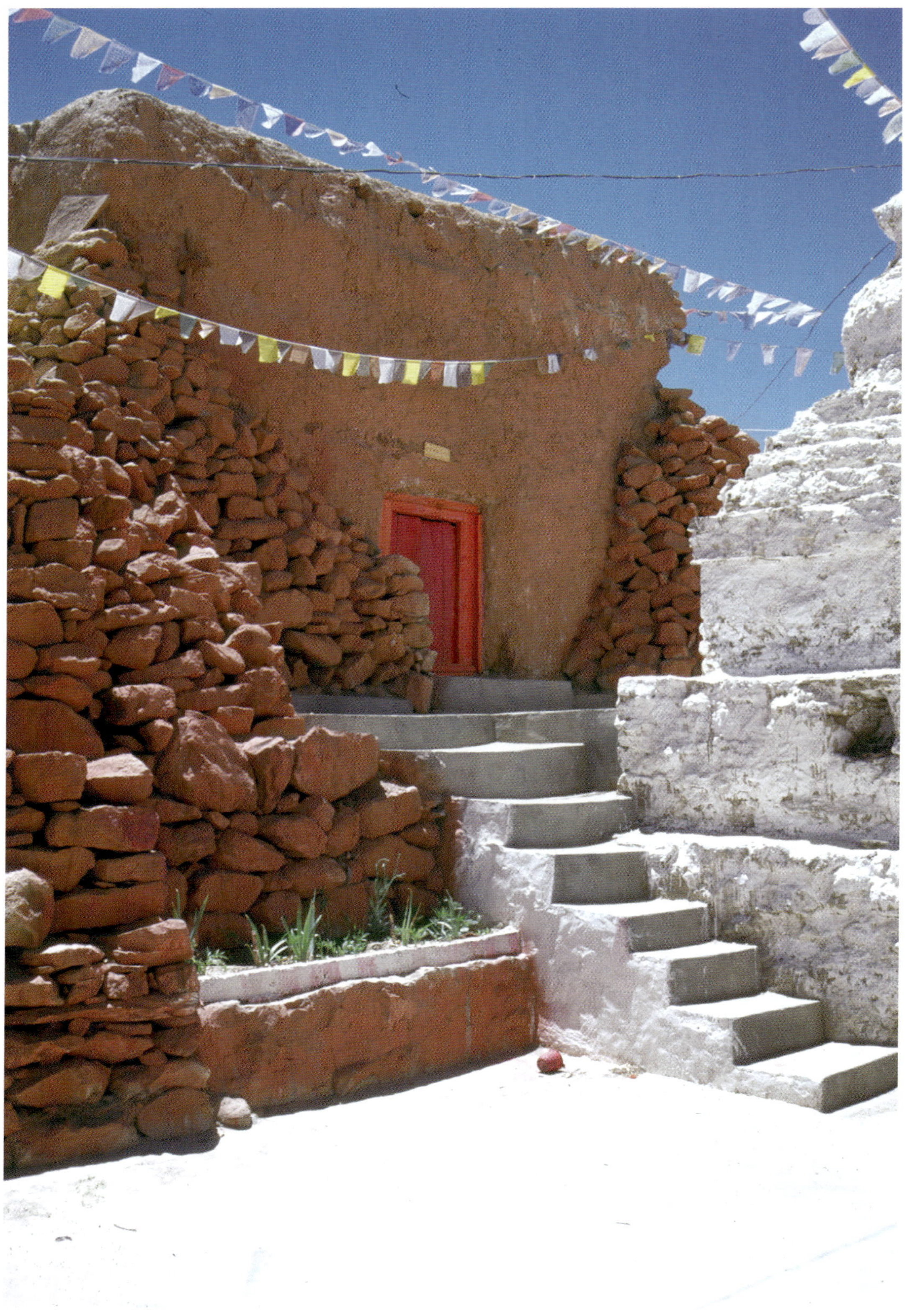

Plate 2. Exterior of Nako's Rgya 'phags pa (Gyapagpa) temple. WHAV CL96 117.

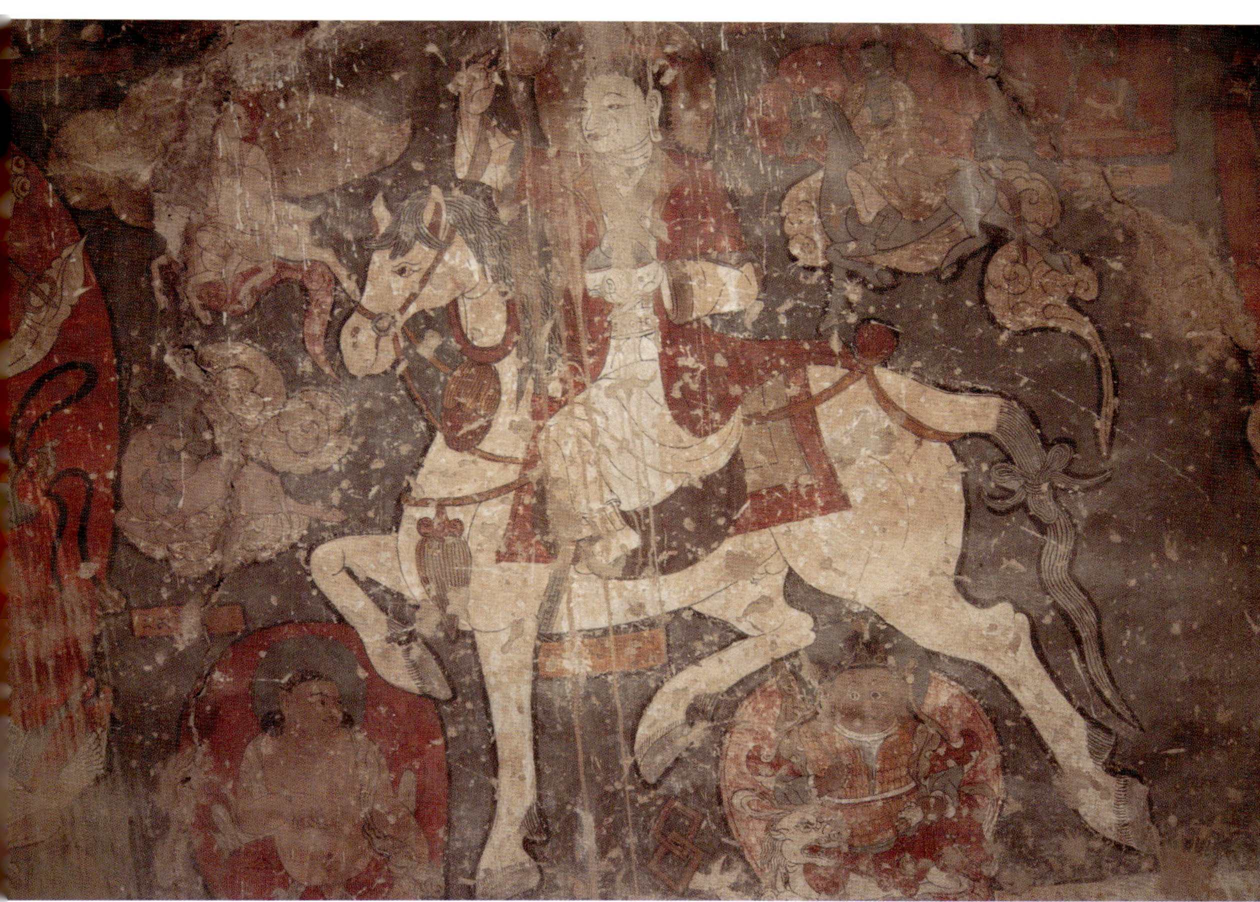

Plate 3. Gyapagpa Temple, west wall: Achi close-up.

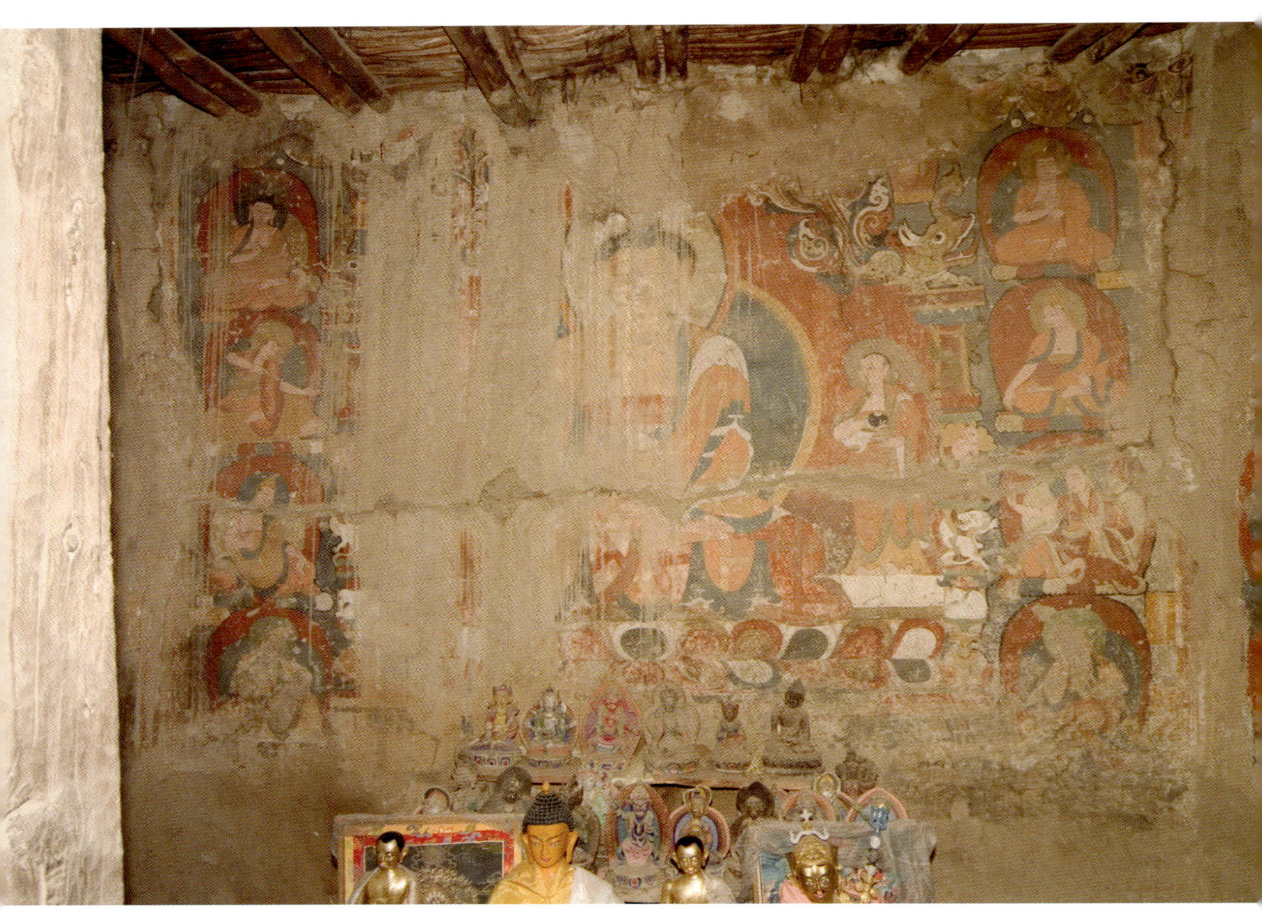

Plate 4. Gyapagpa Temple, east wall.

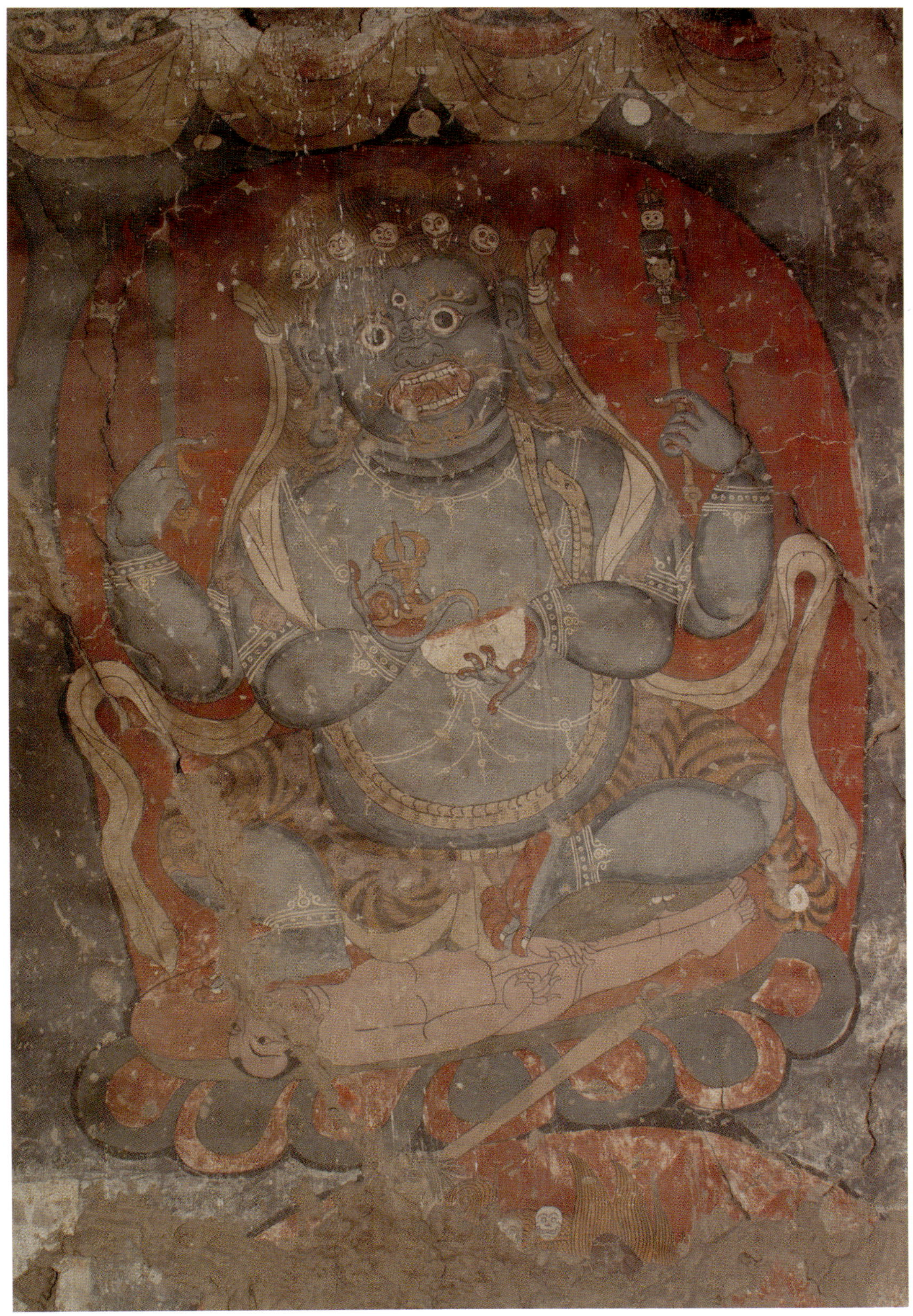

Plate 5. Gyapagpa Temple, west wall: four-armed Mahākāla.

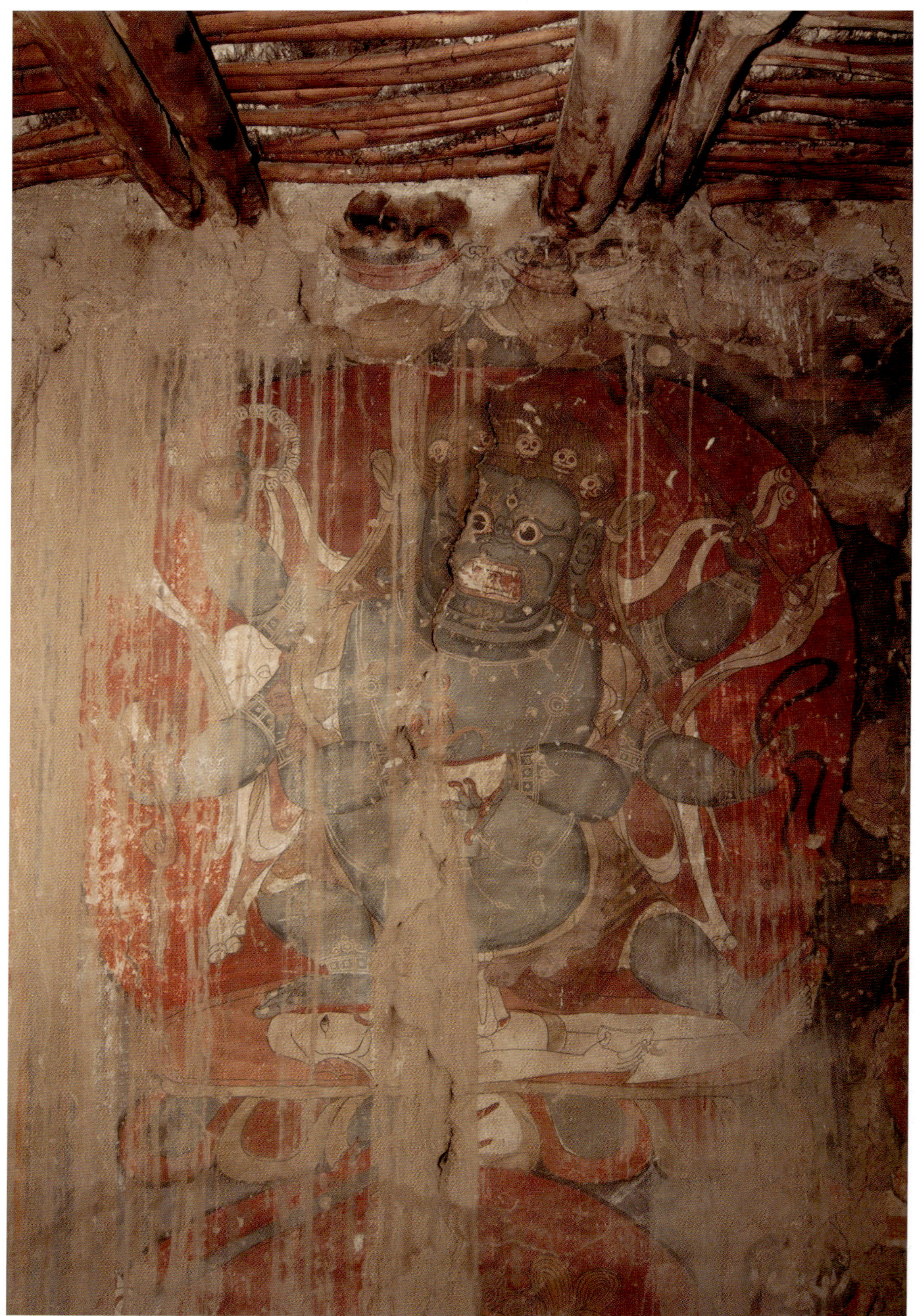

Plate 6. Gyapagpa Temple, west wall: six-armed Mahākāla.

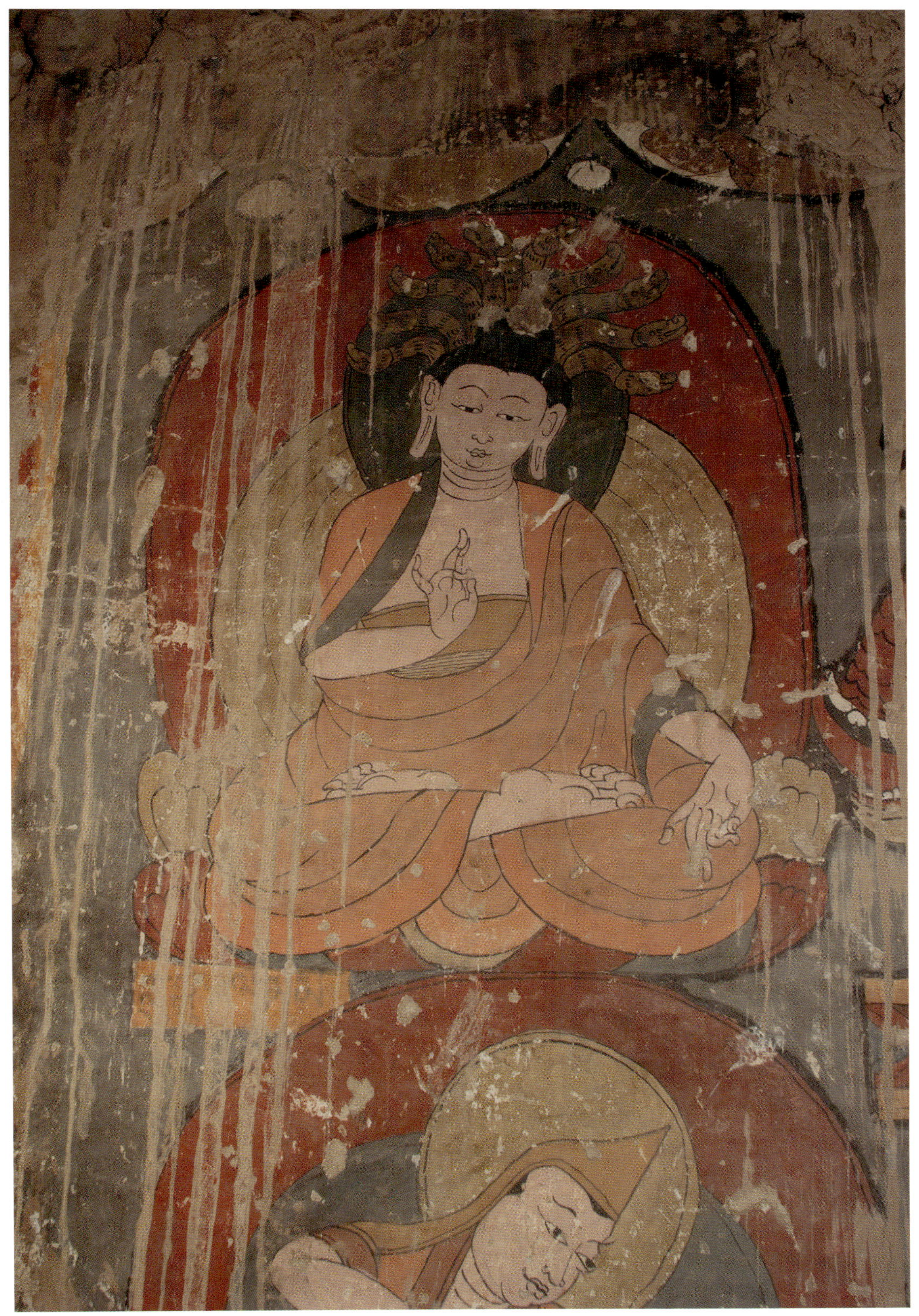

Plate 7. Gyapagpa Temple, east wall: Nāgārjuna portrait.

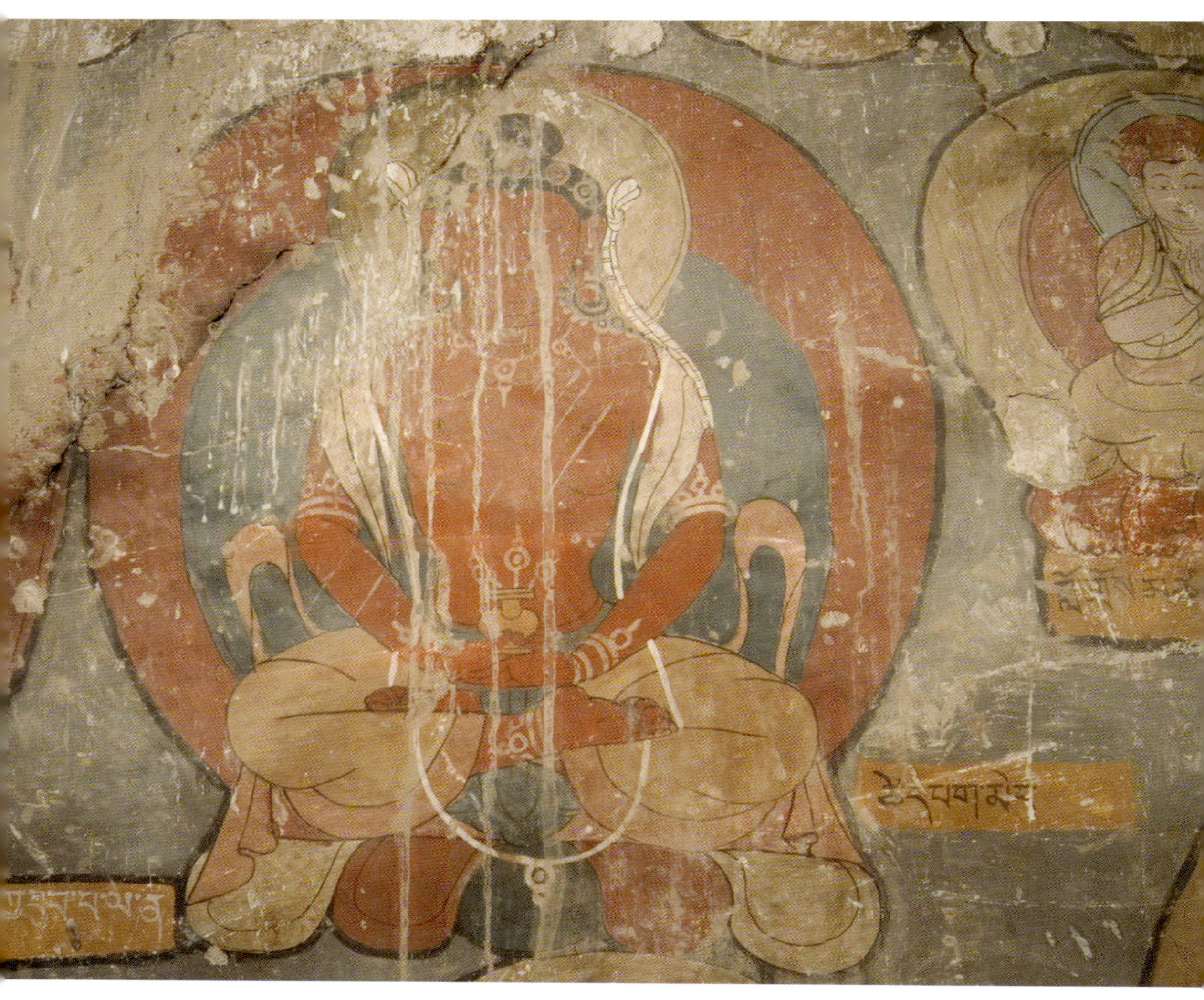

Plate 8. Gyapagpa Temple, south wall: Amitāyus.

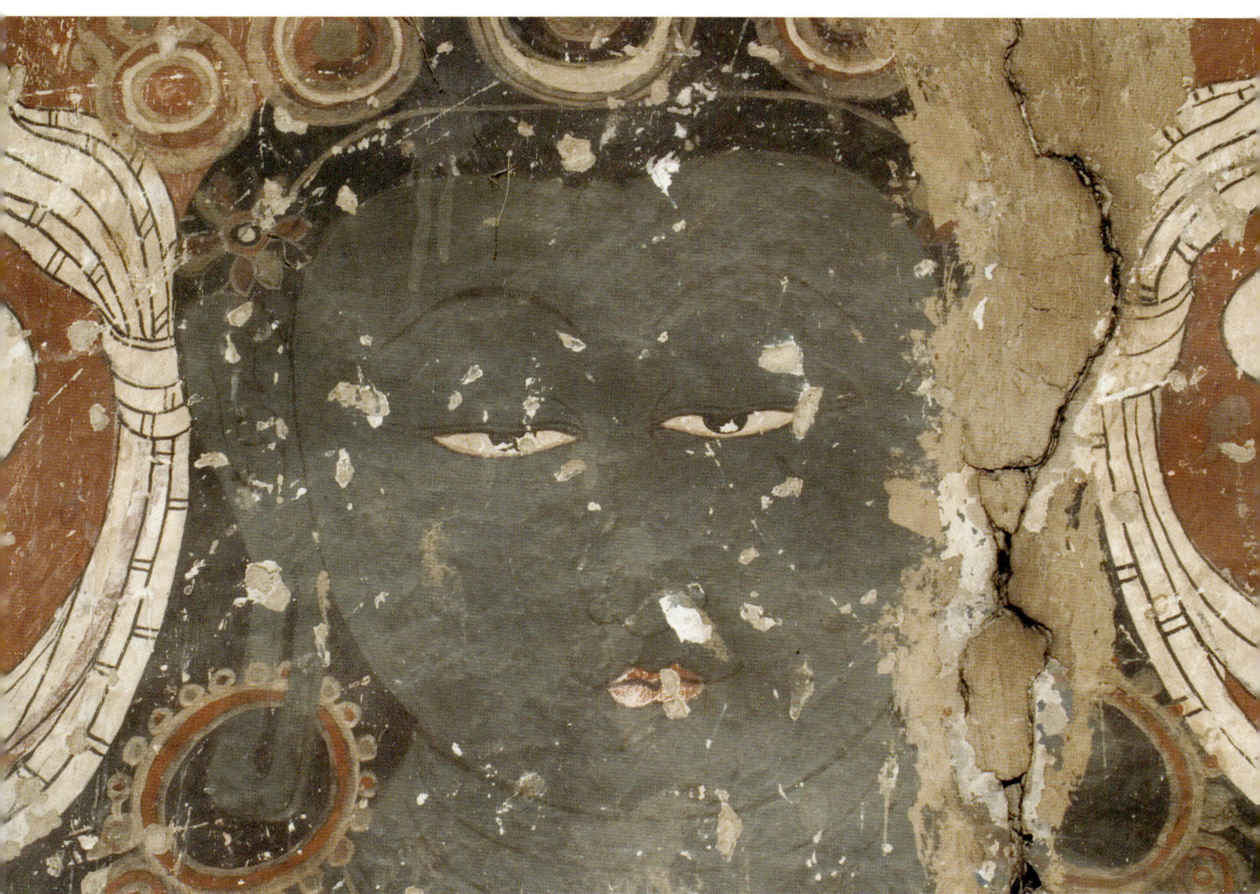

Plate 9. Gyapagpa Temple, north wall: detail of Vajradhara's face.

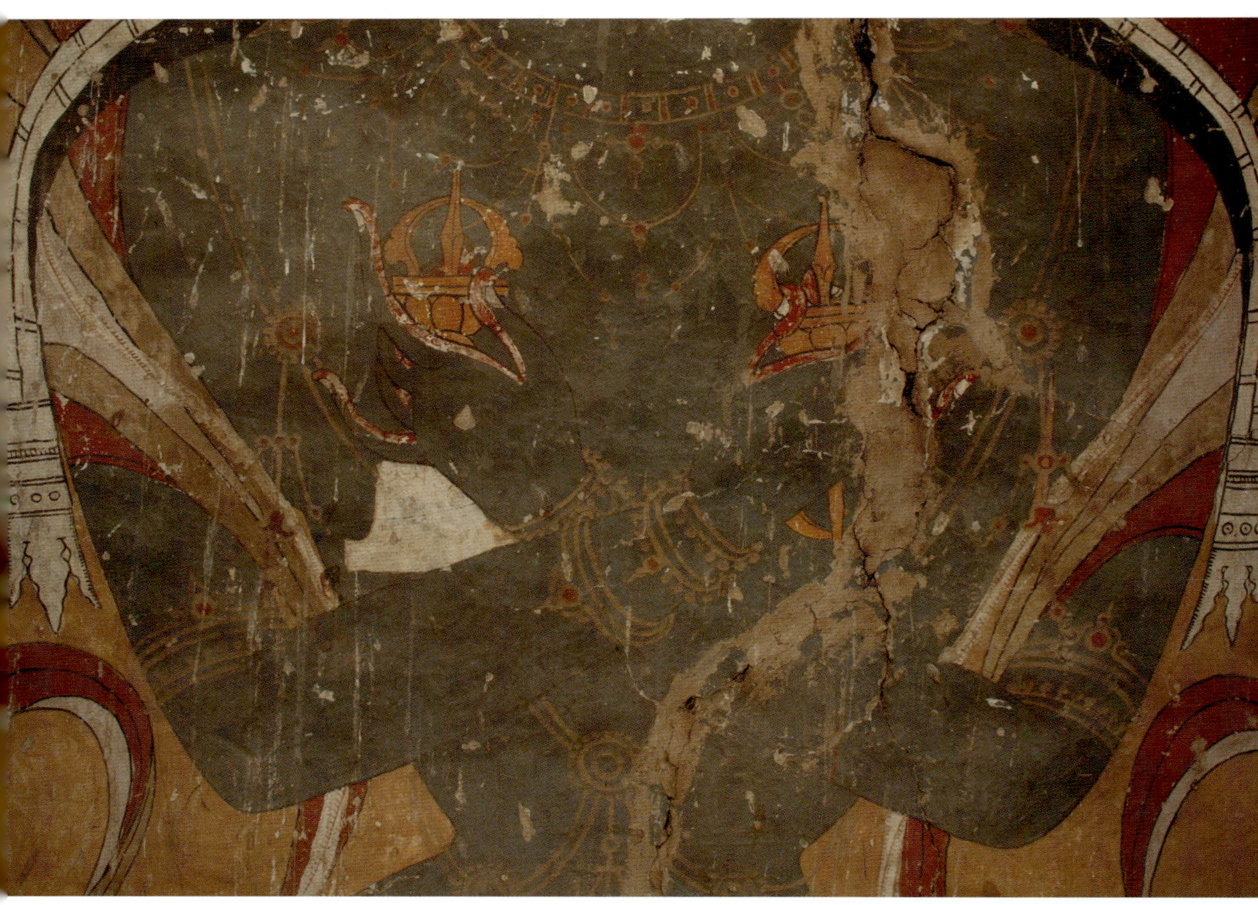

Plate 10. Gyapagpa Temple, north wall: detail of Vajradhara's torso.

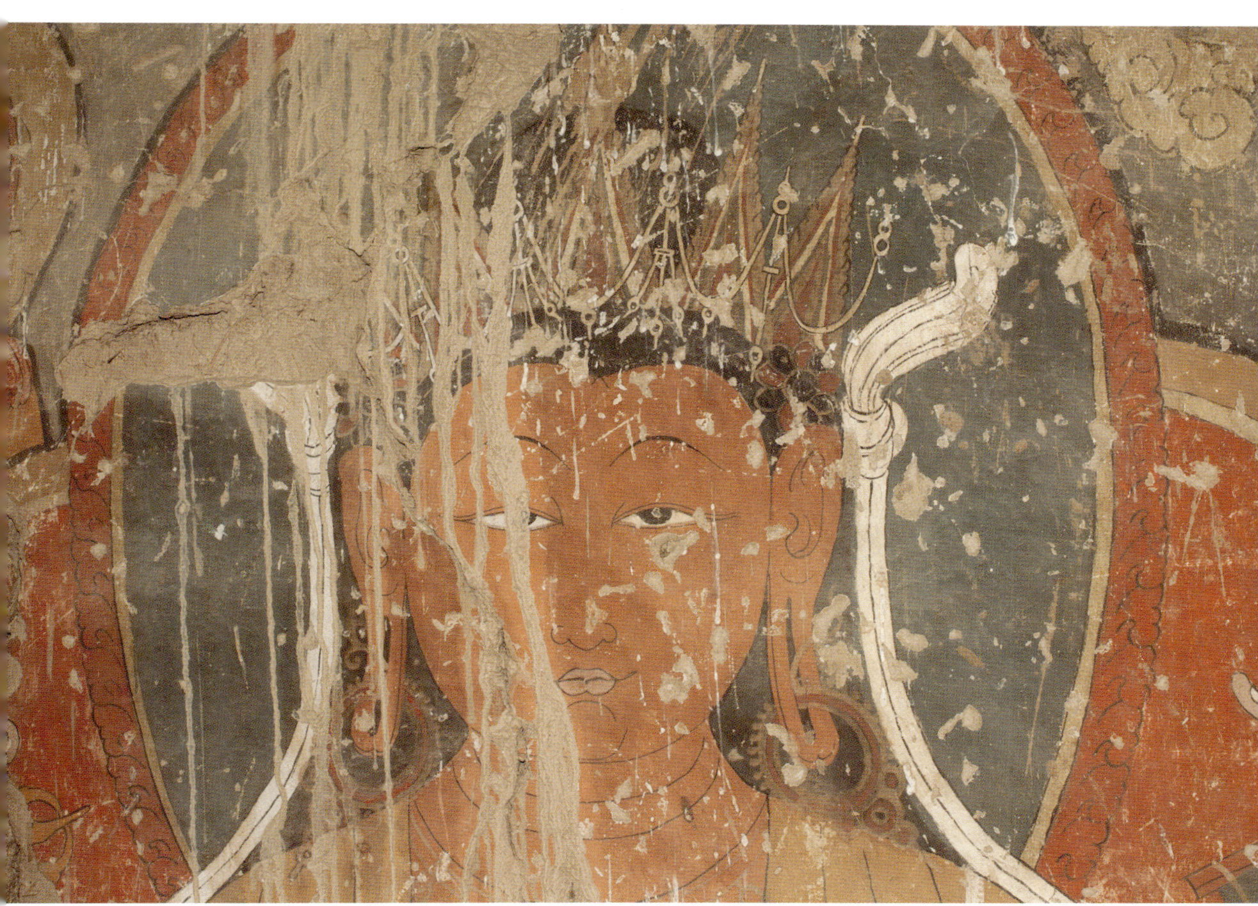

Plate 11. Gyapagpa Temple, south wall: Prajñāpāramitā's head with crown.

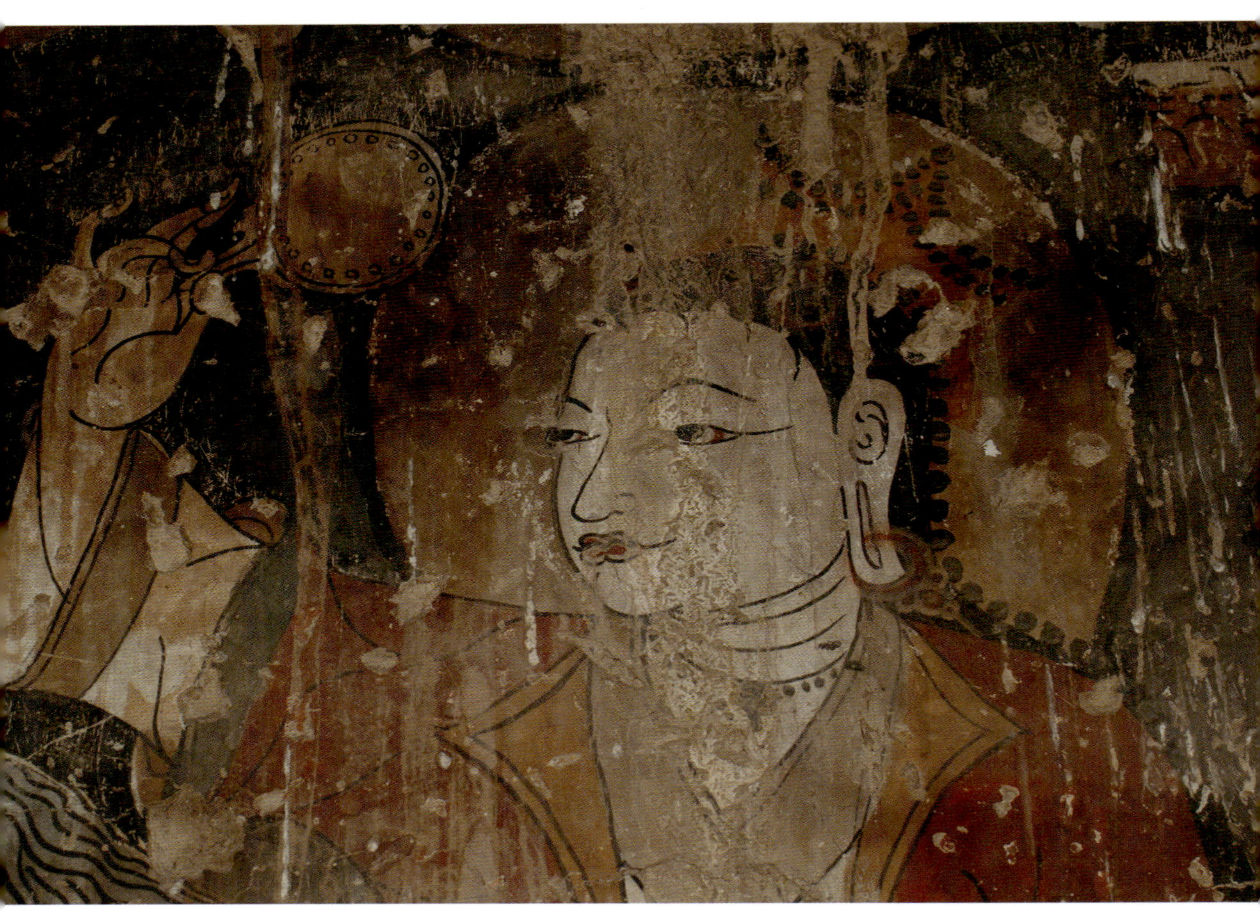

Plate 12. Gyapagpa Temple, west wall: Achi's face.

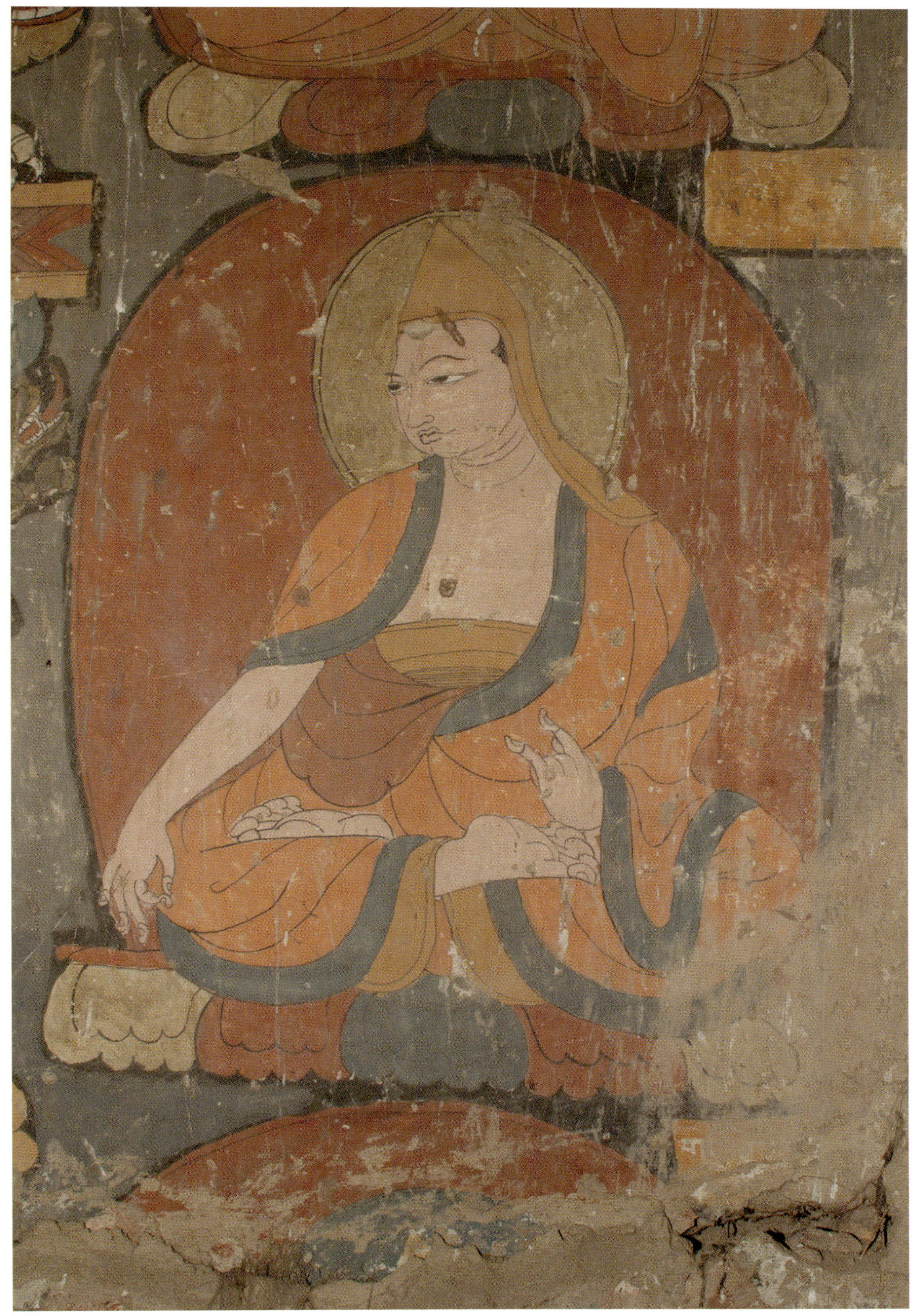

Plate 13. Gyapagpa Temple, east wall: commentator ("Six Ornaments and Two Supreme Ones").

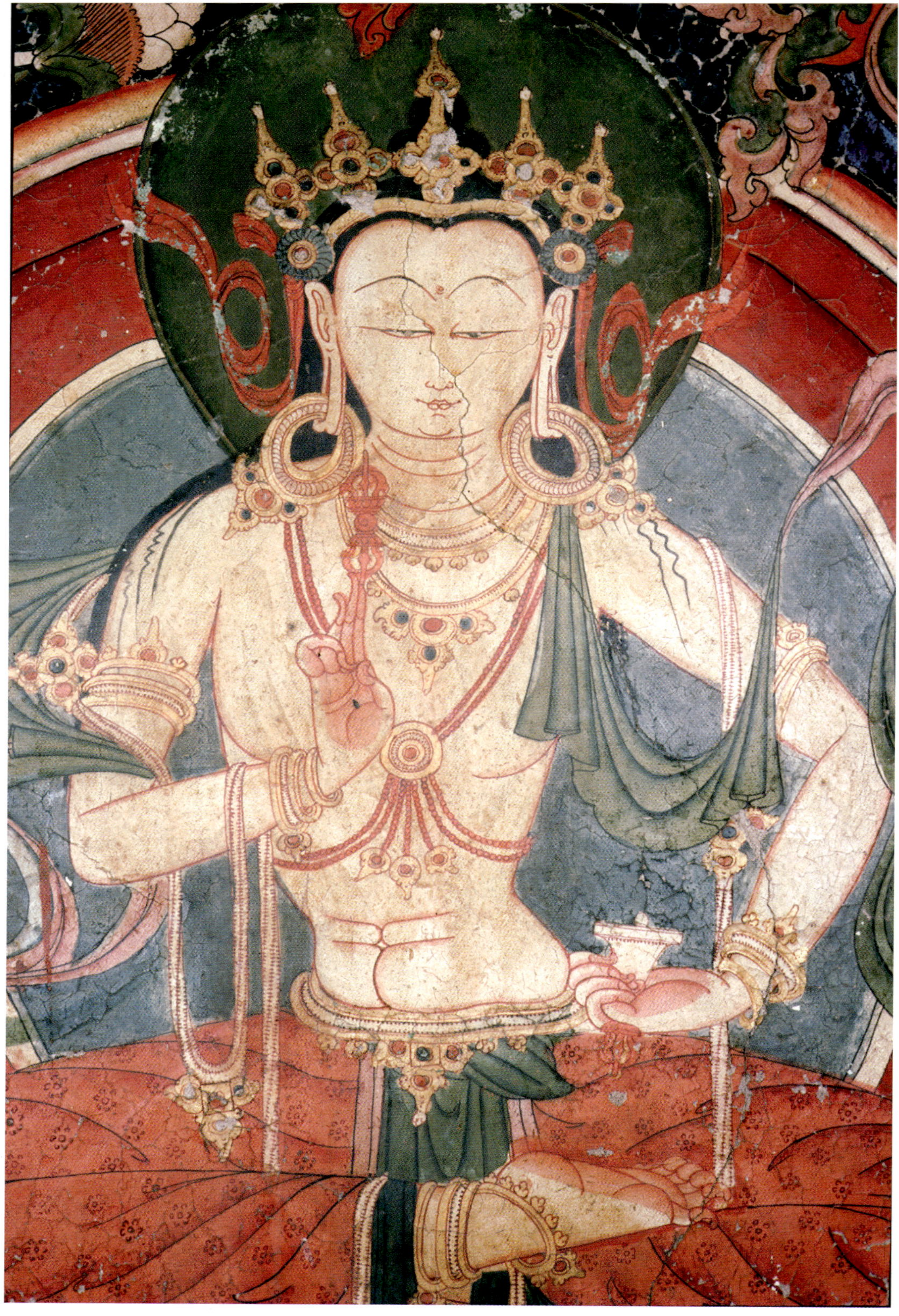

Plate 14. Tholing (West Tibet), Red Temple: white subsidiary deity,
c. fifteenth century. WHAV JP93 479.

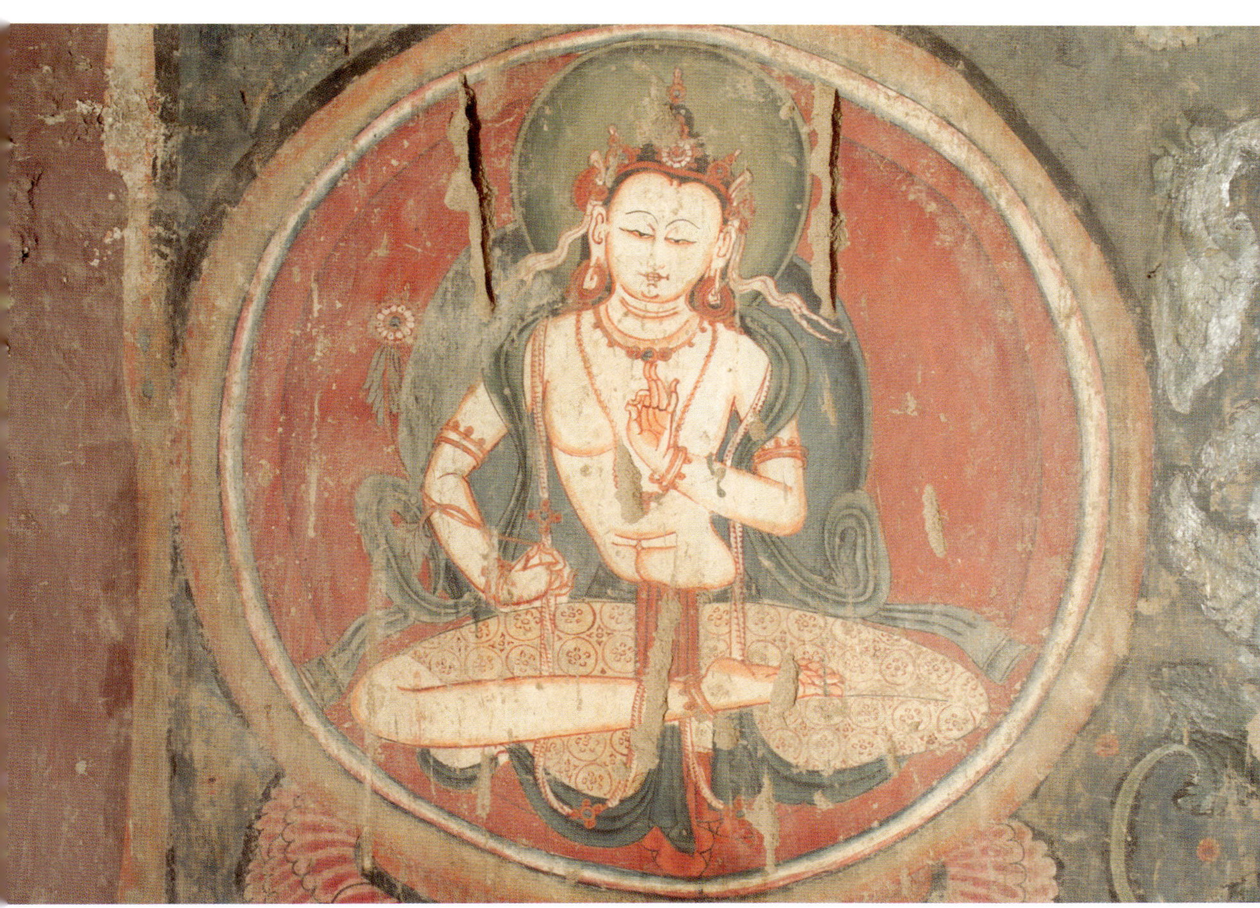

Plate 15. Tabo (Lahaul Spiti Dist., H.P.), Golden Temple: white subsidiary bodhisattva, early sixteenth century.

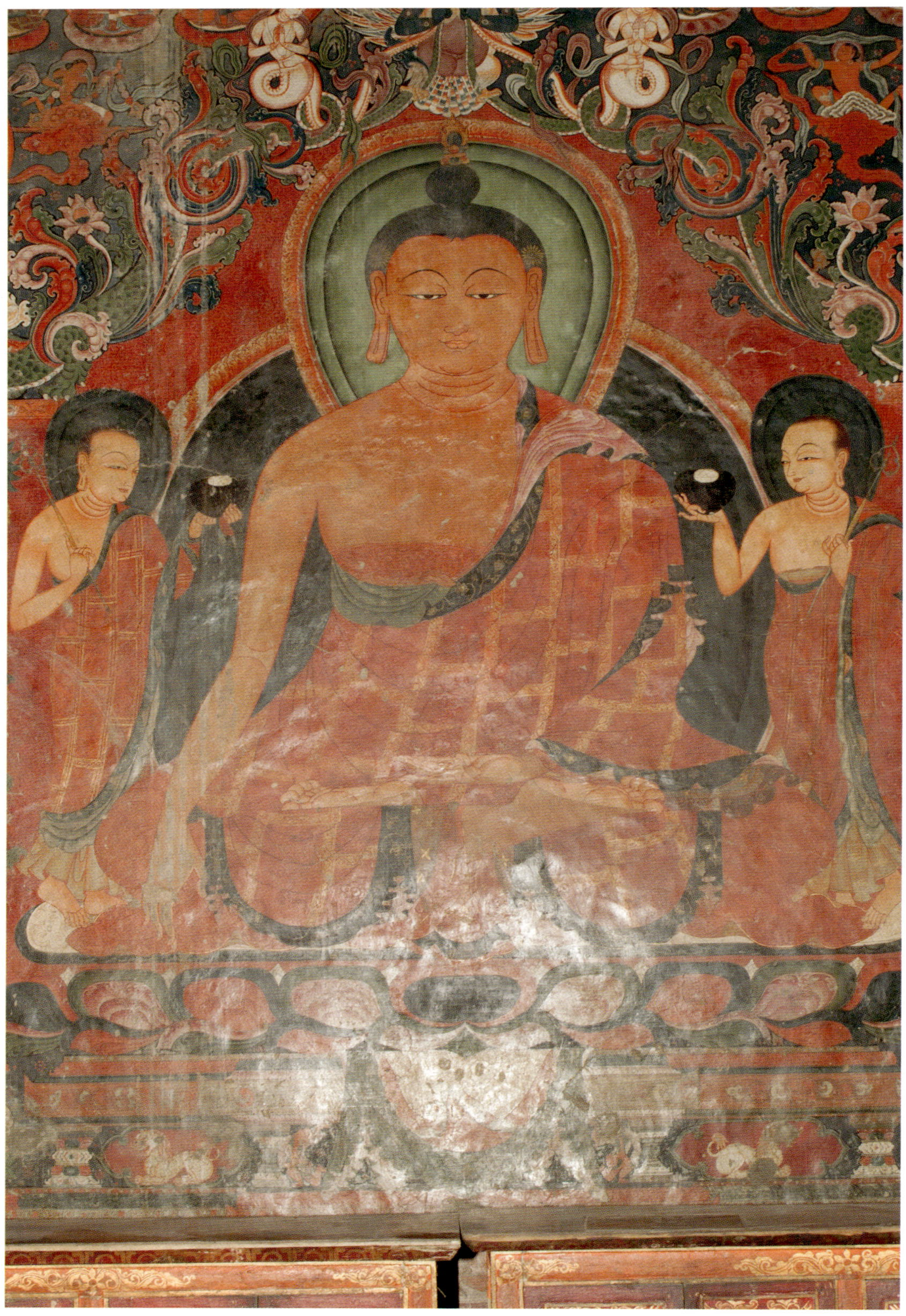

Plate 16. Tabo (Lahaul Spiti Dist., H.P.), Golden Temple: Śākyamuni Buddha, early sixteenth century.

crown types in common, as well as various necklace designs and garment designs.

In the analysis that follows I will examine in greater detail the shared visual vocabulary mentioned above, as well as the strong formal elements connecting the painting programs at Nako's Gyapagpa and Tabo's Golden Temples. In discussing these similarities, it will become evident that the later generation of artists at the Gyapagpa Temple looked to the wall paintings of Tabo's Golden Temple to inform their painting style. In fact, I suggest that Nako's artists referred to Tabo's paintings above and beyond the painting programs at the Red Temples of Tsaparang and Tholing. Although Nako's artists would have had an awareness of the painting programs at all three Buddhist centers—Tabo, Tholing, and Tsaparang—they had immediate access to Tabo, which was only sixty-five kilometers from Nako. This relative proximity to the religious and political hub of Tabo, despite the fact that it followed Gelug instead of Nako's Drigung tradition, allowed Nako's late-sixteenth-century artists access to a specific iteration of the courtly style.

The most compelling visual comparison can be made between the Śākyamuni Buddha figures of the Gyapagpa Temple and Tabo's Golden Temple. Both Śākyamuni Buddha figures are enthroned on an ornate lotus pedestal with a surrounding throneback composed of scrolling *makara* tails. Both figures wear robes rendered with similar drapery and folding patterns at the chest, proper left shoulder and elbow, and at the legs (plates 4 and 16). Looking carefully at the drapery over the Buddha's left shoulder we see a lighter underside of the garment revealed. At Tabo it is rendered in a pinkish hue, and at Nako the underside is painted in an eggshell color. From this crescent-shaped swatch of color, the garment falls into a tiered pattern near the elbow. This similarity in drapery is particularly noteworthy when one considers how different the Buddha's drapery at Tabo is from that of Tsaparang's Buddha figure.

Correspondences are also evident when comparing the faces of two Śākyamuni Buddhas from the Golden Temple and the Gyapagpa Temple (figs. 4.5 and 4.26). Here the most striking parallel is in the shape of their eyes. Following the courtly idiom, the eyebrows arch over long, heavily lidded eyes. Their ears are the same basic shape, with the edge of the upper portion of the ear, known as the helix, curving into a slight indentation. The elongated fleshy lobes flare out slightly from the face and are rendered with a second line to indicate their width. Where the helix and lobe meet, approximately three-quarters of the distance down the ear, is the exact point where the outer hairline ends. Some paintings executed in this style, such as at Tsaparang's Red Temple, show the hairline to continue past this point and only taper at the lobe. This particular detail reveals just how closely the artists of the Gyapagpa Temple were referencing the paintings at Tabo's Golden Temple. Unfortunately, mud covers much of the Gyapagpa Buddha, preventing a fuller visual analysis of the lips, jawline, and neck.

Two types of attendant figures from the Gyapagpa Temple reveal other close connections to Tabo's Golden Temple. The white attendant on the north wall of the Gyapagpa Temple displays a particularly strong association with one of the attendant figures at Tabo's Golden Temple (figs. 4.8 and 4.31). In comparing both, it is clear that they share certain idiosyncrasies, such as positions of their hands, indentations at the forearm and bicep on their proper right arms, torque in the waist, and navel articulation. Moreover, their dhotis are rendered in a similar fashion, with a low waistline that undulates and is tied with a large stylized bow below the navel. Both figures wear a knotted sash that hovers at the sides of their thighs. Lastly, these two attendants wear distinctive white, beaded necklaces that fall below the knee.

Although the Tabo attendant is painted with more closely observed facial features than that of the Gyapagpa Temple, the two figures share similar features—such as the double widow's peak, bow-shaped eyes, small nose, and lobed lips, as well as indented earlobes—all of which are typical of the style. It should be noted that the attendant figure's face from Tabo's Golden Temple (see fig. 4.31) is a basic type used throughout the program, as is clear when one compares the attendant figure's face to the faces of bodhisattvas painted on the west wall (plate 15). While the bodhisattva figure's face at Tabo's Golden Temple is modeled and more subtly rendered, its basic proportions and features are seen in the white attendant figure. At the Gyapagpa Temple this face type is also seen on another figure—Nāgārjuna on the east wall. In comparison, the Gyapagpa paintings are more simply executed, as there are no flourishes in the line work or in modeling. Nonetheless, there is, without a doubt, a resonance among these faces.

As for the jewelry motifs of the Gyapagpa Temple, it is clear that the artists were working with an awareness of various motifs in circulation at places such as Tholing, Tsaparang, and Tabo. Especially interesting is the connection between Vajradhara's jewelry from the Gyapagpa Temple, which is typical of most of the jewelry types and motifs found in this temple, to figures painted in Tholing's and Tsaparang's Red Temples. Plate 14, for instance, reveals the commonalities in the teardrop-shaped motif used on the bracelets and torso chain, as well as the similarly fashioned earrings and crown. Although the delicacy of Vajradhara's necklace and hanging pendant from the torso chain are not exactly the same in Tholing's figure, there are still strong connections between the designs of the two, suggesting that each workshop was working with an

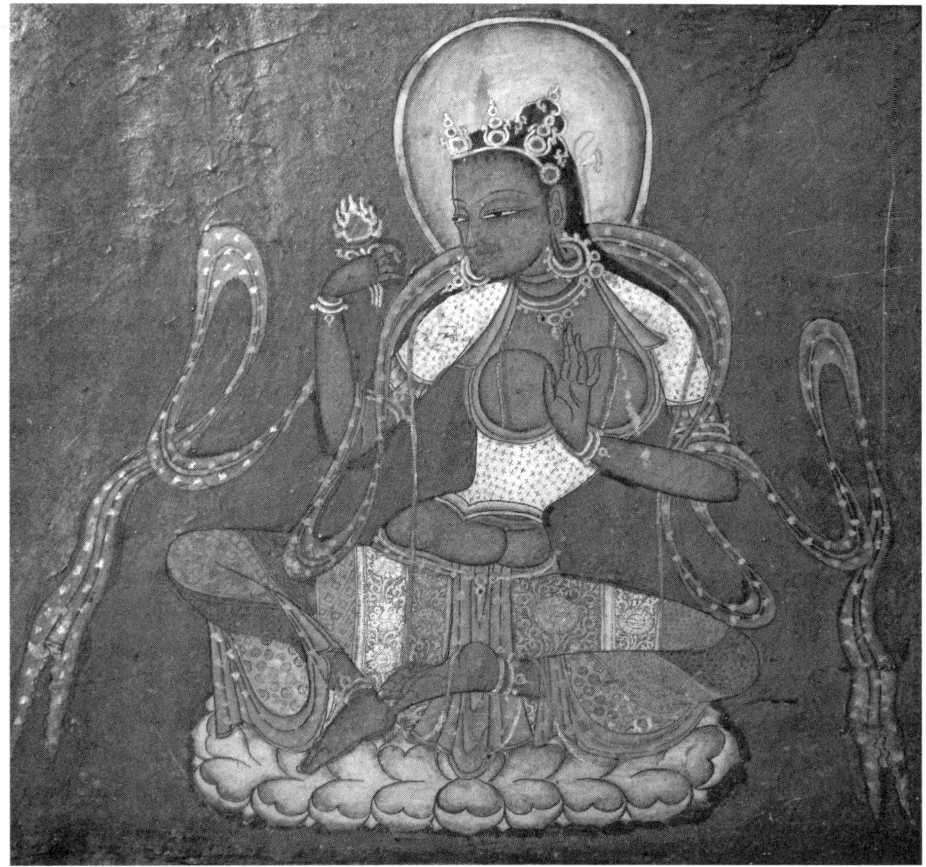

Figure 4.36. Tsaparang (West Tibet) Red Temple: deity with crown,
c. fifteenth century, RNL.

awareness of certain motifs. This is true when one considers the crown
motifs used at the Gyapagpa Temple. Particularly notable is the similarity
between the crown Vajradhara wears in the Gyapagpa Temple (fig. 4.2)
and that featured on one of the female subsidiary deities in Tsaparang's
Red Temple (fig. 4.36). This crown is a variation of one of the three crown
types previously discussed. What makes Nako's crown slightly different
from Tsaparang's is the way each round medallion is teardrop shaped and
embellished with a foliate framing device. Prajñāpāramitā, painted on
Gyapagpa's south wall, wears a crown of five pointed triangular-shaped
plaques (plate 11). This is one of the most common crown types of this
West Tibetan painting style (figs. 4.23, 4.24, and 4.33).

This comparison between the painting programs at the Gyapagpa
Temple and those executed in the courtly idiom demonstrate that the
Gyapagpa paintings are in keeping with the larger Ngari painting tradi-
tion. The painterly particulars of thick and sometimes uneven outlining,

unmodulated color, simple textile patterning, and lack of modeling characteristic of the artists at the Gyapagpa Temple reveal the very specific ways in which the style morphs over the century it is in use. We must keep in mind that the Gyapagpa Temple was painted nearly one hundred years after the establishment of this style's high point, and therefore the Gyapagpa paintings were certainly executed by a later generation of artists who likely were not as well trained. Moreover, Nako's artists did not have access to high quality materials as can be seen in the faded. The difference in materials and skill may have been a result of patronage, although this remains speculative.

The Missing Link: Tabo Cave Paintings

In order to understand better the *formenspaltung* between the Gyapagpa paintings and those at Tabo, Tholing, and Tsaparang, I address another site: Tabo's Cave Temple. Hewn out of the living limestone and quartzite rock,[36] meditation caves dot the hillside northeast of the main village of Tabo.[37] Amid these single-cell meditation caves is a larger complex of four interconnected rooms. These rock-hewn rooms, unlike the meditation cells, were dug deeper into the rock, creating comparatively more spacious environs that could accommodate several people at once. One of the four rooms likely functioned as a dining area, another was for food preparation, a third for large gatherings, and the last of these rooms served as a small temple or prayer hall with an extensive painting program.

Composition and Iconography

Due to significant water damage, the current iconographic program only spans portions of three walls: north, west and east; the south wall, which is also the entrance/exit wall, is completely damaged. The paintings that still exist provide information about the iconographic and religious history of the cave temple as well as its various painting phases. Upon entering the temple, one sees the north wall, which is organized around three images. Centrally positioned is a figure of Śākyamuni with an attendant on either side (fig. 4.37). To the left of center is a depiction of Maitreya, the Buddha of the future, and to the right is Mañjuśrī, the bodhisattva of wisdom. This triad is commonly depicted in post-fifteenth-century paintings in Tabo's temple complex located in the village below. On the west wall there appear to be three bodhisattvas, one Buddha, and finally a historical figure, which can be identified as Tsongkapa, flanked by his two students: Mkhas grub rja (Kedrup [1385–1438]) and Rgyal tshab rje (Gyaltsab [1364–1432]). To the left of Tsongkapa is positioned Amitābha, who is pictured in his Pure Land abode; Avalokiteśvara, in

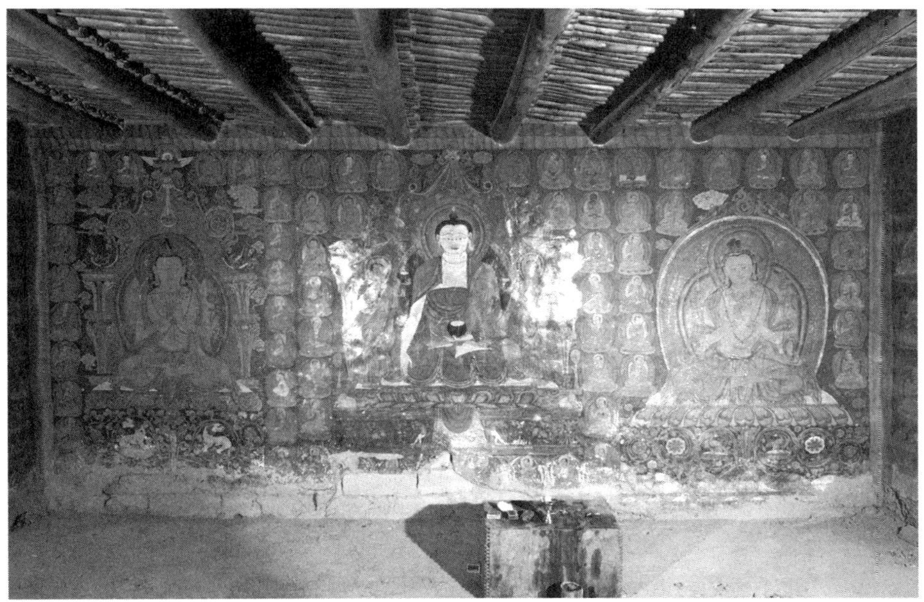

Figure 4.37. Tabo (Lahaul Spiti Dist., H.P.), Cave Temple, central (north) wall, c. late sixteenth century.

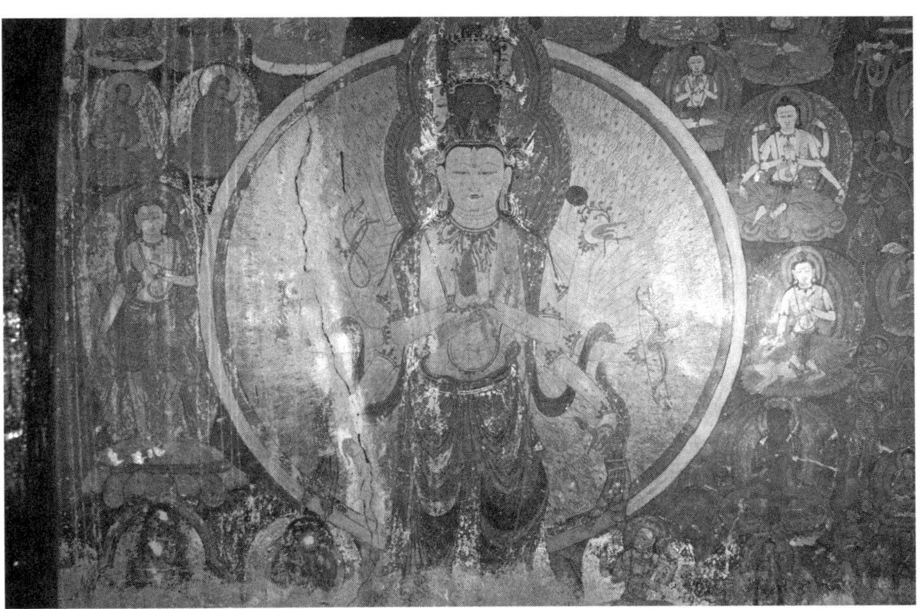

Figure 4.38. Tabo (Lahaul Spiti Dist., H.P.), Cave Temple, west wall: Avalokiteśvara, c. late sixteenth century.

his eleven-faced and thousand-armed manifestation (fig. 4.38), follows Amitābha. Water damage and poor repainting prevent one from accurately determining the identities of the next two female deities. On the east wall there seems to be a Gelugpa figure with a Tibetan Buddhist text in his lap. The only other images that have survived water damage are the Medicine Buddha, flanked by two attendants, and a partial image of another Buddha.

Style

Stylistically, the cave-temple paintings should be understood as part of the larger Ngari painting tradition of the fifteenth and sixteenth centuries; they are not, however, part of the courtly idiom. As the cave temple has no extant inscriptional evidence that would help to date the temple, I suggest that the painting cycle in the cave temple postdates the style's courtly idiom by a half a century, which dates it to the middle or late period of the sixteenth century. These cave paintings can be associated with the larger Ngari tradition because the painting program displays many of the same features as this larger style from West Tibet during the fifteenth through seventeenth centuries. These paintings are particularly useful in tracing the process of this style's gradual morphological disassociation from its high point, the courtly idiom. This can be seen, in particular, in the figural forms and decorative motifs. When one examines the image of the bodhisattva Avalokiteśvara figure in the cave temple, it is clear that this figure shares many of the same features that define this style, such as the long, thin eyes; double widow's peak; gap between the neck and jaw lines; and ears with thick lobes (fig. 4.38). Also, the navel is articulated in the same way as in the other figures from Tabo, Tholing, and Tsaparang. Many of the jewelry and decorative motifs of this figure are also consonant with the larger style, such as the distinctive pointed-plaque crown type. Differences are also discernible, as seen in the use of line and color; both are simplified. As noted earlier in this chapter, the formal elements of line and color are abbreviated as the style morphs and changes from its courtly idiom to its larger regional idiomatic expressions.

There are many bodhisattva attendant types at Tabo's cave temple, but here I focus on one (fig. 4.39) to demonstrate the ways in which the cave temple attendant falls within the parameters of the figural type and decorative motifs of the larger Ngari painting tradition. This figure is closely aligned with the figural type also found at Tabo's Golden and Nako's Gyapagpa Temples, as can be seen in the facial features, widow's peak, jaw delineation, and garment type. This attendant also illustrates

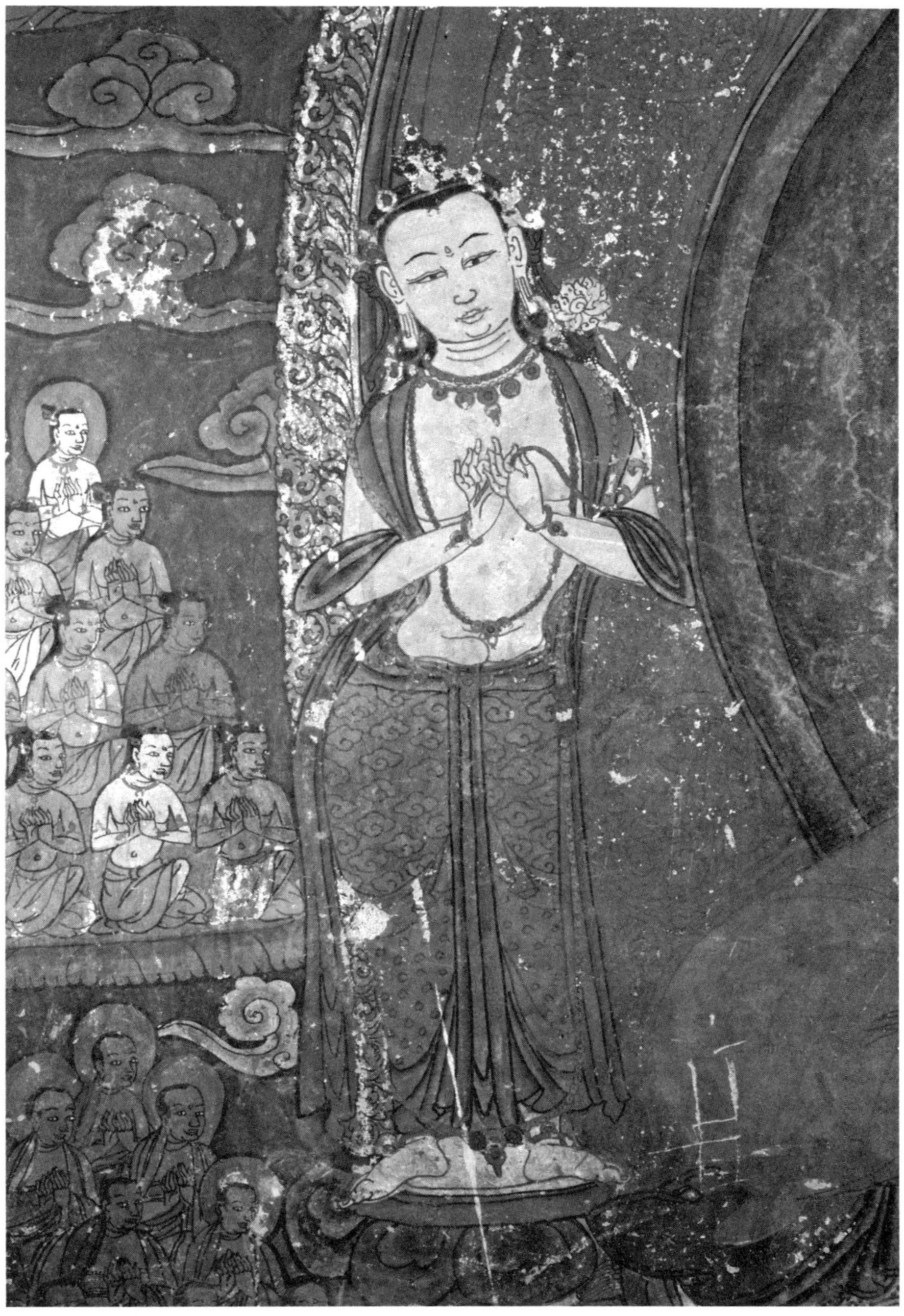

Figure 4.39. Tabo (Lahaul Spiti Dist., H.P.), Cave Temple: attendant figure,
c. late sixteenth century.

an important development: a shift in body proportions. The figure in figure 4.39 has shorter legs, which is an alteration also evident at Nako's Gyapagpa Temple paintings, especially the bodhisattva attendants located on the south wall (fig. 2.24).

Changes to this regional style can be traced by analyzing the slight but significant differences between the paintings comprising the apogee style with those of the later expression of the style, such as Nako or Tabo's cave temple. Lack of modeling ranks as one of the most significant alterations noticed in the later paintings. The omission of shading and highlighting creates a flatter figural form. Another change easily traced from the beginning to end of this style can be seen in the irregular use of textile patterns. In place of detailed patterning there is an increased reliance on simplified marks and designs such as hatch marks, circles, and cloud motifs. In many cases patterns are rejected in favor of a simple, undecorated cloth (fig. 4.35). These pared-down textiles do not convey the same symbolic valence as did the textile patterns of the courtly idiom found at Tholing, Tsaparang, and Tabo. The painters and patrons of the earlier expression of the Ngari painting tradition seemed to have a vested interest in replicating intricate textile patterns. Rich textiles such as these were unmistakably luxury goods that served to symbolize—in real life, as well as in the painted rendition—cosmopolitan and transregional awareness that likely reflected elite concerns and sensibilities.

It is among the subsidiary figures that one finds other painterly abbreviations and changes made to the style. Siṃhanāda Lokunātha sits fully frontal on his lion vehicle with his left hand brought up to his chest (fig. 4.35). The split widow's peak, navel articulation, dhoti type, body form, and jewelry adornment are all quite similar to the apogee style. One of the significant differences between this and the Tabo, Tsaparang, or Tholing images is that the Tabo cave painting is much more simplified; there is no modeling or detailing of the dhoti. The simplification of textile depiction is especially seen at the point of drapery folds. Folds and creases have been reduced to a recurring Z pattern (see fig. 4.35). Moreover, the body nimbus and lotus pedestals of the Tabo cave bodhisattva figure are drastically more simplified than what we see during the earlier phase of the courtly idiom.

These paintings at Tabo's cave temple reveal an important step away from the courtly idiom in terms of the manner in which figural forms are rendered and the level of detail with which the paintings are executed. It is this sort of simplification of decorative motifs and figural forms that continues at the Gyapagpa Temple paintings—where there is no modeling, except for wrathful deities, and no attempt at replicating textile patterning.

Conclusion

This examination of the painting programs at these five temples and the stylistic relationships that these programs have to one another begins to address the geographic, artistic, and temporal span of this Ngari painting tradition. Moreover, by discussing more than the two or three painting programs for which it is best known, this extended visual analysis helps to redress the usual perfunctory manner in which this style is treated. The material evidence explored in this chapter reveals that the larger painting tradition of West Tibet was sustained for over a century and was patronized in Kinnaur, Spiti, and Guge—all areas that were at one time or another part of the Ngari region and fell within the earlier Pu hrang–Guge (Purang) or later Guge kingdoms. More analysis, however, needs to be carried out in order to determine the style's full geographic breadth and its complete stylistic scope. Nonetheless, the five programs addressed in this chapter and in particular those temples that I consider as the apogee of the court style display some degree of variation, which most likely is due to the number of workshops employed at the sites from the late fifteenth into the mid-sixteenth century, when this style was heavily patronized. Further variation, of course, is evident when considering sites such as the Gyapagpa and Tabo cave temples. Through an analysis of these two sites, it is apparent that palette, textile design, modeling, figural types, and the general quality of the paintings change as the painting tradition is employed over the hundred years after its initial application at Tholing and Tsaparang.

There are, of course, numerous other painting programs executed in this style, including other temples at Tabo, Tholing, Tsaparang, and fragmentary remains at sites such as Mangnang. Until now, the Gyapagpa Temple had been overlooked and never considered as a part of this stylistic range. Despite the poor condition of these paintings, it should be clear through this visual analysis that the wall paintings of the Gyapagpa Temple were executed by artists who worked within the visual vocabulary of the late medieval Ngari painting tradition. More specifically, the stylistic resonances between the paintings at Nako's Gyapagpa Temple and Tabo's Golden Temple further illustrate that the Gyapagpa artists were clearly referencing Tabo's paintings. By the time this style is used at the Gyapagpa Temple, however, it diverges in both form and meaning from the apogee of the court idiom. In fact, I suggest that the Gyapagpa paintings at Nako represent one of the last phases of this regional style's life span, although there may have been some paintings still executed in a version of this style as late as the seventeenth century.[38] Once Central Tibet took over this region in the seventeenth century, as a result of the

Tibet-Ladakh-Mughul War discussed in chapter 3, the painting styles began to reflect aesthetic concerns resonant with Central Tibet. The late-sixteenth-century wall paintings at Nako, therefore, are one of the latest examples of the Ngari painting tradition.

While this chapter establishes that Nako's artists used a regional expression of the Ngari painting tradition to fashion the Gyapagpa paintings, a question remains why the artists or patrons chose this style to illustrate Drigung affiliation. Without surviving sixteenth-century stylistic *comparanda,* it is difficult to know what stylistic choices were available to artists and patrons in and around Nako. Was the style at the Gyapagpa Temple used because it was regional? Might there have been any other meaning or purpose for its employment? The next chapter addresses this style's shifting meaning over the one hundred years and more that it was used. Here, I will simply explain that by the time this style is used at Nako, it likely carried with it, though perhaps limitedly, residual associations of royalty and courtly patronage. Such undertones of legitimacy may have been beneficial for a religious group that would have been a minority in an area and at a time when Gelug and Drukpa factions were gaining strength.[39]

5

Origin and Meaning of a Revival Painting Tradition

With stylistic connections made between the Gyapagpa Temple paintings and the larger Ngari style of the fifteenth and sixteenth centuries, this chapter will address the origin of this style, its shifting significations, and the multiple ways in which it has been used and interpreted. Central to this discussion is my argument that this late medieval painting tradition is in fact a revival of the eleventh-century style from the same area. A review of the scant scholarship about fifteenth-century painting traditions of Mnga' ris (Ngari) reveals that scholars have differing opinions about this subject. A critical dichotomy surfaces, which tends to present the later Ngari painting tradition as either a continuation of the eleventh-century style or as a separate style altogether. This difference between these positions is a critical one. Based on analyses of both visual and textual evidence, I argue that the fifteenth- and sixteenth-century painting style was indeed a separate style, which was a revival of the eleventh-century Khache painting tradition. I suggest further that the fifteenth-century resuscitation of this older painting style is reflective of the Guge kingdom's objective to fashion itself as a continuation of the former dynasty. In so doing the later kingdom is communicating an ideological message about its connection to, and continuity with, its predecessor of the eleventh century. Based on this hypothesis, we can understand the fifteenth-century painting style as a carefully constructed visual system that worked to signify the fifteenth-century kingdom's legitimacy and legacy through its association with the eleventh-century dynasty.

At the heart of this hypothesis lies the assumption that style is not arbitrarily determined, but can be a consciously crafted method of communicating. This does not mean, however, that the same message is being expressed over the more than one hundred years that this style was in use. The original valence of the style, as I have interpreted it, changes with the generations of artists and patrons using the style. As a result, by the time this style is used at Nako's Gyapagpa Temple in the late sixteenth century, it maintains a formal relationship with the original Ngari painting tradition, but its meaning, symbolic function, and reception have altered.

Scholarship

Giuseppe Tucci first addressed the Gyapagpa paintings in his multivolume 1935 publication *Indo-Tibetica*. The primary focus of his discussion was the Golden Temple at Tabo, about which he writes that these fifteenth-century murals are related to the larger artistic phenomenon of Guge. According to Tucci, they are "a document of the second period of the art of Guge."[1] Later Tucci treats this western Tibetan stylistic tradition a bit more thoroughly:

> [T]he Guge artists, interpreting with a certain freedom imported inspirations, succeeded, perhaps earlier than other parts of Tibet, in creating a style of their own. For these reasons we are entitled to speak of a Western Tibetan school, born about the XIth century, which had a life of its own until it was completely exhausted by the political decay of the Kingdom of Guge, crumbling under the armed attack of Seng ge rnam rgyal of Ladakh in the XVIIth century.[2]

This earlier period of eleventh-century painting is commonly referred to as either "Indo-Tibetan" or "West Tibetan," and sometimes by the Tibetan name *Kha che lugs* (Khache lug), which translates as "Kashmiri style" and refers to the primary aesthetic tradition that helped shape this eleventh-century style.[3] Although each of these designations is problematic for various reasons, I will use the term "Kashmir" or "Khache" style to refer to this earlier eleventh-century painting style. The Pu hrang (Purang)–Guge kingdom was established in the tenth century, but there is not sufficient material evidence of the Khache style in the western Himalaya until the eleventh century.[4] In 1042, for instance, the royal family of Purang–Guge patronized the elaborate repainting and renovation of Tabo's 'Du khang (Dukhang) in the Khache style and its substyles. These paintings will be cursorily addressed later in this chapter.

Since Tucci, several other scholars have upheld the same position that the fifteenth-century paintings are a continuation of the eleventh-century Khache style. For instance, in 1972 John Huntington suggested that the "Gu-ge bris," or Guge style, began in the tenth century and had a terminus ad quem of the mid-seventeenth century.[5] Huntington argues that the fifteenth-century painting style is in fact a continuation of the earlier eleventh-century style, though with some modifications. About the circa fifteenth-century painting program at Tabo's Golden Temple he writes that it "demonstrates both the stability of the Gu-ge traditions and the ability of the Gu-ge artists to assimilate new elements into their vocabulary of forms."[6] According to Huntington, the "stability of tradition" is reflected in the continued Kashmiri elements that directly relate to the Kashmir-informed eleventh-century, but the new elements he mentions are the Newar and Central Tibetan aesthetics. In 1999 Helmut Neumann also attributed the stylistic consonance between the eleventh- and fifteenth-century material to a continuation of the style; he states that "[a]rtistic traditions must have been kept alive in the intervening centuries, since the style of the grandiose paintings which were to cover the walls of all these new temples, although easily recognizable as later in date, is based on the same characteristics as the earlier works."[7] Indeed, Neumann raises a practical point about training and the sustainability of a style over hundreds of years.

Laxman Thakur posits a clear position on this issue, which relates to Neumann's interpretation. According to Thakur, the paintings of the fifteenth century were part of a continuous style that emerged in the "second half of the tenth century"[8] and ended "when the region was dominated both culturally and politically by Central Tibet."[9] This is generally understood to have been in the mid- to late seventeenth century.

Another set of scholars has proposed that this late medieval painting style was a separate artistic episode with aesthetic antecedents outside of West Tibet. In a brief 1984 essay entitled "Thankas from Western Tibet: Fifteenth and Sixteenth Centuries," Pratapditya Pal proposes that the paintings, both *thangkas* and murals, from this period represent the "emergence of a new style in western Tibet," and argues that the fifteenth-century painting tradition is related to "Sakyapa," or Central Tibet aesthetics, instead of the Khache style of the eleventh century:

> [A] glance at the Khache-Tibetan style murals will also reveal that almost nothing of that style had survived in the Guge style thangkas of the fifteenth century. As Huntington has demonstrated, in some of the Tabo murals one can discern some archaisms, only in the figurative form, from the earlier style, but by and large, the primary inspiration of the Guge style appears to have been the Sakyapa tradition.[10]

Although Pal makes an interesting connection between the "Sakyapa" artistic tradition and the fifteenth-century style, his assertion that almost nothing of that earlier eleventh- and twelfth-century "Khache-Tibetan" style survives in the fifteenth-century style is problematic. He does not provide any stylistic analysis to support his thesis; the reader is expected to go to Huntington's 1972 article in order to construct Pal's visual argument—which, it should be noted, is slightly different than Huntington's thesis.

Marilyn Rhie's assessment of this West Tibetan style echoes Pal's sentiments. She suggests that the fifteenth-century Guge style is the "true inheritor of the Gyantse Kumbum style," which is an example of Sakya-patronized painting.[11] She goes on to say that the painting tradition combined the elegance of the Gyantse style with the "charming styles characteristic of the Western Tibetan tradition that had flowered so brilliantly in the eleventh century."[12] According to Rhie, the hybrid approach apparent in the fifteenth-century Guge style was most discernible in the paintings. The paintings of the Gyantse Kumbum Stūpa are undoubtedly what Pal had in mind when he referred to the "Sakyapa" artistic tradition, because Gyantse was one of the most important Sakya centers in Tibet at this time. Thus, Rhie and Pal seem to share a very similar perspective on the stylistic origins of the fifteenth-century Guge paintings. In my opinion, however, the likelihood of Guge being the inheritor of the Gyantse style is quite slim given the hundreds of miles that separate them. Nonetheless, I think Rhie's insight into hybrid forms is of great significance and will be taken up briefly later in the chapter.

The two styles under discussion—Ngari's painting tradition of the fifteenth to sixteenth centuries and Gyantse's fifteenth-century Kumbum paintings—share some formal aspects due to Ngari's previous exposure to Newar, or as David Jackson refers to it, "Beri," aesthetic traditions; they are nonetheless two different styles. As I have elucidated, the artists of the Ngari tradition of the late medieval period likely appropriated and reused Newar motifs, popular because of Mustang's fourteenth- and fifteenth-century royal wall painting projects, but this does not mean that these artists were adopting the Newar style. Rather, as I interpret the style, the artists integrated parts of Newar aesthetics within their dominant Khache revival style (see my discussion about this in chapter 4). Such a hypothesis allows style to be the organic, evolving phenomenon that it is. Artists of West Tibet in the fifteenth century were readily informed by the rich artistic traditions around them, past and present.

This is not to say, however, that the Beri style (which also overlaps with the Central Tibetan Style) did not exist in West Tibet. It certainly did, as Jackson illustrates, but Jackson goes further to suggest that Guge's court style of the fifteenth to sixteenth century is derived from the Beri style. Based on his analysis of three Sakya-patronized, circa fifteenth-century *thangkas* of supposed West Tibetan provenance, Jackson concludes

that the Guge style "descends" from Beri models;[13] "[F]or many fifteenth-
and sixteenth-century murals of Tsaparang (Guge) can be seen to descend
neither from Kashmiri nor Pāla models but rather mainly from Newar
ones."[14] While his hypothesis would have been complicated had he conducted a close visual comparison of eleventh-century Khache paintings,
such as at Tabo, with fifteenth-century wall paintings at Tsaparang and
Tholing, the stylistic connections he makes between Guge's courtly style
with Beri styles are important and point to motif borrowing. As I have
explained, these motif borrowings do not warrant the conclusion that
the Guge courtly style was a version of the Beri style. The artists of the
Ngari courtly style were looking to the Kache style, a visual vocabulary
and style that carried meanings of ancestry, lineage, and royal authority.[15] Although Jackson misreads the origins of the Guge courtly style, his
close reading of Roberto Vitali's translation and analysis of the fifteenth-
century Guge royal chronicle, *Mnga' ris rgyal rabs,* reveals that there were
at least two different styles in circulation during this late medieval period
in the Guge region.[16] That there was more than one style in circulation
during the fifteenth and sixteenth centuries in West Tibet raises important
questions about why certain painting styles were used, by whom, when,
and in what regions.

Although Pal, Rhie, and Jackson minimize the stylistic connection between Guge's eleventh- and fifteenth-century painting traditions, Michael
Henss lingers on these formal resonances. Like Huntington, he notices
the stylistic resonances between eleventh- and fifteenth-century painting
styles, saying that the latter "preserved" older West Tibetan idioms.[17] He
seems to vacillate between conceiving of the later painting tradition as a
continuation of an earlier style or as a distinct stylistic expression temporally limited to the fifteenth through seventeenth centuries.

Deborah Klimburg-Salter is the first scholar to interpret what these
formal similarities between the eleventh- and fifteenth-century painting
styles might mean. Although her visual analysis is limited, it is poignantly
executed and supports her hypothesis that these fifteenth-century paintings are a *revival* of the Khache style. She writes, "In the 15th century
there is a revival of a very elegant painting style in Guge which has many
of the characteristics of the earlier Indo-Tibetan school of western Tibet.
Both wall paintings and thangkas are known. It would be interesting
to explore the reasons for this renewed interest in the earlier art of the
Kingdom of Purang-Guge."[18] Like Klimburg-Salter, I do not consider the
fifteenth-century Guge paintings as a continuation or preservation of the
eleventh-century style. Nor do I group this late medieval painting tradition as a Nepalese (Beri) derivative peppered with Khache archaisms.
Rather, the fifteenth-century style is a renaissance tradition born out

of a very specific set of sociopolitical circumstances. Indeed, it is in this chapter that we will "explore the reasons for this renewed interest in the earlier art of the Kingdom of Purang-Guge."[19]

Context

After nearly a century of political unrest and instability in Ngari, a powerful new regional kingdom emerged in the early fifteenth century[20] and with it a new era in trans-Himalayan history. No longer under the control of the Yuan dynasty,[21] the newly independent Guge kingdom in Ngari could afford to support religious activity, resulting in its prodigious patronage of Buddhist temples and art. As Vitali has deduced from his analysis of *Mnga' ris rgyal rabs,* "When lasting security was finally achieved by means of an adequate defensive system and increased military strength, renewed prosperity gave rise to a phase of religious activity that led to a renewal of Buddhist practice and temple foundations."[22] The Guge kingdom's reign, spanning the fifteenth through seventeenth centuries,[23] generated one of the most artistically productive and sophisticated periods in the history of Himalayan art. During this period of florescence there was a deliberate and calculated renaissance of the eleventh-century Khache painting style. I suggest that this style was selected and used by the newly established fifteenth-century dynasty as a way of evoking the piety, political successes, and legitimacy of that earlier period—the eleventh- and twelfth-century Purang-Guge dynasty.

My thesis of dynastic emulation is supported by visual and textual sources. This chapter assesses the painting traditions used in Ngari between the late twelfth and the fourteenth centuries and demonstrates that the fifteenth-century painting tradition was not part of a single, continuous style originating in the eleventh century. The visual evidence reveals instead that there was a pervasive use of the Central Tibetan Style during the intervening centuries and that this was indeed a break from the Khache style. I then consider the textual evidence of the fifteenth century, in particular *Mnga' ris rgyal rabs,* supposedly written in 1497, to demonstrate the ways in which the fifteenth-century dynasty defined and fashioned itself.[24] Analysis of the fifteenth-century murals of royally patronized sites, such as Tsaparang's Red Temple, corroborates the textual evidence: the fifteenth-century dynasty had a vested interest in remembering and resuscitating the image of the successful Purang-Guge dynasty of the tenth through twelfth centuries. The renascent painting style effectively produced a visual vocabulary that tapped into this potent past. Lastly, this chapter considers the paintings of Nako's Gyapagpa Temple and how they fit into or challenge the intended meanings of the courtly idiom of the Ngari style of the fifteenth and sixteenth centuries.

Twelfth- through Fifteenth-Century Artistic Activity in Ngari

During the twelfth through fourteenth centuries, the dominant painting style in the western Himalaya, such as in West Tibet, Zangskar, and Ladakh, can be grouped within a stylistic trend from Central Tibet. The Central Tibetan Style is a rubric largely defined by its stylistic resonances with the Newar aesthetic traditions as well as those from Northeast India during the Pāla period.[25] The development of the western Himalayan iterations of the Central Tibetan Style is strongly associated with the migration of important religious traditions, such as Drigung, from Central to West Tibet and beyond in the thirteenth century. As the painting style spread from West Tibet to Ladakh and Zangskar many substyles developed. This widespread distribution of shared motifs attests to vital artistic, but also religious and commercial, corridors of transregional exchange. In the Spiti, Khu nu, and Ngari regions, there are several extant sites with wall paintings executed in this style.

Wall Paintings

Located in India's Spiti region is the large monastic complex of Tabo, the various temples of which were painted in a number of different styles over the centuries. Currently, very little of the Central Tibetan Style exists there. In Tabo's Maitreya Temple, a few fragments of this style can be found, which merit additional scholarly attention. The majority of the temple was repainted in a twentieth-century style, but parts of the western apse have circa fourteenth-century paintings, which is where the fragments of the western Himalayan iteration of the Central Tibetan Style are found.[26] The largest fragment is on the northwest wall of the apse, which features an image of Green Tara (fig. 5.1). The *hamsas'* spiraling tails that adorn her head nimbus, the shape of the flowers she holds, the dominant red and blue palette, and the horseshoe shape of the body nimbus are all unmistakable indicators that this section of painting was executed by artists versed in a local expression of the Central Tibetan Style. Another segment of the same painting program can be found on what is now the base of the Maitreya sculpture. Here, a six-armed figure sits on a small, lotus-petaled pedestal that has a throneback with jeweled triangular plaques typical of the style (fig. 5.2). The form of the figure and

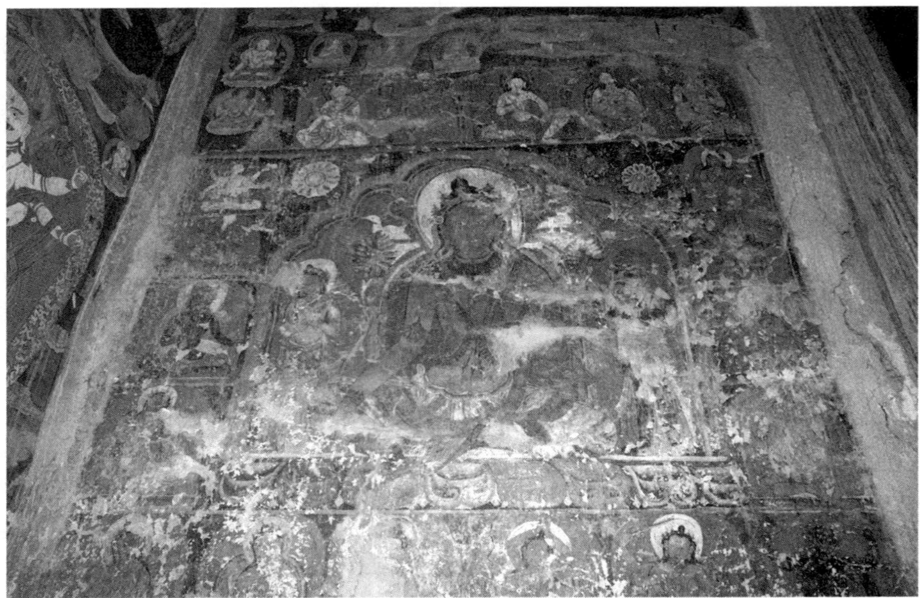

Figure 5.1. Tabo (Lahaul Spiti Dist., H.P.), Maitreya Temple: Green Tara, c. fourteenth century).

the palette in which it is painted match the images painted in a row above Green Tara, indicating that they were executed by the same workshop, if not by the same artist.

Other fragments are found in the Tabo stūpa.[27] These represent a slightly different variation of the Central Tibetan Style from those in the Maitreya Temple. Although they are in poorer condition, the stūpa paintings are a bit more refined in their execution, as is evidenced by their detailed jewelry and crown decorations (fig. 5.3). These minor differences indicate that another workshop was undoubtedly responsible for their execution, though the paintings in general share the same overall stylistic conventions of the twelfth through fourteenth centuries.[28]

Nako, which is about sixty-five kilometers down the valley from Tabo, has a small temple named after Guru Rinpoche. The murals of this temple are yet another variation of this Central Tibetan–informed style. They were first noted by Tucci in 1932: "Though the status of maintenance of the little temple is very unhappy, it is evident that the pictures that once covered the entire temple would not have been without worth. As they are now, they seem to go back to the XIV or XV centuries."[29] The Guru Rimpoche Temple's paintings are stylistically aligned with the Central Tibetan Style, as seen in the composition, decorative motifs, and figural forms. Soot and water damage have badly obscured these paintings, but the general composition of some of the walls can still be discerned. The

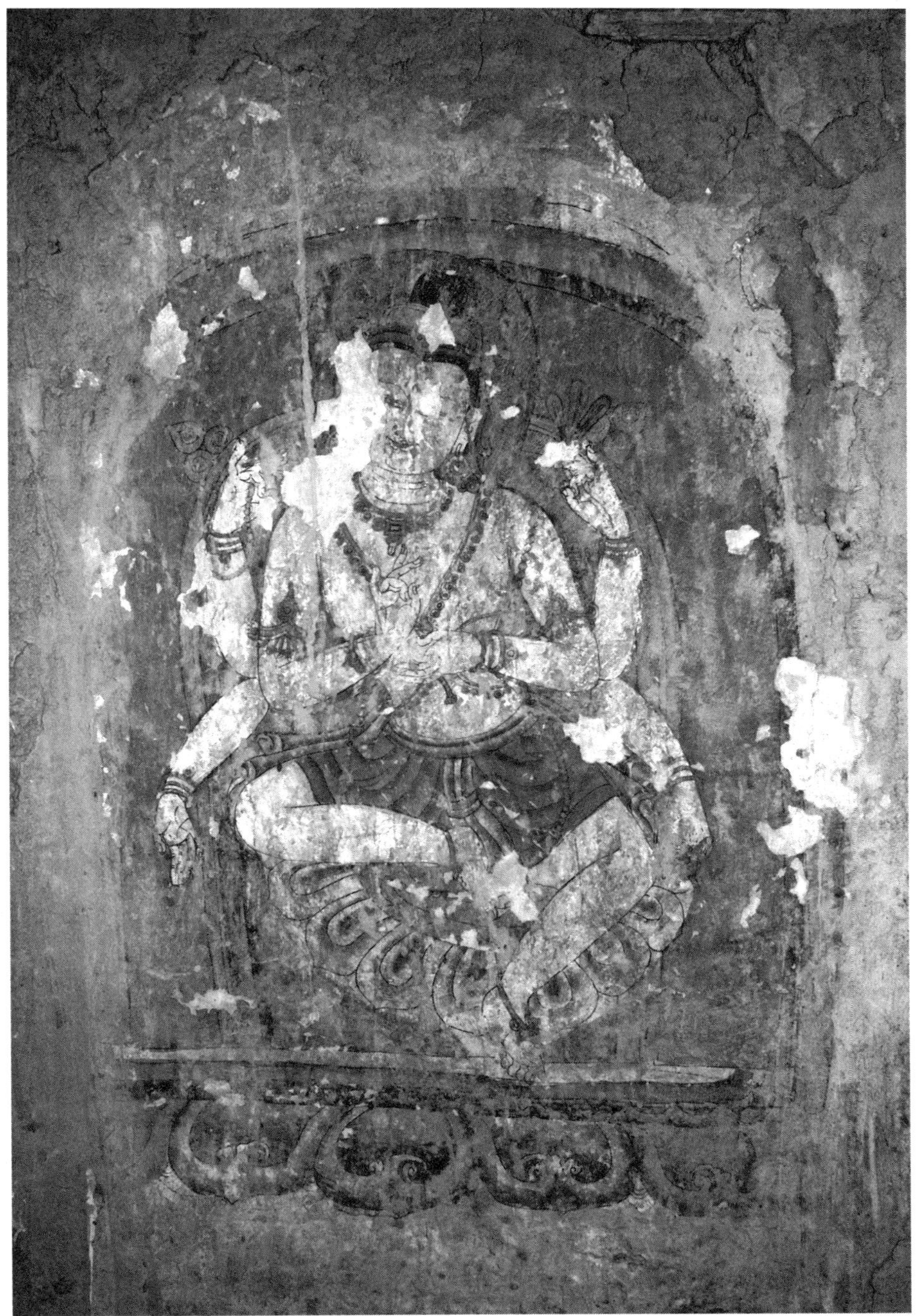

Figure 5.2. Tabo (Lahaul Spiti Dist., H.P.), Maitreya Temple: six-armed figure, c. fourteenth century.

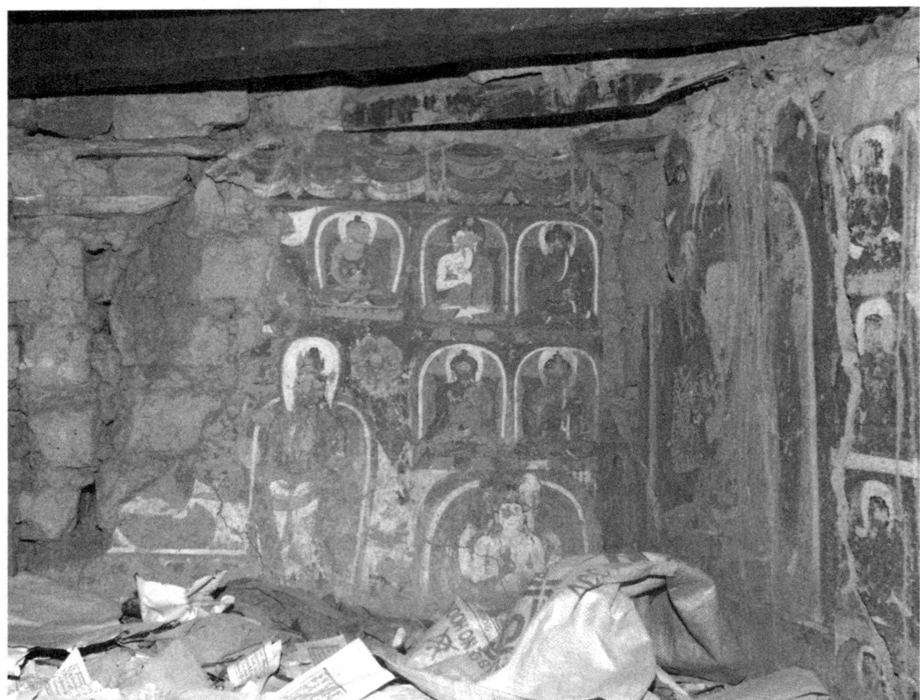

Figure 5.3. Tabo's stūpa (*Mchod rten*), c. fourteenth century.

southern and western walls feature large tathāgata figures surrounded by scores of small Buddhas. These large iconic figures are framed by rainbow-colored arches and scrollwork decorating their oval head nimbi. Their tiered crowns are rendered with pear-shaped golden plaques, and upturned flower blossoms adorn the shoulders of the thronebacks. All of these stylistic flourishes are part of the larger visual vocabulary of the Central Tibetan Style.

Also fragmentary, but of critical importance to this discussion, are the circa twelfth-to-fourteenth-century wall paintings from Tholing's Maṇḍala Temple (fig. 5.4).[30] Although these paintings are badly faded and worn, they retain enough visual information to connect them with the Central Tibetan Style. The Buddha figures wear simple monastic robes with their proper right shoulders unveiled. This type of Buddha figure is also seen at Nako's Guru Rimpoche Temple. The nimbi are horseshoe shaped, and the triangular plaques of the thronebacks can be seen above their shoulders. The faces of the Buddha figures are typically rendered with bow-shaped eyes and strong square jaws.

There are newly discovered sites in Ngari and Purang with paintings in idioms of the Central Tibetan Style, such as the murals of the Sib-Chu cave. Recently, Tsering Gyalpo brought to light these fantastic circa

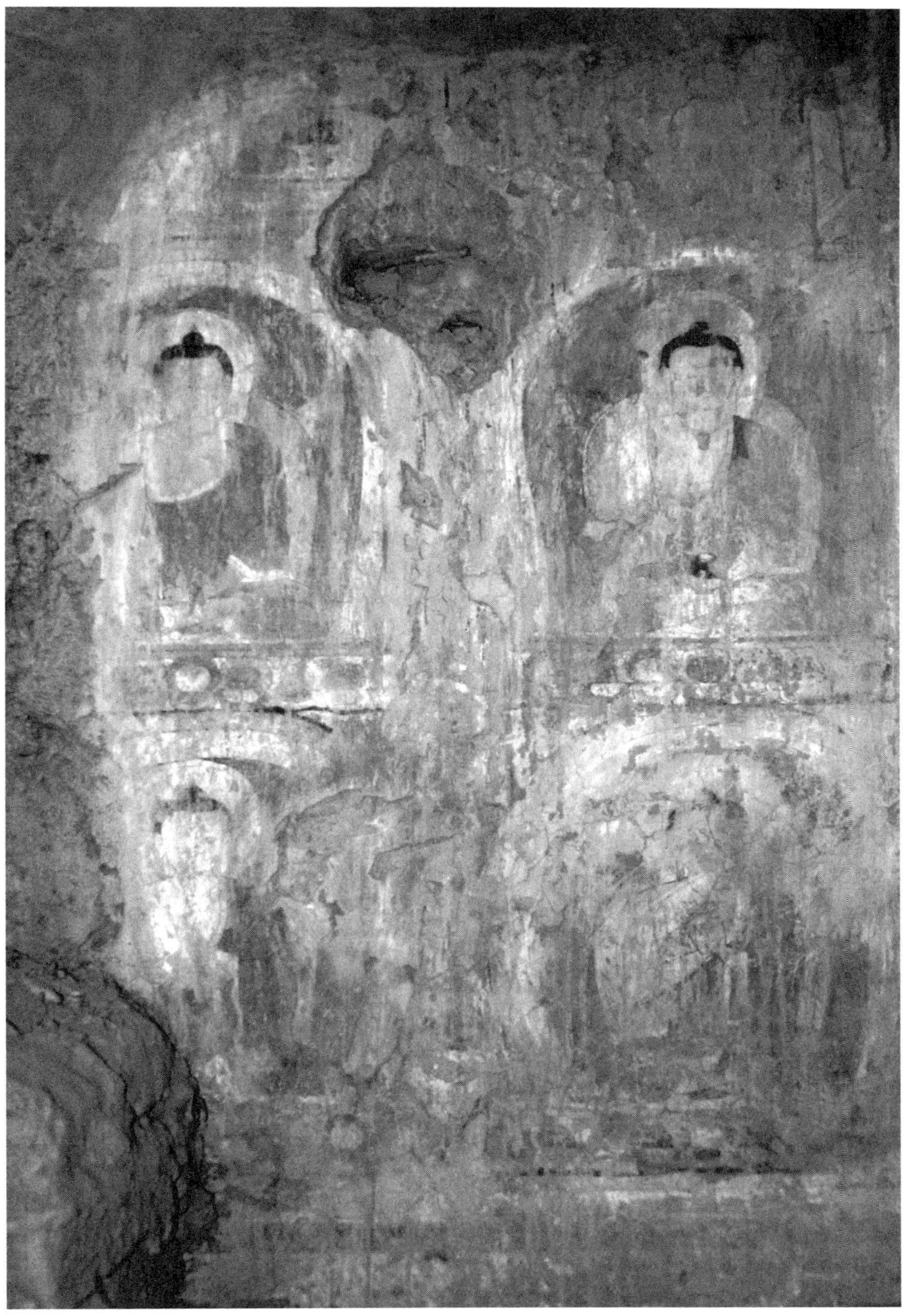

Figure 5.4. Tholing (West Tibet), Maṇḍala Temple, c. fourteenth century. MRK.

fourteenth-century paintings from a cave temple in Dram, approximately ninety kilometers southeast of Tholing.[31] Recently discovered cave paintings in Mustang, an area that was once part of the Purang-Guge region, seem to be from a similar period and style.[32]

Scroll Paintings

Further evidence of the predominance of the Central Tibetan Style in Ngari comes from portable images, such as *thangkas,* although the provenance of such pieces is always questionable—particularly for those collected in India after the 1972 Antiquities and Art Treasures Act went into effect. This act did not necessarily deter collecting, but did prompt people to conceal or fabricate collection points and acquisition dates. Even so, collection points do not always mean creation points, as small images were often in circulation via pilgrims and artists. Working with a valuable set of provenanced paintings from the Spiti valley, Klimburg-Salter was able to determine that they shared stylistic features. Consequently, she was able to classify the "Spiti Valley Painting Tradition" as a subset or idiom of the larger stylistic phenomenon of the Central Tibetan Style.[33] While conducting fieldwork in Spiti and Khu nu, I also found several paintings that should be considered a subset of the same style.[34] One rather large *thangka* painting, the canvas of which roughly measures sixty-five centimeters high and fifty-six centimeters wide, shares the same compositional arrangement, palette, figural types, and decorative motifs as those originally grouped with the "Spiti Valley Painting Tradition."[35] Another local version of this Central Tibetan Style was used to paint a small, banner-like object made of strips of painted canvas. It is approximately forty-five centimeters tall and fifteen centimeters wide, and each canvas panel is painted with five small figures, many of which are wrathful or semiwrathful. These paintings are executed on a reduced scale, necessitating abbreviation of detail, but the manner in which they were painted reveals connections to the Central Tibetan Style, as in the horseshoe-shaped nimbi, triangular plaques used in the crowns, flower blossoms decorating the backgrounds, and palettes dominated by red, green, and blue.

These varied examples of the western Himalayan iterations of the Central Tibetan Style used in both wall paintings and *thangkas* illustrate that a well-developed stylistic tradition had spread throughout the Ngari region from at least the twelfth through the fourteenth centuries.[36] In fact, based on the extant material evidence, one can reasonably posit that the Central Tibetan Style was the predominant painting tradition in the western Himalaya at this time. We do not see, for instance, the continued use of the Khache or Kashmiri-based painting style popular in the eleventh century. Consequently, it seems reasonable to conclude that the Kashmiri-based style was not robustly patronized past the twelfth century.

The fifteenth century in West Tibet marks a new phase in which the rulers of the Guge kingdom sought to reclaim their august heritage, so strongly associated with the monk-ruler Ye shes 'Od (Yeshe Od) and his family. Based on this visual evidence, it is accurate to posit that the new Ngari painting tradition of the fifteenth-century was not an uninterrupted continuation of the previous Kashmiri-based style. Neither was it a permutation of the Newar or "Beri" style. Rather, this later style is a revival of the Kashmiri style used in West Tibet and its environs during the eleventh and twelfth centuries. The artists of the fifteenth-century Guge paintings at the royal and religious centers of Tsaparang, Tholing and Tabo deliberately evoked the earlier eleventh- and twelfth-century style through the careful and intentional reuse of figural types, decorative motifs, textile patterns, and drapery folds, among other formal elements. These artists, especially those working in the courtly idiom, captured the earlier style while also inflecting it with new trends and developments in decorative motifs. Their ability to create a renaissance style that so faithfully looks back to its referent, and in some cases surpasses it, is noteworthy.

Analysis of textual sources helps to reveal why emulation and mimesis of the earlier period were of interest to the fifteenth-century Guge kingdom. The tenth- through twelfth-century dynasty becomes for the neophyte fifteenth-century rulers a bulwark that at once stabilizes and legitimizes them.

Textual Evidence

The only existing royal chronicle for the fifteenth-century Guge kingdom is the *Mnga' ris rgyal rabs*, which was allegedly written in 1497 by Ngag dbang grags pa (Ngawang Dragpa), a disciple of Tsongkapa who founded the Gelug tradition. The chronicle provides a glimpse into the ways in which the newly revitalized suzerainty fashioned itself. A close reading of the text reveals that the Guge kingdom was invested in modeling itself after the Purang-Guge kingdom of the tenth and twelfth centuries, and in particular after the famous ruler Yeshe Od. Their objective was accomplished through evocative statements about and explicit connections to Yeshe Od and his successful kingdom of the eleventh and twelfth centuries.

The fifteenth-century Guge dynasty emerged on the heels of the century-long Yuan dynasty's control, which the Sakya-dominated Central Tibetan feudatories supported and implemented. The new political power, which began to develop in the mid- to late fourteenth century, was eager to express, both textually and visually, its new-fangled political authority. As Vitali explains,

> I believe that the resurgence of West Tibet in the late 14th–early 15th century was the result of the recovery of some form of independence from the dBus gTsang powers which had held Gu.ge for hundreds of years. The end of the rule of the Sa.skya.pa-s and their feudatories (Zhwa.lu.pa-s, Gung.thang.pa-s; see Addendum Three) created an opportunity for the rebirth of local principalities (Gu.ge, La.dwags. Glo. bo). The existence of records of local dynasties in these regions during that time, and their absence for the preceding period, testifies to local resurgence.[37]

The political power of the Guge kingdom represented a refreshing phase of prosperity and strength, as well as military might.[38] Unfortunately, little is known about its ruler, Rnam rgyal lde (Namgyalde [born 1372]), who is credited with heralding a new era for Guge with fortified military and expanded borders that included parts of Ladakh.[39]

Although King Namgyalde is recognized as having spearheaded the expansion and security of this new West Tibetan kingdom, it was his son, Nam mkha'i dbang po phun tshogs lde bzang po (Namkhai Wangpo Phuntsogde Zangpo) who masterfully connected this new kingdom with the successes of the old Purang-Guge kingdom.[40] Through both text and image, the rulers of the fifteenth-century dynasty made themselves appear as an undisrupted continuation of Yeshe Od's kingdom. Moreover, Namkhai Wangpo Phuntsogde Zangpo made a critical alliance with a new religious tradition of Tibetan Buddhism, known as Gelug, which penetrated Ngari in the fifteenth century. During this time Guge's royal family welcomed to their capital Ngawang Dragpa, a missionary for the Gelug tradition. It is thought, though not without skepticism, that he wrote the royal chronicle, *Mnga' ris rgyal rabs*.

With the first two pages of the chronicle missing, the text begins with a short history of Tibet before the ruler Yeshe Od came to power in Ngari in the mid-tenth century. As the chronicle explains, there was a period of oppression associated with Glang dar ma (Lang Darma), consequently the [Buddhist] teachings were abandoned for generations.[41] During this period of 146 years Bon and other "dark" practices prevailed. Yeshe Od's altruistic deeds are a direct response to this time of destitution. According to the text, Yeshe Od, whose rule marks the beginning of the Purang-Guge kingdom, sponsored Buddhist temples and images and sent translators to Kashmir to learn and record the proper Buddhist teachings and to disseminate them within the kingdom. He also hosted teachers from Kashmir in Ngari. Moreover he supported the creation of civil laws and implemented the observation of them.[42]

Yeshe Od's accomplishments and commissions were documented in great detail in this fifteenth-century chronicle, written nearly five hundred years after they occurred. No one else in the chronicle—not even the members of the fifteenth-century royal family—is discussed in as much detail as is Yeshe Od and his family. The precise rendering of this early period, which includes information about patronage practices of each of Yeshe Od's children, indicates that the author must have had access to some sort of chronicle or log from this earlier period. The past is idealized in a way that follows established tropes for royal chronicles, especially the notion of a royal lineage having divine origin. The manner in which the author centralizes Yeshe Od's contribution and influence, however, is beyond what one sees in other chronicles from nearby regions, such as the Ladakhi chronicle.[43] The heavy emphasis on Yeshe Od in the *Mnga' ris rgyal rabs* suggests that there was an agenda at work: the text was to insinuate the relationship between the newfangled fifteenth-century kingdom and Yeshe Od.

When the chronicle reaches the early thirteenth century, the level of detail declines and more general information about each ruler's commissions and political pursuits is given. By the late thirteenth century and into the fourteenth century, the genealogy is completely lost. The chronicle simply leaves off with Grags pa lde (Dragpade), who died in 1277, and resumes—without mention of the hundred-year lacuna—with a king born in 1372. It reads as though the next king was Dragpade's son, which is impossible since this "son's" birth date is ninety-five years after Dragpade's death. The gap in documentation is not a mistake on the part of the chronicler. Other texts pertaining to Ngari also include this hundred-year lapse. Luciano Petech has pieced together Ngari's royal history through the use of a number of other chronicles and pilgrimage guides and noticed the same gap. He suggested that these lapses in documentation point to a major political shift in power.[44] Indeed, the Yuan dynasty had secured control of Central Tibet through its alliance with the dominant Tibetan Buddhist power of the time, the Sakya. They took over parts of greater Tibet, including the Ngari region. It would seem that Yuan dynastic control was a primary reason for the interruption in the chronicle.[45] The chronicle, however, does not acknowledge the gap in time and even tries to elide the temporal distance and probable political disturbance by stating that the two framing kings were father and son.

The "son" born in 1372 was Namgyalde, whose own son, Namkhai Wangpo Phuntsogde Zangpo, marks the true beginning of the new dynasty. In addition to commissioning the chronicle, he and his wife forged new relations with the early formation of the Gelug tradition as well as initiated the construction of temples and images.[46] The chronicler describes the coronation of Namkhai Wangpo Phuntsogde Zangpo—the only coronation included in detail in the text, which explicitly aligns the new king with Yeshe Od:

> He (Phun-tshogs-lde) was enthroned (dbang-bskur) as king, excellent protector of the vast kingdom, to sit on the elephant throne (gnyis-'thung dbang-po'i khri), which is the worthy companion, dust of the feet of the endless successors of the solar race (nyi-ma'i rigs) [descending] from the ancestor lha-bla-maYe-shes-'od, the greatest [of the Guge kings], [which was placed] in the center of the entire assembly of secretaries and retinues filling the [space around the throne].[47]

Clearly this dynasty had an awareness of its past and was making a conscious effort to fashion a place for itself within this "solar race," which was "descended" from Yeshe Od. Thus, the coronation is presented as emblematic of the continuation of Yeshe Od's kingdom.

The fifteenth-century Guge dynasty also sought to define itself in relation to its predecessors through the adoption and revision of civil law and religious vows. The chronicler clearly links the initial implementation of these rules to Yeshe Od. Further, the author seems to make a concerted effort to show that King Namgyalde acted in accordance with these laws. For instance, the king took monastic vows, just as Yeshe Od and other kings of the Purang-Guge kingdom had done.[48] The fifteenth-century royal chronicle noticeably does not highlight the variances or changes that Namgyalde made to the religious vows and civil rules, but only mentions that "he performed deeds in accordance with *mi chos* (civil law) and *Lha dam* (religious vows)."[49] By emphasizing the use of these laws in the late fourteenth century, the chronicler creates an image of this Guge kingdom as a law-abiding and pious community acting in accordance with their august lineage.

Oddly, one of the greatest oversights of the chronicle is its lack of detail regarding artistic patronage practices during the fifteenth century. Specifics of the earlier Purang-Guge dynasty's patronage practices are elucidated in great detail, whereas those of the fifteenth-century dynasty are never mentioned. This omission is particularly odd as the chronicler, Ngawang Dragpa, was supposedly the abbot of the monastic complex of Tsaparang, which was being renovated in the fifteenth century. The Red Temple, discussed in chapter 4, was one of these new building projects. It is not clear why he would have omitted such meritorious acts by the royal family. The patronage practices of the fifteenth-century Guge royals can be deciphered, however, from a seventeenth-century text known as *Vaiḍūrya ser po bai ser*, often referred to by its abbreviated name, *Bai ser*, which primarily served as an outline of the monastic sites under Gelug control. The omission of royal patronage practices in the *Mnga' ris rgyal rabs* chronicle is brought into sharper focus when one considers the seventeenth-century Ladakhi royal chronicle in which the various "statues, manuscripts and mani-walls [are] listed."[50]

In *Mnga' ris rgyal rabs,* the fifteenth-century Guge dynasty was projecting an image of itself as a pious yet politically powerful and historically minded dynasty. As a way of legitimizing their rule, they cultivated links that directly connected them with the Purang-Guge dynasty. I argue that the art of the fifteenth century was intended to communicate a similar message via images of a powerful, pious kingdom deeply connected to the former Purang-Guge dynasty.

Visual Evidence

The fifteenth-century visual vocabulary used to express the ideological message of an unbroken royal lineage was based on the style and forms of the eleventh- and twelfth-century Khache painting tradition. Some scholars have erroneously assumed, however, that the fifteenth-century material was either an uninterrupted continuation of this tradition or a derivative of Nepalese painting styles. I propose that the fifteenth-century visual evidence corroborates what the textual evidence suggests: the fifteenth-century Guge dynasty was modeling itself upon and as an extension of the Purang-Guge dynasty of the tenth through twelfth centuries. One of the more powerful and direct ways in which they executed this objective was to create a visual system that evoked the Khache style that the Purang-Guge dynasty was known to have patronized centuries before. To illustrate this stylistic consonance, I will briefly compare the paintings from the renovation period at Tabo's Dukhang, which dates to the eleventh century, with the fifteenth-century paintings of Tholing's Red Temple, also known as the Dukhang.[51] I have chosen these two sites for several reasons. Tabo's Dukhang is the best preserved example of eleventh-century Khache painting patronized by the Purang-Guge royal family. There are other sites, which were executed in the Khache Style, such as the cave temples of Dungkar, Phyiang, Pedongpo (Pad ma'i sdong po), and Khartse, but these cannot be securely attributed to royal patronage of the Purang-Guge dynasty.[52] Without inscriptional evidence, Tholing's Red Temple cannot be securely dated. Nonetheless, it does provide the most intricate and detailed of the painting programs executed in the courtly idiom. It faithfully follows and replicates some of the intricacies of the earlier Khache style. Consequently, I date it as one of the earliest examples of the fifteenth-century Khache revival style. The following comparisons are simply meant to illustrate that in the fifteenth century artists were clearly reviving the older style, as can be seen in the shared figural forms and decorative motifs.[53] It should be kept in mind, though, that the Khache style of the eleventh century had a number of substyles, as can be seen at Tabo's Dukhang. Tholing's fifteenth-century artists were looking to the substyle executed in Tabo's Dukhang, and were seemingly less interested in faithfully emulating the substyle represented in the Dukhang's Cella. The following analysis begins with an image from the Dukhang, proceeds with a discussion of material from the Cella, and returns to the Dukhang for a general discussion of Buddha and Bodhisattva figural types. The last part of the comparison addresses painted textile motifs and throne designs.

The first comparison is between two offering deities. The eleventh-century female figure at Tabo's Dukhang is greenish in color, seated on a lotus with its seedpod visible and holding in her proper left hand a slim piece of incense, the smoke of which curls upward to her right shoulder (fig. 5.5). The fifteenth-century offering deity at Tholing's Red Temple is blue in color and stands in a dynamic dancelike position while playing a two-stringed wooden instrument, which looks similar to a *ghijak,* an instrument associated with Kashmir and Central Asia (fig. 4.25).[54] Although there are some immediate differences between the two figures, such as body posture, the two figures exhibit many more critical similarities and stylistic consistencies than differences. The greatest similarity between them, though, is the manner in which their volume and form are rendered. Moreover, textile patterns, garment types, and body adornments for each are faithfully articulated in exquisite detail. These similarities are especially noteworthy considering that the image at Tholing was painted over 450 years after the paintings we see at Tabo's Dukhang. Their faces, shown at different angles, display strong shared features: elongated, almond-shaped eyes, dramatic modeling, strong, arching eyebrows, and small pursed mouths. One can easily see how the blue attendant figure from Tholing (figs. 4.24 and 4.27) also shares these stylistic elements. Each offering deity is depicted with a strong torque in the waist and modeling that accentuates each female figure's voluminous form. Their hairstyles are also similarly rendered with large ornamented hair rolls, while their faces are framed by a row of hair ringlets. Upon each of their heads rests a golden crown with pointed plaques. The Tholing image has two large flowers tucked in her hair, but even this flower type is based on the eleventh-century model at Tabo, as can be seen in the similarly rendered blue flower with pointed petals and red stamen, which hovers to the Tabo figure's left side.

A comparison between an eleventh-century image of Mahābodhi-sattva Śreṣṭin, on the south wall of the Cella's ambulatory at Tabo (fig. 5.6), and a fifteenth-century painting from Tholing's Red Temple (plate 14) illustrates that the fifteenth-century artists replicated some of the decorative motifs, such as floral motifs, textile patterns, and body adornment

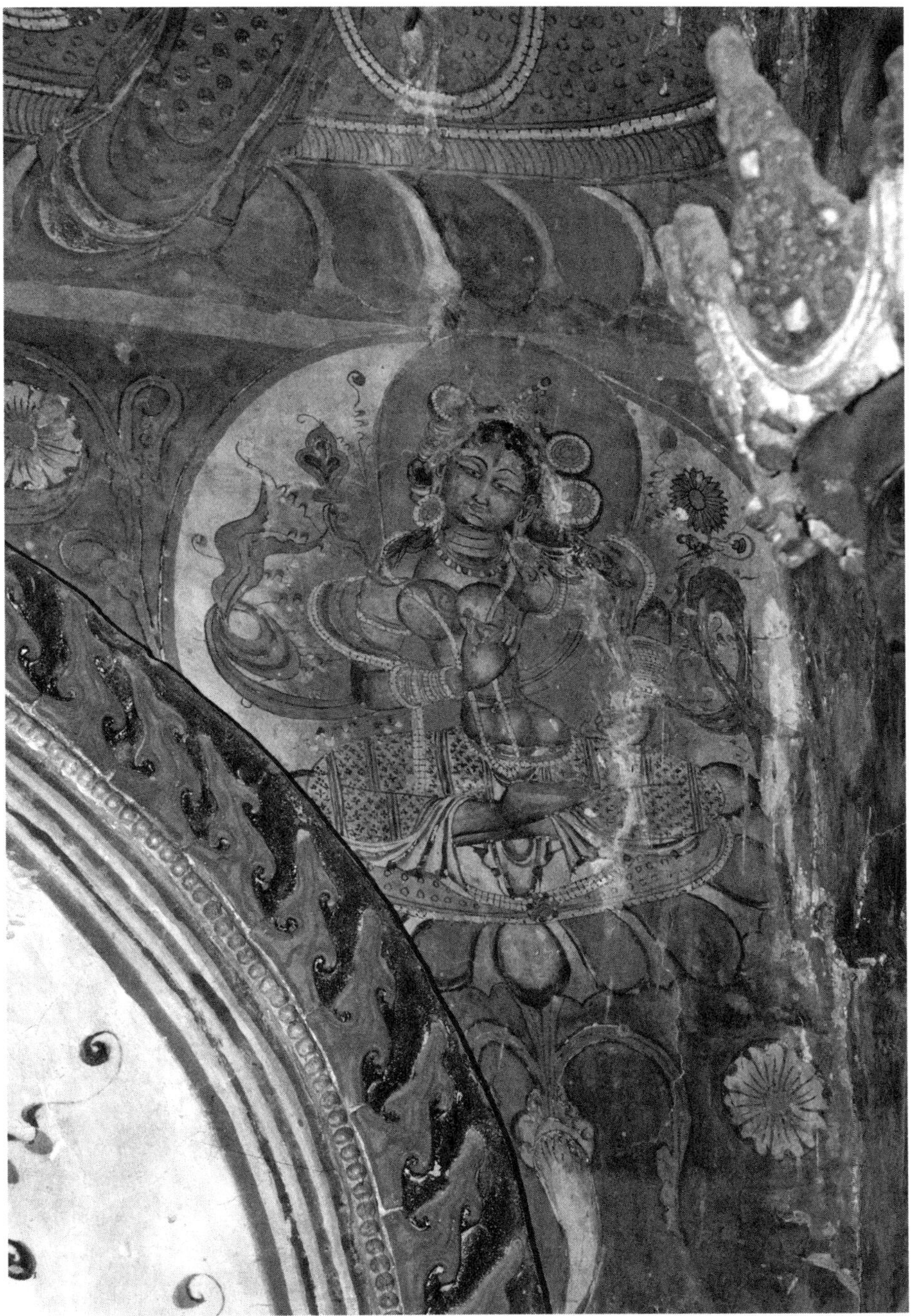

Figure 5.5. Tabo (Lahaul Spiti Dist., H.P.), Dukhang: offering deity,
c. eleventh century.

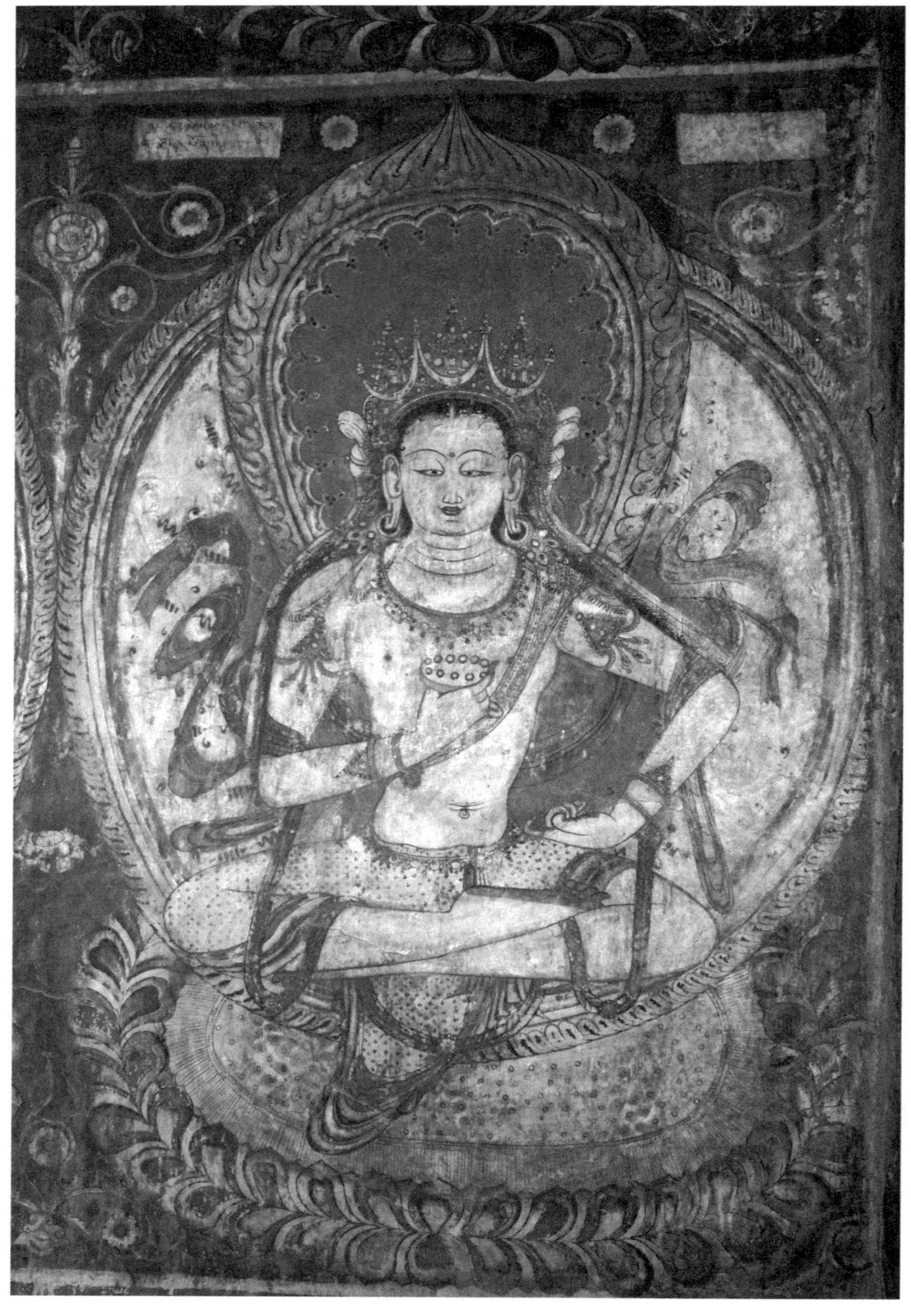

Figure 5.6. Tabo (Lahaul Spiti Dist., H.P.), Cella ambulatory in Dukhang ('Du khang): Mahābodhisattva Śreṣṭin, c. eleventh century.

of the cella substyle. While this comparison between fig. 5.6 and plate 14 demonstrates certain resonances, as will be demonstrated below, the fifteenth-century artists of the revival style were looking at the stylistic vocabulary found in the Dukhang, as evinced by the last comparison, and will be further discussed later in the chapter. Each figure wears a similarly fashioned blue-petaled blossom over each ear. Both have split widow's peaks, thin, arching eyebrows, and rather small noses and defined lips. Their physical forms are similarly fashioned with long torsos torqued to one side, although the eleventh-century figure has a slightly more rigid form with broader shoulders. The fingers of both figures exude a sense of dexterity. While their crowns and much of their jewelry differ, there is one piece that is common to both: the long, bejeweled necklace that falls from the neck and shoulders down to the ankles. On the eleventh-century figure, this garland rests at the crook of each arm and loops around the calf of each leg, whereas on the fifteenth-century figure, the garland is draped over the proper right forearm and loops around each leg. This long, calf-length decorative garland is common in early Kashmiri art.[55] A visual reference to it in the fifteenth century, when such a decorative motif had been long out of circulation, strongly suggests that artists were looking to a body of work influenced by early Kashmiri aesthetics.

The fifteenth-century artists, while obviously aware of the Cella, more closely replicated the forms and motifs found in the Dukhang. The fifteenth-century figure's eyes are rendered with a flat upper lid instead of the almond-shaped eyes of Mahābodhisattva Śreṣṭin. This dramatic eye shape, although not evident in this bodhisattva figure from Tabo's Cella, was readily used throughout the eleventh-century painting program and can easily be seen, for instance, on most of Tabo's Dukhang Buddhas and Bodhisattvas, such as the Maitreya figure.[56] In fact, when comparing the figural forms of Tabo's eleventh-century Dukhang and Tholing's fifteenth-century wall paintings, it is evident that the Buddha and Bodhisattva forms, as well as monastic attendants are quite resonant with one another. This can be seen, for instance, when comparing figs. 25, 25, 109, 162, 188, and 189 from *Tabo: A Lamp for the Kingdom* with figures 4.11, 4.21, 4.22, 4.26, 4.37, and plate 16 in this volume. In comparing Buddha types from both periods, one will notice that the Buddha figures all share the strong horizontal upper lids of the eye and heavy modeling around the eyes. The face is often modeled with a gap between the neck and jaw, which is subtly filled in with shading. Lastly, the ears are rendered to show their thickness. Looking at the monastic attendants of the eleventh and fifteenth centuries, they are depicted in the same distinctive three-quarter profile with the far projecting eye and full cheek and small, rounded chin. The eleventh-century hairline pattern is also echoed in the fifteenth century, as is the simple monastic dress bearing one shoulder.

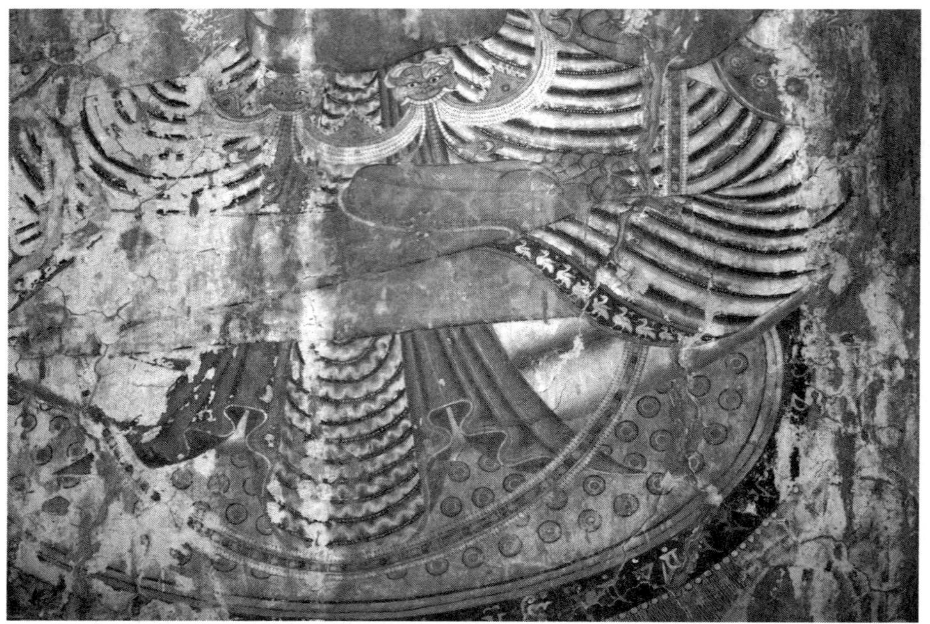

Figure 5.7. Tabo (Lahaul Spiti Dist., H.P.), Cella ambulatory: Mahābodhisattva's dhoti, c. eleventh century.

One of the telltale signs of the eleventh-century style and its fifteenth-century revival is the articulation of the jawlines. On the eleventh-century offering deity at Tabo's Dukhang (fig. 5.5), the jawline never fully extends to meet either side of the face. The chin and jaw of this offering deity are marked by a clear black line, but they are given dimension and shape through shading and highlighting. This technique seems to have been used primarily so that modeling, instead of a hard line, would indicate the true contour of the face. The courtly idiom of the fifteenth-century painting tradition initially employed this labor-intensive technique, as has been discussed in chapter 4.

Another characteristic trait of the eleventh century that is replicated in the fifteenth-century revival style is the depiction of elaborate textiles. Cottons or silks with intricate patterns were luxury goods imported from both Persia and Central India during the eleventh century and frequently depicted in the art of the time.[57] Deities painted in Tabo's Cella are rendered with exquisite textiles, as in a figure of Mahābodhisattva Vimala, who wears a dhoti decorated with red, white, and blue flower medallions. Another Mahābodhisattva figure from Tabo's Cella wears a lovely striped textile bordered with geese (fig. 5.7).[58] Figure 5.5 from the Dukhang illustrates a more complex textile pattern. This emphasis on multiple dyeing techniques and highly detailed designs may indicate the richness of luxury textiles that were in circulation during the eleventh century.

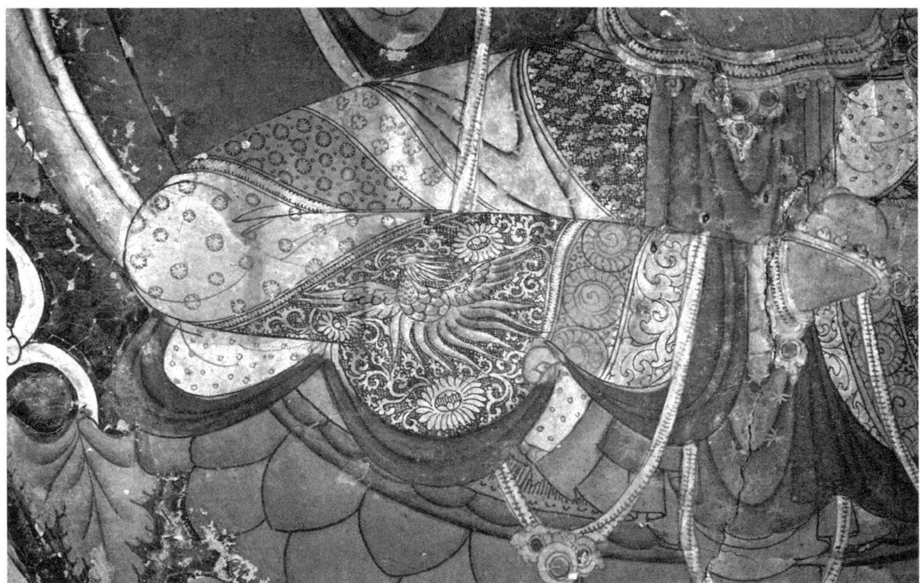

Figure 5.8. Tholing (West Tibet), Red Temple: subsidiary deity's dhoti, c. fifteenth century. WHAV JP93 463.

The artists of the fifteenth-century paintings replicate these multiple hues and intricate patterns with incredible precision, yet they also create innovative patterns. In the fifteenth-century Tholing and Tsaparang paintings, the same resist-dyed techniques and multicolored patterns of the older luxury textiles of the eleventh- and twelfth-century period are replicated as seen in figures 4.27, 4.29, 4.36, and 5.8. A close-up of a dhoti painted in Tholing's Red Temple allows us to see the complexity of design and color scheme with chrysanthemum and phoenix motifs paired with vegetal scrolling patterns, dots, and cloud formations. A more comprehensive study of the textiles from this and other fifteenth-century temples demonstrates that the patterns and motifs replicated are generally more aligned with the Chinese motifs of flying phoenixes and floating clouds, which were popular by the fifteenth and well into the eighteenth century.[59] In figure 5.8, for instance, the dhoti retains some of the dotted and medallion patterns of the eleventh century but also exhibits clouds, phoenixes, and peonies. By contrast, figure 5.9 reveals a more faithful adherence to textile patterns of the eleventh century. The reverse-dye technique can be seen in a red and blue section at the upper left of the image. Below this is a band of geese, which clearly recalls the pattern seen on the eleventh-century wall paintings in figure 5.7. Perhaps one of the noticeable changes to the fifteenth-century textile patterning can be seen in the two bands of vegetal scrolling, a decorative motif popular during the fifteenth century and strongly associated with the Newar or Beri style.

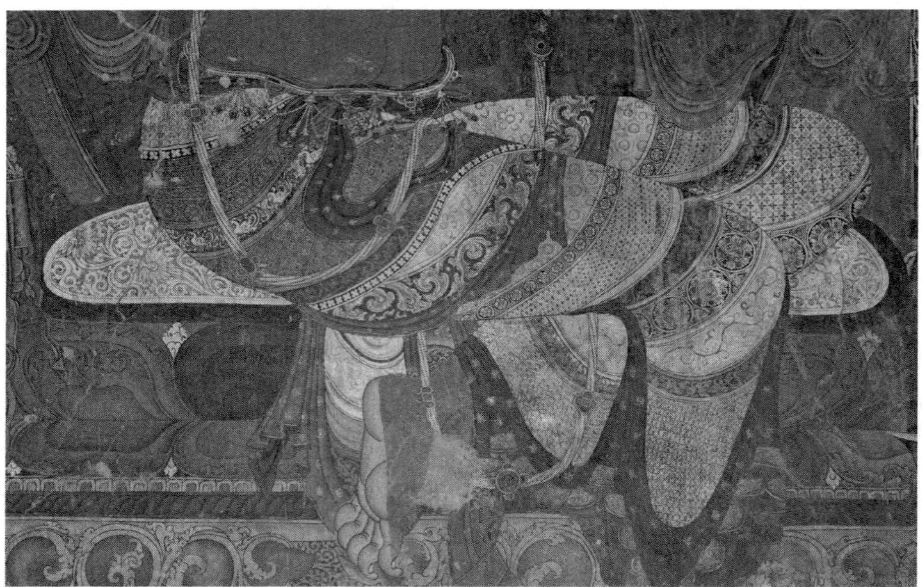

Figure 5.9. Tabo (Lahaul Spiti Dist., H.P.), Golden Temple, c. early sixteenth century: close-up of Maitreya's dhoti.

This shift in the patterns and motifs that were used in textile depictions may well be indicative of larger patterns of change regarding cultural interaction between the Ngari kingdom and other regions in Asia. Although the western Buddhist world of Kashmir was a cultural and religious hub of great significance during the tenth through twelfth centuries, its influence in West Tibet slowly faded after the thirteenth century due to Kashmir's growing Islamic presence. As previously discussed, by the fourteenth century, Tibet and China were politically and religiously involved. Connections, especially religious, were well maintained into the Ming (1368–1644) and Qing (1644–1911) dynasties. Aesthetically, these cultural interactions are borne out in such details as painted renderings of textile motifs.[60] Although Chinese motifs—such as flying phoenixes and chrysanthemums—were referenced in the fifteenth-century paintings, this aesthetic awareness was limited to textiles. It seems that the textiles replicated in the fifteenth-century Ngari paintings came to represent a hybrid of old Persian and Indian aesthetics and textile techniques of the eleventh century combined with Chinese motifs popular in the fifteenth century. These paintings are a product of the complex and rich dialogue between archaisms and contemporary motifs.

Another eleventh-century motif that makes a reappearance in the fifteenth-century paintings is the contorted, weight-bearing figure, such as those painted at the juncture of the wall and ceiling of such sites as the Dungkar caves (briefly mentioned in chapter 4 in relation to figs. 4.18,

4.19, and 4.20). This decorative feature is a typically Ngari motif that was initially used in the horizontal band of painting between the wall and ceiling. In Dungkar Cave 1, a number of figural types are used; one appears to hold the weight of the lantern ceiling on his shoulder, another squats with his hands fully extended above his head, and yet another is in a deep backbend while his hands hold the weight of the ceiling. These same contorted, stout, and muscled figures who strike positions that defy laws of gravity and balance reappear in the fifteenth-century Guge style, but become part of the decorative scheme of the thronebases upon which deities are positioned. In these later versions, the weight-bearing figures are rendered in even more knotted and contorted positions, with arms stretched upward to bear the weight of the throne.[61]

Lastly, another eleventh-century stylistic element that only briefly appears in the fifteenth-century style is the presence of heavenly architectural frames. In the early period, these forms are quite regularly depicted on the walls at Tabo and even at Nako, as Klimburg-Salter has pointed out:

> In painting, fanciful architecture in heavenly environments is used as a frame for a seated Buddha and less frequently a Bodhisattva figure. This type of lobed arch covered by a multi-tiered roof and topped by a dome or round finial is found only in heavenly architecture. . . . The roofs are decorated in a variety of ways, either with multicoloured tiles or painted with a floral motif, a row of wooden dangles always hangs under the eaves, and often there is a bell at the corners. These same wooden dangles are still found today on all temples in Kinnaur as well as other parts of Himachal Pradesh.[62]

At Tholing's Red Temple, there is an abbreviated fifteenth-century version of this form. While this heavenly architectural surround has the same kind of multitiered roof that is topped with a finial and even has white-painted wooden dowels, or "dangles,"[63] there are some differences to note as well. Most significant is the way the fifteenth-century heavenly architectural environment is subsumed within a larger physical structure, the elaborate throne in which Vairocana sits. These architectural structures form the columns for the massive throneback comprised of various bejeweled levels that serve as platforms on which *makaras* sit and offerings are presented. These architectural forms, however, do not remain long within the Guge style of the fifteenth through seventeenth centuries. These are mostly seen in the courtly idiom, which is most faithful to its eleventh- and twelfth-century antecedents.

These examples of stylistic resonance between the eleventh-century and fifteenth-century paintings provide strong evidence of the motifs and patterns to which these later artists were looking for inspiration. While I emphasize the Kashmir roots of the courtly idiom of the Ngari painting tradition in this chapter, I do not want to eclipse the complicated developments of this style. As ateliers continued to use the style, especially in the sixteenth and seventeenth centuries, they drew from other local and transregional styles, creating hybrid styles. A good example of such hybrids are found in Ladakh's Temo temple in Leh.

Multivalency of a Revival Style

The idea of a Tibetan painting style carrying a specifically constructed meaning or a particular semiotic value is not original to the fifteenth century.[64] As Klimburg-Salter has suggested, the art of the eleventh and twelfth centuries carried ideological messages that associated the Purang-Guge kingdom with Kashmiri religion and civilization, which at the time was heralded as the apex of Buddhist culture.[65] This Kashmiri-associated style, as patronized by the Purang-Guge royals, was used as a way to legitimize their new reign. Similarly, the fifteenth-century Guge kingdom employed this renascent style to express the message that they were inheritors of an intellectually and spiritually advanced culture. In considering this possibility one must keep in mind the original environment in which these paintings would have been engaged.

Tabo and Tholing would have had both the Khache style and the fifteenth-century renascent style existing in separate, but neighboring, temples.[66] Both Tabo and Nako are good examples of sites with various temples that housed painted programs spanning multiple centuries. This juxtaposition of old and new would have powerfully underscored the intended ideological message that the Guge kingdom of the fifteenth century had hoped to impart. This specific content was undoubtedly meant for the ruling elite, who likely were agents in the creation of the style and patrons of these programs.[67] The paintings would have functioned as a reflexive sign for the elite viewer, royal and monastic alike, expressing a message of legitimacy and ancestry.

There is a larger issue concerning the fifteenth-century Guge dynasty's reclamation of religious and political sites once associated with the Purang-Guge kingdom. The renascent style used in the fifteenth and sixteenth centuries can be found at many of the places initially patronized by the Purang-Guge dynasty, such as Tsaparang, Tholing, Tabo, and Mangnang.[68] It is impossible to say at this point whether all these sites were royally patronized in the fifteenth and sixteenth centuries, as there is a dearth of textual and inscriptional information to support such a claim. Nonetheless, given the interest that the fifteenth-century kingdom had in modeling itself after its predecessors, it is probable that their choice in both style of painting and sites of patronage was well considered. I am tentatively suggesting that the choice of specific locales worked in tandem with the style in order to impart a message of dynastic and cultural continuity.

While I suggest that these temples and their fifteenth-century painting programs were patronized by and intended for the ruling elite, they were undoubtedly open to the entire community, who composed the majority of the viewing public.[69] The question arises, therefore, about how this majority would have interpreted these images. Based on their "horizon of expectation," which would have been different than the social elite who wanted to position themselves in a place of authority, it is likely that the other viewers generally engaged these religious images less as political and more as religious images. According to the modern-day reception of painting programs at religious sites such as Nako, most adherents are not concerned with the style, chronology, or political message of paintings. This is not to say that such issues were beyond the scope of their comprehension. Rather, the concept of determining a specific date or political motive for the construction of a temple and its painted program can be an arbitrary undertaking because many adherents consider temples and religious art as timeless or divinely constructed, as is the case for Nako's Gyapagpa Temple.[70]

This trope of divine favor and manifestation with regard to religious images and sites is a prominent one throughout South Asia and Tibet. It highlights an important incongruity in the ways in which religious objects are understood as both manmade and divinely crafted. While these two understandings seem irreconcilable, the dissonance reveals multiple yet coexisting meanings and functions of religious images within the Tibetan Buddhist context. As such, the intended message and actual reception of these images do not comply with what Jan Mukarovsky posited when he wrote, "[T]here is nonetheless always something aimed at by the sign; and this arises very naturally from the fact that the sign must be understood in the same way by both its emitter and its receiver."[71] Rather, I consider these medieval Tibetan Buddhist images to be open, not closed, signs. Although the intended message may have been singular, there was likely a plurality in the reception of these images depending upon the viewers and their interpretive framework.

*　*　*

As the previous section illustrated, by "examining the social factors that frame the signs"[72] we are able to discern the multiple, as opposed to singular, meanings of this style. I further suggest that the social factors framing the use of this style change diachronically. Thus, while the textual and visual evidence suggests that the fifteenth-century Guge kingdom carefully and methodically resuscitated older visual forms to create a vocabulary expressing a specific political and religious ideological message, this semiotic message altered as the reproduction practices were temporally removed from their original patrons' intents and therefore referents. One of the most fundamental changes that we can consider in this process of reproduction is that over time artists from outside the cosmopolitan and courtly centers of Tsaparang and Tholing emulated this style, and in so doing effectively transformed the style from a courtly to a regional one, with more ateliers and a wider circulation. Consequently, there are, by the later part of the sixteenth century, a number of variations of this style. The painted program at Nako's Gyapagpa Temple is but one of these variations. Thus, by the time the style is used at the Gyapagpa Temple, it is largely divorced from the messages of royal inheritance and continuity.

Conclusion

*I*n tracing the artistic practices and devotional affiliations at Nako's Gyapagpa Temple, this book elucidates the social history of a Buddhist temple in the Indian Himalaya. Such a microhistory deepens understandings of both art and devotion. More than simple representations of Buddhist devotional subject matter, these paintings in the Gyapagpa Temple are emblematic of the intricate web of polity, economy, and religion that connected the village of Nako to the neighboring political and religious centers of Ladakh to the north and West Tibet (Mnga' ris [Ngari]) to the east. Addressing a neglected period and body of work, this book contributes to reshaping our understanding of India's western Himalayan religious and artistic landscapes in several significant ways. Firstly, the reestablishment of the Gyapagpa Temple's sixteenth-century affiliation with the Drigung school of the Bka' brgyud (Kagyu) tradition has brought into focus a slightly more extensive history of Drigung activity in this part of the western Himalayan region. Moreover, the identification of this temple as a Drigung site has also helped to nuance the ever-developing Drigung landscape of Ladakh, Ngari, and now Khu nu (Kinnaur). In terms of the religious history of Kinnaur and the larger Spiti valley, the extant material evidence allows us to speak of a religiously plural and dynamic environment that has no easily identifiable primary allegiance. Such religious syncretism can be unsettling because specific religious affiliations often help to determine political alliances. Kinnaur, however, resists such clear definitions, which I take to be indicative of the ways in which the region's political and religious identities have overlapped and shifted over the centuries.

Secondly, I hope this book has helped to refine the definition and extent of the transregional dynamics that influenced western Himalayan art production and reception in both the late medieval and present-day milieux. The stylistic analysis of the Gyapagpa paintings has revealed significant connections to the Ngari painting tradition of the fifteenth and sixteenth centuries. This in turn has permitted a deeper investigation of the painting style's vocabulary of forms, idiomatic expressions, and chronological development. Amittedly, much more work along these lines needs to be done. Ultimately, though, these iconographic and stylistic analyses of the Gyapagpa Temple and other related material have helped to illuminate the religious identities and political ideologies of Nako and the larger cultural environs of Ngari to which it was associated in the fifteenth and sixteenth centuries.

Lastly, by employing an interdisciplinary approach that combines traditional art historical methodologies—which considers both formalist and iconographic analysis—with inscriptional translation, ethnographic documentation, and theoretical inquiry, this book reveals the multilayered contexts, both diachronic and synchronic, that circumscribe these polysemic images. I hope this book serves to broaden art historical discussions regarding western Himalayan and Tibetan art with regard to the complex relationships of art to ideology, identity formation, and religious praxis. Moreover, this project contributes to a body of recent scholarship that is based on integrated methodological approaches, firmly grounded in context, for the study of religious images that remain in active use within their communities.

Introduction

1. A. H. Francke, *Antiquities of Indian Tibet,* 2 vols. (Calcutta: Superintendent Government Printing, India, 1914–26); Giuseppe Tucci, *Indo-Tibetica,* vol. 3, *The Temples of Western Tibet and Their Artistic Symbolism,* English edition, ed. Lokesh Chandra (1932; repr. New Delhi: Aditya Prakashan, 1988).

2. As a cursory overview of Indian history textbooks reveals, the majority of histories dealing with the medieval period rarely address material north of the Pratihara kingdom. This lacuna is due in part to the fact that the plethora of principalities and fiefdoms of these northern regions do not follow a model of a well-chronicled, large-scale suzerainty, which makes documentation of these areas very difficult. There are a few textual and art historical studies that have helped to flesh out our otherwise limited understanding of some of these northern kingdoms. See, for instance, Ron Inden, "Imperial Purāṇas: Kashmir as Vaiṇava Center of the World," in *Querying the Medieval: Texts and the History of Practices in South Asia,* ed. Ronald Inden, Jonathan Walters, and Daud Ali (Oxford University Press, 2000), 29–98; Michael Meister, "Mountain Temples and Temple-Mountains: Masrur," *Journal of the Society of Architectural Historians* 65, no. 1 (March 2006): 26–49; Mandavi Mehta, "The Mouse Who Would Be King: Innovating Tradition in the State of Chamba" (Ph.D. diss., University of Pennsylvania, 2011); Romila Thapar, "The Vamshavali from Chamba," *Himāl South Asian,* March 2010, www .himalmag.com/component/content/article/87.html.

3. S. Rickerby, "Nako Temple Complex: Himachal Pradesh, India Preliminary Inspection of the Wall Paintings," conservation report, Courtauld Institute of Art, London, 2003, 4.

4. Rickerby, "Nako Temple Complex," 4. The three other twelfth-century temples mentioned in this conservation report are the Lotsawa, Gongma, and Karchung.

5. Although it was a very short lived war, the conflict resulted in parts of the border area being declared contested zones, which are still tensely monitored by both Indian and Chinese troops stationed along the border. Consequently, the rich trade-life that once existed because of the channels

of commercial exchange running between India and Tibet has been cut off completely since 1962. For more on this see A. K. Dave, *The Real Story of China's War on India, 1962* (New Delhi: Centre for Armed Forces Historical Research, United Service Institution of India, 2006); and D. K. Palit, *War in High Himalaya: The Indian Army in Crisis, 1962* (London: Hurst, 1991).

6. Robert Jan Jauss, *Toward an Aesthetic of Reception* (Minneapolis: University of Minnesota Press, 1982). Several articles in *Art Journal* 57, no. 1 (1998), have been helpful to my thinking about reception theory in relation to religious art. See, for instance, Pamela M. Jones, "The Reception of Christian Devotional Art: The Renaissance to the Present"; and Gauvin Alexander Bailey, "The Indian Conquest of Catholic Art: The Mughals, the Jesuits, and Imperial Mural Painting."

7. This idea is the converse of many concepts about the role of memory and identity formation. See, for instance, Jan Assmann, "Collective Memory and Cultural Identity," *New German Critique* 65 (Spring–Summer 1995): 125–33. In this article he cites the seminal work of Aby Warburg, who specifically addressed this issue in relation to art.

8. Tsering Gyalpo, scholar of West Tibet, provided me with this information on Drigung temples in the westernmost part of Ngari. Conversation with author, Lhasa, Tibet, June 2006.

9. It is quite likely that this style was used well into the seventeenth century; however, I primarily focus on material up to the end of the sixteenth century.

10. Luciano Petech, *Central Tibet and the Mongols: The Yüan-Sa-skya period of Tibetan history* (Rome: Istituto Italiano per il Medio ed Estremo Oriente, 1990). For more on this see Roberto Vitali, "A Chronology (bstan rtsis) of Events in the History of Mnga' ris skor gsum (Tenth–Fifteenth Centuries)," in McKay, *The History of Tibet*, 2:77–79.

11. I construe social history of art to mean, in this case, an analysis of the shifting meanings, uses, and contexts of art objects over time. At the Gyapagpa Temple, I further consider how alterations in meaning, use, and context directly bear on a devotee's or ritual agent's reception.

12. Donald S. Lopez, Jr., *Prisoners of Shangri-La: Tibetan Buddhism and the West* (Chicago: University of Chicago Press, 1998): 146, 150.

13. David Carrier, "What Happens When Art History Travels," in *Is Art History Global?* ed. James Elkins (New York and London: Routledge, 2007), 286–89.

14. Ronald B. Inden, *Imaging India* (Bloomington: Indiana University Press, 2000), 2.

15. This trend in scholarship is not limited to western Himalayan art. As Robert Sharf has explained, art historians and buddhologists have, for different reasons, skirted issues pertaining to the function of Buddhist objects. See introduction to *Living Images: Japanese Buddhist Icons in Context,* ed. Robert H. Sharf and Elizabeth Horton Sharf (Stanford, Calif.: Stanford University Press, 2001), 4. My study, as do other recent books and studies focused on Buddhist art, elucidates the multivalent relationships between devotee and art object in order to articulate the manifold complexities around Buddhist art's changing functions and meanings.

16. Richard Davis, *Lives of Indian Images* (Princeton, N.J.: Princeton University Press, 1997), 7–8.

17. Christian Luczanits writes, "It is thus not surprising that most of the major recent publications are dedicated to objects relatively recently acquired by private collectors and museums on the art market, while studies of monuments and artifacts still in their context remain in the background" ("Methodological Comments Regarding Recent Research on Tibetan Art," *Wiener Zeitschrift für die Kunde Südasiens* 45 [2001]: 126). He then lists four such studies that have focused on sites as a whole.

18. Michael Meister, "Sweetmeats or Corpses? Art History and Ethnography," *RES: Anthropology and Aesthetics* 27 (1995): 118–32; and *Ethnography and Personhood: Notes from the Field* (Jaipur, India: Rawat Publications, 2000). See also Cynthea J. Bogel, "Canonizing Kannon: The Ninth-Century Esoteric Buddhist Altar at Kanshinji," *Art Bulletin* 84, no. 1 (March 2002): 30–64; Sherry Fowler, *Murōji: Rearranging Art and History at a Japanese Buddhist Temple* (Honolulu: University of Hawai'i Press, 2005); and Gregory P. Levine, "Switching Sites and Identities: The Founder's Statue at the Japanese Zen Buddhist Temple Kōrin'in." *Art Bulletin* 83 (March 2001): 72–104.

1. Nako's Sociopolitical History and Artistic Heritage

1. Jogishvar Singh, "A Brief Survey of Village Gods and Their Moneylending Operations in Kinnaur District of Himacha Pradesh; Along with Earlier Importance of Trade with Tibet," in *Wissenschaftsgeschichte und Gegenwärtige Forschungen in Norwest-Indien,* ed. Lydia Icke-Schwalbe and Gudrun Meier (Dresden: Staatliches Museum für völkerkunde, 1990), 244–58.

2. For more information on the various routes connecting Kinnaur to Spiti see Deborah Klimburg-Salter, *Tabo: A Lamp for the Kingdom: Early-Indo-Tibetan Buddhist Art in the Western Himalaya* (New York: Thames and Hudson, 1998), 31–32.

3. Jogishwar Singh, *Banks, Gods and Government: Institutional and Informal Credit Structure in a Remote and Tribal Indian District (Kinnaur, Himachal Pradesh) 1960–1985* (Stuttgart: Steiner Verlag Wiesbaden GMBH, 1989), 5. This extreme landscape raises the question of water access and irrigation systems in villages located along the Sutlej River in Upper Kinnaur. In Nako, Chango, and other villages, water is gathered from precipitation, as well as snow melt. Water collected above the village is then channeled into the fields through an irrigation system. For more on water and irrigation systems in the Himalayas, see Kim Gutschow and Niels Gutschow, "A Landscape Dissolved: Households, Fields, and Irrigation in Rinam, Northwest India," in *Sacred Landscape of the Himalaya, Proceedings of an International Conference at Heidelberg, May 1998,* ed. Niels Gutschow et al. (Vienna: Verlage der Österreische Akademie der Wissenschaften, 2003), 111–136.

4. The exchange of goods between Tibet and the Indian western Himalayan regions, however, has come to a halt since the 1962 Sino-Indian Border Conflict. See the introduction.

5. Singh, *Banks, Gods, and Government,* 10. Singh suggests that other occupations included animal husbandry, horticulture, and moneylending.

6. Guge Tsering Gyalpo addresses this issue of the difficulty of establishing boundary lines between Kinnaur and West Tibet. See Gu ge tshe ring rgyal po, *Gu ge thse ring rgyal po'i ched rtsom phyogs bsgrigs* [Guge Tsering

Gyalpo's collection of essays] (Lhasa: Tibetological Publishing House of China, 2004), 175–77.

7. Deborah Klimburg-Salter, "Ribba: The Story of an Early Buddhist Temple in Kinnaur," in *Buddhist Art and Tibetan Patronage, Ninth to Fourteenth Centuries: PIATS 2000, Proceedings of the Ninth Seminar of the International Association for Tibetan Studies*, ed. Deborah E. Klimburg and Eva Allinger (Leiden and Boston: Brill, 2002), 4; Roberto Vitali, *The Kingdoms of Gu.ge Pu.hrang According to mNga'.ris rgyal.rabs by Gu.ge mkhan. chen Ngag.dbang grags.pa* (New Delhi: Indraprasha Press, 1996), 126. Vitali wonders if the site *Khur shud* might be the same as *Kinnaur shod*. Indeed, it would be important to know if Kinnaur was also known as Khur and if there was such a designation of "lower" Kinnaur, as the Tibetan word *shod* would suggest.

8. Roberto Vitali, *The Kingdoms of Gu.ge Pu.hrang,* 126.

9. Tucci, "Travels of Tibetan Pilgrims in the Swat Valley," in *Opera Minora* (Rome: Giovanni Bardi, 1971), 2:384.

10. Elena De Rossi Filibeck, *Two Tibetan Guide Books to Ti Se and La Phyi* (Bonn: VGH Wissenschaftverlag, 1988), 77.

11. Klimburg-Salter, "Ribba," 4.

12. For a detailed discussion of the ways in which Khu nu was variously incorporated into Zhang Zhung territories—and specifically West Tibet's fifteenth-century purview—see Vitali, *The Kingdoms of Gu.ge Pu.hrang,* 126, 158, 167.

13. J. Singh, *Banks, Gods, and Government,* 74. Singh also writes, however, that there is no actual written proof or documentation of the Bashahr kingdom in Kinnaur until the end of the seventeenth century (54). See Mandavi Mehta, "The Mouse Who Would Be King: Innovating Tradition in the State of Chamba" (Ph.D. diss., University of Pennsylvania, 2011).

14. J. Singh, *Banks, Gods, and Government,*

15. Christian Jahoda, "Political Space and Socio-Economic Organization in the Lower Spiti Valley (Early Nineteenth to Late Twentieth Century)," *Journal of the International Association of Tibetan Studies* 4 (December 2008): 8. See also Luciano Petech, "Historical Introduction," in *Inscriptions from the Tabo Main Temple, Texts and Translations,* ed. Luciano Petech and Christian Luczanits (Rome: Istituo italiano per l'Africa e l'Oriente, 1999), 2. It should also be noted that A. H. Francke mentions a lineage of chiefs that resides at Nako and ruled over the district of Li. He does not, however, provide a date for this activity. See Francke, *Antiquities of Indian Tibet* (Calcutta: Superintendent Government Printing, India, 1914–26), 2:276.

16. Vitali, *The Kingdoms of Gu.ge Pu.hrang,* 130.

17. Luciano Petech, for instance, expressed some hesitation about this point. See *The Kingdom of Ladakh, c. 950–1842 A.D.* (Rome: Istituto Italiano per il Medio ed Estremo Oriente, 1977), 22. Petech's hesitation can likely be attributed to the fact that little was known about West Tibet and its relation to Central Tibet. The later discovery of the Ngari Chronicle (*Mnga' ris rgyal rabs*) furnishes a bit more insight.

18. Giuseppe Tucci, *Tibetan Painted Scrolls* (Rome: Libreria dello Stato, 1949), 671–72.

19. Luciano Petech, "The 'Bri-Guṅ-Pa Sect in Western Tibet and Ladakh," in Petech, *Selected Papers on Asian History* (Rome: Istituto Italiano per il Medio ed Estremo Oriente, 1988), 366; Petech, *The Kingdom of Ladakh,* 30.

20. Luciano Petech, "The Tibetan-Ladakhi Moghul War of 1681–83," *Indian Historical Quarterly* 23, no. 3 (1947): 198.

21. Luciano Petech, "Western Tibet: Historical Introduction," in Klimburg-Salter, *Tabo,* 248.

22. Nachiket Chanchani's "Fording and Frontiers: Architecture and Identities in the Central Himalayas" (Ph.D. diss., Univerity of Pennsylvania, 2012), although focused on an earlier period, may help to illuminate the intersections and interactions among sacred centers in the Himalayan region.

23. Such an intermixing of religious practices is not unique to the Upper Kinnaur region. Areas in Uttar Pradesh also practice a mixture of Hinduism and Buddhism. For more on this, see T. S. Maxwell, "Lakhamandal and Trilokinath: The Transformed Functions of Hindu Architecture in the Cross-Cultural Zones of the Western Himalaya," *Art International* 24, nos. 1–2 (September–October 1980): 9–74.

24. Stylistically the temple paintings could be dated to roughly the nineteenth and twentieth centuries, yet the temple may be much earlier, even perhaps to the period of Rinchen Zangpo (958–1055). See Christian Luczanits, *Buddhist Sculpture in Clay: Early Western Himalayan Art, Late 10th to Early 13th Centuries* (Chicago: Serindia, 2004), 57–62.

25. For more on this, see Anne-Marie Blondeau, ed., *Tibetan Mountain Deities, Their Cults and Representations: Papers Presented at a Panel of the 7th Seminar of the International Association for Tibetan Studies, Graz, 1995* (Vienna: Verlag der Osterreichischen Akademie der Wissenschaften, 1998).

26. This romanization is based on an inscription found in a Dung 'gyur temple in Chango, a village just north of Nako. Although the romanization is not recognized in Tibetan dictionaries, I use it because it addresses a very specific type of temple in the Kinnaur and Spiti regions.

27. S. Rickerby, "Nako Temple Complex: Himachal Pradesh, India Preliminary Inspection of the Wall Paintings," conservation report, Courtauld Institute of Art, London, 2003, 7.

28. Luczanits, *Buddhist Sculpture in Clay,* 89.

29. Padmasambhava, an Indian ascetic practitioner, is thought to have introduced institutionalized Tantric practice to Tibet in the eighth century. He is a much beloved figure in Tibetan Buddhism and is strongly associated with one of the oldest schools of Tibetan Buddhism known as Nyingma. He is an incredibly popular figure in this part of northern India. See also Tucci, "Travels of Tibetan Pilgrims," 370. In this essay, Tucci briefly comments on how the Kagyu tradition, especially the Drukpa and Kar ma (Karma) schools, are strongly associated with the figure of Padmasambhava and his birthplace—known in Sanskrit as Uḍḍiyāna or Oḍiyāna (Tibetan: O rgyan or U rgyan)—which is located in the Swat valley, in present-day Pakistan. This is of particular relevance as there are several sites in the Spiti valley, including Nako, which combine Kagyu iconography with images of Guru Rimpoche. For a more detailed discussion on this topic in relation to Drigung practice see Petech, "The 'Bri-Guṅ-Pa Sect," 355–68.

30. Based on limited stylistic analysis, I would date these paintings to circa eighteenth century.

31. This number of monastics was based on an interview I had with one of
the monks in residence.

32. Petech, "The 'Bri-Gung-Pa Sect," 355–68. Petech discusses the gradual
doctrinal amalgamation that happens between the Drigungpa school and
Nyingma tradition in the sixteenth century in Ngari. Based on the iconographic evidence, it seems that this same syncretism may have occurred with
the Nyingma tradition and the 'Brug pa school as well as the early Dge lugs
pa tradition in the Kinnaur and Spiti regions. This hybrid approach may have
developed only on the devotional level and therefore there may be no textual
sources that corroborate the visual evidence.

33. Deborah Klimburg-Salter, personal communication, May 2008. According to Klimburg-Salter, the *mani* stones (rocks carved with the prayer *Oṃ ma
ṇi pad me hūṃ*) and rock inscriptions in and around Nako give the name of
the village as Gnas sgo.

34. Laxman S. Thakur, *Buddhism in the Western Himalaya: A Study of
the Tabo Monastery* (New Delhi: Oxford University Press, 2001), 43. Thakur
mentions, for instance, that Rinchen Zangpo (958–1055) traveled to Kashmir
for Buddhist teachings and had to pass through Kinnaur to get there. This
information, however, is not exactly corroborated when one refers to Rinchen
Zangpo's biography; there is no direct reference to Kinnaur that I could find.
See the oft-quoted biography translation in David L. Snellgrove and Tadeusz
Skorupski, *The Cultural Heritage of Ladakh*, vol. 2, *Zangskar and the Cave
Temples of Ladakh* (Warminster, UK: Aris and Phillips, 1979–80). There are
several redactions of Rinchen Zangpo's biography, which ideally should be
collected, analyzed, and consulted for information on his travels through this
region. They may shed light on routes traveled or regions visited.

35. Tucci, "Travels of Tibetan Pilgrims," 384.

36. Tucci, "Travels of Tibetan Pilgrims," 384. The date of the text with the
thirteenth-century pilgrim's itinerary is not explicitly given by Tucci and it
cannot be assumed that it dates to the thirteenth century.

37. Tucci, "Travels of Tibetan Pilgrims," 375. Tucci, in fact, uses two texts
related to this figure's life and travels. The larger biography, which Tucci
found in Spiti, is the primary source for the quoted material. The title of this
text is *Rgyal ba rgod tsang pa mgon po rdo rje'i rnam t'ar mthong ba don
ldan nor bui phreng ba.*

38. Tucci, "Travels of Tibetan Pilgrims," 377.

39. Tucci, "Travels of Tibetan Pilgrims," 377.

40. Tucci, "Travels of Tibetan Pilgrims," 407.

41. Deborah Klimburg-Salter's interpretation of the seventeenth-century
pilgrim's travel itinerary is different from mine; cf. Klimburg-Salter, "The
Nako Preservation Project," *Orientations* (May 2003): 40. She writes that the
pilgrim travels from the Charang Pass to "Poo and Namgia en route to Lahaul." Indeed, if the pilgrim came upon Poo first and then Namgia, this would
indicate a northerly route. Tucci's translation inverts that order, however. The
pilgrim first comes to Rnam rgyal, which Klimburg-Salter and I both construe
as Namgia, and proceeds to Poo. To confuse matters, there are two villages
known as Poo. One lies north and the other south of Namgia, and this very
well may be the root of the confusion over the pilgrim's route (fig. 1.1). Based
on the other places the pilgrim travels, I suggest that the "Poo" he visits is
along the southern route as he then proceeds to So rang, which if Tucci is

correct, is Sarahan (see fig. Intro.3). In other words, I think the pilgrim does not go through Lahaul as Klimburg-Salter suggests. This southern route running along the Sutlej is not as well known for its fervent Buddhist activity as is Spiti and Lahaul. Why this path would have been preferred over the northern route, which would have taken the pilgrim through places like Tabo, is unclear.

42. Thakur, *Buddhism in the Western Himalaya*, 13–15.

43. Singh, *Banks, Gods and Government*, 25.

44. Singh, *Banks, Gods and Government*, 21.

45. Singh, *Banks, Gods and Government*, 11. Singh notes, "Over time trade patterns stabilized in such a way that traders from particular villages in Kinnaur would trade only with particular correspondents in Western Tibet or other areas year after year" (11).

46. Klimburg-Salter, *Tabo*, 34.

47. Thakur, *Buddhism in the Western Himalaya*, 13–15.

48. J. Singh, *Banks, Gods and Government*, 24. This is a good example of the vast trade routes east and west between northern India and Tibet, as well as extending north into Ladakh.

49. J. Singh, "A Brief Survey of Village Gods," 245.

50. Although the whole community uses these temples, the responsibility of maintaining them falls on individual families. For instance, this temple and the four temples of the religious compound are maintained by Tenzin Lama, commonly referred to as Lama ji. He is thought of as the ritual master of the village. Although he is not currently a monk, he was trained as one earlier in his life and is one of the most knowledgeable people in the village about the temples and their histories.

51. Occurrences of Guru Rimpoche's footprints in rock and the veneration of these touch-relics are well known throughout the Tibetan cultural zone. See, for instance, Janet Gyatso, *Apparitions of the Self: The Secret Autobiography of a Tibetan Visionary* (Princeton, N.J.: Princeton University Press, 1998), 18–19.

52. For more on this style, see chapters 3 and 4. I am aware that nomenclature and taxonomy of style are particularly knotty issues in the study of Tibetan and more broadly Himalayan art history. In fact, in 2011 Rob Linrothe and I organized and co-chaired "What's in a Name: Reconsidering Tibetan Stylistic Taxonomies," a panel presented at the 99th College Art Association conference in New York City. I thank Rob for his continued discussions about the topic. An example of such complicated stylistic taxonomies relevant to this book relates to the terms Inner Asian international style and Central Tibetan Style. The umbrella term "Inner Asian International Style," coined in 1998 by Deborah Klimburg-Salter ("Is There an Inner Asian International Style 12th to the 14th Centuries? Definition of the Problem and Present State of Research," in Klimburg-Salter and Allinger, *Inner Asian International Style*, 1–12) had been used to name and define multivarious Pāla-derived painting traditions of Inner Mongolia, Tibet, Nepal, and Burma. Since that publication, however, scholars, including Klimburg-Salter, have moved away from the concept of an international style when addressing the Pāla-derived painting styles of Central Tibet and their different, and often far-flung regional interpretations. For the purposes of this book, Central Tibetan Style is used to

refer to the western Himalayan iterations of the Central Tibetan Pāla-derived style of the twelfth to fourteenth centuries.

53. Klimburg-Salter, "The Nako Preservation Project," 45.

54. For more information on this temple and its inscription see Kurtis Tropper, "On an Inscription in the Guru Rimpoche Lha Khang at Nako, Kinnaur," in *Tibetan Art and Architecture in Context: PIATS 2006, Tibetan Studies: Proceedings of the Eleventh Seminar of the International Association for Tibetan Studies, Königswinter 2006,* ed. Erberto F. Lo Bue and Christian Luczanits ([Andiast]: International Institute for Tibetan and Buddhist Studies, 2010), 122–43.

55. It is unclear when or why the monastic community died out at Nako. It seems that monks were active in the village during A. H. Francke's visit in the early 1900s. He does not mention a sectarian affiliation for the monastery, although Francke clearly states that Nako village was affiliated with the 'Brug pa school of the Bka' brgyud pa tradition. Tucci makes no mention of monastic life in his description of his fieldwork in Nako in 1931, which would suggest that it had died out by that time. See Francke, *Antiquities of Indian Tibet* (Calcutta: Superintendent Government Printing Office, India, 1914–26), 1:32–33; and Giuseppe Tucci, *Indo-Tibetica,* vol. 3, *The Temples of Western Tibet and Their Artistic Symbolism,* English edition, ed. Lokesh Chandra (1932; repr. New Delhi: Aditya Prakashan, 1988).

56. The pitched metal roof is a rather recent preservation measure taken by the village in an attempt to minimize water leakage caused by rain and snow accumulation. Although architecturally incongruent, these stopgap measures are affordable for the village and fairly effective in protecting the structure from continued damage in the short term.

57. Kunchok Ngodrub (temple caretaker), in discussion with the author (Rinchen Namgyal, translator), May 2005. Rinchen Namgyal is the artist who was commissioned to repaint the sculptures on either side of the prayer wheel in the Dung 'gyur. He organized this interview and kindly served as translator. All the interviews conducted in Nako became public events, with people dropping in and out of the conversations.

58. Despite numerous requests, Ani Kuntsog declined to be recorded.

59. Given the style of painting in these two temples, a rough date of the nineteenth century would be appropriate.

60. I went to each Tungyur temple but found no concrete proof that they had all been sponsored by Lobsang Chodak. Further, those at Chango and Dankar had been renovated and repainted. Chango's Tungyur has a newly painted Nyingma iconographic program, perhaps obliterating old 'Brug pa iconography. There is an inscription by the door of the temple with a painted image of three women, all of whom are named. Part of the inscription reads, "Ne srang dpen shes rab . . . su dung 'gyur 'di bzhengs pa yin." Although the entire name is not legible, the inscription indicates that the temple was "built by" Ne srang dpen shes rab. While Shes rab is a common name, Ne srang is not. Ne srang may refer to the village of Nisang, which is south of Nako. Nonetheless, this clearly is not the name of Lobsang Chodak.

61. Rickerby, "Nako Temple Complex," 7.

62. André Alexander, *The Temples of Lhasa: Tibetan Buddhist Architecture from the 7th to the 21st Centuries* (Chicago: Serindia, 2005); Romi Khosla,

Buddhist Monasteries of the Western Himalaya (Kathmandu: Ratna Pustak Bhandar, 1979).

63. Francke, *Antiquities of Indian Tibet*, 1:32.

64. It is difficult to know if Francke was writing about the two *Mchod rten* located immediately outside of the compound since he did not include a plan of the site.

65. Note that the site plan does not include this new Dung 'gyur temple, which must have been constructed after the plan was drafted.

66. Francke, *Antiquities of Indian Tibet*, 1:32. It is interesting to note that Francke uses the word *monastery* instead of *temple* to describe these structures. It seems that these words are still often interchanged in scholarship on the area.

67. For information on the stylistic and iconographic information about these two temples see Klimburg-Salter, "The Nako Preservation Project"; Christian Luczanits, "The 12th Century Buddhist Monuments of Nako," *Orientations* (May 2003): 46–53.

68. Luczanits, "The 12th Century Buddhist Monuments," 52.

69. The connection between Ngari and the Bka' gdams pa tradition is due in large part to one of its most venerated teachers, Atiśa, who taught and wrote while staying in Tholing in the eleventh century.

70. Rickerby, "Nako Temple Complex," 4.

71. These paintings will be briefly discussed in chapter 4. It should be noted that the east wall (the entrance/exit) features paintings of the nineteenth century. These wall paintings are discussed in Melissa Kerin, "Post-Fifteenth-Century Wall Paintings of Nako's Religious Compound," in *Nako*, ed. Lisa Gräber (Vienna: Böhlau Verlag Wien Köln, forthcoming).

72. Interestingly, it seems that the Upper Temple is the only one in the compound that does not have extensive repainting. I did not, however, have the opportunity to study the Upper Temple during my two seasons of fieldwork in Nako (2004–5) because it was being renovated. As the roof was taken off and replaced, the paintings were covered in plastic sheets to prevent any damage. Consequently, I could not study the painting programs of this temple as carefully as the others. Nonetheless, the photos of this temple, which are housed at the Western Himalayan Archive Vienna at the University of Vienna indicate that there is no later painting campaign.

73. Rickerby, "Nako Temple Complex," 4, 8. Although these technical similarities are important for gauging a date for these two temples, their exact chronology in relation to the other two temples, the Upper and Translator Temples, cannot yet be clearly determined.

74. Francke, *Antiquities of Indian Tibet*, 1:33.

75. Tucci, *Indo-Tibetica*, 3, bk. 1, *The Monasteries of Spiti and Kunavar*, 171.

76. Klimburg-Salter, "The Nako Preservation Project," 44.

2. Forgetting to Remember

1. Janet Gyatso, *In the Mirror of Memory: Reflections on Mindfulness and Remembrance in Indian and Tibetan Buddhism* (Albany: State University of New York Press, 1992).

2. Matthew Kapstein uses this term in the chapter "The Amnesic Monarch and the Five Mnemic Men," in *The Tibetan Assimilation of Buddhism:*

Conversion, Contestation, and Memory (Oxford: Oxford University Press, 2000), 178–96. Admittedly, Kapstein's notion of "mnemic engagement" in relation to Dzokchen practice is different from my employment here, but the term is a useful one that underscores the active processes of remembering.

3. Gregory Schopen coined the phrase "on the ground" in his efforts to high light the disparity between textual and archaeological evidence. According to Schopen, the latter provides concrete information for understanding how early Buddhism functioned "on the ground" (*Bones, Stones and Buddhist Monks: Collected Papers on the Archaeology, Epigraphy and Texts of Monastic Buddhism in India* [Honolulu: University of Hawai'i Press, 1997], 114).

4. While in Dehra Dun, the director of the Songtsen Library, Dr. Tashi Sampel, mentioned that there was another analysis of this temple written in Hindi by a professor at Himachal Pradesh University of Shimla. Unfortunately, I have not been able to locate a copy of this article.

5. A. H. Francke, *Antiquities of Indian Tibet* (Calcutta: Superintendent Government Printing Office, India, 1914–26), 1:32.

6. Francke, *Antiquities of Indian Tibet,* 1:32.

7. Francke, *Antiquities of Indian Tibet* 1:33.

8. Giuseppe Tucci, *Indo-Tibetica*, vol. 3, *The Temples of Western Tibet and Their Artistic Symbolism*, bk. 1, *The Monasteries of Spiti and Kunavar*, English edition, ed. Lokesh Chandra (1932; repr. New Delhi: Aditya Prakashan, 1988), 171.

9. Laxman S. Thakur, "Nako Monastery: Archaeological Notes from an Account of the Western Himalayan Expeditions," *East and West* 46, nos. 3–4 (1996): 349.

10. Thakur, "Nako Monastery," 349.

11. Deborah Klimburg-Salter, "The Nako Preservation Project," *Orientations* (May 2003): 43.

12. Tibetan Buddhist nuns in the western Himalayan region often work fields and tend children. This engagement with the quotidian world forces them to bridge the worlds of householder and renunciant. For more on Himalayan female monasticism, see Kim Gutschow, *Being a Buddhist Nun: The Struggle for Enlightenment in the Himalaya* (Cambridge, Mass.: Harvard University Press, 2004).

13. Ani Samten Wangmo (Buddhist nun), in discussion with the author, May 2005. The primary interview took place at her home in Nako on May 30, 2005. Rinchen Namgyal, an artist from Malling who was repainting some of the family's small clay sculptures at the time, helped translate some of the interview.

14. Moni (owner of Nas Go Restaurant, Nako), in discussion with the author, June 4, 2006. As several people casually joined the conversation at various points throughout this interview, it was difficult to document the names of all those who contributed. In my written rendition, I have tried to retain this spontaneous and interactive quality.

15. Samten Karmay, "The Theoretical Basis of the Tibetan Epic, with Reference to a 'Chronological Order' of the Various Episodes in the Gesar Epic," *Bulletin of the School of Oriental and African Studies, University of London* 56, no. 2 (1993), 234–46.

16. Kunchok Ngodrub (temple caretaker), in discussion with the author (Rinchen Namgyal, translator), May 2005. Unfortunately, this Buddha

remained unnamed. At the same time that these temples were erected, Kunchok said that an eight-kilometer canal was also built. There were no other specifics mentioned about this canal; it may very well have something to do with their irrigation systems upon which agriculture depends in the high altitude desert.

17. It should be noted that even the Tungyur temples at Nako participate in this trope, as it is thought that the patron was an incarnation of Spyan ras gzigs (Chenrezig) a form of Avalokiteśvara (see chapter 1).

18. J. P. Vogel, *Antiquities of Chamba State* (Calcutta: Superintendent Government Print, 1911–57); Francke, *Antiquities of Indian Tibet*, 2:7. Vogel includes the Chamba Vaṃśāvalī, which outlines the history of Chamba's royal lineage that claims divine ancestry. Francke makes an apt comparison between the royal chronicles of Ladakh and India revealing their similarities in proclaiming divine origin. He writes, "It is very probable that some of the early historians of Ladakh or Tibet took Indian Vaṃśāvalī as their model. The Vaṃśāvalī of Chamba, for instance, as published by Dr. J. Ph. Vogel . . . bears a strong resemblance to the older portions of the La-dvags-rgyal-rabs. Both productions begin with an introductory hymn. . . . Then, both books contain a long list of names of mythological beings, the supposed supernatural ancestors of the race of kings, and, in a third part, the names of the actual human kings are given" (2:7).

19. "2002 World Monuments Watch." World Monuments Fund website, January 2002, www.wmf.org/sites/default/files/wmf_publication/Watch _Catalog_2002.pdf.

20. For information about Drigung's "decline" after the thirteenth century in West Tibet, see Luciano Petech, "The 'Bri-Guṅ-Pa Sect in Western Tibet and Ladakh," in Petech, *Selected Papers on Asian History,* 361. He locates the decline of Drigung spiritual life and scholarship to the fifteenth century when Drigung relinquished control of various hermitages and property to Drukpa. This is also a period when the Sa skya (Sakya) tradition (in particular the Ngor school) received political favor by the Sman tang (Mustang) kingdom. As a result, patronage was directed to either Drukpa or Sakya affiliations. This trend would change very briefly in the sixteenth century, when the charismatic Drigung teacher, Ldan ma kun dga' grags pa (Danma Kunga Drakpa), gained tremendous support in West Tibet and Ladakh.

21. This is all the more shocking when one considers that Kinnaur's neighboring areas of Ladakh, Zangskar, and West Tibet have valuable material evidence supporting Drigung activity. The primary Drigung sites in Ladakh are Alchi, Phyiang, Lamayuru, Kanji, Wanla, and Tangtse. There are several other dis- or reused sites that still provide critical material evidence for Drigung activity. These are located in Photoksar, Lingshet, Urbis, and Senge. As for Tibet, there are several well-known Drigung temples in West Tibet, but these do not retain original paintings or sculpture. One temple that has preserved an eighteenth-century Drigung painting program is known as the Tsegu Monastery in Purang. The dearth of in situ material evidence in Tibet may be due in part to large-scale changes in religious practice. For instance, widespread conversion to Drukpa and Gelug in the seventeenth century may have resulted in repainting old Drigung sites. For a case study of the conversion of a Drigung site in Ladakh, see Rob Linrothe, "A Winter in the Field," *Orientations* (May 2007): 40–53.

22. For comparison see Himalayan Art Resources #90715, www
.himalayanart.org.

23. The Drigung school claims Achi, who lived in the eleventh century, as
the great-grandmother of its founder, Jigten Gonpo. It should be noted that
the inscription is a specific and perhaps archaic rendering of the protector's
name. More commonly one will see either A chi chos kyi sgrol ma or A phyi
chos kyi sgrol ma. Each renders the second syllable differently: chi vs. phyi.
They both, however, share the ending of sgrol ma, which evokes the name
of the bodhisattva Tara. The ending used in the Gyapagpa inscription reads:
sgron ma, which translates as "torch," "lamp," or "light." In this context her
name could be translated as "Lamp or light of the Dharma, Achi." Lastly,
one should be aware that *la na mo* is an honorific salutation and not a specific
part of her name.

24. As there is very little in situ material evidence that survives featuring Achi, it is difficult to find visual correspondences. There are a couple
nineteenth-century paintings in the Himalayan Art Resource to which one
can refer. See, for instance, items numbered 73896 and 1034. I thank Meghan
Howard for discussions about Achi iconography in 2006.

25. I thank Dr. Jamyang Samten of the Central Institute for Higher Tibetan
Studies for having brought this text to my attention. I worked with Terrence
Barrett on a translation of the following: "A phyi chos kyi sgrol ma sku mdog
dkar la dmar ba'i mdangs dang ldan / zhi zhing cung zad khro ba'i nyams can
/ dbu la dung thod dang rin po ches brgyan pa / dar sna tshogs kyi cod pan
rna ltag tu 'pur ba dbu skra ral pa'i thor tshugs can / sku la lha rdzas kyi na
bza' bklubs pa / phyag gyas stong nyid kyi rang bzhin dā ma ru drag tu 'grol
bas ye shes kyi dā kī tshogs rnams dbyings nas bskul ba . . . phyag gyon bdud
khrag gis gang ba'i thod pa thugs kar bsnams shing snying rjes zhal du gsol ba
/ zhabs gnyis drag shul chen po'i stabs kyis gung gnyis la gling bzhi khyab par
nyul pa'i cang shes gro sngon myur mgyogs shugs can la rab tu mdzes pa'i za
'og gi dar chen gyis glo bsdams pa / O rgyan bstan dzin, *Rgyal b'i bstan srung
dbyings phyug chos kyi sgrol ma'i bskang mdos rgyas pa'i phyug len grigs su
bkod pa thub bstan snyan pa'i dbyar rnga bzhugs so*" (O rgyan bstan 'dzin,
*Rgyal ba'i bstan srung dbyings phyug chos kyi sgrol ma'i bskang mdos rgyas
pa'i phyug len grigs su bkod pa thub bstan snyan pa'i dbyar rnga bzhugs so*
[Bir, Himachal Pradesh: D. Tsondu Senghe, 1998], 29–30).

26. In trying to find visual *comparanda,* I could not locate any sixteenth-
century image of Achi. Rather, the majority of imagery relating to Achi comes
from the nineteenth century or later. In studying these forms and in looking at
various textual descriptions of her, it became clear that there are many iconographic forms for Achi as well as variant spellings of her name. Clearly, what
is depicted at Nako is but one of her manifestations. Moreover, it should be
noted that the spelling of her name at Nako may be an older form of her now
common name: A chi chos kyi sgrol ma (Achi choski drol ma).

27. Very little is published about Achi and her personas as both historical
person and divinized being. A very useful master's thesis does just this. See
Kristen Kail Muldowney, "Outward Beauty, Hidden Wrath: An Exploration
of the Drikung Kagyü Dharma Protectress Achi Chökyi Drölma," M.A. thesis, Florida State University, 2011.

28. The west wall does not have any lineage portraits.

29. David Jackson, "Lineages and Structures in Tibetan Buddhist Painting: Principles and Practice of an Ancient Sacred Choreography," *Journal of the International Association of Tibetan Studies*, no. 1 (October 2005): 15, www.thdl.org?id=T1220.

30. The beginning of the lineage is determined by the ritual clockwise movement through the temple.

31. This idea is the converse of many concepts about the role of memory and identity formation. See for instance, Jan Assmann, "Collective Memory and Cultural Identity," *New German Critique* 65 (Spring–Summer 1995): 125–33. In this article he cites the seminal work of Aby Warburg, who specifically addressed this issue in relation to art.

32. There is a nineteenth-century pilgrimage text that mentions Kinnaur's thirteenth-century Drigung affiliation, but there is no extant painting or architectural evidence for this activity. See Elenda De Rossi Filibeck, *Two Tibetan Guide Books to Ti se and La Phyi* (Bonn: VGH Wissenschaftverlag, 1988), 38, 77.

33. Christian Luczanits, "A First Glance at Early Drigungpa Painting," in *Studies in Sino-Tibetan Buddhist Art* (Beijing: China Tibetology, 2006): 459–88; Luczanits, "The Eight Great Siddhas in Early Tibetan Painting," in Linrothe, *Holy,* 78; Deborah Klimburg-Salter, "Lama, Yidam and Protectors," *Orientations* (April 2004): 48–53. It should be noted that Cakrasaṃvara is also used by other schools of the Kagyud tradition, as well as other Vajrayāna traditions.

34. This pairing of Namtose (Sanskrit: Vaiśravama) manifestations is notable because a single manifestation of Namtose is often depicted with three other important protectors. Together they form the quadrumvirate that protects the cardinal directions and the Buddhist teachings. In mural paintings such as these, this grouping of four is usually positioned on the wall with the portal. The fact that Namtose is depicted without the other three but with another manifestation of himself raises the question of when and where the tradition of depicting these four cardinal deities on the portal wall became popular. Given the visual evidence in Nako and the Spiti Valley in general, it seems that this was not a common practice in the area until the late seventeenth and eighteenth centuries.

35. Christian Luczanits, "The Wanla Bkra shis gsum brtegs," in Klimburg-Salter and Allinger, *Buddhist Art and Tibetan Patronage,* 119–20.

36. Linrothe, *Holy Madness,* 88, 95, 106.

37. The "v" sound is commonly replaced by the "b" in Tibetan transliterations of Sanskrit.

38. At first glance, this animal might not be identified as a tigress. After studying many other Ḍombi Heruka paintings, however, it is evident that depictions of tigers were not mimetic in any way. At best, most are suggestions of the animal, its stripes being the most easily identifying aspect. This is due, in large part, to the fact that there are no jungle animals in Tibet. Elephants are another example of an animal that was poorly rendered by Tibetan artists.

39. Although Indrabhūti is often positioned next to Virūpa, here Indrabhūti is alone and clad in voluminous robes. For more on the pairing of Indrabhūti and Virūpa see Luczanits, "The Eight Great Siddhas," 87.

40. The discrepancies in the color of the inscriptions and handwriting styles, as well as the presence of underwriting that is apparent in places, such as on

Choje Darma's inscription, raises concerns about the date of the inscriptions. At this point I cannot do more than note the inconsistencies.

41. Martin Willson and Martin Brauen, *Deities of Tibetan Buddhism* (Boston: Wisdom, 2000), 568.

42. Francke, *Antiquities of Indian Tibet*, 1:33.

43. Tucci, *Indo-Tibetica*, 3, bk. 2, *Tsaparang*, 71.

44. Lokesh Chandra, *Dictionary of Buddhist Iconography* (New Delhi: International Academy of Indian Culture and Aditya Prakashan, 1999), 1:226–28.

45. "Prajñāpāramitā," in Chandra, *Dictionary of Buddhist Iconography*.

46. For more on Mañjuśrī's association with Prajñā, see Jacob Kinnard, *Imaging Wisdom: Seeing and Knowing in the Art of Indian Buddhism* (Richmond, UK: Curzon, 1999), 158–163. See also himalayanart.org/pages /wisdomdeities/index.html.

47. See Lokesh Chandra, *Buddhist Iconography: Compact Edition* (New Delhi: International Academy of Indian Culture and Aditya Prakashan, 1999). See also www.himalayanart.org/news/post.cfm/medicine-buddha-main-page -updated.

48. Luczanits, "The Eight Great Siddhas," 91. He writes, "All Kagyud traditions share the generic lineage commencing with Tilopa and Naropa."

49. Michael Meister, "Sweetmeats or Corpses? Art History and Ethnography," *RES: Anthropology and Aesthetics* 27 (1995): 118–32; Meister, "Ethnography, Art History, and the Life of Temples," in Meister, *Ethnography and Personhood Notes from the Field* (Jaipur, India: Rawat, 2000), 17–45.

50. This phrase comes from Cynthea J. Bogel, "Canonizing Kannon: The Ninth-Century Esoteric Buddhist Altar at Kanshinji," *Art Bulletin* 84, no. 1 (March 2002): 30–64.

51. A. H. Francke, *A Lower Ladakhi Version of the Kesar Saga* (1905–9; repr., New Delhi: Asian Educational Services, 2000), xxviii.

52. Certainly, the number of phonetic spellings in the Gyapagpa Temple indicates that accurate writing was not strongly emphasized in this village.

53. Roland Barthes, "Rhetoric of the Image," in *Image, Music, Text* (New York: Hill and Wang, 1977), 39. I am referring here to Barthes's suggestion that "The denominative function [of the text] corresponds exactly to an anchorage of all the possible (denoted) meanings of the object by recourse to a nomenclature."

54. Richard Davis, *Lives of Indian Images* (Princeton, N.J.: Princeton University Press, 1997), 54–57.

3. Mapping Drigung Activity at Nako and in the Western Himalaya

1. Dkon mchog rgya mthso, *'Bri gung chos 'byung* (Beijing: Mi rigs dpe skrun khang, 2004); Bstan 'dzin padma'i rgyal mshtan, *Nges don bstan pa'i snying po mgon po 'bri gung pa chen po'i gdan rabs chos kyi byung tshul gser gyi phreng ba zhes bya ba bzhugs so* (repr., Lhasa: Bod ljongs bod yig dpe rnying dpe skrun khang, 1989). Since completing this manuscript, David Jackson published *Painting Tradition of the Drigung Kagyu School*, New York: Rubin Museum of Art, 2015. While his catalogue does not bear on Drigung history in West Tibet, he does speculate on the identities of the lineage portraits in the Gyapagpa Temple.

2. Dr. Jamyang Samten of the Central Institute for Higher Tibetan Studies, Sarnath; Dr. Tashi Sampel of the Songtsen Library, Dehra Dun; Venerable Thogden Rimpoche, Ladakh; Dr. Tsering Gyalpo of the Tibet Academy of Social Sciences, Lhasa; and Venerable Rase Konchog Gyatso, Lhasa.

3. For more on the founding of 'Bri gung mthil see Kuo-wei Liu, "'Jig rten mgon po and the 'Single intentions' (Dgongs gcig): His View on Bodhisattva Vow and Its Influence on Medieval Tibetan Buddhism" (Ph.D. diss., Harvard University, 2002), 79–85.

4. Roberto Vitali, *The Kingdoms of Gu.Ge Pu.Hrang According to mNga'. ris rgyal.rabs by Gu.ge mkhan.chen Ngag.dbang grags.pa* (New Delhi: Indraprasha Press, 1996), 372–73.

5. Vitali, *The Kingdoms of Gu.ge Pu. Hrang,* 380, 406. Dngos grub mgon (Ngodrub Ngon), the king of Ladakh ("Mar Yul," and briefly of Pu hrang [Purang]) patronized Gyuyasangpa in the thirteenth century. Gyuyasangpa enjoys the patronage of several other royal figures: Guge king Bkra shis lde (Tashide), and Purang kings Stag thse Khri 'bar (Tagthse Dri) and Gnam lde mgon (Namde Gon).

6. Vitali, *The Kingdoms of Gu.ge Pu. Hrang,* 407–9.

7. Vitali, *The Kingdoms of Gu.ge Pu. Hrang,* 407–9.

8. It is worth noting that not all western Tibetan kingdoms supported Drigung at this time. There is, for instance, a conspicuous omission of the capital Tholing, which was the royal seat of the Guge-Purang kingdom. Located only 150 kilometers west of Kailash, a stronghold of Drigung activity, it seems likely that the Purang-Guge kingdom were not Drigung benefactors. On this issue Vitali writes, "It is somewhat surprising that Tho.ling is not mentioned in the 'Bri.gung.pa sources during the period in which this sect exercised supremacy in West Tibet. It seems, therefore, that Tholing was not 'Bri.gung.pa during the period from iron pig 1191, the date of the earliest 'Bri.gung.pa expedition to Ti.se, until the third quarter of the twelfth century, these being the decades in which the 'Bri.gung.pa exercised preeminence in sTod. In particular, it seems that the centre of the 'Bri.gung.pa activities was outside Gu.ge" (Roberto Vitali, *Records of Tho.ling: A Literary and Visual Reconstruction of the "Mother" Monastery in Gu.ge* [New Delhi: High Asia, 1999], 34).

9. Vitali, *The Kingdoms of Gu.ge Pu. Hrang,* 376.

10. Vitali, *The Kingdoms of Gu.ge Pu. Hrang,* 129. In the chronicle it is mentioned that Dragpade was enthroned after Chos rgyal grags pa (Chogyal dragpe) and died in 1277 at the age of forty-eight.

11. Roberto Vitali, "A Chronology (bstan rtsis) of Events in the History of Mnga' ris skor gsum (Tenth–Fifteenth Centuries)," in McKay, *The History of Tibet,* 2:77; Vitali, *The Kingdoms of Gu.ge Pu. Hrang,* 129.

12. Elenda De Rossi Filibeck, *Two Tibetan Guide Books to Ti Se and La Phyi* (Bonn: VGH Wissenschaftverlag, 1988), 77.

13. It might be that the boundaries of Kinnaur have changed or that Kinnaur was referred to by another name. At this point, there are only three documented names in English-language sources for this district: Kunawar, Khu nu, and Kinnaur. As Deborah Klimburg-Salter suggests, it may have been part of a territory known as Rong chung, though this is not clear either. On this see Klimburg-Salter, "Ribba: The Story of an Early Buddhist Temple in Kinnaur," in *Buddhist Art and Tibetan Patronage: Ninth to Fourteenth Centuries, PIATS 2000, Proceedings of the Ninth Seminar of the International Association*

for Tibetan Studies, ed. Deborah Klimburg-Salter and Eva Allinger, *Buddhist Art and Tibetan Patronage* (Leiden and Boston: Brill, 2002), 4.

14. Kurt Tropper, "The Historical Inscription at the Sum Brtsegs Temple at Wanla, Ladakh," in *Word, Image and Song in Transdisciplinary Dialogue: Proceedings of the 10th Seminar of the International Association of Tibetan Studies, Oxford, 2003,* ed. Deborah E. Klimburg-Salter, Kurt Tropper, and Christian Jahoda (Leiden: Brill, 2007), 111.

15. It is worth noting that there is some disagreement around the date of this temple's construction. Kurt Tropper analyzes the various interpretations of the inscription and then provides his own reading. See Tropper, "The Historical Inscription," 105–50. Roberto Vitali suggests that it can be dated to 1240. See Alex McKay, *The History of Tibet,* vol. 2, *The Medieval Period: C. 850–1895: The Development of Buddhist Paramountcy* (London and New York: Routledge Curzon, 2003), 75. Based on inscriptional material found within the temple and on stylistic analysis, Luczanits ultimately posits a date of the late thirteenth century to mid-fourteenth century for the construction of this Drigung temple at Wanla. For more on this see Luczanits, "The Wanla Bkra shis gsum brtegs," in Klimburg-Salter and Allinger, *Buddhist Art and Tibetan Patronage,* 115–25.

16. Roger Goepper, *Alchi: Ladakh's Hidden Buddhist Sanctuary: Sumtsek* (Chicago: Seridia, 1996). This same date is also posited for the architecture and murals of Alchi's Great Stūpa (Goepper, "Great Stupa at Alchi," *Artibus Asiae* 53, nos. 1–2 (1993): 116).

17. Rob Linrothe, "A Winter in the Field," *Orientations* (May 2007): 40–53.

18. Martin A. Mills, *Identity, Ritual and State in Tibetan Buddhism: The Foundations of Authority in Gelukpa Monasticism* (London and New York: Routledge Curzon, 2003), 20.

19. Linrothe, "A Winter in the Field," 52.

20. At this point it is not known who was responsible for boarding up these Drigung temples. The question, however, raises others about why it would have been necessary to decommission the temples instead of reuse them. Moreover, when did this process of omitting Lingshet's Drigung past occur? Were, for instance, these dramatic efforts of shutting down temples part of the Gelug conversion?

21. For other 'Bri gung pa sites in Ladakh, see the Achi Association website (www.achiassociation.org), which provides a synopsis of various 'Bri gung pa temples, such as Photoksar and Urbis.

22. For more on this see Luciano Petech, *Central Tibet and the Mongols: The Yuan-Sa-skya Period of Tibetan History* (Rome: Istituto Italiano per il Medico ed Estremo Oriente, 1990).

23. Vitali, *Records of Tho.ling,* 36. *Khab gung* can be construed as a ranking official in the Tibetan government. See, for instance, "Historical Tibetan Dictionary," Tibetan and Himalayan Library website, www.thlib.org/reference/dictionaries/tibetan-dictionary/index.php.

24. Giuseppe Tucci, *Tibetan Painted Scrolls* (Rome: Libreria dello Stato, 1949), 671–72. See also Luciano Petech, *The Kingdom of Ladakh, c. 950–1842 A.D.* (Rome: Istituto Italiano per il Medio ed Estremo Oriente, 1977), 22. While Petech questions whether West Tibet fell under Sa skya

administration, the Zha lu documents that Tucci translated clearly indicate that West Tibet was indeed an area controlled by the Yuan Empire.

25. Vitali, "A Chronology (bstan rtsis) of Events," 2:79–80. "The 'Bri gung pa temples in Gelug pa skor gsum and elsewhere continued prospering under the eighth 'Bri gung abbot bCu gnyis pa rDo rje rin chen (1278–1314, in office during those years)" (2:79).

26. I thank Tsering Gyalpo for making me aware of this portrait.

27. As I use the term here, inclusive suggests that preference is given to a primary tradition, which in this case, would be Gelug. Thus, this central tradition would be open to the inclusion of other traditions at the periphery. An ecumenical approach, however, would be less focused on a central tradition.

28. Vitali, *The Kingdoms of Gu.ge Pu. Hrang,* 507, 510.

29. Vitali, *The Kingdoms of Gu.ge Pu. Hrang,* 507.

30. Based on several resources, chief among them the *Chronicle of Ladakh* and *Vaidurya ser po* (commonly referred to as Vaiser or Baiser), Petech determined that the Ladakhi royal community supported the newly developed Gelug tradition. See Petech, *The Kingdom of Ladakh,* 22–23.

31. Linrothe, "A Winter in the Field," 52. Some of the other monasteries associated with Changsem Sherab Zangpo's missionary work are found in Karsha and Phuktal. See also Linrothe, "Portraiture on Periphery."

32. Petech, *The Kingdom of Ladakh,* 23–24.

33. Petech, *The Kingdom of Ladakh,* 22–23, 26.

34. Petech, *The Kingdom of Ladakh,* 23.

35. Petech, *The Kingdom of Ladakh,* 26.

36. Petech, *The Kingdom of Ladakh,* 27–28. The most effective, though short-lived, of these raids was in 1548.

37. Petech, *The Kingdom of Ladakh,* 167–69.

38. Luciano Petech, "The 'Bri-Guṅ-Pa Sect in Western Tibet and Ladakh," in Petech, *Selected Papers on Asian History,* 355–68.

39. Petech, *The Kingdom of Ladakh,* 355–68.

40. Petech, *The Kingdom of Ladakh,* 29.

41. The names of the two kings Petech cites, based on his translation of the nineteenth-century Ti-Se pilgrimage guide, are different from the king's name as given in Dkon mchog (Konchog) Namgyal, *A History: Blue-Ridge Monastery, Phiyang* (Ladakh: Government Institute of Buddhist Culture, 1989). This book identifies the king who invited him to Ladakh as 'Jam dbyang rnam rgyal (Jamyang Namgyal) instead of Tashi Namgyal. I am grateful to Terence Barrett for his translation.

42. For a brief history of this monastery and Danma's role in its founding see Namgyal, *A History.*

43. Petech, *The Kingdom of Ladakh,* 29; Dkon mchog (Konchog) Namgyal, *A History: Blue-Ridge Monastery, Phiyang* (Ladakh: Government Institute of Buddhist Culture, 1989).

44. Although there was likely a fair amount of lay (as opposed to royal) patronage, at present there is no inscriptional or textual evidence to identify patrons.

45. Jürgen C. Aschoff, *Tsaparang—Königsstadt in Westtibet: Die vollständigen Berichte des Jesuitenpaters António de Andrade und eine Beschreibung vom heutigen Zustand der Klöster* (Munich: MC Verlag, 1997); Petech, *The Kingdom of Ladakh,* 41–42; Cornelis Wessels, *Early Jesuit Travelers in*

Central Asia, 1603–1721 (1924; repr., New Delhi: Asian Educational Services, 1992); Petech, *The Kingdom of Ladakh,* 41–42.

46. Petech, *The Kingdom of Ladakh,* 42.

47. Petech, *The Kingdom of Ladakh,* 43.

48. Petech, *The Kingdom of Ladakh,* 43.

49. Petech, *The Kingdom of Ladakh,* 53.

50. Petech, *The Kingdom of Ladakh,* 53.

51. There are conflicting dates for this war. Luciano Petech states that it was fought from 1681–83 while Zahiruddin Ahmad suggests a slightly early date of 1679–84. Petech, "The Tibetan-Ladakhi Moghul War of 1681–83," *Indian Historical Quarterly* 23, no. 3 (1947): 169–99; Zahiruddin Ahmad, "New Light on the Tibet-Ladakh-Mughal War of 1679–84," *East and West* 18, nos. 3–4 (1968): 340–61.

52. Petech, "The Tibetan-Ladakhi Moghul War," 173.

53. Petech, "The Tibetan-Ladakhi Moghul War," 173. Petech mentions that the area west of Ladakh, known as Purig (which is now the area including Kargyil), was primarily a Muslim chiefdom in the seventeenth century, which is why the "Moghuls" would have been strongly invested in the trade routes running south into India, as well as east into Tibet. See Petech, *The Kingdom of Ladakh,* 49.

54. Petech, *The Kingdom of Ladakh,* 71.

55. Petech discusses the manner in which Ladakh gradually shifted to 'Brug pa adherence, and how by the mid-seventeenth century there was a connection between Ladakh's royal family and the Drukpa Kagyu that continues today. See Petech, *The Kingdom of Ladakh,* 71, 168–69.

56. Gerhard Emmer, having consulted the Fifth Dalai Lama's autobiography, expands on the possible motives for the Fifth Dalai Lama's war with Ladakh. One possible reason relates to the Dalai Lama's interest in asserting Gelug dominance in a region that had become saturated with Drukpa supporters. That Ladakh supported Drukpa made them a threatening presence in this area and to the Central Tibetan governing power of the time. Interestingly, Emmer mentions that war was started under the pretense of Ladakh's failure to supply oil for butter lamps to Gelug monasteries in the Ngari area. See Gerhard Emmer, "Dga' ldan tshe dbang Dpal Bzang po and the Tibet-Ladakh-Mughal War of 1679–84," in *The Mongolia-Tibet Interface: Opening New Research Terrains in Inner Asia,* ed. Uradyn E. Bulag and Hildegard G. M. Diemberger (Leiden: Brill, 2003), 87, 93.

57. Petech, "The Tibetan-Ladakhi Moghul War," 175.

58. Petech, "The Tibetan-Ladakhi Moghul War," 181. This is also mentioned in the Namgia Document: "The army was drawn up against the kind of Ladakh. [There were] the camps of the Government official dGa-ldan Ts'e-dbang and of the Bashahr minister acting as general. At the place called Go-ro in Ladakh" (199).

59. Petech, *The Kingdom of Ladakh,* 72.

60. Petech, "The Tibetan-Ladakhi Moghul War," 199.

61. Petech, "'Bri-Guṅ-Pa Sect in Western Tibet and Ladakh," 361, 365.

4. Gyapagpa Temple's Painting Style and Its Antecedents

1. See, for instance, David Jackson, *A History of Tibetan Painting: The Great Tibetan Painters and Their Traditions* (Vienna: Verlag der Österreichischen Akademie der Wissencheften, 1996); and Rob Linrothe, "Stretched on a Frame of Boundless Thought: Contemporary Religious Painting in Rebgong," *Orientations* 33, no. 4 (2002): 48–56.

2. My ideas on style are strongly influenced by Meyer Schapiro's essay "Style," in *Theory and Philosophy of Art: Style, Artist, and Society* (New York: George Braziller, 1994), 51–102. Of particular relevance was his discussion about variations and substyles of larger styles.

3. Rob Linrothe and Jeff Watt, *Demonic Divine: Himalayan Art and Beyond* (New York and Chicago: Rubin Museum of Art and Serindia, 2004).

4. This inscription is a misspelling of the name, which is usually rendered Tshe dpag med.

5. The crown of the blue attendant seems to have been slightly retouched. The foliate setting (seen on the Vajradhara figure) has been painted in white, but only on the central three tines of the crown.

6. As will become clear later in the chapter, I suggest that these shorter legs and stockier figures are a later development in the sixteenth-century iteration of this style, as seen at Tabo's Cave Temple.

7. Instrumental to my thinking about this has been Michael Meister's scholarship. See "Regions and Indian Architecture," *Nirgrantha* 2 (1996): 87–91; "Style and Idiom in the Art of Uparamāla," *Muqarnas: An Annual on Islamic Art and Architecture* 10 (1992): 344–54.

8. Chapter 5 addresses how and why this painting style is a revival. Please note that my use of revival is different from Marilyn Rhie and Robert Thurman's use of renaissance in the term "Guge renaissance style." Although Rhie explains that the term "renaissance" refers to the so-called renaissance under the Guge during the fifteenth through seventeenth centuries, there is no explanation of what exactly was rebirthed. See Rhie and Thurman, *Wisdom and Compassion: The Sacred Art of Tibet* (New York: Harry N. Abrams, 1991), 58.

9. For the purposes of this chapter, it was important to articulate the difference between the courtly and regional idioms of this style, but I do so with the understanding that there are, within each of these categories, numerous other related idioms that need to be documented and properly analyzed. Although he discusses idiom in terms of Indian temple architecture, Michael Meister's conception of idiom and multiple idiomatic expressions is pertinent here. He writes, "'Idiom' however, in my experience is site and guild related, rooted in a place (or region) through local population and tradition. Thus many 'idioms' make up the basis for 'styles'; the gradations are located in the continuum of local idioms. As political hegemony expands, as 'centers' for conventional norms shift under such patronage, local idioms rooted in local craft can sway from affiliation with one 'style' to affiliation with another." See Meister, "Regions and Indian Architecture," 89.

10. Giuseppe Tucci, *Indo-Tibetica*, vol. 3, *The Temples of Western Tibet and Their Artistic Symbolism*, bk. 2, *Tsaparang*, English edition, ed. Lokesh Chandra (1932; repr. New Delhi: Aditya Prakashan, 1988).

11. Laxman S. Thakur, *Buddhism in the Western Himalaya: A Study of the Tabo Monastery* (New Delhi: Oxford University Press, 2001), 84.

12. See, for example, Pratapditya Pal, *Tibetan Paintings: A Study of Tibetan Thankas, Eleventh to Nineteenth Centuries* (Basel, Switzerland: Ravi Kumar; London: Sotheby, 1984), 99; Michael Henss, "Wall Paintings in Western Tibet: The Art of the Ancient Kingdom of Guge, 1000–1500," *Marg* 48, no. 1 (1996): 57.

13. Sangs rgyas rgya mtsho, *Dga' ldan chos 'byung bai du rya ser po* (Zi ling, Tibet: Krung go bo kyi shes rig dpe skrun khang, 1989).

14. "De'i btsun mo don grub mas mchod hang dmar po kha bsu[m] cu'i khyon ldan dang / thub dbang / byams pa / rigs gsum mgon po / rje btsong kha pa yab sras rnams kyi snang brnyan dang sku gsung thugs rten brten par bcas pa bzhengs" (Sangs rgyas rgya mtsho. *Dga' ldan chos "byung bai du rya ser po*, 222). Just after this it reads that several generations later, her great grandson, 'Jig rten dbang pyug constructed the White Temple and the Yamataka Temple at Tsaparang, which would date these temples to the sixteenth century. For more on questions about the chronology of the Red and White Temples at Tsaparang and Tholing see Kurt Tropper, "The Buddha-Vita in the White Temple of Tsaparang," in *Tibetan Inscriptions: Proceedings of a Panel Held at the Twelfth Seminar of the International Association for Tibetan Studies, Vancouver 2010*, ed. Kurt Tropper and Cristina Scherrer-Schaub (Leiden-Boston: Brill, 2013), 43–106. Page 51 is especially relevant. See also Christian Luczanits, "Styles in Western Himalayan Art," in *Han Zang Fo jiao mei shu yan jiu: 2007 [sic] di san jie Xizang kao gu yu shu guo ji xue shu tao lun hui lun wen ji*, ed. Jisheng Xie, Wenhua Luo, and Anning Jing, (Shanghai: Shanghai Guji Chuban She, 2009), 133–50. In this article, Luczanits suggests that the Red Temple is later than the White Temple despite what the seventeenth-century *Vaiser* says about them.

15. Giuseppe Tucci, "Tibetan Notes," in *Opera Minora* (Rome: Giovanni Bardi, 1971), 2:478.

16. Luciano Petech, "Ya-ts'e, Gu-Ge, Pu-Raṅ: A New Study," *Central Asiatic Journal* 24, nos. 1–2, (1980): 104–5.

17. Roberto Vitali, *The Kingdoms of Gu.Ge Pu.Hrang According to mNga'. ris rgyal.rabs by Gu.ge mkhan.chen Ngag.dbang grags.pa* (New Delhi: Indraprasha Press, 1996), 528.

18. Henss, "Wall Paintings in Western Tibet," 44.

19. Although this idea of an apogee is informed by Kubler's "prime object," it is necessarily different in a number of ways. It is impossible for me to argue that all three of these temples can function as the prime object; only one, according to Kubler's conception, can be designated as such. Without knowing the chronology of these sites, it is too speculative for me to suggest, for instance, that Tholing's Red Temple serves as the prime object and the other sites are products of emulation. Thus, the notion of the acme or apogee of a style allows me to think more broadly about a set of paintings as the model for subsequent variations. See George Kubler, *The Shape of Time: Remarks on the History of Things* (New Haven, Conn.: Yale University Press, 1962), 39–53.

20. One should note that Tucci suggests that this artistic tradition reached its summit at the time of Seng ge rnam rgyal (Senge Namgyal) (*Indo-Tibetica*, 3, bk. 1, *The Monasteries of Spiti and Kunavar*, 91). Senge Namgyal was the

king of Ladakh who invaded and took over Guge in the seventeenth century. This is a period more correctly associated with the demise of Ngari's political supremacy and artistic proliferation, not its summit. Elsewhere Tucci suggests that the art of Ngari was "completely exhausted" after the attack of Senge Namgyal; see Tucci, *Tibetan Painted Scrolls* (Rome: Libreria dello Stato, 1949), 275. The point of mentioning this confusion is to demonstrate that even at its inception, the scholarship has suffered from inconsistencies with regard to chronology.

21. Thomas Da Costa Kaufmann, *Toward a Geography of Art* (Chicago: University of Chicago, 2004), 225. Da Costa Kaufman's use of Goldschmidt's idea of *formenspaltung* and Kubler's "morphological disassociation" has helped me formulate my own understanding of this style's development and transformations.

22. Since the eleventh century, Vairocana has been a deity of critical importance at Tabo. For more on this deity's maṇḍala formations and other iconographic issues, see Deborah Klimburg-Salter, *Tabo: A Lamp for the Kingdom: Early-Indo-Tibetan Buddhist Art in the Western Himalaya* (New York: Thames and Hudson, 1998); and Christian Luczanits, *Buddhist Sculpture in Clay: Early Western Himalayan Art, Late 10th to Early 13th Centuries* (Chicago: Serindia, 2004).

23. For more information on religious architecture, see André Alexander, *The Temples of Lhasa: Tibetan Buddhist Architecture from the 7th to the 21st Centuries* (Chicago: Serindia, 2005).

24. Bautze-Picron, "The Elaboration of a Style: Eastern Indian Motifs and Forms in Early Tibetan (?) and Burmese Painting." In Klimburg-Salter and Allinger, *Inner Asian International Style,* 15–65.

25. See, for instance, David Jackson, *The Nepalese Legacy in Tibetan Painting* (New York: Rubin Museum of Art, 2010), 9, 86, 160.

26. For more on Guge's relationship with Mustang and the Sa skya connection in the Mustang kingdom, see Petech, "Ya-Ts'e, Gu-ge, Pu-rang," 103; and Vitali, *The Kingdoms of Gu.ge Pu.hrang,* 483–84. Here, Vitali addresses the sometimes intertwined political relationships among Guge, Pu hrang (Purang), and Mustang in the fourteenth and fifteenth centuries.

27. Keith Dowman, "The Mandalas of the Lo Jampa Lhakhang," in *Tibetan Art: Towards a Definition of Style,* ed. Jane Casey Singer and Philip Denwood (London: Laurence King, 1997), 186–95. This turn toward a Newar style of painting was likely deliberate; the royals of Mustang were patrons of the Sa skya (Sakya) tradition, which was strongly associated with the patronage of Newar artists. Jackson discusses the artists and date of these murals in *Nepalese Legacy,* 151–153.

28. The Red Temples at Tsaparang and Tholing both feature narrative scenes of the Buddha's life story painted in narrow horizontal bands below the larger iconic images. Although these narrative scenes are of critical importance, I will not address this genre of painting in this chapter. Stylistically, these Buddha figures, and the three-quarter profiles that are featured in these narrative scenes, are consonant with the rest of the temples' painting programs.

29. I thank Dr. Verena Widorn of the University of Vienna for this insight.

30. At Tsaparang and Tholing there are numerous portraits of laypeople congregated in assembly scenes featuring royal and other personages clad in

various ethnic dress. All of these figures, while differentiated by distinctive hair styles, hats, clothing, and postures, are rendered in the same three-quarter profile; their eyes are almond shaped and the far eye projects outward. The only difference from the other previously discussed portrait types is that the portraits of the lay community are not painted with any noticeable modeling.

31. Inscriptions are indeed plentiful at Tsaparang's Red Temple, for instance, but little has been done to document and translate them. When I was there in 2006, I was forbidden from taking photographs of them

32. See Phuntsok Namgyal, *Ntho-Ling Monastery* (Beijing: Encyclopedia of China, 2001), 33.

33. For more on this type of textile depiction in paintings, see Erna Wandl, "The Representation of Costumes and Textile," in Klimburg-Salter, *Tabo,* 179–88.

34. See Klimburg-Salter, *Tabo,* figs. 103, 104, 119.

35. See Namgyal, *Ntho-Ling Monastery,* 28–29. In this image, the grisaille-like table is located at the center of the photo.

36. Augusto Gansser, *Geology of the Himalayas* (London: Interscience, 1964), 68–73.

37. Tucci, *Indo-Tibetica,* vol. 3, bk. 2. Tucci suggests that these caves were the summer residence of the monks at Tabo. I posit, however, that they were used as retreat caves, which is how many of them are still used today. In fact, there is a well-established tradition of cave asceticism practiced in and around Tabo. For instance, in the hills past Lari, a village approximately 6 km east of Tabo, a number of ascetic caves are in constant use.

38. Tucci initially suggested that this painting style lasted until the end of the Guge kingdom, roughly the late seventeenth century. "When the province was incorporated into Greater Tibet at the end of the seventeenth century, its individuality was completely lost and the new manner of the Tibetan 'settecento' triumphed in Guge too" (*Indo-Tibetica,* 3:275).

39. Tucci, *Indo-Tibetica,* 3:42, 53.

5. Origin and Meaning of a Revival Painting Tradition

1. Giuseppe Tucci, *Indo-Tibetica,* vol. 3, *The Temples of Western Tibet and Their Artistic Symbolism,* bk. 1, *The Monasteries of Spiti and Kunavar,* English edition, ed. Lokesh Chandra (1932; repr. New Delhi: Aditya Prakashan, 1988), 91.

2. Giuseppe Tucci, *Tibetan Painted Scrolls* (Rome: Libreria dello Stato, 1949), 275.

3. This early West Tibetan painting style was also informed by Central Asian and possibly Indian aesthetics (Deborah Klimburg-Salter, *Tabo: A Lamp for the Kingdom: Early-Indo-Tibetan Buddhist Art in the Western Himalaya* [New York: Thames and Hudson, 1998], 210–14). Elsewhere I have favored the term "Western Tibetan" to describe this early style. Such a general geographic designation does not work, however, when addressing various styles from the same region. See Melissa R. Kerin, "Faded Remains: Little-Known 12th Century Wall Paintings in Ladakh's Markha Valley," *Orientations* (May 2007): 54. For a discussion of "Kashmiri" style painting from the tenth through twelfth centuries, see Rob Linrothe, "A Winter in the Field," *Orientations* (May 2007): 40–53.

4. According to Klimburg-Salter, "The true Indo-Tibetan style begins in the 11th century (Tabo Phase ii) and has a homogenous stylistic evolution through the 11th–12th centuries in monuments associated with the kings of Purang-Guge" (*Tabo*, 210).

5. John Huntington, "Gu-ge Bris: A Stylistic Amalgam," in *Aspects of Indian Art,* ed. Pratapaditya Pal (Leiden: Brill, 1972), 106–107. He suggests the specific date of 1655.

6. Huntington, "Gu-Ge Bris," 115.

7. Helmut F. Neumann, "Wall Paintings of Western Tibet: A Stylistic Analysis," *Orientations* (October 1999): 81.

8. Laxman S. Thakur, *Buddhism in the Western Himalaya: A Study of the Tabo Monastery* (New Delhi: Oxford University Press, 2001), 220.

9. Thakur, *Buddhism in the Western Himalaya,* 219.

10. Pratapditya Pal, *Tibetan Paintings: A Study of Tibetan Thankas, Eleventh to Nineteenth Centuries* (Basel, Switzerland: Ravi Kumar; London: Sotheby, 1984), 102; see also Huntington, "Gu-ge Bris."

11. Marilyn M. Rhie and Robert A. F. Thurman, *Wisdom and Compassion: The Sacred Art of Tibet* (New York: Harry N. Abrams, 1991), 57.

12. Rhie and Thurman, *Wisdom and Compassion,* 57.

13. Jackson, *The Nepalese Legacy,* 160: "Otherwise, the style obviously descends, in general, from the Beri."

14. Jackson, *The Nepalese Legacy,* 160.

15. Melissa R. Kerin, "From Emulation to Interpretation: Trends in the Late Medieval Ngari Painting Tradition in the Guge Kingdom and Beyond," in *Collecting Paradise: Buddhist Art of Kashmir and Its Legacy,* ed. Rob Linrothe with contributions by Melissa R. Kerin and Christian Luczanits (New York: Rubin Museum of Art, 2015), 152–161.

16. Jackson, *The Nepalese Legacy,* 225n338.

17. Michael Henss, "Wall Paintings in Western Tibet: The Art of the Ancient Kingdom of Guge, 1000–1500," *Marg* 48, no. 1 (1996): 57.

18. Klimburg-Salter, *Tabo,* 226–27.

19. Klimburg-Salter, *Tabo,* 226–27.

20. The beginning of this new kingdom actually dates to the end of the fourteenth century and into the early fifteenth century under the rule of Rnam rgyal lde (Namgyalde), who made tremendous efforts to fortify the kingdom's militia. This military presence, combined with the fact that there were reportedly fewer famines and plagues, as well as no foreign power diverting their resources, allowed for a new level of prosperity for Ngari. It seems that Namgyalde's son, Nam mkha'i dbang po phun tshogs lde bzang po (Namkhai Wangpo Phuntsogde Zangpo), was able to reap the benefits of this new era of peace and prosperity, which culminated in the wonderful artistic and architectural undertakings that we now associate with the fifteenth-century Guge period. For more details on this kingdom's history see Roberto Vitali, *The Kingdoms of Gu.Ge Pu.Hrang According to mNga'.ris rgyal.rabs by Gu.ge mkhan.chen Ngag.dbang grags.pa* (New Delhi: Indraprasha Press, 1996), 131–34.

21. For more information on foreign control of Ngari during the thirteenth and fourteenth centuries see Roberto Vitali, *Records of Tho-Ling: A Literary and Visual Reconstruction of the "Mother" Monastery in Gu.ge* (New Delhi: High Asia, 1999). "Immediately after the end of Grags.pa.lde's reign,

in the years 1277–1280, Gu.ge passed under the Sa.skya.pa-s, who ruled locally by means of their Khab Gung.thang and Zhwa.lu feudatories. This is the
most obscure period in the history of Ngari skor gsum and other territories
of sTod" (36). Luciano Petech also mentions this period of Yuan/Sa.skya.ya
control over West Tibet. He writes, "During the years 1268–1368 central Tibet, including Lower (sMad) mNga'-ris, was governed by the Yüan (Mongol)
dynasty of China in partnership with the Sa-skya-pa sect" ("Western Tibet:
Historical Introduction," in Klimburg-Salter, *Tabo*, 241). See also Luciano
Petech, *Central Tibet and the Mongols: The Yüan-Sa-skya Period of Tibetan
History* (Rome: Istituto Italiano per il Medio ed Estremo Oriente, 1990)

   22. Vitali, *The Kingdoms of Gu.ge Pu.hrang*, 501.

   23. Petech, "Western Tibet," 229–56.

   24. The date and author for this text have been contested by Luciano Petech.
See Petech, "A Regional Chronicle of Gu ge pu hrang," *Tibet Journal* 22, no.
3 (1997): 106–11.

   25. As discussed in chapter 1 and specifically in note 52, this term flags a
style of painting that has a wide temporal and regional span. As I use it here,
Central Tibetan Style refers to the western Himalayan iterations of the Central Tibetan Pāla-derived style of the twelfth through fourteenth centuries.

   26. There are also sections painted in a later eighteenth-century style, a style
also used in the wall paintings of a neighboring site, Nadang.

   27. Klimburg-Salter, "Is There an Inner Asian International Style?," 4.

   28. It should also be noted that there is carving-work at Tabo's monastic
complex that can be associated with the Central Tibetan Style of the twelfth
to fourteenth centuries. "The door to the ['Brom-ston] temple however still
retains much ruined traces of carving which can be dated to the 13th or 14th
century" (Klimburg-Salter, *Tabo*, 66).

   29. Tucci, *Indo-Tibetica,* vol. 3, bk. 1, *The Monasteries of Spiti and Kunavar,* 172.

   30. Klimburg-Salter, "Is There an Inner Asian International Style?," 5.

   31. This information was presented by Tsering Gyalpo, scholar on West Tibet, at the 11th conference for the International Association of Tibetan Studies, Bonn, Germany, August 2006.

   32. Gopal Sharma, "Explorers Find Ancient Caves, Paintings in Nepal,"
Reuters, May 3, 2007, www.reuters.com/article/2007/05/03/us-nepal
-idUSB50593420070503; BBC News, "'Stunning' Nepal Buddha Art Find,"
May 4, 2007, news.bbc.co.uk/2/hi/6624117.stm. Although a great deal of stylistic analysis needs to be conducted on this new cache of images, the limited
photographic material published by Reuters and the BBC would indicate that
these paintings are part of the Central Tibetan Style.

   33. It should be noted, however, that Klimberg-Salter refers to this style as
the Inner Asian International Style. Deborah Klimburg-Salter, "A Thangka
Painting Tradition from the Spiti Valley," *Orientations* (November 1997):
40–47. It is worthwhile for me to stress the distinction between the descrip-
tor "Inner Asian International Style" and Jackson's use of the term "Beri."
The term Beri is derived from Tibetan source material *(Bal ris* or *bris* meaning "Nepal art/painting"), and as Jackson uses it, refers to Newar-inspired
Tibetan painting (xi). Klimburg-Salter's art historical terminology of the Inner
Asian International Style suggests that the style is not primarily Nepalese in
derivation. Rather, her discussion of this style recognizes Pāla aesthetics of the

tenth through twelfth centuries as the primary source for its visual vocabulary. Jackson, on the other hand, separates Pāla- from Newar-inspired styles.

34. These two objects have been analyzed in another publication. See Melissa R. Kerin, "Materiality of Devotion: Tibetan Buddhist Shrines of the Western Himalaya," in *Art of Merit: Proceedings of the First Buddhist Forum, The Courtauld Institute, 2012,* ed. David Park and Kuenga Wangmo (London: Archetype, 2013), 286–96, figs. 3, 4, and 5.

35. I first discussed this piece in "New Evidence for the Spiti Valley Painting Style," presented at the Association of Southern Asian Arts, San Diego, October 22, 2005.

36. It has been well proven that this Central Tibetan Style, and its various localized and regional expressions, were in use from Burma all the way to the Lamayuru in Ladakh and various places through Zangskar. See Christian Luczanits, "On an Unusual Painting Style in Ladakh," in Klimburg-Salter and Allinger, *Inner Asian International Style,* 151–69; Rob Linrothe and Melissa Kerin, "Deconsecration and Discovery: The Art of Karsha's Kadampa Chorten Revealed,"*Orientations* (December 2001): 52–63.

37. Vitali, *The Kingdoms of Gu.ge Pu.hrang,* 501.

38. Vitali, *The Kingdoms of Gu.ge Pu.hrang,* 83, 500–504.

39. According to Vitali's calculations, Namgyalde was supposedly born in 1372 (*The Kingdoms of Gu.ge Pu.hrang,* 130). As for Namgyalde's reign over Ladakh, see *The Kingdoms of Gu.ge Pu.hrang,* 492.

40. He was probably born in 1408.

41. Vitali, *The Kingdoms of Gu.ge Pu.hrang,* 108 (his translation). It should be mentioned that there is a fair amount of contention over whether or not the Dark Ages after Lang Darma's rule actually happened. Matthew Kapstein makes a compelling argument that there was not enough of a decrease in literary material and writing skills to indicate such a dark period. See Kapstein, *The Tibetan Assimilation of Buddhism: Conversion, Contestations, and Memory.* (New York: Oxford University Press, 2000). Ronald Davidson, on the other hand, accepts that there was indeed such a Dark Age in Tibetan history in *Tibetan Renaissance: Tantric Buddhism in the Rebirth of Tibetan Culture* (New York: Columbia University Press, 2005).

42. Vitali, *The Kingdoms of Gu.ge Pu.hrang,* 209.

43. See, for instance, Luciano Petech, *A Study on the Chronicles of Ladakh* (Calcutta: Calcutta Oriental Press, 1939).

44. Petech, "Western Tibet," 229–51. See Vitali, *The Kingdoms of Gu.ge Pu.hrang,* 129–30, for specific mention of Ngawang Dragpade's death and the birth of Ngawang Namgyalde, 129–130.

45. Vitali, *The Kingdoms of Gu.ge Pu.hrang,* 501.

46. The chronicle, unfortunately, does not mention any of their patronage practices. This information is gleaned from the *Bai Ser* text of the seventeenth century.

47. Vitali, *The Kingdoms of Gu.ge Pu.hrang,* 133.

48. Vitali, *The Kingdoms of Gu.ge Pu.hrang,* 472 and 502, "Among his great achievements, rNam rgyal lde is reported to have revised the corpus of laws laid down by his ancestors (*mNgas' ris rgyal rabs,* p. 83, lines 3–5). He updated the ancient code to meet the requirements of his time, but no details were given as to the content of the laws he issued" (502).

49. Vitali, *The Kingdoms of Gu.ge Pu.hrang,* 130.

50. Giuseppe Petech, *The Kingdom of Ladakh, c. 950–1842 A.D.* (Rome: Istituto Italiano per il Medio ed Estremo Oriente, 1977), 52.

51. As discussed in chapter 4, these temples have either inscriptional or textual accounts that help to date them fairly accurately and to prove that they were royally patronized.

52. The fact that these sites were not mentioned in the fifteenth-century chronicle as having been royally patronized by the earlier Guge-Purang dynasty is not proof that they were not the result of royal patronage. Rather, it is entirely possible that some sites have escaped documentation. For instance, according to Vitali's reading of the *Bai Ser,* Yeshe Od's daughter Lha'i me tog (Lemeto) became a nun and is thought to have built a monastery at Dungkar. This is an example, therefore, of circa eleventh-century royal patronage not having been documented in the fifteenth-century chronicle. This would make it highly probable that this village received royal patronage and attention in the eleventh century (Vitali, *The Kingdoms of Gu.ge Pu.hrang,* 274–75). Helmut Neumann and Thomas Pritzker have each individually discovered and documented other eleventh- and twelfth-century style murals at cave sites located within the Guge-Pu rhang kingdom's region. Of course, without adequate inscriptional or textual evidence patronage remains a question. See Helmut Neumann, "The Wheel of Life in the Twelfth Century Western Tibetan Cave Temple of Pedongpo," in Klimburg-Salter and Allinger, *Buddhist Art,* 75–84; and Thomas Pritzker, "The Wall Paintings of Nyag Lhakhang Kharpo," *Orientations* (March 2008): 102–12.

53. For a more substantive and heavily illustrated essay about this very topic see Melissa R. Kerin, "From Emulation to Interpretation: Trends in the Late Medieval Ngari Painting Tradition in the Guge Kingdom and Beyond," in *Collecting Paradise: Buddhist Art of Kashmir and Its Legacy,* ed. Rob Linrothe with contributions by Melissa R. Kerin and Christian Luczanits (New York: Rubin Museum of Art, 2015).

54. I thank Rob Linrothe for this identification.

55. See, for instance, Klimburg-Salter, *The Silk Route and the Diamond Path: Esoteric Buddhist Art on the Trans-Himalayan Trade Routes* (Los Angeles: USLA Art Council, 1982) 104–5 (pl. 30), 134 (pl. 32).

56. Klimburg-Salter, *Tabo,* 168.

57. Erna Wandl, "The Representation of Costumes and Textile," in Klimburg-Salter, *Tabo,* 179–88.

58. For photographic evidence, please see Klimburg-Salter, *Tabo,* 160, 164, 166.

59. For more on Chinese textiles in Tibetan culture see Rob Linrothe, *Paradise and Plumage: Chinese Connections in Tibetan Arhat Painting* (New York and Chicago: Rubin Museum of Art and Serindia, 2004), 29–31.

60. Linrothe, *Paradise and Plumage,* 10–44.

61. For an image of Dungkar Cave 1 please see Kerin, "From Emulation to Interpretation," fig. 3.20, 170.

62. Klimburg-Salter, *Tabo,* 216.

63. The inclusion of these wooden dowels hanging from the eaves in the fifteenth-century paintings is a point that Vitali addresses in a footnote. He uses these "pendants hanging from the roof gutters" as art historical proof that the Tabo Golden Temple should be dated to the later part of the fifteenth century. It seems, though, that he is not aware of the longevity of this decorative motif,

which was clearly in circulation during the eleventh century, as Klimburg Salter points out. Vitali also points out that these dowels can be seen on Tholing's Golden Temple in one of Ghersi's photos published in Giuseppe Tucci's *Transhimalaya,* trans. James Hogarth (Geneva: Nagel, 1973), pl. 68. This is particularly interesting as it would mean that this architectural detail, often associated with Himachal Pradesh and not with the Tibetan plateau, was indeed used in Guge. See Vitali, *The Kingdoms of Gu.ge Pu.hrang,* 526n.897.

64. Another set of paintings whose style was deliberately crafted to express a certain sensibility, if not a specific message, were those at Jo nang phun tshogs gling, which were commissioned by Tāranātha (1575–1634). See Rob Linrothe, "Polishing the Past: The Style of a Seventeenth-Century Tibetan Mural" (paper presented at the Center for East Asian Art, University of Chicago, April 2008).

65. Deborah Klimburg-Salter writes, "The choice of the Kashmiri mode of representation demonstrates that the patrons allied themselves with Indian *Mahāyāna* traditions as known in Kashmir" ("Style in Western Tibetan Painting: The Archaeological Evidence," *East and West* 46, nos. 3–4 [1996]: 336).

66. Although the fifteenth-century material is still in situ, the earliest paintings from the eleventh century are no longer extant at Tholing. The reason for their demise is not clear. It has, in the past, been blamed on the Cultural Revolution, but this would not explain why the other temples survived.

67. Although the patronage practices of the Guge kingdom are not well documented, there is mention of them in the seventeenth-century text *Bai ser,* in which several members of the royal family are said to have commissioned the construction and renovation of various temples in Tsaparang, the capital of the fifteenth-century kingdom. See chapter 4. Also see Giuseppe Tucci, "Tibetan Notes," in *Opera Minora* (Rome: Giovanni Bardi, 1971), 2:471–88; Petech, "Ya-ts'e, Gu-Ge, Pu-Raṅ: A New Study," *Central Asiatic Journal* 24, nos. 1–2 (1980): 104–5; and Vitali, *The Kingdoms of Gu.ge Pu.hrang,* 528.

68. Mangnang, a place that was once a seat for Guge-Pu hrang royalty, became the location for Rnam rgyal lde's palace in the fourteenth and fifteenth centuries (Vitali, *The Kingdoms of Gu.ge Pu.hrang,* 503). As I was not allowed to travel to Mangnang in 2007, my photographic evidence is limited to the few illustrations in a Chinese publication, but it seems as though Mangnang also had sets of fifteenth-century paintings. See Administration Commission of Cultural Relics of the Tibetan Autonomous Region, *Xizang Fojiao siyuan bihua yishu / Xizang Zizhiqu wenwu guanli weiyuanhui bian(Fresco Art of the Buddhist monasteries in Tibet / Compiled by the Administration Commission of Cultural Relics of the Tibetan Autonomous Region),* in Chinese, English, and Tibetan (Chengdu: Sichuan renmin chubanshe, 1994), 151.

69. Although Tsaparang was the capital of the new Guge kingdom in the fifteenth century (after Namgyalde), there is no evidence that I know of to suggest that the audience at Tsaparang's temples was restricted to the elite or royal communities. The temples' locations on the plain—rather than on the surrounding hills, which is where the royal compounds were established— would also suggest that although these temples were royally patronized, they were accessible to the whole community.

70. As mentioned in chapter 2, several Nako villagers expressed their views about the miraculous construction of the Gyapagpa Temple, which took place thousands of years ago.

71. Jan Mukarovsky, "Art as Semiological Fact," in *Essays in New Art History from France,* ed. Norman Bryson (Cambridge: Cambridge University Press, 1988), 3.

72. Mieke Bal and Norman Bryson, "Semiotics and Art History," *Art Bulletin* 73, no. 2 (1991): 175.

Books and Articles

Ahmad, Zahiruddin. "New Light on the Tibet-Ladakh-Mughal War of 1679–84." *East and West* 18, nos. 3–4 (1968): 340–61.

Aldenderfer, Mar. "Piyang: A Tibetan Buddhist Temple and Monastic Complex of the 10th–11th Centuries AD in Far Western Tibet." *Archaeology, Ethnology and Anthropology of Eurasia* 4, no. 8 (2001): 138–46.

Alexander, André. *The Temples of Lhasa: Tibetan Buddhist Architecture from the 7th to the 21st Centuries.* Chicago: Serindia, 2005.

Alsop, Ian. "The Wall Paintings of Mustang." In *Nepal: Old Images, New Insights,* edited by Pratapaditya Pal, 128–39. Mumbai: Marg, on behalf of the National Centre for the Performing Arts, 2004.

Aschoff, Jürgen C. *Tsaparng—Königsstadt in Westtibet: Die vollständigen Berichte des Jesuitenpaters António de Andrade und eine Beschreibung vom heutigen Zustand der Klöster.* Munich: MC Verlag, 1997.

Aschoff, Jürgen C., and Helfried Weyer. *Tsaparang: Tibets grosses Geheimnis.* Freiburg: Eulen Verlag, 1987.

Assmann, Jan. "Collective Memory and Cultural Identity." *New German Critique* 65 (Spring–Summer, 1995): 125–33.

Bailey, Gauvin Alexander. "The Indian Conquest of Catholic Art: The Mughals, the Jesuits, and Imperial Mural Painting." *Art Journal* 57, no. 1 (Spring 1998): 24–30.

Bajpai, S. C. *Lahaul–Spiti: A Forbidden Land in the Himalayas.* New Delhi: Indus, 1987.

Bal, Mieke, and Norman Bryson. "Semiotics and Art History." *Art Bulletin* 73, no. 2 (1991): 174–298.

Barthes, Roland. "Rhetoric of the Image." In *Image, Music, Text,* translated by Stephen Heath, 32–51. New York: Hill and Wang, 1977.

Bautze-Picron, Claudine. "The Elaboration of a Style: Eastern Indian Motifs and Forms in Early Tibetan (?) and Burmese Painting." In *Inner Asian International Style, 12th–14th Centuries: Papers Presented at a Panel of the 7th Seminar of the International Association for Tibetan Studies, Graz, 1995,* edited by Deborah E. Klimburg-Salter and Eva Allinger, 15–65. Vienna: Verlag der Österreichischen Akademie der Wissenschaften, 1998.

BBC News, "'Stunning' Nepal Buddha Art Find," May 4, 2007, news.bbc.co
.uk/2/hi/6624117.stm.

Béguin, Gilles. *Art ésotérique de l'Himâlaya: Catalogue de la donation Lionel Fournier.* Paris: Réunion des musées nationaux, 1990.

———. *Tibet, art et méditation: Ascètes et mystiques au Musée Guimet.* Paris: Editions Findakly, 1991.

Berger, Patricia. *Empire of Emptiness: Buddhist Art and Political Authority in Qing China.* Honolulu: University of Hawai'i Press, 2003.

Binczik, Angelika, and Roland Fischer. *Verborgene Schätse aus Ladakh / Hidden Treasures from Ladakh.* Munich: Otter Verlag, 2002.

Blondeau, Anne-Marie, ed. *Tibetan Mountain Deities, Their Cults and Representations: Papers Presented at a Panel of the 7th Seminar of the International Association for Tibetan Studies, Graz, 1995.* Vienna: Verlag der Osterreichischen Akademie der Wissenschaften, 1998.

Bogel, Cynthea J. "Canonizing Kannon: The Ninth-Century Esoteric Buddhist Altar at Kanshinji." *Art Bulletin* 84, no. 1 (March 2002): 30–64.

Bray, John., ed. *Ladakhi Histories: Local and Regional Perspectives.* Leiden: Brill, 2005.

Carrier, David. "What Happens When Art History Travels." In *Is Art History Global?* edited by James Elkins, 286–89. New York: Routledge, 2007.

Chanchani, Nachiket. "Fording and Frontiers: Architecture and Identities in the Central Himalayas." Ph.D. diss. Univerity of Pennsylvania, 2012.

Chandra, Lokesh. *Buddhist Iconography: Compact Edition.* New Delhi: International Academy of Indian Culture and Aditya Prakashan, 1999.

———. *Dictionary of Buddhist Iconography,* vol 1. New Delhi: International Academy of Indian Culture and Aditya Prakashan, 1999.

Chayet, Anne. *Art et archéologie du Tibet.* Paris: Picard, 1994.

Craig Clunas, "Social History of Art." In *Critical Terms for Art History,* edited by Robert S. Nelson and Richard Schiff, 465–76. Chicago: University of Chicago Press, 2003.

Dave, A. K. *Real Story of China's War on India, 1962.* New Delhi: Centre for Armed Forces Historical Research, United Service Institution of India, 2006.

Davidson, Ronald. *Tibetan Renaissance: Tantric Buddhism in the Rebirth of Tibetan Culture.* New York: Columbia University Press, 2005.

Davis, Richard. *Lives of Indian Images.* Princeton, N.J.: Princeton University Press, 1997.

Debreczeny, Karl. "Sino-Tibetan Artistic Synthesis in Ming Dynasty Temples at the Core and Periphery." *Tibet Journal* 28, nos. 1–2 (2003): 49–108.

Deva, Krisna. *Temples of North India.* New Delhi: National Book Trust, India, 1969.

Dowman, Keith. "The Mandalas of the Lo Jampa Lhakhang." In *Tibetan Art: Towards a Definition of Style,* edited by Jane Casey Singer and Philip Denwood, 186–95. London: Laurence King, 1997.

Eckel, Malcolm D. *To See the Buddha: A Philosopher's Quest for the Meaning of Emptiness.* Princeton, N.J.: Princeton University Press, 1992.

Elkins, James, ed. *Is Art History Global?* New York and London: Routledge, 2007.

Gerhard Emmer, "Dga' ldan tshe dbang Dpal Bzang po and the Tibet-Ladakh-Mughal War of 1679–84." In *The Mongolia-Tibet Interface:*

Opening New Research Terrains in Inner Asia, edited by Uradyn E. Bulag and Hildegard G. M. Diemberger, 81–108. Leiden: Brill, 2003.

Essen, Gerd-Wolfgang, and Tsering T. Thingo. *Die Götter des Himalaya: Buddhistische Künst Tibets. Die Sammlung Gerd-Wolfgang Essen.* 2 vols. Munich: Prestel-Verlag, 1989.

Filibeck, Elenda De Rossi. "A Description of Spyi ti by J. Gergan." In *Territory and Identity in Tibet and the Himalayas,* edited by Katia Buffetrille and Hildegard Diemberger, 313–24. Leiden: Brill, 2002.

———. *Two Tibetan Guide Books to Ti Se and La Phyi.* Bonn: VGH Wissenschaftverlag, 1988.

Fowler, Sherry. *Murōji: Rearranging Art and History at a Japanese Buddhist Temple.* Honolulu: University of Hawai'i Press, 2005.

Francke, A. H. *Antiquities of Indian Tibet.* 2 vols. Calcutta: Superintendent Government Printing, India, 1914–26.

———. *A Lower Ladakhi Version of the Kesar Saga.* 1905–9. Reprint, New Delhi: Asian Educational Services, 2000.

Gansser, Augusto. *Geology of the Himalayas.* London: Interscience, 1964.

Goepper, Roger. "The Great Stūpa at Alchi." *Artibus Asiae* 53, nos. 1–2 (1993): 111–43.

Goepper, Roger, and Jaroslav Poncar. *Alchi: Ladhak's Hidden Buddhist Sanctuary: The Sumstek.* Chicago and London: Serindia, 1996.

Goetz, Herman. *The Early Wooden Temples of Chamba.* Leiden: E. J. Brill, 1955.

———. *Studies in the History and Art of Kashmir and the Indian Himalaya.* Wiesbaden: Harrassowitz, 1969.

Gutschow, Kim. *Being a Buddhist Nun: The Struggle for Enlightenment in the Himalaya.* Cambridge, Mass.: Harvard University Press, 2004.

Gutschow, Kim, and Niels Gutschow. "A Landscape Dissolved: Households, Fields, and Irrigation in Rinam, Northwest India." In *Sacred Landscape of the Himalaya, Proceedings of an International Conference at Heidelberg, May 1998,* edited by Niels Gutschow et al., 111–36. Vienna: Verlage der Österreische Akademie der Wissenschaften, 2003.

Gyatso, Janet. *Apparitions of the Self: The Secret Autobiography of a Tibetan Visionary.* Princeton, N.J.: Princeton University Press, 1998.

———. "Image as Presence." In *Catalogue of the Tibetan Collection of the Newark Museum,* 3:171–76. Newark, N.J.: Newark Museum, 1999.

———. *In the Mirror of Memory: Reflections on Mindfulness and Remembrance in Indian and Tibetan Buddhism.* Albany: State University of New York Press, 1992.

Ham, Peter van, and Aglaja Stirn. *The Forgotten Gods of Tibet: Early Buddhist Art in the Western Himalyas.* Paris: Menges, 1997.

Handa, Omacanda. *Buddhist Monasteries in Himachal Pradesh.* New Delhi: Indus, 1987.

———. *Buddhist Western Himalaya.* New Delhi: Indus, 2001.

———. *Tabo Monastery and Buddhism in the Trans-Himalaya: Thousand Years of Existence of the Tabo Chos-khor.* New Delhi: Indus, 1994.

Harcourt, Alfred Fredrick Pollock. *The Himalayan Districts of Kooloo, Lahoul, and Spiti.* 1871. Reprint, Delhi: Vivek, 1972.

Hein, Ewald, and Günther Boelmann. *Tibet—Der Weisse Tempel von Tholing.* Ratingen, Germany: Melina-Verlag, 1994.

Heller, Amy. "Indian Style, Kashmiri Style: Aesthetic of Choice in Eleventh Century Tibet." *Orientations* (December 2001): 18–23.

———. *Tibetan Art: Tracing the Development of Spiritual Ideals and Art in Tibet, 600–2000 A.D.* Milan and Wappingers Falls, N.Y.: Jaca Book and Antique Collectors' Club, 1999.

Henss, Michael. "Wall Paintings in Western Tibet: The Art of the Ancient Kingdom of Guge, 1000–1500." *Marg* 48, no. 1 (1996): 32–61.

Huntington, John. "Gu-ge Bris: A Stylistic Amalgam." In *Aspects of Indian Art,* edited by Pratapaditya Pal, 105–17. Leiden: Brill, 1972.

Huntington, Susan, and John Huntington. *Leaves from the Bodhi Tree: The Art of Pāla India (8th–12th Centuries) and Its International Legacy.* Dayton, Ohio: Dayton Art Institute with the University of Washington Press, 1989.

Inden, Ronald, B. *Imaging India.* Bloomington: Indiana University Press, 2000.

———. "Imperial Purāṇas: Kashmir as Vaiṭnava Center of the World." In *Querying the Medieval: Texts and the History of Practices in South Asia,* edited by Ronald Inden, Jonathan Walters, and Daud Ali, 29–98. Oxford: Oxford University Press, 2000.

Jackson, David. "The Early History of Lo (Mustang) and Ngari." *Journal of the Institute of Nepal and Asian Studies* 4 (1976): 39–56.

———. *A History of Tibetan Painting: The Great Tibetan Painters and Their Traditions.* Vienna: Verlag der Österreichischen Akademie der Wissenscheften, 1996.

———. "The Identification of Individual Masters in Paintings of Sa-skya-pa Lineages." In *Indo-Tibetan Studies: Papers in Honour and Appreciation of Professor David L. Snellgrove's Contribution to Indo-Tibetan Studies,* edited by Tadeusz Skorupski, 129–44. Tring, England: Institute of Buddhist Studies, 1990.

———. "Lama Yeshe Jamyang of Nyurla, Ladakh: The Last Painter of the 'Bri gung Tradition." *Tibet Journal* 27, nos. 1–2 (Spring–Summer 2002): 153–76.

———. "Lineages and Structure in Tibetan Buddhist Painting: Principles and Practice of an Ancient Sacred Choreography." *Journal of the International Association of Tibetan Studies,* no. 1 (October 2005): 1–40, www.thdl.org?id=T1220.

———. *The Nepalese Legacy in Tibetan Painting.* New York: Rubin Museum of Art, 2010.

———. *Painting Tradition of the Drigung Kagyu School.* New York: Rubin Museum of Art, 2015.

Jahoda, Christian. "Political Space and Socio-Economic Organization in the Lower Spiti Valley (Early Nineteenth to Late Twentieth Century)." *Journal of the International Association of Tibetan Studies* 4 (December 2008). www.thlib.org/collections/texts/jiats/#!jiats=/04/jahoda.

Jauss, Robert Jan. *Toward an Aesthetic of Reception.* Minneapolis: University of Minnesota Press, 1982.

Jina, Prem Singh. *Religious History of Ladakh.* Delhi: Sri Satguru, 2001.

———. *Some Monasteries of Drigungpa Order in Central Ladakh.* Delhi: Sri Satguru, 1999.

———. *Tibetan Manuscripts and Inscriptions of Ladakh Himalaya*. Delhi: Sri Satguru, 1998.

Jina, Prem Singh, with Konchok Namgyal. *Lamayuru Monastery of Ladakh Himalaya*. Faridabad, India: Om, 1999.

Jones, Pamela M. "The Reception of Christian Devotional Art: The Renaissance to the Present." *Art Journal* 57, no. 1 (Spring 1998): 2–4.

Kanamaru, Atsushi. *Mapping the Tibetan World*. Reno, Nev.: Kotan, 2001.

Kapstein, Matthew. *The Tibetan Assimilation of Buddhism: Conversion, Contestations, and Memory*. New York: Oxford University Press, 2000.

———. "Weaving the World: The Ritual Art of the Pata in Pala Buddhism and its Legacy in Tibet." *History of Religions* 34 (1995): 241–62.

Karmay, Samten. "The Theoretical Basis of the Tibetan Epic, with Reference to a 'Chronological Order' of the Various Episodes in the Gesar Epic." *Bulletin of the School of Oriental and African Studies, University of London* 56, no. 2 (1993), 234–46.

Kaufmann, Thomas Da Costa. *Toward a Geography of Art*. Chicago: University of Chicago Press, 2004.

Keilhauer, Anneliese, and Peter Keilhauer. *Ladakh and Zangskar: Lamaistiche Klosterkulter in Land Zwischen Indien und Tibet*. Cologne: DuMour, 1982.

Kerin, Melissa R. "From Emulation to Interpretation: Trends in the Late Medieval Ngari Painting Tradition." In *Collecting Paradise: Buddhist Art of Kashmir and Its Legacies*, Rob Linrothe, with contributions by Melissa R. Kerin and Chritian Luczanits, 151–95. New York: Rubin Museum of Art, 2015.

———. "Faded Remains: Little-Known 12th Century Wall Paintings in Ladakh's Markha Valley." *Orientations* (May 2007): 54–59.

———. "Nako's Post-Fifteenth-Century Painting Traditions." In *Nako*, edited by Lisa Gräber. Vienna: Böhlau Verlag Wien Köln, forthcoming.

———. "New Evidence for the Spiti Valley Painting Style." Paper presented at the Association of Southern Asian Arts, San Diego, October 22, 2005.

———. "Visual Evidence of 'Bri-Gung Activity in Nako, Kinnaur." In *Proceedings of the 11th Seminar of the International Association of Tibetan Studies, Bonn, 2006*, edited by Erberto Lobue and Christian Luzcanits, 175–96. Leiden: Brill, 2010.

———. "Materiality of Devotion: Tibetan Buddhist Shrines of the Western Himalaya." In *Art of Merit: Proceedings of the First Buddhist Forum, The Courtauld Institute, 2012*, edited by David Park and Kuenga Wangmo, 286–96. London: Archetype, 2013.

Khosla, Romi. *Buddhist Monasteries of the Western Himalaya*. Kathmandu: Ratna Pustak Bhandar, 1979.

Kinnard, Jacob. *Imaging Wisdom: Seeing and Knowing in the Art of Indian Buddhism*. Richmond, UK: Curzon, 1999.

Klimburg-Salter, Deborah. "A Decorated Prajnaparamita Manuscript from Poo." *Orientations* (June 1994): 54–60.

———. "Indo-Tibetan Miniature Painting from Himachal Pradesh." In *Tibetan Studies, PIATS 1992: Proceedings of the 6th Seminar of the International Association for Tibetan Studies, Fagernes, 1992*, edited by Per Kvaerne, 1:441–53. Oslo: Institute for Comparative Research in Human Culture, 1994.

———. "Is There an Inner Asian International Style 12th to the 14th Centuries? Definition of the Problem and Present State of Research." In *Inner Asian International Style, 12th–14th Centuries: Papers Presented at a Panel of the 7th Seminar of the International Association for Tibetan Studies, Graz, 1995*, edited by Deborah E. Klimburg-Salter and Eva Allinger, 1–12. Vienna: Verlag der Österreichischen Akademie der Wissenschaften, 1998.

———. "Lama, Yidam and Protectors." *Orientations* (April 2004): 48–53.

———. "The Nako Preservation Project." *Orientations* (May 2003): 39–45.

———. "Reformation and Renaissance: A Study of Indo-Tibetan Monasteries in the Eleventh Century." In *Orientalia Iosephi Tucci Memoria Dicata*, edited by G. Gnoli and L. Lanciotti, 683–702. Rome: Istituto Italiano per il Medio ed Estremo Oriente, 1987.

———. "Ribba: The Story of an Early Buddhist Temple in Kinnaur." In *Buddhist Art and Tibetan Patronage: Ninth to Fourteenth Centuries, PIATS 2000, Proceedings of the Ninth Seminar of the International Association for Tibetan Studies*, edited by Deborah E. Klimburg-Salter and Eva Allinger, 1–28. Leiden: Brill, 2002.

———. "Some Thoughts on Style in Tibetan Art." *Tibet Journal* 25, no. 4 (1999/2000): 83–90.

———. "Style in Western Tibetan Painting: The Archaeological Evidence." *East and West* 46, nos. 3–4 (1996): 319–36.

———. *Tabo: A Lamp for the Kingdom: Early Indo-Tibetan Buddhist Art in the Western Himalaya*, Deborah E. Klimburg-Salter, with contributions by Christian Luczanits, Luciano Petech, Erst Steinkeller, and Erna Wandl, 179–88. New York: Thames and Hudson, 1998.

———. "A Thangka Painting Tradition From the Spiti Valley." *Orientations* (November 1997): 40–47.

———. "Tucci Himalayan Archives Report, 1: The 1989 Expedition to the Western Himalayas, and a Retrospective View of the 1933 Tucci Expedition." *East and West* 40, nos. 1–4 (1990): 145–71.

Klimburg-Salter, Deborah, and Eva Allinger, eds. *Buddhist Art and Tibetan Patronage: Ninth to Fourteenth Centuries, PIATS 2000, Proceedings of the Ninth Seminar of the International Association for Tibetan Studies*. Leiden: Brill, 2002.

———. *Inner Asian International Style, 12th–14th Centuries: Papers Presented at a Panel of the 7th Seminar of the International Association for Tibetan Studies, Graz, 1995*. Vienna: Verlag der Osterreichischen Akademie der Wissenschaften, 1998.

Klimburg-Salter, Deborah, et al. *The Silk Route and the Diamond Path: Esoteric Buddhist Art on the Trans-Himalyan Trade Routes*. Los Angeles: USLA Art Council, 1982.

Kossak, Stephen M., and Jane Casey Singer. *Sacred Visions: Early Paintings from Central Tibet*. New York: Metropolitan Museum of Art and Harry N. Abrams, 1999.

Krasser, Helmut, and Ernst Steinkellner, Ernst, eds. *Tibetan Studies, Proceedings of the 7th Seminar of the International Association of Tibetan Studies, Graz 1995*. Vienna: Verlag der Österreichischen Akademie der Wissenschaften, 1997.

Kreide-Damani, Ingrid, ed. *Dating Tibetan Art: Essays on the Possibilities and Impossibilities of Chronology from the Lempertz Symposium, Cologne.* Wiesbaden: Reichert, 2003.

Kubler, George. *The Shape of Time: Remarks on the History of Things.* New Haven, Conn.: Yale University Press, 1962.

Kulke, Hermann, and Dietmar Rothermund, *History of India.* 3rd ed. London and New York: Routledge, 1998.

Kvaerne, Per. "The Ideological Impact on Tibetan Art." In *Resistance and Reform in Tibet,* edited by Robert Barnett, 166–85. Bloomington: Indiana University Press, 1994.

Kvaerne, Per, ed. *Tibetan Studies: Proceedings of the 6th Seminar of the International Association for Tibetan Studies, Fargernes 1992,* vol. 1. Oslo: Institute for Comparative Research in Human Culture, 1994.

Levine, Gregory P. "Switching Sites and Identities: The Founder's Statue at the Japanese Zen Buddhist Temple Kōrin'in." *Art Bulletin* 83 (March 2001): 72–104.

Levy, Megan. "Tibetan Art." Seminar paper, Skidmore College, December 2007.

Linrothe, Rob. "Mapping the Iconographic Programme of the Sumtsek." In *Alchi, Ladakh's Hidden Buddhist Sanctuary: The Sumtsek,* edited by Roger Geopper and Jaroslav Poncar, 269–72. London: Serindia Publications, 1996.

———. "The Murals of Mangyu: A Distillation of Mature Esoteric Buddhist Iconography." *Orientations* (November 1994): 92–102.

———. *Paradise and Plumage: Chinese Connections in Tibetan Arhat Painting.* New York and Chicago: Rubin Museum of Art and Serindia, 2004.

———. "Polishing the Past: The Style of a Seventeenth-Century Tibetan Mural." Paper presented at the Center for East Asian Art, University of Chicago, April 2008.

———. "Portraiture on the Periphery: Recognizing Changsem Sherab Zangpo." *Archives of Asian Art* 63.1 (2013): 59–86.

———. *Ruthless Compassion: Wrathful Deities in Early Indo Tibetan Esoteric Buddhist Art.* Boston: Shambhala, 1999.

———. "Strengthening the Roots: An Indian Yogi in Early Drigung Paintings of Ladakh and Zangskar." *Orientations* (May 2007): 65–71.

———. "Stretched on a Frame of Boundless Thought: Contemporary Religious Painting in Rebgong." *Orientations* 33, no. 4 (2002): 48–56.

———. "A Winter in the Field." *Orientations* (May 2007): 40–53.

Linrothe, Rob, ed. *Holy Madness: Portraits of Tantric Siddhas.* New York and Chicago: Rubin Museum of Art and Serindia, 2006.

Linrothe, Rob, and Melissa Kerin. "Deconsecration and Discovery: The Art of Karsha's Kadampa Chorten Revealed." *Orientations* (December 2001): 52–63.

Linrothe, Rob, and Jeff Watt. *Demonic Divine: Himalayan Art and Beyond.* New York and Chicago: Rubin Museum of Art and Serindia, 2004.

Liu, Kuo-wei. "'Jig rten mgon po and the 'Single intentions' (Dgongs gcig): His View on Bodhisattva Vow and Its Influence on Medieval Tibetan Buddhism." Ph.D. diss., Harvard University, 2002.

Lo Bue, Erberto. "A 16th-Century Ladakhi School of Buddhist Painting." In *Buddhist Art, Form and Meaning*, edited by Pratapaditya Pal, 102–15. Mumbai: Marg, 2007.

———. "Iconographic Source and Iconometric Literature in Himalayan Art." In *Indo-Tibetan Studies*, edited by Tadeusz Skorupski, 171–98. Tring, UK: Institute of Buddhist Studies, 1990.

Lopez, Donald S., Jr. *Prisoners of Shangri-La: Tibetan Buddhism and the West*. Chicago: University of Chicago Press, 1998.

Luczanits, Christian. "Alchi and the Drigunpa School of Tibetan Buddhism: The Teacher Depiction in the Small Chorten at Alchi." In *Festschrift in Honour of Roger Goepper: Long Life*, edited by Jeong-hee Lee-Kalisch, Antje Papist-Matsuo, Willibald Veit, and Roger Goepper, 181–96. New York: Peter Lang, 2006.

———. "Another Rin chen bzaṅ po Temple?" *East and West* 44, no. 1 (1994): 83–98.

———. *Buddhist Sculpture in Clay: Early Western Himalayan Art, Late 10th to Early 13th Centuries*. Chicago: Serindia, 2004.

———. "The Eight Great Siddhas in Early Tibetan Painting." In *Holy Madness: Portraits of Tantric Siddhas*, edited by Rob Linrothe, 76–91. New York/Chicago: Rubin Museum of Art and Serindia Publications, 2006.

———. "A First Glance at Early Drigungpa Painting." In *Studies in Sino-Tibetan Buddhist Art: Proceedings of the Second International Conference on Tibetan Archaeology & Art, Beijing, September 3–6, 2004*, edited by Xie Jisheng, Shen Weirong, and Liao Yang. 459–88. Beijing: China Tibetology, 2006.

———. "Methodological Comments Regarding Recent Research on Tibetan Art." *Wiener Zeitschrift für die Kunde Südasiens* 45 (2001): 125–45.

———. "A Note on Tholing Monastery." *Orientations* (June 1996): 76–77.

———. "On an Unusual Painting Style in Ladakh." In *Inner Asian International Style, 12th–14th Centuries: Papers Presented at a Panel of the 7th Seminar of the International Association for Tibetan Studies, Graz, 1995*, edited by Deboarh Klimburg-Salter and Eva Allinger, 151–69. Vienna: Verlag der Osterreichischen Akademie der Wissenschaften, 1998.

———. "Style in Western Himalayan Art." In *Han Zang Fo jio mei shu yan jiu: 2007 [sic] di san jie Xizang kao gu yu yi shu guo ji xue shu tao lun hui lun wen ji* [Proceedings of the Third International Symposium of Tibetan Art and Archaeology, Beijing, October 2006], edited by Xie Jisheng, Xiong Wenbing, et al. 133–50. Shanghai: Shanghai Guji Chuban She, 2009.

———. "The 12th Century Buddhist Monuments of Nako." *Orientations* (May 2003): 46–53.

———. "The Wanla Bkra shis gsum brtegs." In *Buddhist Art and Tibetan Patronage: Ninth to Fourteenth Centuries, PIATS 2000, Proceedings of the Ninth Seminar of the International Association for Tibetan Studies*, edited by Deborah E. Klimburg-Salter and Eva Allinger, 119–20. Leiden: Brill, 2002.

Martin, Dan. "Padampa Sangye: A History of Representation of a South Indian Siddha in Tibet." In *Holy Madness: Portraits of Tantric Siddhas*, edited by Rob Linrothe, 108–23. New York/Chicago: Rubin Museum of Art and Serindia Publications, 2006.

Maxwell, T. S. "Lakhamandal and Trilokinath: The Transformed Functions of Hindu Architecture in the Cross-Cultural Zones of the Western Himalaya." *Art International* 24, nos. 1–2 (September–October 1980): 9–74.

McKay, Alex. *The History of Tibet,* vol. 2, *The Medieval Period: C. 850–1895: The Development of Buddhist Paramountcy.* London and New York: Routledge Curzon, 2003.

Mehta, Mandavi. "The Mouse Who Would Be King: Innovating Tradition in the State of Chamba." Ph.D. diss., University of Pennsylvania, 2011.

Meister, Michael W. "Ethnography, Art History, and the Life of Temples." In *Ethnography and Personhood: Notes from the Field,* edited by Michael W. Meister, 17–45. Jaipur, India: Rawat, 2000.

———. "Mountain Temples and Temple-Mountains: Masrur." *Journal of the Society of Architectural Historians* 65, no. 1 (March 2006): 26–49.

———. "Regions and Indian Architecture." *Nirgrantha* 2 (1996): 87–91.

———. "Seeing and Knowing: Semiology, Semiotics and the Art of India." In *Los Discursos Sobre el Arte,* edited by Juana Gutiérrez Haces, 193–207. México: Universidad Nacional Autónoma de México Instituto de Investigaciones Estéticas, 1995.

———. "Style and Idiom in the Art of Uparamāla." *Muqarnas: An Annual on Islamic Art and Architecture* 10 (1992): 344–54.

———. "Sweetmeats or Corpses? Art History and Ethnography." *RES: Anthropology and Aesthetics* 27 (1995): 118–32.

Meister, Michael W., ed. *Ethnography and Personhood: Notes from the Field.* Jaipur, India: Rawat, 2000.

Mignucci, Aldo. "Three Thirteenth Century Thangkas: A Rediscovered Tradition from Yazang Monastery?" *Orientations,* 32, no. 10 (December 2001): 24–32.

Mills, Martin A. *Identity, Ritual and State in Tibetan Buddhism: The Foundations of Authority in Gelukpa Monasticism.* London and New York: Routledge Curzon, 2003.

Morgan, David. *The Sacred Gaze: Religious Visual Culture in Theory and Practice.* Berkeley: University of California Press, 2005.

Mukarovsky, Jan. "Art as Semiological Fact." In *Essays in New Art History from France,* edited by Norman Bryson, 3. Cambridge: Cambridge University Press, 1988.

Muldowney, Kristen Kail. "Outward Beauty, Hidden Wrath: An Exploration of the Drikung Kagyü Dharma Protectress Achi Chökyi Drölma." M.A. thesis, Florida State University, 2011.

Nagar, Shanti Lal. *The Temples of Himachal Pradesh.* New Delhi: Aditya Prakashan, 1990.

Namgyal, Dkon mchog (Konchog). *A History: Blue-Ridge Monastery, Phiyang* (Ladakh: Government Institute of Buddhist Culture, 1989).

Neumann, Helmut F. "The Cave of the Offering Goddesses: Early Painting in Western Tibet." *Oriental Art* 44, no. 4 (1998–99): 52–60.

———. "Shalu's Hidden Treasure: The Paintings of the Shadakshari Chapel." *Orientations* (December 2001): 33–43.

———. "Wall Paintings of Western Tibet: A Stylistic Analysis." *Orientations* (October 1999): 74–83.

———. "The Wheel of Life in the Twelfth Century Western Tibetan Cave Temple of Pedongpo." In *Buddhist Art and Tibetan Patronage: Ninth to*

Fourteenth Centuries, PIATS 2000, Proceedings of the Ninth Seminar of the International Association for Tibetan Studies, edited by Deborah E. Klimburg-Salter and Eva Allinger, 75–84. Leiden: Brill, 2002.

Pal, Pratapditya. *Art of the Himalayas: Treasures from Nepal and Tibet.* New York: Hudson Hills Press, 1991.

———. *Tibetan Paintings: A Study of Tibetan Thankas, Eleventh to Nineteenth Centuries.* Basel, Switzerland: Ravi Kumar; London: Sotheby, 1984.

Palit, D. K. *War in High Himalaya: The Indian Army in Crisis, 1962.* London: Hurst, 1991.

Panofsky, Erwin. *Renaissance and Renascences in Western Art.* New York: Harper and Row, 1972.

Petech, Luciano. "The 'Bri-Guṅ-Pa Sect in Western Tibet and Ladakh." In *Selected Papers on Asian History,* edited by Luciano Petech, 355–68. Rome: Istituto Italiano per il Medio ed Estremo Oriente, 1988.

———. *Central Tibet and the Mongols: The Yüan-Sa-skya Period of Tibetan History.* Rome: Istituto Italiano per il Medio ed Estremo Oriente, 1990.

———. "Historical Introduction." In *Inscriptions from the Tabo Main Temple, Texts and Translations,* edited by Luciano Petech and Christian Luczanits, 1–9. Rome: Istituo italiano per l'Africa e l'Oriente, 1999.

———. *The Kingdom of Ladakh, c. 950–1842 A.D.* Rome: Istituto Italiano per il Medio ed Estremo Oriente, 1977.

———. "A Regional Chronicle of Gu ge pu hrang." *Tibet Journal* 22, no. 3 (Autumn 1997): 106–11.

———. *Selected Papers on Asian History.* Rome: Istituto Italiano per il Medio ed Estremo Oriente, 1988.

———. *A Study on the Chronicles of Ladakh.* Calcutta: Calcutta Oriental Press, 1939.

———. "The Tibetan-Ladakhi Moghul War of 1681–83." *Indian Historical Quarterly* 23, no. 3 (1947): 169–99.

———. "Western Tibet: Historical Introduction." In *Tabo: A Lamp for the Kingdom: Early Indo-Tibetan Buddhist Art in the Western Himalaya,* Deborah E. Klimburg-Salter, with contributions by Christian Luczanits, Luciano Petech, Erst Steinkeller, and Erna Wandl, 229–55. New York: Thames and Hudson, 1998.

———. "Ya-ts'e, Gu-ge, Pu-raṅ: A New Study." *Central Asiatic Journal* 24, nos. 1–2, (1980): 104–5.

Postel, M., A. Neven, and K. Mankodi. *Antiquities of Himachal,* vol. 1. Bombay: Franco-Indian Pharmaceuticals, 1985.

Pritzker, Thomas J. "A Preliminary Report on Early Cave Paintings of Western Tibet." *Orientations* (June 1996): 26–47.

———. "The Wall Paintings of Nyag Lhakhang Kharpo." *Orientations* (March 2008): 102–13.

Quintman, Andrew. "Milarepa's Many Lives: Anatomy of a Tibetan Biographical Corpus." Ph.D. diss., University of Michigan, 2006.

Rechung, J. K. "The Buddhist Paintings and Iconography According to Tibetan Sources." *Bulletin of Tibetology* 26, nos. 1–3 (1990): 55–63.

Rhie, Marilyn M. "Tibetan Painting: Styles, Sources, and School." In *Worlds of Transformation: Tibetan Art of Wisdom and Compassion,* edited by

Marylin M. Rhie and Robert A. F. Thurman, 45–74. New York: Tibet House New York and The Shelly and Donald Rubin Foundation, 1999.

Rhie, Marilyn M., and Robert A. F. Thurman. *Wisdom and Compassion: The Sacred Art of Tibet*. New York: Harry N. Abrams, 1991.

———. *Worlds of Transformation: Tibetan Art of Wisdom and Compassion*. New York: Tibet House New York and The Shelly and Donald Rubin Foundation, 1999.

Ricca, Franco, and Erberto Lo Bue. *The Great Stupa of Gyantse: A Complete Tibetan Pantheon of the Fifteenth Century*. London: Serindia, 1993.

Rickerby, S. "Nako Temple Complex: Himachal Pradesh, India: Preliminary Inspection of the Wall Paintings." Photocopy. Conservation Report, Courtauld Institute of Art, London, 2003.

Schaffer, Kurtis R. *Dreaming the Great Brahmin: Tibetan Tradition of the Buddhist Poet-Saint Saraha*. Oxford: Oxford University Press, 2005.

Schapiro, Meyer. "Style." In *Theory and Philosophy of Art: Style, Artist, and Society*, 51–102. New York: George Braziller, 1994.

Schopen, Gregory. *Bones, Stones and Buddhist Monks: Collected Papers on the Archaeology, Epigraphy and Texts of Monastic Buddhism in India*. Honolulu: University of Hawai'i Press, 1997.

Sharf, Robert. Introduction. In *Living Images: Japanese Buddhist Icons in Context*, edited by Robert H. Sharf and Elizabeth Horton Sharf, 1–18. Stanford, Calif.: Stanford University Press, 2001.

Sharma, Gopal. "Explorers Find Ancient Caves, Paintings in Nepal," Reuters, May 3, 2007, www.reuters.com/article/2007/05/03/us-nepal -idUSB50593420070503.

Shuttleworth, H. Lee. *Lha-luṅ Temple, Spyi-ti*. Memoirs of the Archaeological Survey of India 39. Calcutta: Government of India, Central Publication Branch, 1929.

Singer, Jane Casey. "Painting in Central Tibet, ca. 950–1400." *Artibus Asiae* 54, nos. 1–2 (1994): 87–136.

Singh, Ajay Kumar. "Rangrig Rtse: An Early Buddhist Temple in Kannaur, Western Himalayas." In *Tibetan Studies,* International Association for Tibetan Studies, Seminar, Helmut Krasser, 883–90. Vienna: Verlag der Osterreichischen Akademie der Wissenschaften, 1997.

———. *Trans-Himalayan Wall Paintings: 10th to 13th century A.D.* Delhi: Agam Kala Prakashan, 1985.

Singh, Jogishvar. *Banks, Gods and Government: Institutional and Informal Credit Structure in a Remote and Tribal Indian District (Kinnaur, Himachal Pradesh) 1960–1985*. Stuttgart: Steiner Verlag Wiesbaden GMBH, 1989.

———. "A Brief Survey of Village Gods and Their Moneylending Operations in Kinnaur District of Himachal Pradesh; Along with Earlier Importance of Trade with Tibet." In *Wissenschaftsgeschichte und Gegenwärtige Forschungen in Nordwest-Indien*, edited by Lydia Icke-Schwalbe and Gudrun Meier, 244–58. Dresden: Staatliches Museum Für Völkerkunde, 1990.

Singh, Mian Goverdhan. *Art and Architecture of Himachal Pradesh*. Delhi: B. R. Publishing, 1983.

Smith, E. Gene. *Among Tibetan Texts: History and Literature of the Himalayan Plateau*. Edited by Kurtis R. Schaeffer. Boston: Wisdom, 2001.

Snellgrove, David L., and Tadeusz Skorupski. *The Cultural Heritage of Ladakh*. 2 vols. Warminster, UK: Aris and Phillips, 1979–80.

Spengen, Wim van. *Tibetan Border Worlds: A Geohistorical Analysis of Trade and Traders*. London and New York: Kegan Paul International, 2000.

Stoddard, Heather. "'Bri gung, Sa skya and Mongol Patronage: A Reassessment of the Introduction of the Newar 'sa skya' Style in Tibet." In *Dating Tibetan Art: Essays on the Possibilities and Impossibilities of Chronology from the Lempertz Symposium, Cologne*, edited by Ingrid Kreide-Damani, 59–69. Wiesbaden: Dr. Ludwig Reichert Verlag, 2003.

———. "Early Tibetan Paintings: Sources and Styles (Eleventh–Fourteenth Centuries A.D.)." *Archives of Asian Art* 49 (1996): 26–50.

Tanaka, Kimiaki. "The Buddhist Sites of Tholing Monastery and the White Temple at Tsaparang (Western Tibet): Their Present Condition and an Analysis of the Iconography of the Yoga Tantras." In *Tibetan Studies: Proceedings of the 6th Seminar of the International Association for Tibetan Studies, Fargernes 1992*, edited by Per Kvaerne, 1:863–72. Oslo: Institute for Comparative Research in Human Culture, 1994.

Thakur, Laxman S. *Buddhism in the Western Himalaya: A Study of the Tabo Monastery*. New Delhi: Oxford University Press, 2001.

———. "Exploring the Hidden Buddhist Treasures of Kinnaur (Khu nu): A Study of the Lha khang chen mo, Ribba." In *Buddhist Art and Tibetan Patronage: Ninth to Fourteenth Centuries, PIATS 2000, Proceedings of the Ninth Seminar of the International Association for Tibetan Studies*, edited by Deborah E. Klimburg-Salter and Eva Allinger, 337–52. Leiden: Brill, 2002.

———. "Nako Monastery: Archaeological Notes from an Account of the Western Himalayan Expedition." *East and West* 46, nos. 3–4 (1996): 337–52.

———. "Pagoda Temples of the Western Himalaya." *Journal of Indian History* 62 (1984): 127–38.

———. "Tibetan Historical Inscriptions from Kinnaur and Lahaul-Spiti: A Survey of Recent Discoveries." In Krasser, *Tibetan Studies*, 29–44.

Thapar, Romila. "The Vamshavali from Chamba." *Himāl South Asian* (March 2010), www.himalmag.com/component/content/article/87.html.

Tropper, Kurt. "The Buddha-Vita in the White Temple of Tsaparang." In *Tibetan Inscriptions. Proceedings of a Panel Held at the Twelfth Seminar of the International Association for Tibetan Studies, Vancouver 2010*, edited by Kurt Tropper and Cristina Scherrer-Schaub. Leiden: Brill, 2013.

———. "The Historical Inscription at the Sum Brtsegs Temple at Wanla, Ladakh." In *Text, Image and Song in Transdisciplinary Dialogue: Proceedings of the 10th Seminar of the International Association of Tibetan Studies, Oxford, 2003*, edited by Deborah E. Klimburg-Salter, Kurt Tropper, and Christian Jahoda, 105–50. Leiden: Brill, 2007.

———. "On an Inscription in the Guru Rimpoche Lha Khang at Nako, Kinnaur." In *Tibetan Art and Architecture in Context: PIATS 2006, Tibetan Studies: Proceedings of the Eleventh Seminar of the International Association for Tibetan Studies, Königswinter 2006*, edited by Erberto F. Lo Bue and Christian Luczanits, 122–43. [Andiast]: International Institute for Tibetan and Buddhist Studies, 2010.

Tucci, Giuseppe. "Indian Paintings in Western Tibetan Temples." *Artibus Asiae* (1937): 191–204.

———. *Indo-Tibetica*, vol. 3, *The Temples of Western Tibet and Their Artistic Symbolism*. 1932. English edition, edited by Lokesh Chandra. New Delhi: Aditya Prakashan, 1988.

———. "Tibetan Notes." In *Opera Minora*, 2:471–88. Rome: Giovanni Bardi, 1971.

———. *Tibetan Painted Scrolls*. Rome: Libreria dello Stato, 1949.

———. *Transhimalaya*. Translated from the French by James Hogarth. Geneva: Nagel, 1973.

———. "Travels of Tibetan Pilgrims in the Swat Valley." In *Opera Minora*, 2:471–88. Rome: Giovanni Bardi, 1971.

Vitali, Roberto. "A Chronology (bstan rtsis) of Events in the History of Mnga' ris skor gsum (Tenth–Fifteenth Centuries)." In McKay, *The History of Tibet*, 2:53–89. London and New York: Routledge Curzon, 2003.

———. *The Kingdoms of Gu.ge Pu.hrang According to mNga'.ris rgyal.rabs by Gu.ge mkhan.chen Ngag.dbang grags.pa*. New Delhi: Indraprasha Press, 1996.

———. "Ladakhi Temples of the 13th–14th Centuy: Kan-ji Lha-khang in sPurig and Its Analogies with Gu-ru Lha-khang." *Kailash* 18, no. 6 (1996): 93–106.

———. *Records of Tho.ling: A Literary and Visual Reconstruction of the "Mother" Monastery in Gu.ge*. New Delhi: High Asia, 1999.

Vogel, J. P. *Antiquities of Chamba State*. Calcutta: Superintendent Govt. Print, 1911–57.

Wandl, Erna. "The Representation of Costumes and Textile." In *Tabo: A Lamp for the Kingdom: Early Indo-Tibetan Buddhist Art in the Western Himalaya*, Deborah E. Klimburg-Salter, with contributions by Christian Luczanits, Luciano Petech, Erst Steinkeller, and Erna Wandl, 179–88. New York: Thames and Hudson, 1998.

———. "Textile Depictions from the 10th/11th Century in the Tabo Main Temple." In *Tabo Studies II: Manuscripts, Texts, Inscriptions, and the Arts*, edited by C. A. Scherrer-Schaub and E. Steinkellner, 277–98. Rome: Istituto Italiano per L'Africa e L'Oriente, 1999.

Wessels, Cornelius. *Early Jesuit Travelers in Central Asia, 1603–1721*. 1924. Reprint, New Delhi: Asian Educational Services, 1992.

Willson, Martin, and Martin Brauen. *Deities of Tibetan Buddhism*. Boston: Wisdom, 2000.

Xin, Yang. "The Ming Dynasty (1368–1644)." In *Three Thousand Years of Chinese Painting*, edited by Richard M. Barnhart et al., 197–249. New Haven, Conn.: Yale University Press, 1997.

Yoritomi Motohiro, trans. *Nishi Chibetto sekkutsu iseki* [Cave temples of West Tibet]. Tokyo: Shūeisha, 1997.

Tibetan Sources

Bstan 'dzin padma'i rgyal mtshan. *Nges don bstan pa'i snying po mgon po 'bri gung pa chen po'i gdan rabs chos kyi byung tshul gser gyi phreng ba zhes bya ba bzhugs so*. Reprint, Lhasa: Bod ljongs bod yig dpe rnying dpe skrun khang, 1989.

Dkon mchog Namgyal. *Chags Rabs sgang sngon dGon pa Phyi dbang dkon mchog rnam rgyal dbus gzhung nang pa'i rig gnas khang chen po* [A History: Blue-Ridge Monastery, Phiyang]. Ladakh: Government Institute of Buddhist Culture, 1989.

Dkon mchog rgya mthso. *'Bri gung chos 'byung*. Beijing: Mi rigs dpe skrun khang, 2004.

Gu ge tshe ring rgyal po, *Gu ge thse ring rgyal po'I ched rtsom phyogs bsgrigs* [Guge Tsering Gyalpo's Collection of Essays]. Lhasa: Tibetological Publishing House of China, 2004.

Namgyal, Phuntsok. *Ntho-ling Monastery*. Beijing: Encyclopedia of China, 2001.

O rgyan bstan 'dzin. *Rgyal ba'i bstan srung dbyings phyug chos kyi sgrol ma'i bskang mdos rgyas pa'i phyug len grigs su bkod pa thub bstan snyan pa'i dbyar rnga bzhugs so*. Bir, Himachal Pradesh: D. Tsondu Senghe (Yorey Tsang), 1998.

Sangs rgyas rgya mtsho. *Dga' ldan chos "byung bai du rya ser po*. Zi ling, Tibet: Krung go bo kyi shes rig dpe skrun khang, 1989.

Chinese Sources

Administration Commission of Cultural Relics of the Tibetan Autonomous Region, comp. *Xizang Fojiao siyuan bihua yishu / Xizang Zizhiqu wenwu guanli weiyuanhui bian (Fresco Art of the Buddhist monasteries in Tibet / Compiled by the Administration Commission of Cultural Relics of the Tibetan Autonomous Region)*. In Tibetan, English, and Chinese. Chengdu: Sichuan renmin chubanshe, 1994.

Huo Wei and Li Yongxian. *Xizang Xibu Fojiao yishu* [Buddhist art in Western Tibet]. Chengdu: Sichuan People's Publishing House, 2001.

Jin Weinuo and Qing Baiyin. *Zhongguo bihua quanji 32: Zangchuan siyuan 2*. Tianjin: Renmin meishu chubanshe, 1991.

Nian Xin and Li Shumin. *Xiangxiong bihua* [Xiangxiong murals]. Tibetan Folk Art Series. Chongqing: Chongqing Publishing House, 2003.Xizang Zizhiqu wenwu guanli weiyuanhui [The Administrative Committee of Archaeology of the Tibet Autonomous Region], ed. *Guge gucheng* [The site of the ancient Guge kingdom]. 2 vols. Beijing: Wenwu chubanshe, 1991.

Interviews

Ani Samten Wangmo (Buddhist nun), in discussion with the author, May 2005.

Kunchok Ngodrub (temple caretaker), in discussion with the author, May 2005. Rinchen Namgyal, translator.

Moni (owner of Nas Go Restaurant, Nako), in discussion with the author, June 4, 2006.

Tenzin (caretaker of Nako's religious compound and the Guru Rimpoche Temple), in discussion with the author, May 28, 2005.

Guge Tsering Namgyal (Scholar on West Tibet, Lhasa), in discussion with the author, June 2006.

Archives, Databases, and Websites

Achi Association, www.achiassociation.org.
Giuseppe Tucci Photographic Archives, Museo Nazionale d'Arte Orientale,
    Rome, Italy. March 2003; March 2005.
Himalayan Art Resources, www.himalayanart.org.
"2002 World Monuments Watch." World Monuments Fund website, January
    2002, www.wmf.org/sites/default/files/wmf_publication/Watch
    _Catalog_2002.pdf.
Western Himalayan Art Archive, Universität Wien, Vienna, Austria. February
    2005; June 2007.

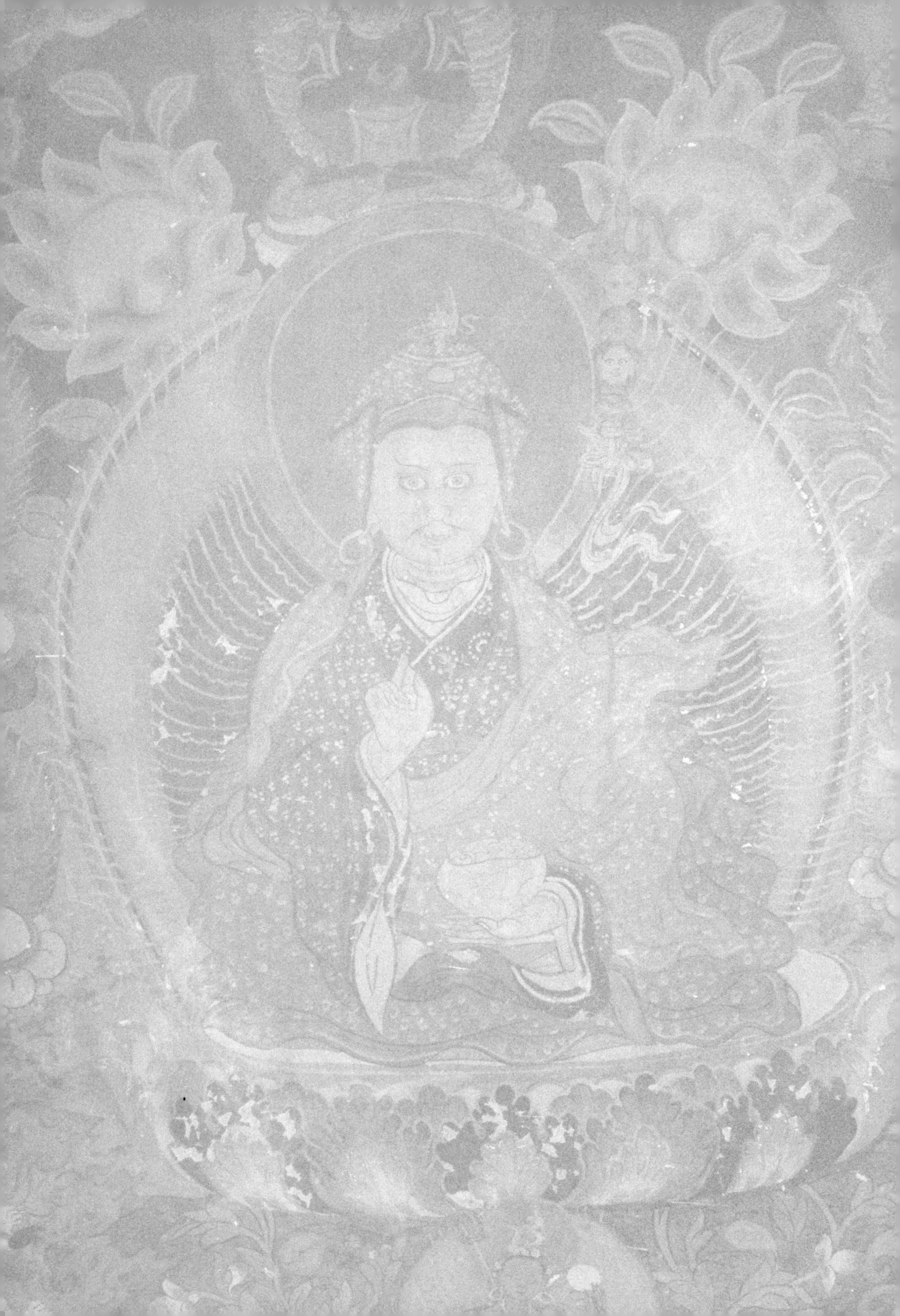

51, 52, 105, 111, *112, 113,* 114–15;
Mahāyāna tradition and, 75; religious history of, 79–80; resurgence of, 85–87; revival in sixteenth century, 8, 85; royal patronage of, 82

Drukpa Kagyu ('Brug pa bka' brgyud) tradition, 7, 19–20, 76, 193n29; growing strength of, 158; Guge kingdom antagonism with, 87–88; Gyapagpa Temple iconographic program and, 48–49, 57, 77; monastic complex at Nako and, 44, 45; Nako temple painting programs and, 34–35; Nangasan Temple images and, 27, 28

Dukhang ['Du khang] (Tabo), 96, 120, 160, 175; Cella substyle in, 176, 179; Mahābodhisattva Śreṣṭin, 176, *178,* 179, *180;* offering deity in, 176, *177*

Dungkar caves, 127, 175, 182–83

Durgā (Hindu deity), 22

Dzogchen (Rdsogs chen), 31

Emmer, Gerhard, 206n56

ethnography, 9, 11

forgetfulness/forgetting, 7, 42, 43, 57, 83

Francke, August Herman, 36, 39, 71, 192n15, 196n55; Gesar as preoccupation of, 76–77; on monastic complex at Nako, 43–44; on the Translator Temple, 37, 197n66

Gadan Tsewang Palzang (Dga' ldan tshe dbang dpal bzang), 89

Gelug (Dge lugs) tradition, 7, 22, 49, 82, 172; decline of Drigung and, 83–84; formation of, 173; growing strength of, 158; iconography in Chango temples, 24; Ki (Kye) monastery, 28; Ladakhi royal patronage of, 205n30; Nangasan Temple images and, 28; Tsongkhapa as founder of, 84; yellow hats associated with, 136

Gesar [Ge sar] (protector deity), 44, 45–48, 49, 76–77

Ghaṇṭāpa (Tibetan: Dril bu pa), 67

Ghuyasangpa (Ghu ya sgang pa), 81, 203n5

Golden Temple (Tabo), 8, 40, 118, 120, 149, 154; architectural structure of thronebase, *126;* bodhisattva attendants in, *139–140,* 141, 150; Guge style ("Gu-ge bris") and, 161; Maitreya (detail of dhoti), *182;* monastic attendants in, 141, *142;* Śākyamuni Buddha images, 127, *133,* 136, 149–150; Vairocana image, 122, *125;* Vajradhara (detail of dhoti), *144, 147;* wooden dowels as decorative motif, 214n63

Gotsangpa (Rgod tshang pa), 30–31

Great Maitreya Temple, 128

Green Tara, 165, 166, *166*

Guge kingdom, 6, 8, 19, 85, 92, 157, 171; beginnings of, 164, 171–72, 211n20; Danma Kunga Dragpa and, 85–86; dissolution of, 89; Drigung community and, 84; Drukpa population tension with, 87–88; Ladakhi invasion of, 87; legacy of Purang (Pu hrang) kingdom and, 19; Ngari painting tradition and, 117; political relations of seventeenth century and, 20; Purang-Guge as model for, 171, 172, 174, 175, 184; royal chronicles of, 9, 11, 12

"Guge style," 162–63, 183, 207n8

Guling monastery, 28

Guṇaprabha, 71

Guru Rimpoche Temple (Nako), 33, 166, 168

Gyadrag monastery (Mount Kailash), 82

Gyalpo, Guge Tsering, 80, 86, 168, 212n31

Gyaltsab (Rgyal tshab rje), 152

Gyalwang Kunga Rinchen, 85

Gyangdrag (Gyang grags) monastery, 81, 86

Gyandrug Chogni [Rgyan drug mchog gnyis] (Six Ornaments and Two Supreme One), 71, 109, 111–15, *114*

phun tshogs lde bzang po), 172,
173–74, 211n20
Nangasan Temple (Dankar), 24,
26–27, 28
Naropa, 75
Nepalese painting. *See* Beri painting
style
Neumann, Helmut, 161, 214n52
Newar painting style, 128, 129, 161,
162, 209n27; Central Tibetan Style
and, 165; as revival of Khache
(Kashmiri) style, 171; vegetal scrolling motif, 181. *See also* Beri painting style
Ngari (Mnga' ris [West Tibet]), 5,
6, 18, 22, 159, 199n20; Drigung
network in, 12, 49, 81, 87, 199n21;
Guge kingdom of, 8; Kashmir and,
30; map, 2; political structure of,
18; Sakya control of, 83; undocumented period in history of, 19;
Yuan dynasty and, 19
Ngari painting tradition (eleventh–fifteenth centuries), 92, 117, 146, 154,
157–58, 165; courtly and regional
idioms of, 117–120, 183–84, 186,
207n9; decorative forms between
basement levels, 126–27, *126*; form
splitting (*formenspaltung*) of, 121–
22, 152; Newar/Beri tradition and,
129, 162; problems in defining style
of, 117–120. *See also* Gyapagpa
Temple iconographic program;
Tholing-Tsaparang-Tabo courtly
idiom (post-fifteenth century)
Ngari painting tradition, later
(fifteenth–sixteenth centuries),
159–160, 188; ideology of unbroken
royal lineage, 175–184, *177–78*,
180–82; in political and historical
context, 164–65; as revival of Khache Style, 159, 163, 175; scholarship on, 160–64
Ngawang Dragpa (Ngag dbang grags
pa), 119, 171, 172
Ngodrub Ngon (Dngos grub mgon),
203n5
Nyingma (Rnying ma) tradition, 22,
28, 30, 193n29

Ogyanpa Ngawang Gyatso (O rgyan
pa ngag dbang rgya mtsho), 17, 30
oral tradition, village, 30, 35
Orientalism, 10

Pal, Pratapditya, 161–62
Pāla period/style, 123, 163, 195n52;
Central Tibetan Style and, 165,
212n25; Newar painting style and,
212n33
patronage, courtly, 1, 3, 21, 199n20;
dependence on economic prosperity,
32; Ghuyasangpa and, 203n5; of
Guge kingdom, 215n67; Gyapagpa
Temple iconographic program and,
77–78, 152; Khache (Kashmir)
style and, 170–71; lay patronage
and, 205n44; *Mnga' ris rgyal rabs*
(Ngari Chronicle) and, 174–75; of
Purang-Guge kingdom, 184
Pedongpo (Pad ma'i sdong po) cave
temple, 175
Persia, 180, 182
Petech, Luciano, 80, 85, 120, 192n17,
204n24; on Ladakhi patronage of
Drigung, 88; on lapses in documentation of Ngari royal lineage, 173;
on Tibet-Ladakh-Mughal War, 88,
89, 206n51; on Yuan/Sakya rule in
West Tibet, 212n21
Phuktal temple (Zangskar), 119
Phyiang cave temple, 175
pilgrimage routes, 15, 18, 21, 30,
194n41
Pin valley, 28, 31
Prajñāpāramitā (Tibetan: Yum chen
mo), 71, 74, 75; crown of, 151;
painting style of Gyapagpa Temple
images, 96, 97, 98, 99, 116, 147,
151; in schematic drawing of
Gyapagpa south wall, *73*; in White
Temple (Tholing), 118
prayer wheels, 22, 23, 196n57
Pritzker, Thomas, 214n52
provenance, obscured or uncertain, 14
Purang-Guge (Pu hrang-Guge) kingdom, 9, 19, 36, 157, 164, 203n5;
Danma Kunga Dragpa and, 85–86;
establishment of, 160; as model for

MELISSA R. KERIN is Assistant Professor of Art History
at Washington and Lee University.